IVORY & SLAVES
IN EAST CENTRAL AFRICA

IVORY AND SLAVES

Changing Pattern of International Trade in East Central Africa to the Later Nineteenth Century

Edward A. Alpers

UNIVERSITY OF CALIFORNIA PRESS

BERKELEY AND LOS ANGELES

1975

University of California Press
Berkeley and Los Angeles, California

ISBN 0–520–02689–6
Library of Congress Catalog Card Number: 73–93046

Printed in Great Britain

To Annie   *To My Parents*

Acknowledgements

Few works of scholarship are the sole responsibility of a single person and this one is no different in that respect. My attention was first directed towards this general area by Professors Roland Oliver and Richard Gray. To Richard Gray, who supervised the original thesis, I owe my sincerest thanks, not only for his keen scholarly counsel, but also for his friendship and encouragement.

The original research was undertaken with the aid of a small grant from the Research Fund of the University of London and the generous support of my parents. Travel to and research in Goa in 1967 was supported by a grant from the Research Committee of the University of California, Los Angeles. The final writing was indirectly, though substantially, made possible by a grant from the Humanities Institute of the University of California, and another from the Ford Foundation, through the African Studies Center of the University of California, Los Angeles. I am also grateful to the Directors of the various archives in which I worked in England, France, Portugal, India, and Tanzania, and particularly to those junior members of staff who so often came to my aid. To Professor C. R. Boxer and the Marquesa da Cadaval I am especially indebted for allowing me to use documents in their private libraries. I am also grateful to Professor Ronald E. Gregson for providing me with the text of an interview he conducted in Malawi, and even more so to Lance J. Klass, who generously agreed to let me make use of his enterprising unpublished research among the Machinga Yao of Kasupe District, Malawi. Finally, I wish to thank my good friend, Professor Allan F. Isaacman, for offering to synopsize his oral data on Yao trade among the Chewa of Makanga, so that I could make use of it at my convenience.

The process of revising the original thesis has benefited from the comments of several readers, including Professors Gray, Boxer, Isaacman, and George Shepperson. I have been especially fortunate to have had a close and careful critique of a major section of my thesis done by Dr. Abdul M. H. Sheriff as part of his own dissertation. The benefit that I have gained from this, and from further discussions with him in Dar es Salaam, is considerable. More generally, the shape of this book owes a great deal to many discussions with various colleagues and students at both the University of Dar es Salaam and the University of California, Los Angeles, among whom I wish to name Professor Walter Rodney, Dr. Andrew Roberts, and Professor T. O. Ranger, who has also commented on it directly in most of its transitional stages.

Finally, in her unhistorical way, the most important contributor to the general intelligibility of this book—my most persistent critic, chief editor, and major source of comfort and encouragement—has been my wife. That she has inevitably surrendered some of her own independence so that I could do my work is to be expected; that we have enjoyed every minute of it together is a joy, for which I thank her with all my love.

Contents

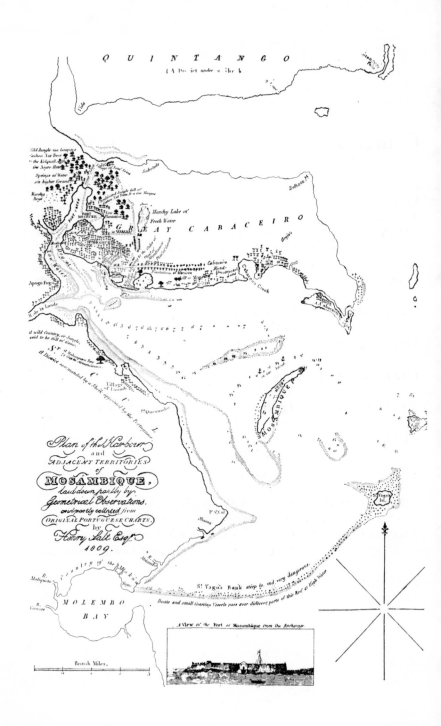

QUINTANGO

GREAT CABACEIRO

Plan of the Harbour
and
ADJACENT TERRITORIES
of
MOSAMBIQUE,
laid down partly by
Geometrical Observations,
and partly collected from
ORIGINAL PORTUGUESE CHARTS.
by
Henry Salt Esqr.
1809.

MOLEMBO
BAY

British Miles.

A View of the Port of Mosambique from the Anchorage.

Illustrations

Frontispiece and page vi are details from View of the Government House at Mesuril, published in Henry Salt, *A Voyage to Abyssinia . . . in the Years 1809 and 1810. . . .*, London, 1814. Plan of the Harbour at Mosambique, p. x, also from Henry Salt.

Maps

Tables

Graph

Abbreviations

A.C.	*Arquivo das Colónias*
A.C.L.	Academia das Ciências de Lisboa
A.C.U., p.n.o.	*Annaes do Conselho Ultramarino*, parte não official
Add. Mss.	Additional Manuscripts
A.H.U.	Arquivo Histórico Ultramarino
A.N.F.	Archives Nationales de France
A.N.T.T.	Arquivo Nacional da Tôrre do Tombo
B.M.	British Museum
B.N.L.	Biblioteca Nacional de Lisboa
C.O.	Colonial Office
Cod.	Códice
Cx.	Caixa
F.G.	Fundo Geral
fl.	folha
F.O.	Foreign Office
Gov.	Governor
Jl.	Journal
L.M.	Livro das Monções
Moç.	Moçambique
M.R.	Ministério do Reino
N.A.I.P.G.	National Archives of India, Panaji, Goa
P.R.O.	Public Record Office
Prov. Govt.	Provisional Government
Sec. St.	Secretary of State
T.N.A.	Tanzania National Archives
T.N.R.	*Tanganyika Notes and Records*
U.M.C.A.	Universities' Mission to Central Africa
U.S.P.G.	United Society for the Propagation of the Gospel

A Note on Names and Spelling

I have attempted to modernize all Portuguese personal names, while refraining from the Anglo-American practice of citing Portuguese by their last name only, when a multiple name is preferred. Wherever practical, I have rendered African names in a standard Bantu form, but in most cases I have simply adopted the most common contemporary Portuguese spelling. For example I prefer Makua to Macua, Lomwe to Lomue, Lujenda to Lugenda, but retain Mauruça and Uticulo in the absence of a more widely recognized Bantu spelling. I have also chosen to reserve use of the name Maravi for the peoples who compose that socio-linguistic group, while using that of Malawi for the modern state only. And I have preferred Nyasa to Malawi for the name of the lake, since that is the name by which it was known to most people during the period of this study. Somewhat differently motivated is my decision to employ the name Zimbabwe for the white minority ruled territory presently known as Rhodesia. The famous stone ruins located near the town of Fort Victoria are distinguished as Great Zimbabwe. A finer point concerns my retention of the convenient term *prazero*, which M. D. D. Newitt points out in an appendix to his major study of *Portuguese Settlement on the Zambesi* does not exist in the Portuguese language. Finally, since positional inheritance was an important feature of traditional political structure in the societies of East Central Africa, I have always given the titular names of chiefs as 'the Lundu' or 'the Mucutomuno', unless a personal or any other distinguishing name is also given, as in 'Kalonga Muzura' or 'Mwene Mutapa Gatsi Rusere'.

Glossary of Principal Portuguese Terms

Devassa—a special judicial investigation

Estado da Índia—State of India, the name applied to the Portuguese possessions east of the Cape of Good Hope, of which Mozambique formed a part until 1752

Junta do Comércio—Board of Trade

Machila—a rough, durable cotton cloth woven by the people of Zambesia

Patamar, patamares—an African or mulatto trading agent, usually a slave, who travelled in the interior on behalf of his master at the coast

Prazo—Portuguese Crown Estate, a major Afro-Portuguese political institution in Zambesia and the Kerimba Islands, the title-holder of which is usually known as a *prazero*

Residência—a judicial investigation conducted at the completion of an official's tenure of office to see if he had fulfilled, or contravened, his instruction

Santa Casa da Misericórdia—Holy House of Mercy, a charitable brotherhood

Senado da Câmara—Municipal Council

Velório—glass trade beads, usually Venetian

Weights

Arrátel—0·459 kg

Arroba: 32 *arráteis*—14·688 kg

Bar: 20 *faraçolas*—247·860 kg

Bar: 4 *quintais*—234·900 kg

Faraçola: 27 *arráteis*—12·393 kg

Maina: $\frac{1}{12}$ *faraçola*—1·03275 kg

Onça: $\frac{1}{16}$ *arrátel*—0·0287 kg

Quintal: 4 *arrobas*—58·725 kg

Rubo: $\frac{1}{4}$ *maina*—0·25819 kg

Currencies

Cruzado—a silver coin equal to 400 *réis*

Dollar—either the Spanish or Austrian Maria Theresa dollar, both of which were basic trading currencies in the Western Indian Ocean region.

Pataca—the Portuguese name for a dollar, equal in the eighteenth century first to three, then to four, and finally, when marked at Mozambique, to six *cruzados*

Piastre—the French name for dollar

Real—the basic Portuguese monetary unit

Introduction

East Central Africa is an area which has been largely ignored by historians of Africa until very recently, particularly for the period before the late nineteenth century. Bounded on one side by the East African coast between Kilwa and the mouth of the Zambesi River, and on the other by the Luangwa River, it includes what is today southern Tanzania, northern Mozambique, Malawi, and north-eastern Zambia. The entire region lies north of the Zambesi. Those scholars who have previously studied East Central Africa have concentrated their energies on specific problems in specific localities. Thus the works of José Justino Teixeira Botelho, Alexandre Lobato, and Eric Axelson focus on the history of the Portuguese in this region, and only marginally consider that of the African peoples in whose country the Portuguese had established themselves. Similarly, the work of A. J. Hanna deals with African trade and politics only insofar as they provide the background to the struggle for European control of what is today Malawi and north-eastern Zambia. This Eurocentric focus has recently begun to be corrected by the work of Harry Langworthy on the Chewa and Leroy Vail on the Tumbuka, while similar studies of other particular African peoples are currently in progress. Finally, the remarkable work of J. M. Schoffeleers on Maravi religious history and of Allen Isaacman on the Zambesi *prazos* (which in turn builds upon and extends the work done by M. D. D. Newitt) marks an important step forward both conceptually and methodologically. Still, no one has attempted to examine the history of the entire region over an extended period of time. This is one of the tasks which I have set myself in writing this book.

The first scholars who recognized the unity of East Central Africa were anthropologists, who included it in the even larger Central African culture area of Bantu-speaking peoples.[1] The historical unities which exist in this vast region are several. Given the proper sources, an historian could probably reconstruct a regional history focusing on state-building, on resistance to colonial domination, or on religious development, among other topics. The topic which dominates this book is primarily that of African activities within the framework of international trade, which began to penetrate East Central Africa from about 1400 and became particularly intensive and widespread during the eighteenth and nineteenth centuries. More specifically, this book focuses on the roles played first by the Maravi, and then by the Yao and Makua.

This emphasis has been determined partly by my own interests and partly by the sources available for such a study. The initial research for this study was undertaken from 1964 to 1966, and the findings were submitted as a Ph.D. thesis for the School of Oriental and African Studies, University of London, in 1966. The principal source was contemporary Portuguese documentation, both published and unpublished, which was available in Lisbon and London. This was supplemented valuably by material in the French national archives relating to the Mascarene Islands during the eighteenth century and, to a lesser extent, by British documentation concerning the early nineteenth century. The overwhelming emphasis of this documentation, so far as it concerned Africans directly, was economic, since the primary involvement of Europeans in this part of Africa was international trade. The original dissertation bears the much different title of 'The role of the Yao in the development of trade in East Central Africa, 1698–c. 1850', although it also deals extensively with Maravi expansion in the sixteenth and seventeenth centuries. In its original form, the thesis reflects the predominant trend in studies on pre-colonial African trade in the mid-1960s, when the assumptions were that entrepreneurial skills and economic development were inevitably linked in a positive relationship, and that the initiative which Africans demonstrated in their trading with non-Africans was above all else a verification of the role which Africans played in making their own history. The present book no longer shares those assumptions.

The basic argument of this study is that the changing patterns of international trade in East Central Africa during these centuries, including the initiatives taken by Africans themselves, must be set within the context of the historical roots of underdevelopment in Africa. I have elsewhere argued the case for this perspective at length.[2] It is an argument which is beginning to gain a foothold among students of Africa and does not bear repeating here, except as it becomes possible to do so within the context of the evidence presented in the study which follows. What does need to be pointed out, however, are the limitations which the original sources for this study impose upon the book as it now stands. (Although I conducted research in the National Archives of India, Panaji, Goa, in 1967, the nature of that documentation was identical to the material from the European archives.) Basically, the character of these sources is such that there is almost no contemporary evidence of changes within African societies during the period of richest documentation, during the eighteenth century. Africans were generally treated as anonymous bodies of people bearing very inclusive names. Details emerge from this picture only where they concern political, military, and trading relations between the various European and African peoples. In an attempt to probe beneath the often superficial level of this evidence, I have made several major changes in and additions to the original thesis.

First, I have excised a mass of detailed material relating to the trading relations of the French with the Portuguese and, to a much lesser extent, with the Swahili rulers of the Kilwa coast in the eighteenth century.[3] At the same time, however, I have retained an equally detailed body of material on the Indian trading community at Mozambique Island, primarily because of its critical significance to the pattern of African trade during the eighteenth century.

Second, I have added an entirely new chapter which deals exclusively with the economic, social, and political structures of the three main African socio-linguistic groups with whom this book is concerned. Most of the evidence in this chapter dates from the nineteenth and twentieth centuries, and great care has been taken not to overspeculate about the interaction between pre-existing socio-economic structures of the Makua-Lomwe, Yao, and Maravi peoples and the historical developments which constitute the larger part of the book. In the present stage of research, such an historical synthesis can only be attempted for the nineteenth century, as I have demonstrated elsewhere.[4] Nevertheless, it seems to me that the process of beginning to think about the historical impact of international trade on African systems of production can be valuably informed by this sort of exercise, so long as its inherent limitations are clearly recognized.

Third, I have greatly extended the scope of the final chapter, so as to take advantage of the more vivid published evidence which becomes available for the internal history of the peoples of East Central Africa during the nineteenth century. Had time, money, and historical circumstances permitted, this chapter would certainly have been the richer for research conducted in the Mozambican archives and in the field. Nevertheless, this restructuring has made it possible to demonstrate more clearly than in the original thesis some of the nineteenth-century consequences of the long historical involvement in international trade in this part of Africa. And it has also allowed me to indicate the legacy of this history for the period of modern colonial rule.

To reiterate, the argument of this book is that the history of international trade between the peoples of East Central Africa and the Europeans, Indians, and Arabs who came to their land was a decisive factor leading to their present underdevelopment. Far from producing healthy economic, social, and political development, this historical process contributed instead only to an increasingly divisive differentiation within and between the peoples of East Central Africa. If any progress is made by this book towards understanding these fundamental problems, and therefore towards dealing with them, then its purpose will have been achieved.

E. A. A.

1. See H. Baumann and D. Westermann, *Les Peuples et les civilisations de l'Afrique*, trans. L. Homburger (Paris, 1948), pp. 146–70; G. P. Murdock, *Africa—Its Peoples and their Culture History* (New York, 1959), pp. 290–306; A. I. Richards, 'Some Types of Family Structure amongst the Central Bantu', in A. R. Radcliffe-Brown and D. Forde (eds.), *African Systems of Kinship and Marriage* (London, 1950), pp. 207–51; M. Douglas, 'Matriliny and Pawnship in Central Africa', *Africa*, XXXIV, 4 (1964), pp. 301–13.
2. E. A. Alpers, 'Re-thinking African Economic History: a contribution to the discussion of the roots of underdevelopment', *Ufahamu*, III, 3 (1973), pp. 97–129.
3. Alpers, 'The French Slave Trade in East Africa (1721–1810)', *Cahiers d'Études Africaines*, X, 37 (1970), pp. 80–124.
4. Alpers, 'Trade, State, and Society among the Yao in the Nineteenth Century', *Jl. of African History*, X, 3 (1969), pp. 405–20, and 'Towards a History of the Expansion of Islam in East Africa: The Matrilineal Peoples of the Southern Interior', in T. O. Ranger and I. N. Kimambo (eds.), *The Historical Study of African Religion* (London, 1972), pp. 172–201.

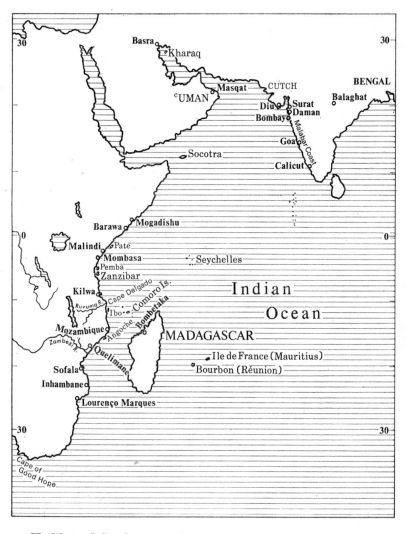

I   The Western Indian Ocean

CHAPTER ONE

Economy and Society in East Central Africa

The sources for reconstructing this chapter present particular problems in a study which is organized principally as a narrative analysis of changes in the commercial history of East Central Africa over the course of some four centuries. Ideally, one would like to be able to begin with an overview of African institutions before 1498 and then to follow it with an integrated discussion of their adjustments to the demands of international trade until the later nineteenth century. At the very least it would be desirable to establish a diachronic model of change from the beginning to the end of this period. But presently available sources simply do not admit either of these possibilities. Necessarily, then, this chapter is largely a synchronic reconstruction of Makua-Lomwe, Yao, and Maravi economy and society during the nineteenth century. It is based mainly on contemporary and twentieth-century accounts, both African and European, professional and amateur. Even for this more limited exercise great caution must be employed in the use of the more modern materials which purport to describe various aspects of 'traditional' African society. It is therefore hoped that this chapter will not give the impression of a timeless African past which has somehow maintained its 'traditional' institutions over several hundreds of years with little or no significant change. Indeed, where the evidence warrants such treatment, an attempt is made here to trace the changes that produced some of the characteristics of nineteenth-century economy and society, while subsequent chapters argue that these African societies were regularly adjusting their patterns of trade to the increasingly pressing demands of the international market. They were anything but static.

What this first chapter does propose tentatively, however, is that while the specific reconstructions of Makua-Lomwe, Yao, and Maravi economy and society represent the state of affairs at the end of the period examined in this book, certain underlying characteristics of regional and institutional variation were probably operative throughout (if not necessarily before) these centuries. What I am offering, then, is a hypothesis about the influence of economy and society on the history of international trade after 1498 in East Central Africa by an *ex post facto* examination of the shape of economy and society among the principal societies involved in that commerce. This may seem a risky venture, but it is better conceived than a less tentative, pseudo-historical treatment of the same subject.

The Environment and the People

The different responses of the peoples of East Central Africa to the penetration of international trade were shaped by several independent factors, not least of which was the environment which each inhabited. Considering the region as a whole, the dominant climatic feature is the air-masses of the Western Indian Ocean. From November to March the climate takes its character from the north-east trade winds or monsoon, which blows in from the Arabian peninsula. From April to October the region is subject to the south-east trade winds which come in off the Indian Ocean and then sweep back up towards Arabia, the Persian Gulf, and western India as the south-west monsoon. These winds have also had a major impact on the trading history of the region, for it was the mastery of the monsoons and their associated currents which enabled the Arab and Indian traders of the Western Indian Ocean to come to East Africa in order to exploit its natural resources.

Although it is theoretically practical to utilize these trade winds throughout each season, voyages were generally made only once each monsoon, after the wind was well established in either direction. During the north-east monsoon vessels left port around mid-November and for perhaps a month afterwards. Similarly, since the winds of the south-west monsoon are especially violent in July and August, traders attempted to leave either at the very beginning or very end of the seasonal winds.[1] Once arrived from their home ports, these Arab and Indian traders encountered a coastline which is marked by many serviceable natural harbours

2

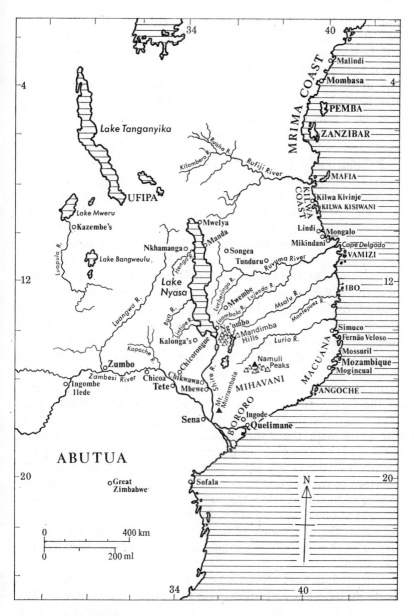

34

40

Malindi

Mombasa

PEMBA

ZANZIBAR

MRIMA COAST

Lake Tanganyika

Kilombero R.

Ruaha R.

Rufiji River

MAFIA

Kilwa Kivinje

KILWA KISIWANI

KILWA COAST

UFIPA

Lake Mweru

Kazembe's

Mwelya

Manda

Lindi

Mongalo

Luapula R.

Lake Bangweulu

Nkhamanga

Songea

Tunduru

Mikindani

Cape Delgado

VAMIZI

Ruvuma River

Hengo R.

Luangwa R.

Lake
Nyasa

Lucheringo R.

Lujenda R.

Msalu R.

IBO

Bua R.

Luambala R.

Montepuez R.

Mwembe

Ng'ombo

Lintipe R.

Kalonga's

Chicoronge

Mandimba
Hills

Lurio R.

MACUANA

Simuco

Fernão Veloso

Mossuril

Mozambique

Mogincual

Kapoche

Zumbo

Namuli
Peaks

Zambesi River

Ingombe
Ilede

Chicoa

Tete

Chikwawa

Mbewe

Shire R.

Mt.
Murrambala

MIHAVANI

BORORO

ANGOCHE

Sena

Ingode

Quelimane

ABUTUA

Great
Zimbabwe

Sofala

N

0   400 km

0   200 ml

20

20

12

12

4

4

34

40

2   East Central Africa

and a number of offshore islands which either protected mainland roadsteads or themselves provided safe ports. Zanzibar is both the largest and most important of these islands, but others of great significance include the Lamu archipelago, where Pate was the main town, Mombasa, the Mafia Islands, Kilwa Kisiwani, the Kerimba Islands, Mozambique Island, Angoche, and the mainland port of Sofala. Before the end of the fifteenth century all of these would be connected outposts of the Afro-Islamic civilization which later became known as Swahili (see Chapter 2).

Rainfall throughout East Central Africa is limited to a single rainy season spanning about half the year, usually from December to April, with local variations.[2] The rest of the year is marked by a single dry season during which all major social activities, most iron smelting and salt extraction, and long-distance trading expeditions to the coast took place. It is important to note that the dry season on the continent coincides with the south-west monsoon in the ocean, so that there was a fairly closely coordinated rhythm of arriving caravans and departing vessels during the months of August, September, and October at the coast. Except for parts of the extreme south-east of Tanzania, the mouth of the Lurio River, and the lowlands of the Shire River valley (where annual flooding is a compensating factor), the level of annual rainfall reliability is adequate for stable agriculture in the area. Rainfall is generally more abundant to the west of the Lujenda River and to the south of the Lurio. It is heaviest in the highland areas around Lake Nyasa and the mountains to the north-east of the confluence of the Shire with the Zambesi River. Nevertheless, in the lower coastal plains (ranging up to about 185 metres in altitude) and in much of the gently rising plateau up to 915 metres, periodic shortage of rainfall due to meteorological variations, run-off, and evaporation, impose less than ideal conditions on most African farmers at one time or another. Furthermore, as in most of Africa, soils are generally poor and badly leached, although all authorities stress that climate is a much more important factor than soil conditions.

The predominant vegetation of East Central Africa is woodland savanna, both dry and moist, with the latter predominating. The moist woodland savanna in this area is also characterized by abundant Brachystegia and Julbernardia. Near the Kilwa coast this vegetation becomes mixed with the more humid coastal forest, while much of the coast is characterized by mangrove

4

swamps, which are particularly significant at the deltas of the Rufiji and Zambesi Rivers. Nearly all of this country, then, is relatively open to travel by foot. The interior is also penetrable by several major waterways. The Ruvuma River supports small canoe traffic as far as the confluence with the Lujenda, but not much beyond. It never became a major artery of international trade. The Zambesi, on the other hand, is navigable by large canoes some 400 kilometres inland, as far as Tete, while the Shire can bear this traffic 160 kilometres north to Chikwawa, where the Murchison Falls are located. Above these cataracts, however, canoe traffic again becomes possible, and Lake Nyasa has supported a considerable canoe trade for centuries. In the nineteenth century Swahili traders also introduced a dhow traffic across the middle reaches of the lake.

There has probably been little fundamental change in the environment of East Central Africa during the period of this study, but what change has taken place is almost certainly the work of man rather than nature. On a local level, these changes might have been quite significant, as they seem to have been in the later nineteenth century. In general, these changes would have been demographic, caused either by the shifting pattern of agriculture or by larger-scale migrations. Indeed, during the period under consideration there were a number of very important migrations within this part of Africa, each of which undoubtedly played a role in shaping the environment of the country. In some cases, such as the movement of the Makonde from about 1700 on to the plateaux flanking the mouth of the Ruvuma River and that of the Makua in the nineteenth century north across the same river into south-eastern Tanzania, these migrations involved the opening up of previously uninhabited country. In others, such as the sixteenth-century invasion of the Mang'anja eastwards into Makua-Lomwe country and that of the Yao into southern Malawi from about 1860, they meant a rather sudden increase of population in areas which were already settled by agricultural peoples. In the nineteenth century, too, there was considerable local migration as people attempted to move beyond the reach of Ngoni and slave-raiding parties.[3] It would also seem that the extensive hunting out of elephant in the coastal hinterland which was noted in the nineteenth century must have had some effect on the local vegetation pattern.[4]

It is impossible to do more than speculate about the demography of East Central Africa during this period in any absolute sense, but it seems most likely that in the past, as today, both the coast and southern Malawi were relatively more densely populated than the rest of the region. In general, it is the eastern and southern parts of the region which are more densely populated at present, with the area to the west of the middle and upper reaches of the Msalu and Lurio Rivers, and north across the Ruvuma, supporting a population of less than two persons per square kilometre.[5] Because there has been as much movement into this area as there has been out of it since the middle of the nineteenth century, it seems likely that this part of the country has been relatively underpopulated for some time.[6]

It is also important to recognize that two of the most important staple crops in this region belong to the American complex. Maize, which is grown extensively in the Yao highlands to the east of Lake Nyasa, in most of southern Malawi, and in other highland areas of East Central Africa, was certainly known by the mid-eighteenth century, and probably earlier, although its wider distribution may only date to the nineteenth century.[7] Manioc, which is even more widely cultivated, was only introduced on the mainland opposite Mozambique Island in 1768, although it may have spread into the region from other directions as well.[8] Rice, a Malaysian crop which is important in the river beds of southern Tanzania, may have been a relatively late introduction from the coast, as it was in other parts of the Tanzanian interior. Farther south, however, in the Zambesi valley and delta, and around Sofala, it was being grown regularly by the end of the sixteenth century.[9] Of the African cereals, pearl millet is important principally in the lowlands of southern Malawi and in the Zambesi valley. The dominant indigenous cereal is sorghum, which is the staple crop in the eastern half of the region and is widely grown elsewhere. Hunting and fishing were everywhere important in supplementing local diets, but the distribution of tsetse fly over almost the entire savanna region made it impossible for cattle to be kept except in southern Malawi, along the coast, and in the mountainous regions rising above about 1,525 metres.

With the exception of the Swahili of the coast and the intrusive Ngoni groups of the nineteenth century, all of the major sociolinguistic groups of East Central Africa belong to the closely related matrilineal cluster of Central Bantu speakers. The Swahili, as Muslims, and the Ngoni, with their Southern Bantu-speaking background, trace their inheritance patrilineally. For the rest, matrilineality is a major index of a broader cultural similarity among all of them. Patterns of marriage, with cross-cousins being favoured, and of residence, which is overwhelmingly matrilocal, are common throughout this area. Succession to political office is, of course, reckoned through the mother's line, with the preference being for sister's son to succeed mother's brother. Positional inheritance and perpetual kinship relations are also common features among the matrilineal peoples of East Central Africa. Kinship terminology and relations are characterized by the opposition of generations and the close identification of alternating generations. Another common socio-political institution is the payment of debts by pawn. Social tension most commonly manifests itself throughout this area in terms of witchcraft accusations.

The cultural unity of East Central Africa is also attested to in similar modes of religious practice among the three major peoples with whom this study is concerned. Belief in a single High God is universal, with the predominant form of invocation being conducted by the senior member of the matrilineal group through the medium of its dead ancestors. On these occasions the unity of the kin-group is strongly emphasized, and the forms of offering to the ancestral spirits are everywhere similar.[10] The lip-plug (*pelele*) was apparently a much more widely dispersed form of personal adornment in the past than it is today, when its use is confined to more traditionally-oriented Makonde women. Elaborate cicatrization also seems to have been more widespread formerly, although it was concentrated principally among the peoples of northern Mozambique. At the same time, there is strong evidence of a closely related masked dance complex among the Makonde and the Maravi.[11] Similarly, whatever the differences between various authorities may be, there is clearly a general underlying linguistic unity to the region as a whole.[12]

Nevertheless, it would be a great mistake to lump all of these people together on the basis of this general commonality. For the historian, the combined effects of economic, social, and political atomization during these centuries is of far greater significance than the underlying social and cultural unities that existed. One especially vivid index of this phenomenon is the highly ethnocentric terminology used by individual groups to distinguish themselves from all other groups with whom they might come into regular contact. The best known example is the distinction made by the Swahili between *waungwana* or free, civilized people, i.e. Muslims, and *washenzi* or barbarians, but the same sense of superiority is to be found in the Yao use of *walolo* for all Makua-Lomwe speakers and in the Maravi use of *wanguru* to indicate all people living to their east. Similarly, there are sharp distinctions drawn between groups within the broader socio-linguistic conglomerations, so that northern Makonde refer to the southern Makonde as 'Mawia', while these in turn call themselves Makonde, but refer to the Makonde of the Malemia Plateau as 'Ndonde'. Even the names 'Makua' and 'Lomwe' may have their origins in the distinction drawn between Makua-Lomwe speakers living near the coast and those living beyond them in the interior. When one adds to these the distinctions drawn on the basis of chiefdom, clan, and lineage membership, the problem of coming to grips with the particularistic nature of these small-scale societies becomes evident.[13]

The Makua-Lomwe

The Makua-Lomwe peoples speak a number of very distinct dialects of the same language, some of which are said to be mutually unintelligible. Their Adamic origins are traced to the Namuli Mountains which rise to a height of more than 2,440 metres, and are usually identified as being in Lomwe, rather than Makua, country.[14] In the period covered by this study they have been greatly influenced by the Maravi (see Chapter 2), while the issue of Indonesian influence at a much earlier date remains to be investigated. Although they have been agriculturalists for centuries, Whiteley was informed that they 'formerly seem to have subsisted almost entirely on hunting. One of the reasons given for the name Acawa, by which the Yao are known, is that they were the people who "ate their own food" (*anolya acawa*), as opposed to the Makua who had to go out and hunt for theirs.'[15]

Perhaps the situation encountered in 1932 by Vincent among the Lomwe of Namuli, before there had been any penetration by the Portuguese administration when not a single trading store had been established as yet, can be taken as roughly representative of the state of Makua-Lomwe economy before the advent of international trade. Vincent learned that new land had to be cleared after about two to three planting seasons. The sorghum head was cut just before it ripened and after drying was threshed with a

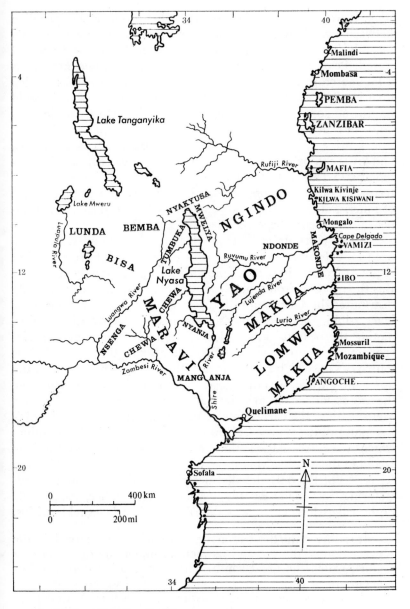

3   *The Peoples of East Central Africa*

stick. It was reduced to flour by pounding in a mortar or grinding between two stones. Little maize was grown, having been only recently introduced. It was eaten green on the cob and was not stored. Pearl millet was grown for making beer, and manioc as a famine crop. Beans and sweet potatoes were grown as garden luxuries. The most popular food, however, was rice, but it could be grown in only a few places in the mountains. Much hunting was done and all flesh was eaten. 'Salt is the principal requirement from outside sources, and quantities of supplies such as flour, eggs, and fowls can be purchased for a few spoonfuls (sic) of this commodity.'[16] This picture corresponds closely to Whiteley's characterization of the economy as one in which there was an absence of inheritable material goods and a closely linked lack of permanent attachment to specific pieces of land.[17]

For the self-contained Makua or Lomwe community, then, the need for salt was a major factor in bringing it into some sort of regular relationship with neighbouring groups. Equally important was the need for iron tools. Iron ore, like salt, was not uniformly distributed in East Central Africa, so that the accessibility or inaccessibility of these two basic commodities were critical in promoting the peaceful integration of otherwise autonomous socioeconomic kinship groups.[18] For the Makua the most obvious source of salt, which in the nineteenth century was a staple of the up-country trade, was the coast. Indeed, in the Makua language the words for 'coast' and for 'salt' are identical, *maka*.[19] As for iron smelting, the earliest notice comes in 1785 from the inquisitive naturalist, Manuel Galvão da Silva, who visited iron mines which were located on the mainland opposite Mozambique Island in the Mutipa Mountains and at the mouth of the Monapo River.[20] But the only detailed description of Makua iron manufacturing was made by the French ethnographer, Eugène de Froberville, who got his information from Makua slaves at Mauritius.

It is during the dry season that the entire tribe is freed for the extraction of the ore and its melting under the direction of a chief, called the great smith. The first step is to erect a vast enclosure of clay earth, in which the chief assigns a space to each man, woman, and child, where they will come to deposit the ore which they collect in the vicinity. Meanwhile, others cut wood and make charcoal. Each person stacks his ore in the enclosure, which he then fills with charcoal. The entire lot is covered over with iron bars and earth, arranging openings from place to place to serve as chimneys; finally the hide bellows are prepared, the bellow pipes are connected to the interior of the furnace, and the fire is lighted, after having removed the women. The greatest activity then reigns among the smiths. The bellows operators, who have no respite either day or night, work in shifts, while others renew the charcoal and still others ascertain that the melting is operating properly. After a fortnight of incessant work, the chief announces that the iron is smelted. The furnace is extinguished by throwing water on it. The workers go to bathe; the married men rejoin their wives who, as soon as the fire is started, do not approach the foundry, because the presence of a woman in a state of impurity may make the ore vanish or change into useless rocks. Finally the furnace is uncovered and each person comes to collect the produce of his ore. The blocks of cast-iron are broken into medium-sized lumps of iron and carried to individual forges, where local smiths manufacture axes, knives, bill-hooks, spear heads, musket balls, rings, etc., which are then exchanged with the neighbouring peoples for muskets, powder, cotton cloths, glass beads, etc.[21]

It is clear that the process described at a remove by Foberville was a very large communal undertaking. In the twentieth century Vincent witnessed Lomwe iron smelting which was a long and inefficient, but essentially localized affair, as was the making of barkcloth.[22] It is likely that the large scale, highly organized and ritualized system described by Froberville may have been associated with a fairly powerful chiefdom. Indeed, there are parallels in Makua elephant hunting for this sort of communal economic activity with important ritual sanctions.

According to Froberville, the Makua had secret societies for the hunting of both elephants and buffalo. Each member of these separate societies had to swear his fidelity to that organization.[23] The fact that there was a distinct society for hunting buffalo, however, suggests that the idea of hunting societies may have its roots in the great dependence of the Makua upon hunting for food, rather than upon the economic significance of hunting for ivory to trade to the coast. If this were so, then the particular organization and prestige of hunting among the Makua before the growth of the ivory trade would have been a significant factor in affecting their ability to respond to that demand, as appears to have been the case also among the Kimbu, Kamba, and Cokwe.[24]

By the mid-nineteenth century, at the latest, the technology of elephant hunting was dominated by firearms. Indeed, a century earlier at least one observer noted their use in the hinterland of Mozambique, but in view of our greater knowledge of the weaponry of eighteenth-century Makua warfare this was very likely a recent innovation.[25] In this respect the Makua also resembled the Cokwe, though not the Kamba, who preferred to hunt with poisoned arrows.

Another aspect of Makua hunting which bears upon this study is the role which groups of hunters played in opening up new territory to settlement. Indeed, hunters appear to have been the vanguard of the migration into southern Tanzania in the nineteenth century.[26] By about 1859 Makua hunters had established themselves as far into Tanzania as western Ugogo, and in the general region of Kilosa.[27] And by the last decades of that century, the name 'Makua' had become a generic term for itinerant professional elephant hunters throughout the interior of Tanzania.[28] Given the tremendous range of their activities and the extensive documentation of Makua ivory trading from the eighteenth century, the taboo on carrying elephant tusks which Câmara Reis cites for the Makua of Mogovolas, in the hinterland of Angoche, was probably an isolated phenomenon.[29]

It appears that the normal division of labour in Makua society made it possible for men to be absent from their homes for long periods of time during the dry season, since their part in the agricultural productive cycle was limited to clearing the heavy bush.[30] But their absence was apparently not without a potential toll in social tension and disequilibrium within the village. In 1878 Cambier encountered a group of Makua hunters to the north-east of Morogoro, in eastern Tanzania. 'These hunters believe that when one of them is killed or wounded in one of their lengthy and perilous expeditions, it is because his wife has forgotten her conjugal duties during his absence and has thereby created a dangerous situation for him. The unfortunate woman is burned alive, as well as her supposed paramour, after having been identified by the "Sorcerer".'[31] While Cambier's account may not be accurate in all of its details, it does serve to reveal the existence of social, as opposed to the lack of economic, problems raised by the prolonged absence of male elephant hunters from the domestic context of Makua life.

For the vast majority of Makua-Lomwe peoples, the basic unit of social organization was the village, which was in more recent times usually composed of several three-generational groups or *oloko*, each of which ideally included a woman, her married daughters and their children, and her sons.[32] The average size of the *oloko* was from one to seven huts, while villages of more than one *oloko* often contained forty or more huts.[33] Villages were by no means permanent, however, and fissiparation generally took place on the basis of *oloko* movements into new territory.[34] Village government usually consisted of a chief and a council of elders.[35] The chief was regarded with considerable respect, as he was political leader, principal judicial authority and the most important intermediary with the ancestors of the village founders, that is, with the ancestors of his own *oloko*. The grave of a former chief was regarded with veneration and according to Vincent was regularly replenished with a supply of beer and food. The one which he visited in Namuli was surrounded by a fence and also included the chief's stool. The preferred succession was from mother's brother to sister's son, and failing that line to a brother of the deceased chief.[36]

Taken together as individual political units, the many Makua-Lomwe chiefdoms impressed a late nineteenth-century outsider like Henry O'Neill as 'a number of petty despotisms', but at the same time it was also clear that there were 'a number of confederations of petty chiefdoms'.[37] In fact, all who have written about the Makua-Lomwe peoples agree on this single point, that over and above the localized village chiefdom there were important superstructures dominated by particularly powerful chiefs who in matters of mutual defence, more than anything else, commanded a following well beyond their daily authority. According to accounts of the Makua of Tanzania, this hierarchical ordering was based upon clan authority, without regard to territorial chiefdoms, but those accounts which pertain to the Makua-Lomwe of Mozambique place more emphasis on the territorial aspects of this form of greater political organization. Clearly the two are interrelated, since the clans themselves seem to have developed as a combination of kinship and territorial organization in Mozambique. Until further clarification can be achieved by basic field research, one must be satisfied to recognize that the dual principles of kinship and territorial organization were at play in shaping the development of these relationships.

It was possible for such a grouping to take shape at any point in time, with outstanding political leadership being the main criterion of genesis. But even when this sort of confederation had a long history it appears that sub-chiefs of the confederation acted quite independently of its paramount chief in most situations. Fighting often took place within these groupings, although in most cases it seems not to have disturbed the structure of the confederation, at least until the middle of the nineteenth century. Matters of general concern were decided in council and sub-chiefs had an important voice in the selection of the paramount chief. At the same time most of these chiefdoms were linked permanently by bonds of perpetual kinship which generally were expressed in the characteristic matrilineal terms of uncle-nephew.[38]

Considering the important role which the belligerency of the Makua played in the economic and political history of northern Mozambique during the period of this study, a word should be said about Makua warfare. Although imported firearms became increasingly important after the middle of the eighteenth century (see Chapter 4), locally manufactured weapons continued to be used extensively. According to Froberville, the Makua were especially known for their ability to handle a spear.[39] Before any major combat could take place, it was necessary to call together the able-bodied men of the chiefdom or confederation and to prepare them for battle. This preparation included ritual cleansing and the administration of charms to protect them in battle. All of this took place in the bush, away from the non-combatant population. The chief had an important role in this preparation, as did a special war-medicineman. On some occasions attacks were launched by surprise, while on others war was officially announced by sending a special emissary (*mamuhupe*) to the enemy, who could respond according to his inclination. Warriors were divided into companies and there was a recognized set of military lieutenants under the chief. According to an anonymous eighteenth-century writer, war could only be declared at certain times of the month, as determined by the position of the moon. Male enemies were frequently decapitated and women and children taken captive. Indeed, Froberville's informants told him that the reason for body cicatrization among the Makua was to aid the identification of victims of battle.[40]

A final institution among the Makua-Lomwe which was potentially of very great importance in the development of trade in northern Mozambique was the system of reciprocal clan relations or *unavili*. Whiteley states that this relationship involved rights and duties associated with funerals and installation ceremonies among the Makua. *Unavili* existed only between pairs of clans, although most clans had more than one such arrangement. No seniority was recognized in *unavili*, while mutual aid in distress was expected and mutual abuse was enjoyed. Two decades ago in southern Tanzania the Makua distinguished between *unavili* between Makua clans and their external joking relationships or *utani* between all Makua and the Ngoni and Ngindo. Nevertheless, Whiteley did note that a full *unavili* relationship existed between the Makua known to him and the Maravi, a peculiarity which may possibly owe its origin to the sixteenth- and seventeenth-century Maravi domination of the Makua-Lomwe peoples. (See Chapter 2.) As for the origins of *unavili* among the Makua themselves, Whiteley has suggested that clan warfare and the need to normalize affairs afterwards was the leading stimulus.[41]

The Yao

The heart of Yao country lies in north-west Mozambique, bounded approximately by the Rivers Lucheringo to the west, Luambala to the south, Lujenda to the east, and Ruvuma to the north. Like the Makua-Lomwe peoples, the Yao also claim a single place of origin in one of the many prominent peaks that dot the region. This hill is called 'Cao', the plural form of which is 'Yao', the name of the people themselves. Yao hill has never been precisely located by any outsider, but it occupies a most important position in Yao mythology.[42] At the same time, however, there is another stream of Yao tradition which claims an origin for man in Lake Bangweulu, although this may well be influenced by Maravi traditions of origin.[43] Abdallah also records the myth that from Yao hill there was a 'very ancient' dispersal—which another Yao source states was caused by the fact that 'they did not have enough land for gardens'—of the eleven major Yao-speaking groups until the Yao had settled the greater part of north-west Mozambique and the Mwera or Chimbanga Yao had moved across the Ruvuma River into southern Tanzania.[44] However unhistorical this dispersal may be, it seems certain that at a very early date—certainly no later than the beginning of the seventeenth century—the Yao had occupied an extensive tract of territory extending from the south-east of Lake Nyasa across the Ruvuma.[45]

Before the days of trading to the coast the Yao were primarily agriculturalists who were able to provide their own needs for themselves. Their staple crop was sorghum, although both maize and manioc were well established by the third quarter of the nineteenth century, if not earlier. According to David Livingstone, ridging to prevent saturation of crops was a common feature of Yao agriculture.[46] A developed drainage and irrigation system was also a prominent feature of Mwembe, the great town of Mataka I Nyambi, the most powerful of the late nineteenth-century Yao chiefs.[47] The fertility of the country around the central Lujenda valley enabled it to support an especially large population in the nineteenth century, and one traveller at the beginning of the twentieth century noted that two crops of maize were raised annually.[48]

The Yao supplemented their diet considerably by hunting and gathering. They hunted with both bow and arrow and dogs and nets; they also set traps and dug pits for big game.[49] Both hunting and fishing could be pursued by individuals, but in recent times the hunter always divided his kill with his chief and headman. When a man either hunted or fished outside his own territory, he was supposed to give a part of his catch to the local headman.[50] Hunting and fishing was the work of the men, while the women did all of the village work. Women also did most of the cultivating. For the early period Abdallah makes no mention of domestic livestock, but by the second half of the nineteenth century there were sheep, goats, and at Mwembe a small breed of humped cattle which were milked.[51] Salt was produced from a variety of grasses and barkcloth was manufactured for clothing. Local trade among the Yao is said to have been very keenly pursued.[52]

Abdallah also implies that the Yao possessed knowledge of iron-working at the beginning of their known history. Iron ore was abundant and easily worked, and the Yao were accomplished smiths. But Abdallah's account of how the Chisi Yao 'started building forges, furnaces and workshops', and manufacturing iron tools, suggests that the Chisi may have been an immigrant group who introduced this vital skill to the Yao. The Chisi were specifically blacksmiths, 'and they dwelt in Yao country, because had they not started forging the country would have been devastated with famine'. As a consequence of their technological skills the

Chisi were 'held in great esteem'. Whatever their origins, the social impact of the Chisi was no less dramatic than their economic contribution. 'So the Wachisi became extraordinarily wealthy, they travelled in every country peddling hoes and other tools . . . When any Wachisi arrived at a village everyone came in from the neighbourhood till it was full up, and the man whose hospitality they had accepted was a lucky fellow. He would run about smiling and telling everybody, "The Wachisi are my guests." ' In the end, however, tradition asserts that this treatment went to their heads, the quality of their work declined, and their exclusive control of iron-smithing was lost, as the rest of the Yao learned to do their own work.[53] Not all of this account of the Chisi may be strictly historical, but it usefully indicates both the significance of iron technology to an agricultural people and the potential for social stratification in a small-scale, agricultural society when such skills were the exclusive possession of a closed group within it.

If iron was plentiful in Yaoland, good salt was not. Salt was a staple of their regional trade with the Mang'anja and was one of the first products sought by the Yao at the coast.[54] Indeed, it seems very likely that the predominant role after 1700 of the Yao in the international trade of East Central Africa may well have its roots in their tradition of an active internal trade and the availability of better quality salt outside their country than they could produce for themselves.

When the Yao were at last drawn into the orbit of international trade it was ivory which overwhelmingly occupied their attention until the growth of the slave trade from the later eighteenth century ultimately came to challenge its supremacy in the middle of the nineteenth century. Elephants seem to have abounded in Yaoland and were still 'fairly numerous' at the beginning of the present century.[55] Elephant hunting among the Yao was not organized in specialized guilds, as it was among the Makua, but instead was more obviously tied to the political structure of the village and chiefdom. Before setting out on a hunting expedition the men involved would go to the chief or headman to see if the time was right for such an undertaking. The chief would make an offering of sorghum flour at the *nsolo* tree where he approached his ancestors. If the signs were good, on the following day the hunters would wash themselves in water to which were added the leaves of various trees which they had collected themselves in the bush. Peirone adds that their guns were protected by the application on the barrel of a smudge of the augural flour, while Stannus mentions that a specific hunting medicine—consisting of pieces of wood threaded on a string or of dried animal blood and charcoal—was tied to the gun barrel. Stannus also states that everyone in the hunting party would have medicine rubbed into small incisions on the arms, shoulders, and occasionally on the body. When hunting was done locally, he adds, the ground tusk of the elephant, i.e. the tusk on the underside of the slain elephant, was the property of the chief. But many hunting parties involved long periods of separation from the village, the men often remaining absent for as many as three months. In this situation, according to Stannus, 'The hunter inaugurating a hunt had the first shot at an elephant, and all the ivory was his till sold at the coast, when the followers got their proportion of calico brought back. . . . The chief has choice of the biggest tusk on the return of the party to the village,' which suggests that this was done normally before setting off to trade at the coast.[56]

It is evident that the two main figures in Yao elephant hunting were the principal hunter and his chief. Moreover, it is possible to see that an enterprising young man could rapidly assert himself through hunting and trading and, if Stannus is correct, accumulate surplus wealth which he could then use to help to establish himself as a chief on his own. It is impossible to project the accounts of Peirone and Stannus back too far beyond the late nineteenth century, but even before firearms became common among the Yao after 1860 it seems reasonable to suggest that this mode of organization might have been operative and that prowess in hunting was a well established route to wider personal political authority. If any tentative contrast is to be drawn with the Makua, it would be that the internal organization of Makua hunting parties may have been more communalistic than was that of the Yao.

There is, however, one striking similarity between Makua and Yao elephant hunting, this being the shared concern for the maintenance of the existing social order during the lengthy absence of the men. Stannus writes that 'Should the wife of anyone of the expedition commit adultery her husband might get killed. A man going to hunt will never have intercourse with his wife the night before, otherwise he would be unsuccessful.' Peirone, too, emphasizes the critical significance of ritual cleanliness, observing that the role of the wife of the main hunter was like that of a queen in the reintegration ceremonies which were observed upon the return of the party to the village. 'Upon the arrival of the caravan, the wife of the man who killed the beast goes to sit upon the tusks, young boys raise the skin of the dead animal on the heads and dance around the wife; the hunter grasps the trunk of the elephant with one hand', to the accompaniment of chanted praises of thanksgiving. A feast followed, after which the hunter took the tusks to the chief and then washed together with his wife in the specially prepared mixture of water and leaves, thereby ending the celebration. This was her reward for maintaining celibacy during her husband's absence.[57]

This same insistence upon ritual purity and village integration was observed in the closely related institution of caravan trade, which Stannus indicates may reasonably be regarded as an extension of elephant hunting in terms of its social implications for the Yao village. Yao caravans were often away from their home for a very long time. Henry Salt met Yao traders at the Mozambique coast in 1809 who had already been gone for two and three months, although one Yao said that the journey to the coast could be accomplished in a little more than six weeks.[58] That the factor of time was of no great consequence in the economic reckoning of the Yao is also witnessed by this traveller's proverb: 'See the caterpillar's leisured gait! / He does not reach his leafy bait / By haste unseemly.'[59] Village headmen or their chiefs controlled the dispatching of caravans, while protective medicines, ritual ablutions, and the avoidance of adultery by the wives of the travellers were essential to their well-being.[60] It is important to recognize, however, that not all caravans obtained their ivory, and later slaves, by hunting or raiding. In time perhaps most Yao became primarily traders, preferring to let others do the actual procurement of the goods for export to the coast. In the last quarter of the nineteenth century, Johnson found that 'Every man had a great ambition to buy an elephant's tusk and then to borrow men to carry such tusks to the coast.' After a trading expedition was over a man would distribute his returns with an eye towards future expeditions.

One would say: 'My Mother, you sent a tusk and I have returned with two or three kegs of gunpowder, such and such gun-caps, so many bags of salt, such and such good cloths.' Then they divided the goods and took an offering to the graves of the village: some cloth to spread over them and some salt to put at the head of the dead. Afterwards salt, &c., was put aside to buy more tusks for future trading.[61]

By this date, and surely much earlier, the Yao had developed a very clear business sense when it came to the financing of their international trading interests.

Salt was a staple of regional trade and it was a source of capitalization for international trade. It was also intimately involved in the rituals surrounding the maintenance of the unity of the matrilineage, which lay at the core of Yao socio-political organization. Yao life centred on the village, which at its smallest was a spatial expression of a single, matrilineally defined, uterine sorority group or *mbumba*. The village headman was also the head of the *mbumba* and was usually the eldest living brother of the core sorority group. Fissiparation was marked among the Yao, with younger brothers always anxious to take advantage of tensions within the growing matrilineage so that they could move away with their sisters and set themselves up as headmen over their own *mbumba*.[62] There was thus a highly developed mystique surrounding the integrity of the matrilineage and one of the major expressions of this mystical concept was the Yao belief in a dread form of edema called *ndaka*.

According to Mitchell, *ndaka* affected sexually inactive people who were 'suddenly brought into contact with a person, or an object which he has touched, after having intercourse'. The usual victims of *ndaka* were the young and the elderly, but sexually active adults were vulnerable during prolonged absence from their normal sexual partners. To protect themselves, people in this last group were supposed to have ritual intercourse with a stranger as a kind of inoculation.[63] The great danger of coming into contact with a sexually active person was that the only people who could become victimized by *ndaka* were the members of his or her own matrilineage. Salt appears to have been regarded as a particularly potent vehicle for the transmission of *ndaka* and therefore for the exacerbation of tensions within the core matrilineage.[64] The mystical relationship of salt and *ndaka* to the social unity of the matrilineage would seem to explain why it was that men who were away on a caravan expedition in the nineteenth century were expressly forbidden to use salt, even though salt might constitute one of the main items of trade for the caravan as an economic extension of the social unit of the village.[65] Similarly, the powerful fear of *ndaka* as an expression of social control makes it easier to appreciate the premium which was placed on conjugal celibacy for those who remained at home during the absence of the men on hunting or trading expeditions.[66]

The Yao *mbumba* was comparable to the Makua-Lomwe *oloko*, but most Yao villages were ideally composed of a single matri-lineage, with average size tending towards about a dozen huts with a population of four or five dozen inhabitants.[67] During the nineteenth century, however, and perhaps earlier, Yao residential patterns were characterized by the growth of large towns, often with closely associated outlying villages.[68] Within the village, the headman never exercised his authority without consulting his advisers, a procedure which the tendency towards fragmentation can only have encouraged for anyone who sought to maintain his political validity. The political structure and administration of the great territorial chiefdoms of the later nineteenth century have been described elsewhere and do not bear reiteration here.[69] For the earlier periods of Yao history it is impossible to do more than speculate as to whether or not such larger political units existed, although Bocarro's account of his travels in 1616 and the size of Yao caravans appearing at Mozambique Island from the middle of the eighteenth century indicate that at the very least there was a considerable degree of economic cooperation between smaller independent villages and chiefdoms.

The only source for social stratification among the Yao in the period before the later nineteenth century, when stratification could be explained in terms of the impact of a long history of international trading and the acquisition of large numbers of slaves, is Abdallah. But Abdallah was very much an aristocrat himself so that his testimony on this score must be treated with particular care.[70] If he is to be believed, the Chisi were perhaps the very first 'aristocracy' among the Yao, but they were not the only group to receive special treatment within Yao society. Before coastal cloths were known, chiefs, elders, and other promi-nent men were distinguished by their exclusive right to wear serval, lion, and leopard skins, while others wore barkcloth and more common animal hides.[71] It is possible, then, that a developed sense of social differentiation had taken place within Yao society before the advent of trading to the coast. Accordingly, when new wealth came into the orbit of the Yao, people already knew how to take advantage of it so as to differentiate themselves from their fellows. Abdallah proudly proclaims that as a result of the ivory and slave trades 'we Yaos became very rich', but he also points out that of the many cloths brought back from the coast 'some cannot be worn by common folk, for whom they are forbidden, but only by nobles' and their families. Among these cloths the most highly prized was a bright red cloth of good quality called *Ndeule*, about which people sang:

> Ndeule, Ndeule, Ndeule,
> Nduele is a lovely cloth;
> When I wear it everyone knows
> As the lord of many I pose.
> It's a lovely cloth, Ndeule.

Again, only the women of chiefs could wear brass wire.[72] Perhaps Abdallah's own sense of aristocracy led him to exaggerate, but there seems little doubt that the Yao were a people who were more than prepared to acknowledge either ascriptive or self-elected leadership when they encountered it in their midst.

A final illustration of this aspect of Yao social structure in the pre-colonial era is the disproportionate social value which was placed on trading and journeying to the coast in a society which was still essentially agrarian. Abdallah quotes several songs which make the distinction between the well-travelled man and the 'pounders of beans' abundantly clear. The most poignant of these runs:

> The traveller's child,
> In accents wild,
> Cries, 'Daddy, calico!'
> But the child of him
> Who bark-cloth wears,
> Cries, 'Tap, tap, tap! you go!'

Indeed, as Abdallah notes, the ideal life for a Yao man was that of a rover. 'Should anybody say, "I am a Yao", not having visited other countries, he is not a Yao at all, and everybody laughs at him, saying, "This is a woman, not a man." '[73]

The Maravi

The nineteenth-century image of the Yao as roving caravaneers stands in marked contrast to that of the Maravi peoples, most importantly for this study the Mang'anja and Chewa, who more than either the Yao or the Makua-Lomwe were a people who traded within the confines of their own country during that period As Livingstone observed of the Mang'anja of the Shire valley they were 'much more fond of the home pursuits of spinning weaving, smelting iron, and cultivating the soil, than of foreign travel'. This he posed in direct contrast to the Yao, who he believed 'had little of a mechanical turn, and not much love for agriculture, but were very keen traders and travellers'.[74]

All nineteenth-century European travellers in the Shire valley were impressed by the fruitfulness of the country. Livingstone remarked upon the ability of the Maravi to cultivate enormous sweet potatoes and to preserve them in the ground for months 'by digging a pit and burying them therein inclosed in wood-ashes'.[75] According to Kirk, however, who served as botanist on Livingstone's Zambesi expedition in the late 1850s, sorghum was still the staple crop in most areas, with maize being grown extensively in the highlands and manioc also having a wide distribution. Pearl millet, yams, bananas, beans, and ground-nuts were also cultivated.[76] Livingstone adds that maize was grown all year round.[77]

According to Morgan, Mang'anja agriculture is marked by the existence of two distinctive types of cultivation. *Mphala* is cultivable land which depends on annual rains, as in most parts of East Central Africa, while *dimba* are dry-season gardens whose existence is made possible by annual flooding in the lowlands. It appears that *dimba* acreage was much more extensive in the nineteenth than in the twentieth century, and provided the Mang'anja with significant protection against dependence on rainfall and crop failure.[78] Concerning the division of labour in Mang'anja cultivation of *mphala*, Livingstone has this to say:

All the people of a village turn out to labour in the fields. It is no uncommon thing to see men, women, and children hard at work, with the baby lying close by beneath a shady bush. When a new piece of woodland is to be cleared, . . . the trees are cut down with their little axes of soft native iron; trunks and branches are piled up and burnt, and the ashes spread on the soil. The corn is planted among the standing stumps which are left to rot. If grass land is to be brought under cultivation, as much tall grass as the labourer can conveniently lay hold of is collected together and tied into a knot. He then strikes his hoe around the tufts to sever the roots, and, leaving all standing,

23

proceeds until the whole ground assumes the appearance of a field covered with little shocks of corn in harvest. A short time before the rains begin these grass shocks are collected in small heaps, covered with earth, and burnt, the ashes and burnt soil being used to fertilize the ground.[79]

Although it still remained for the women to do most of the harvesting of the crops, the cooperation between sexes in planting and cultivating marked Mang'anja agriculture off from that of the Yao and Makua-Lomwe.[80] In these circumstances, it would have been difficult for Mang'anja men to absent themselves from home for the long periods of time that were imposed by elephant hunting and caravan trading. Thus it may well be that the productiveness of the land imposed this closer cooperation in agricultural production on the Mang'anja and thereby created a less marked division of labour between the sexes in their society.

A vivid illustration in support of this argument comes from what Kirk says about the cultivation and processing of cotton in the Shire valley, where it had been introduced by the Arabs before the arrival of the Portuguese in the sixteenth century. At least four varieties of cotton were grown, the most common being the foreign *Tonje Manga* and the indigenous *Tonje Kaja*. *Tonje Manga* was a perennial, but required re-planting after three years. The shorter stapled *Tonje Kaja* had to be re-planted every year in the highlands.[81] Plots of cotton were generally half an acre or more in size.[82] At the beginning of September 1859, a time when the Yao and Makua hunters and traders would have been many weeks away from home, Kirk witnessed the gathering of the local cotton crop at a village in the middle Shire valley.

> The crop of cotton was now coming in. All classes from the poor man to the chief work the cotton. The process is laborious. First the field, after being cleared of grass and weeds, has to be kept so. The cotton is picked as it ripens. The *Tonje Kaja* adhering closely to the seed, requires much labour in separating and the yield is small compared with that of the *Tanje Nianga* [*sic*— read *Tonje Manga*]. Once cleared it has all to be arranged with the hand, piece by piece of 6 inches and spun on a sort of bobbin. This is again changed to another in which process it receives an additional twist. The weaving is simple. The thread is passed from end to end between two horizontal bamboos, supported in the ground. There is thus a double layer of threads. The under ones are attached by *Buaze* or *Musheo* [a local fibre bush] threads to an upper stick which serves to bring them

up or down above the others, while a shuttle consisting of a stick, a little longer than the breadth of the cloth and covered with the cotton thread, is passed from side to side, the thread unwinding as it passes. The resulting fabric is coarse and can never for a moment stand against foreign manufactures. No attempt is made at dyeing, but while it remains of a white colour, the owner seems very proud. The work except the cultivation and even a good deal of that, is done entirely by the men. Indeed we noticed how frequently the men were seen labouring in the fields.[83]

That Mang'anja men were much more closely involved with the agricultural production of their society than were those of the Yao and Makua-Lomwe seems evident. Furthermore, the fact that the coarse cloth which they wove was still in full production in the middle of the nineteenth century eloquently gives the lie to Kirk's assertion that it could not stand the pressure of foreign competition. Livingstone remarked approvingly that the *Tonje Manga* was considered equal to the best New Orleans at Manchester, but he also observed of the *Tonje Kaja* that 'because it makes stronger cloth, many of the people prefer it to the foreign cotton'.[84] Indeed, the Mang'anja canvas cloth or *machila*, as it was known to its makers and to the Portuguese on the Zambesi, was not directly threatened by the Indian trade cloths which had dominated inland trade for centuries precisely because it was so very coarse and tough. The Portuguese used it for their personal litters, which were also called *machilas*, and produced their own *machila* on the Zambesi *prazos*. On occasion there were complaints that the cloth itself was capturing some of the wider Zambesia market from the less durable and more expensive Indian cloths.[85] From a practical point of view, then, *machila* was well worth having, if less prestigious than the more elaborate trade cloths.[86]

Southern Malawi was also blessed with several major sources of high quality salt and an abundance of rich deposits of iron ore. There was a large salt-extractable plain at the south end of Lake Nyasa which was actively exploited in the 1860s, and there were other smaller locations in the Shire valley and along certain river banks flowing into the Zambesi where salt was produced and traded locally.[87] But the major source of salt in Maravi country was the western shore of the shallow and saline Lake Chilwa, to the east of the Shire valley. An account from 1861 mentions that there were three varieties of salt to be had in southern Malawi.

The first and best, though a little darker, is equal to good table-salt in England. This is obtained from the shores of Lake Shirwa. It impregnates the soil, which the natives wash, evaporating the solution twice or thrice. Two yards of calico bought twenty-five pounds of it. The other two kinds are very inferior, and were obtained from certain rushes growing in the marsh lands by the lake. The rush is burnt, the ashes washed, and the solution evaporated several times.[88]

By the 1840s at the very latest salt was being acquired in the valley by both Yao and Bisa traders, the latter coming from west of the Luangwa River, so that they could purchase provisions along the way to the coast. For the return trip salt from the coast would serve the same purpose. Between the coast and the Shire valley, wrote Guillain, 'this country is deprived'.[89] Indeed, Abdallah dates Yao trade in salt with the Mang'anja and Nyasa to before the period of ivory and slaves.[90] Lake Chilwa was also an important source of salt for Makua and Lomwe, who made up special caravans to procure it there.[91]

No less important in the regional trade of East Central Africa was Maravi ironware. According to the Governor of the Rivers of Sena (Zambesia) in 1806, 'The Marave . . . are the only people who work the iron in these hinterlands for trade, exporting from their lands every quality of agricultural and domestic tools which are used in the Rivers of Sena. Hoes are traded to Mozambique, Sofala, Inhambane, and other ports of the coast where this metal is unavailable', and iron bars were also widely current.[92] A half century later the Mang'anja were recognized as better black-smiths than the Yao, and Maravi hoes were a regular item of Yao trading caravans to Quelimane, where the local officials knew they had to be on the look for locally manufactured hoes of inferior quality which the Yao sometimes sought to pass off as being Maravi work.[93] This being the case, it seems quite possible that the hoes which were traded by the Yao to Mozambique Island in the later eighteenth century were also acquired from the Mang'anja, although they were known at the coast as 'Yao hoes'.[94] Closer to home, the Mang'anja themselves seem to have recognized how important their skills in iron working were for the success of their agriculture.[95]

Yet within the Maravi group there were clear distinctions made by those who knew the iron trade of the region. Among the Mang'-anja, for example, it was the people in the hills, where the ore was richer and more abundant, whose work was most highly prized.[96] Rowley made particular note of this phenomenon of uneven distribution of raw materials among the Mang'anja. 'The people in the highlands were rich in iron, those in the valley were poor; so when a highlander wanted cotton to make himself a cloth, he sent down hoes, and such like things, to the valley, and obtained cotton in exchange.'[97] Taken together with the active exchange in foodstuffs and dried fish, the cotton for ironware trade in the valley helped to make the Mang'anja the most self-sufficient people in East Central Africa.[98] No wonder that southern Malawi was as important a meeting ground of regional and international trade as was the coast itself. No wonder, too, that except for the relatively short episode of Maravi trading hegemony in the seventeenth century—itself the product of military conquest and colonization rather than of commercial supremacy—the Mang'anja were content to let others come to them to seek the wealth of their land and to bring them the exotic goods of the coast. Similarly, although less clearly perhaps, this explanation why the Mang'anja were less actively engaged in long-distance caravaneering than were the Yao and even the Makua would seem to apply to the Chewa.[99] Only copper, which came from Katanga and the interior beyond Zumbo and the Luangwa River, was not available in the country of the Maravi.[100] Even gold, for which the Portuguese never ceased searching, was available in the western reaches of Maravi territory.[101]

When it comes to the two items which formed the nub of international trade in East Central Africa—ivory and slaves—southern Malawi was equally provided with great herds of elephant and a particularly dense population. One of the most prominent features of the lower Shire valley was the Elephant Marsh, where in 1859 Livingstone saw 'nine large herds of elephants; they sometimes formed a line two miles long'. On another occasion he believed himself to have counted eight hundred elephant there.[102] Elephant were also plentiful around the Bua River, to the south-west of Lake Nyasa and in the Luangwa River valley on the western border of Maravi territory.[103] The Mang'anja did not hunt elephant on foot, as it was very difficult to move about in the marshy plains which the animals frequented in the valley. Instead they dug deep pits and sometimes attacked elephant from tree-perches by plunging a heavy spear in between the shoulder blades. Stannus also mentions game pits among the

Chipeta.[104] Hunting was also pursued among the Chewa, while around Zumbo, at the confluence of the Luangwa and Zambesi rivers, the method used was to sever the elephant's tendon with a wide-edged axe, a practice which may reflect influences from peoples to the south of the Zambesi.[105] Almost everywhere among the Maravi the ground tusk of a dead elephant was the due of the territorial chief or *mambo* of the district, the lesser chiefs and village headmen not having any such claim to it.[106]

In common with the Makua-Lomwe and the Yao, however, life for the average Maravi focused on the village, which again was primarily a geographical expression of a social unit based on the matrilineage of its founder. Chewa and Mang'anja villages were often composed of several matrilineages, with the founding family providing the headman or *nfumu*, who was also known as the *mwini mudzi* or owner of the village. The Chewa matrilineages or *mbumba* correspond to their Yao counterpart, the *liwele* ('breast'), but in contrast to the Yao and Makua-Lomwe the Chewa matrilineage remained the principal socio-political unit of society rather than the smaller lineage segment or *bele* (cf. Yao *mbumba* and Makua-Lomwe *oloko*). With the possible exception of the Chipeta, however, the Maravi village was usually an administrative unit of a hierarchically ordered chiefdom or kingdom in which there were clearly delegated powers above the level of the village in the person of the territorial chief, *mwini dziko* or *mambo*, and the paramount chief or king, who was also known as *mambo*. Territorial political organization appears to have had a much longer and more firmly entrenched history among the Maravi than among their eastern neighbours. But it must be recognized that the degree of authority which the Maravi kingdoms exercised over individual villages depended very much upon the fortunes of the state. Political power was normally delegated and decentralized among the Maravi and the secession of chiefdoms from kingdoms was a common feature of the political process. Perpetual kinship relations were one mechanism for counterbalancing this tendency towards fragmentation, as were territorial cults associated with the more important paramount chiefdoms. Neither was entirely effective. For the Mang'anja the high point of this political integration was probably in the late sixteenth and seventeenth centuries; for the Chewa it was somewhat later. But for both the authority of the larger political units was much dissipated by the middle of the nineteenth century. Over time, then, the matrilineage-village remained the key institution in Maravi socio-political organization.[107]

Conclusions

This examination of the economic and social systems of the three major peoples of East Central Africa during the nineteenth century suggests several tentative conclusions about the indigenous forces which moulded the pattern of international trade there. It would be very misleading to portray the economies of these people as being based simply upon 'subsistence' agriculture, when in fact there were very significant differences in both productivity of the land and associated modes of production. However, these very differences and the unequal distribution of essential items such as salt and iron on both a local and a regional level nurtured a healthy exchange of goods between these peoples that was a function of production. In this transitional stage of development, to use Rodney's terminology, each one of these societies was beginning to move slowly from communalism towards some other, as yet undefined, stage of development.[108]

Of the three peoples, the Maravi, and particularly the Mang'anja, enjoyed the richest and most varied economy. Their self-sufficiency seems to have imposed a more equitable division of labour between the sexes upon their relations of production, while making it unnecessary for them to seek out their neighbours in search of essential commodities. At the same time, the wealth of their economy made possible the rise of a more highly developed state system than existed among the Makua-Lomwe and the Yao. Surpluses from Mang'anja agriculture, for example, were utilized to support the chiefs' bodyguards.[109] It seems reasonable to suggest that the large armies of the great Maravi paramount chiefs of earlier centuries were at least partially provided for in the same fashion. These armies became the vehicles of Maravi imperial expansion in the sixteenth and seventeenth centuries.

By contrast, the Makua-Lomwe were perhaps only marginally an agricultural people, so that hunting and regular prolonged absences from home on the part of their men were an established feature of the economy quite independent of the demands of international trade. The Makua-Lomwe seem to have been able to produce their own iron implements, although the widespread

29

prestige of Mang'anja wares suggests that they would have obtained these whenever possible. Similarly, high quality salt was a local product for those who inhabited the coastal region, but a rarer commodity for those who lived farther inland. Their tradition of hunting, gathering, and trading with their neighbours undoubtedly faciliated their ability to shift their energies in accordance with the demands of international trade.

The Yao seem to have fallen somewhere between these two poles, both of which were, of course, located within the same economic spectrum. For while the Yao possessed a more abundant agricultural economy than did the Makua-Lomwe, the absence of fine salt within their country, and their more scattered population seem to have fostered a tradition of extensive travelling within and without Yaoland which enabled them to seize the opportunities for trading in luxury items offered by the penetration of the international market economy in East Central Africa. Moreover, their agricultural economy was not so productive as was that of the Mang'anja, so that once men had cleared the fields it was not necessary for them to continue to invest their energy in that direction.[110]

Indeed, in both Yao and Makua-Lomwe societies it seems indisputable that the most productive members of the agricultural economy were the women, upon whose labour the fabric of society was constructed. For it was their concentration on basic food production, particularly among the Yao, where hunting was apparently a less significant means of food production than among the Makua-Lomwe, which freed their men for elephant hunting and trading. Neither the Yao nor the Makua-Lomwe men were exceptional in their exploitation of female labour—it is a phenomenon well known from almost every society in history. But as this point is not often made in studies of trade in Africa, it is important to remember that the far-ranging trading activities of the Yao, in particular, were initially made possible only because there were women at home to tend their crops for them. While women were taking the major responsibility for producing the real wealth in their societies—wealth upon which genuine development, however gradual, could be based—men were beginning to engage themselves in a related set of purely extractive economic activities for the luxury trade in ivory of the Eastern and, much less significantly until the nineteenth century, Western worlds.

Participation in this trade eventually became so important to the Yao that the economic values of their society came to be derived from the wealth and prestige that it brought, rather than from the truly productive aspects of the economy, such as agriculture and manufacturing. Social differentiation and stratification were increased as a result of this trade, although the productive capacity of society was in no way increased, except by the addition of slave labour that was purchased with its profits. This process became even more pronounced with the rise of the slave trade in East Central Africa, which brought in train the inevitable weakening of some victims and the fragile strengthening of others who preyed upon them and accumulated great personal wealth and political power.[111] By the end of the nineteenth century the economic values of people like the Yao had been completely distorted so that this sort of trade was considered the only activity worth pursuing. At the same time, the entire course of their economic development had been disastrously skewed and was already on its way towards an underdeveloped state. Even the Mang'anja, ravaged though they were during the nineteenth century by foreign slave traders, among whom the Yao figured prominently, deluded themselves in the belief that 'the River tribes say that riches come from the Yao'.[112] Indeed, by the late nineteenth century the various trading goods of the international market—virtually all of them consumables or luxury items, none of which contributed positively to African methods of production—had penetrated just about every corner of East Central Africa. In the isolated Lomwe village of Egwoli, north-west of the Inagu Hills in northern Mozambique, O'Neill observed in the 1880s that 'for *one hand-palm's breadth* of the commonest calico, a mat of native make that must have cost many days' labour' could be purchased.[113] The growth of international trade in East Central Africa must be set against this stark reality.

NOTES

1. See Captain Colomb, *Slave-Catching in the Indian Ocean. A Record of Naval Experience* (London, 1873), pp. 24–8.
2. The following paragraphs are based upon Swanzie Agnew, 'Environment and History: the Malawian Setting', in Bridglal Pachai (ed.), *The Early History of Malawi* (London, 1972), pp. 28–48; *Átlas de Moçambique* (Lourenço Marques, 1962); S. J. K. Baker, 'The East African Environment', in Roland Oliver and Gervase Mathew (eds.), *History of East Africa* (Oxford, 1963), I, pp. 1–22; Mário de Carvalho, *A Agricultura Tradicional de Moçambique* (Lourenço Marques, 1970), pp. 13–15, 32–47; and Francis F. Ojany, 'The Geography of East Africa',

in B. A. Ogot and J. A. Kieran (eds.), *Zamani—A Survey of East African History* (Nairobi, 1968), pp. 22–48.

3. See, e.g., Henry E. O'Neill, 'Journey from Mozambique to Lakes Shirwa and Amaramba', *Proceedings of the Royal Geographical Society*, VI (1884), Part I, pp. 632–46.

4. U.S.P.G., U.M.C.A. A/I/iii/2, Edward Steere to R. M. Heanley, London, 21 June 1877; J. F. Elton, *Travels and Researches among the Lakes and Mountains of Eastern & Central Africa*, ed. H. B. Cotterill (London, 1879), p. 206.

5. It is impossible to determine how much the present demographic picture has been altered by the liberation struggle in Mozambique and the Portuguese policy of villagization.

6. Some support for this tentative suggestion may be found in the narrative of Gaspar Bocarro's journey overland from Tete to Kilwa in 1616, which will be discussed in greater detail in Chapter 2.

7. Inácio Caetano Xavier, 'Notícias dos Domínios Portugueses na Costa de África Oriental', *Moç.*, 26 December 1758, in António Alberto de Andrade (ed.), *Relações de Moçambique Setecentista* (Lisbon, 1955), p. 149 (original copy in B.N.L., F.G., Cod. 826; another in A.N.T.T., M.R., maço 604); Marvin Miracle, *Maize in Tropical Africa* (Madison, 1966), p. 97.

8. Joaquim José Varella, 'Descrição da Capitania de Moçambique e suas povoações e produções, pertencentes a Coroa de Portugal', n.d., but dated internally to 1788, in Andrade, *Relações*, p. 378 (original copy in A.N.T.T., M.R., maço 604).

9. João dos Santos, 'Ethiopia Oriental', in George McCall Theal (ed.), *Records of South-East Africa* (London, 1901), VII, pp. 189, 268, 306 (original edition, Évora, 1609).

10. Alpers, 'Expansion of Islam', pp. 173–81.

11. Mary Louise Franz, 'The Masking Complex of the Makonde-Speaking People of East Central Africa', unpublished M.A. thesis, University of California, Los Angeles, 1970, Ch. 3.

12. See Desmond T. Cole, 'Doke's Classification of Bantu Languages', in C. M. Doke and D. T. Cole, *Contributions to the History of Bantu Linguistics* (Johannesburg, 1961), pp. 87–8; Malcolm Guthrie, *The Classification of the Bantu Languages* (London, 1948), pp. 59–64; M. A. Bryan, *The Bantu Languages of Africa* (London, 1959), pp. 133–9.

13. For the sources of these terms and distinctions, see *A Standard Swahili-English Dictionary* (Oxford, 1939), pp. 323, 419; Meredith Sanderson, *A Dictionary of the Yao Language* (Zomba, 1954), p. 43; Thomas Price, 'The Name "Anguru" ', *Nyasaland Jl.*, V, 1 (1952), pp. 23–5; W. H. J. Rangeley, 'The Ayao', *Nyasaland Jl.*, XVI, 1 (1963), pp. 8–9, 13; J. Rebman, *Dictionary of the Kiniassa Language*, ed. J. L. Krapf (St. Chrischona, 1877), p. 120; Jorge Dias, *Os Macondes de Moçambique* (Lisbon, 1964), I, pp. 63–5; Soares de Castro, *Os Achirimas (Ensaio Etnográfico)* (Lourenço Marques, 1941), pp. 8–9; Abel dos Santos Baptista, *Monográfia Etnográfica sobre os Macuas* (Lisbon, 1951), pp. 17–18. A. J. de Mello Machado, *Entre os Macuas de Angoche—Historiando Moçambique* (Lisbon, 1970), pp. 108–9.

14. Castro, *Os Achirimas*, pp. 9–13; O'Neill, 'Journey from Mozambique', pp. 642, 727; T.N.A., Secretariat 42186, 'Preliminary Report on the Makua of S. Province', by W. H. Whiteley, 3 February 1951, p. 9.

15. ibid., p. 11.

16. J. Vincent, 'The Namuli Mountains, Portuguese East Africa', *The Geographical Jl.*, LXXXI, 4 (1933), pp. 317, 323.

17. T.N.A., Secretariat 42186, 'Essays on the Makua. Being the final report presented to the Tanganyika Government on field work in the Masasi district, 1950–1951', by W. H. Whiteley, 5 December 1951, p. 2.

18. An additional factor linking otherwise autonomous communities was marriage,

which was exogamous for each lineage group. And marriage, of course, had an economic function, in terms of the present and future supply of labour, as well as a social function. The most important examination of this problem in Africa has been made by Claude Meillassoux, *Anthropologie Économique des Gouro de Côte d'Ivoire—De l'économie de subsistence á l'agriculture commerciale* (Paris and The Hague, 1970), Ch. 8.

19. Diogo da Câmara Reis, 'Os Macuas de Mogovolas', *Boletim da Sociedade de Estudos de Moçambique*, XXXI, 131 (1962), p. 35.

20. 'This is the exact method which the Makua use for making their spears and their utensils: they take a piece from the mine, fire it, and shake it vigourously so that the pieces fall in flakes, there remaining the completely pure iron, without any other work.' A.H.U., Moç., Cx. 22, Manuel Galvão da Silva, 'Noticia Sobre as duas Minas de ferro, e a mostras de pedro que mando', Moç., 21 August 1785.

21. Eugène de Froberville, 'Notes sur les moeurs, coutumes et traditions des amakoua, sur le commerce et la traite des esclaves dans l'Afrique Orientale', *Bulletin de la Société de Géographie*, 3ᵉ Série, 8 (1847), pp. 322–3.

22. Vincent, 'Namuli Mountains', p. 324.

23. Froberville, 'Notes', p. 322.

24. Aylward Shorter, 'Ukimbu and the Kimbu Chiefdoms of Southern Unyamwezi', unpublished D.Phil. thesis, University of Oxford, 1968, pp. 122, 221–9, noting hunting guilds in general and the distinction drawn between the separate guilds for elephant trappers and elephant hunters, and pp. 247–9, where he observes that 'Members of the elephant hunting and trapping guilds were specialists in this elephant lore [relating to the divination of human affairs], and there was apparently a considerable mystique attached to elephant hunting long before the ivory trade reached Ukimbu at the turn of the eighteenth and nineteenth centuries'. John Lamphear, 'The Kamba and the Northern Mrima Coast', in Richard Gray and David Birmingham (eds.), *Pre-Colonial African Trade* (London, 1970), pp. 79–80; and Joseph C. Miller, 'Cokwe Trade and Conquest in the Nineteenth Century', ibid., pp. 179–80.

25. António Pinto de Miranda, 'Memória sobre a costa de Africa', *c.* 1766, in Andrade, *Relações*, p. 232 (original copy in A.N.T.T., M.R., maço 604). See below, Ch. 4.

26. T.N.A., Masasi and Newala District Books, 'Tribal History and Legends'. This, too, is reminiscent of the history of Kamba and Cokwe expansion in the nineteenth century.

27. John Hanning Speke, *Journal of Discovery of the Sources of the Nile* (London, 1863), p. 63; T.N.A., Kilosa District Book, 'Tribal History and Legends', entry on Makua by J. F. Kenny-Dillon; interviews with Mzee Mbrisho Kipindula, Wami Station, Miono Division, Bagamoyo Area, Coast Region, Tanzania, 14 November 1972, and Mzee Ali Rusewa Pangapanga, Mziha, Turiani Division, Morogoro Area, Morogoro Region, 14 February 1973. Mzee Kipindula's grandfather was a Makua elephant hunter named Fundi Tambuu who came to Udoe from Masasi during the reign of Seyyid Majid bin Sultan of Zanzibar (1856–1870). Fundi Tambuu hunted with guns and had a special medicine for elephant hunting. He and his followers were welcomed by the Doe, and he settled and married a daughter of the local chief. According to Mzee Pangapanga, many of the southern Zigua learned to hunt elephant from the Makua.

28. Andrew D. Roberts, 'Nyamwezi Trade', in Gray and Birmingham, *Pre-Colonial African Trade*, p. 69; see also T.N.A., Secretariat 42186/14, L.C.A. to L.G. 3, 8 February 1954.

29. Câmara Reis, 'Os Macuas de Mogovolas', pp. 33–4.

30. T.N.A., Secretariat 42186, 'Preliminary Report', p. 12; cf. Santos, 'Ethiopia Oriental', p. 306.

31. Ernest Cambier, 'Rapport de l'excursion sur la route de Mpwawa adressé a

l'Association Internationale Africaine', *Bulletin de la Société Belgé de Géographie*, II (1878), p. 203.

32. T.N.A., Secretariat 42186, 'Preliminary Report', p. 28.

33. T.N.A., Secretariat 42186, 'Essays', p. 42; Antonio Camizão, *Indicações Geraes sobre a Capitania-Mór de Mossuril—Governo do Moçambique: Appendice ao Relatorio de 1 de Janeiro de 1901* (Mozambique, 1901), p. 5.

34. ibid., p. 5.

35. Santos in 'Ethiopia Oriental', p. 308, calls the chief *fumo*; N.A.I.P.G., L.M. 125–B, fl. 547, António de Brito Freire to Viceroy, Moç., 19 August 1752, where he calls the chiefs *gummos*. Whiteley states that *mhumu* is 'a rather archaic word for clan head', but he may not have realized that it was also the title for village chief, since the pattern of Makua settlement in southern Tanzania was in *oloko* homesteads, rather than in villages. See T.N.A., Secretariat 42186, 'Preliminary Report', pp. 25, 28. According to Camizão, *Indicações*, the Makua word for chief in the interior was *M'beua*.

36. P.e Gerard, 'Costumes dos Macua do Medo, região de Namuno, circunscrição de Montepuez', *Moçambique*, 28 (1941), pp. 18–19; Vincent, 'Namuli Mountains', p. 327; Santos, 'Ethiopia Oriental', p. 308; Froberville, 'Notes', p. 322; Camizão, *Indicações*, p. 4.

37. O'Neill, 'Journey from Mozambique', p. 635, and 'On the Coast Lands and some Rivers and Ports of Mozambique', *Proceedings of the Royal Geographical Society*, IV, (1882), p. 199.

38. The most important descriptions of this wider political organization among the Makua in Mozambique are Froberville, 'Notes', p. 322; O'Neill, 'Journey from Mozambique', p. 635; Gerard, 'Costumes', p. 18; and Albano Aujustida Portugal Durão, 'Reconhecimento e Occupação dos Territorios entre o Messangire e os Picos Namuli', *Boletim da Sociedade de Geografia de Lisboa*, XX, 7 (1902), p. 12. The analyses available for the Makua of Tanzania are much more detailed and may be found in T.N.A., Masasi District Book, 'Tribal Government', Lindi District Book, 'Laws, Manners, and Customs', and Secretariat 42186, 'Preliminary Report', pp. 22–7, especially p. 26, and 'Essays', pp. 98–100. The literature on Makua clans in Mozambique is fairly useless, but see Gerard, ' "Mahimo" Macuas', *Moçambique*, 26 (1941), pp. 5–22; Castro, *Os Achirimas*, p. 19, and 'Os Lómuès no Larde', *Boletim Geral das Colónias*, 304 (1950), pp. 60–1; Santos Baptista, *Os Macuas*, pp. 22–9.

39. Froberville, 'Notes', p. 313. For the combination of firearms and traditional weaponry, see Gastão de Sousa Dias (ed.), *Silva Porto e a Travessia do Continente Africano* (Lisbon, 1938), p. 156.

40. The major source is Eduardo do Couto Lupi, *Angoche—Breve memoria sobre uma das capitanias-móres do Districto de Moçambique* (Lisbon, 1907), pp. 98–105; also important are Camizão, *Indicações*, p. 4; Froberville, 'Notes', p. 313; and J. Jerónimo de Alcântara Guerreiro, 'Episódios inéditos das lutas contra os macuas no reinado de D. Maria I, segundo o Códice CXVI, fls. 179 a 184 da Biblioteca Pública de Évora', *Boletim da Sociedade de Estudos da Colónia de Moçambique*, XV, 52 (1947), pp. 79–80.

41. T.N.A., Secretariat 42186, 'Preliminary Report', pp. 18–20, and 'Essays', p. 37. For *utani*, see T.V. Scrivenor, 'Some Notes on Utani, or the Vituperative Alliances existing between the Clans in the Masasi District', *T.N.R.*, 4 (1937), pp. 72–4, in which he distinguishes between *utani* between clans and that between peoples.

42. Yohanna B. Abdallah, *The Yaos*, trans. and ed. Meredith Sanderson (Zomba, 1919), p. 7; H. S. Stannus, 'The Wayao of Nyasaland', Harvard African Studies, *Varia Africana III* (Cambridge, Mass., 1922), p. 231; Sanderson, 'Inyago—The Picture-Models of the Yao Initiation Ceremonies', *Nyasaland Jl.*, VIII, 2 (1955), pp. 36–7; N. B. Valdez Thomaz dos Santos, *O Desconhecido Niassa* (Lisbon, 1964), p. 121; cf. A. Sousa Lobato, 'Monográfia Etnográfica Original sobre o Povo

Ajaua', *Boletim da Sociedade de Estudos de Colónia de Moçambique*, XIX, 63 (1949), pp. 7–8.

43. A. Hetherwick, 'Some Animistic Beliefs among the Yaos of British Central Africa', *Jl. of the Anthropological Institute of Great Britain and Ireland*, XXXII (1902), p. 94; S. S. Murray, *A Handbook of Nyasaland* (London, 1932), pp. 86–7.

44. Abdallah, *The Yaos*, pp. 8–10; Lance J. Klass, 'The Amachinga Yao of Malawi: Field Research Papers', Chancellor College Library, University of Malawi, Zomba, interview with Edwin Nyambi, Nyambi Village, Kasupe District, 20 July 1969.

45. See Chapter 2 for the evidence provided by Gaspar Bocarro's journey of 1616 for this conclusion; cf. Thomas Price, 'Yao Origins', *Nyasaland Jl.*, XVII, 2 (1964), pp. 11–16.

46. David Livingstone, *Last Journals*, ed. Horace Waller (London, 1874), I, p. 79.

47. ibid., I, p. 73.

48. J. Stevenson-Hamilton, 'Notes on a Journey through Portuguese East Africa, from Ibo to Lake Nyasa', *The Geographical Jl.*, XXXIV (1909), p. 528.

49. Abdallah, *The Yaos*, p. 11.

50. Sousa Lobato, 'O Povo Ajaua', p. 16.

51. Livingstone, *Last Journals*, I, p. 80; U.S.P.G., U.M.C.A. A/I/iv, anon., 'Up the Lujenda', n.d., but probably by W. P. Johnson and dating to about 1880.

52. Abdallah, *The Yaos*, pp. 11, 25.

53. ibid., pp. 11, 23–4. For two brief accounts of Yao forging in the nineteenth century, see Edward Steere, *The Free Village in Yao Land* (Zanzibar, c. 1876), p. 10, and Charles Alan Symthies, *A Journey to Lake Nyassa, and Visit to the Magwangwara and the Source of the Rovuma, in the Year 1886* ... (Kiungani, n.d.), p. 44.

54. Abdallah, *The Yaos*, p. 28.

55. Stevenson-Hamilton, 'Notes', p. 521.

56. Klass, 'The Amachinga Yao', interview with Chikwisimbi, Kalambo Village, Kasupe District, 2 May 1970; J. F. Peirone, *A Tribo Ajaua do Alto Niassa (Moçambique) e Alguns Aspectos da sua Problemática Neo-Islâmica* (Lisbon, 1967), pp. 61–2; Stannus, 'Some Notes on the Tribes of British Central Africa', *Man*, XL (1910), p. 325.

57. ibid., p. 325; Peirone, *A Tribo Ajaua*, p. 62.

58. Henry Salt, *A Voyage to Abyssinia ... in the Years 1809 and 1810; in which are included, An Account of the Portuguese Settlements on the East Coast of Africa, visited in the Course of the Voyage* (London, 1814), pp. 32–3.

59. Abdallah, *The Yaos*, p. 27.

60. For a more detailed description of the rituals surrounding Yao caravans, see Alpers, 'Trade, State, and Society', pp. 416–17.

61. W. P. Johnson, *Nyasa the Great Water* (London, 1922), pp. 26–8.

62. For more detail, see Alpers, 'Trade, State, and Society', p. 409; J. C. Mitchell, *The Yao Village—A Study in the Social Structure of a Nyasaland Tribe* (Manchester, 1956), Ch. 6.

63. ibid., p. 112, n. 1; see also his 'Marriage, Matriliny and Social Structure among the Yao of Southern Nyasaland', *International Jl. of Comparative Sociology*, III, 1 (1962), pp. 35–6.

64. Mitchell cites the hypothetical example of a man returning from being a migrant labourer who has sexual relations on his way home. He carries some salt in his effects as a present for his kinsmen. 'The salt becomes charged with sexual heat and if he gives any of it to any of his matrilineal relatives to cook with, they will contract this disease. He must therefore give the salt to members of another matrilineage, even if they live in the same village'. Mitchell, *Yao Village*, p. 137.

65. Duff Macdonald, *Africana, or the Heart of Heathen Africa* (London, 1882), I, pp. 80–85; this was a relationship which I did not explain fully in 'Trade, State, and Society', pp. 416–17.

66. Among the Chewa the equivalent disease is called *mdulo*; see António Rita-Ferreira, *Os Cheuas da Macanga* (Lourenço Marques, 1966), pp. 224, 227. I have found no references to this phenomenon among the Makua-Lomwe.
67. Mitchell, *Yao Village*, p. 40.
68. Alpers, 'Trade, State, and Society', pp. 417–18.
69. ibid., pp. 415–16, and Alpers, 'Expansion of Islam', pp. 175–6, 186–7.
70. See Alpers, 'Introduction' to Abdallah's *The Yaos*, second edition (London, 1973).
71. Abdallah, *The Yaos*, pp. 12–13.
72. ibid., pp. 32–4.
73. ibid., p. 29.
74. David and Charles Livingstone, *Narrative of an Expedition to the Zambesi and its Tributaries* . . . (New York, 1866), p. 522.
75. Livingstone, *Missionary Travels and Researches in South Africa* (London, 1857), p. 638. Cf. Santos, 'Ethiopia Oriental', p. 268.
76. Reginald Foskett (ed.), *The Zambesi Journal and Letters of Dr John Kirk, 1858–1863* (Edinburgh, 1965), I, pp. 184–5, 188–9, 238, 244.
77. Livingstone, *Narrative*, p. 231.
78. W. B. Morgan, 'The Lower Shire Valley of Nyasaland: A Changing System of African Agriculture', *The Geographical Jl.*, CXIX (1953), pp. 459–66.
79. Livingstone, *Narrative*, pp. 122–3; cf. Foskett, *Zambesi Journal*, I, p. 238.
80. Stannus, 'Notes', pp. 323–4.
81. Livingstone, *Narrative*, p. 123.
82. Foskett, *Zambesi Journal*, II, p. 363.
83. ibid., I, pp. 240–1; cf. Livingstone, *Narrative*, p. 124.
84. ibid., p. 123.
85. Allen F. Isaacman, *Mozambique—The Africanization of a European Institution: The Zambezi Prazos, 1750–1902* (Madison, 1972), pp. 66, 73, 75.
86. I have not been able to determine how successfully *machila* survived the introduction of the sturdy bleached cotton sheeting (Swahili: *merikani*) which inundated East Africa during the second half of the nineteenth century, which was also a period of severe turmoil in the southern Shire valley.
87. Livingstone, *Last Journals*, I, p. 106, and *Missionary Travels*, p. 643.
88. Henry Rowley, *The Story of the Universities' Mission to Central Africa* (London, 1866), p. 179; cf. Livingstone, *Narrative*, p. 113. For a full description of salt production at Lake Chilwa, with illustrations, see Ernest Gray, 'Notes on the Salt-Making Industry of the Nyanja Peoples near Lake Shirwa', *South African Jl. of Science*, XLI (1945), pp. 465–75.
89. Charles Guillain, *Documents sur l'histoire, la géographie, et le commerce de l'Afrique Orientale* (Paris, 1856), II, p. 377 and n. 2.
90. Abdallah, *The Yaos*, p. 28.
91. U.S.P.G., U.M.C.A. A/I/iv, 'Up the Lujenda'; O'Neill, 'Three Months' Journey', p. 203. In the 1880s salt from Lake Chilwa was also 'a great article of barter on the northern half of the lakeshore' of Lake Nyasa. London Missionary Society, Journal of Alexander Carson, Quelimane to Niomkolo, Tanganyika, 20 December 1886, entry at Bandawe. I am grateful to my colleague, Professor John S. Galbraith, for showing me a copy of this manuscript which is in his possession.
92. António Norberto das Vilasboas Truão, 'Extracto do Plano para um Regimento ou Nova Constituição Económica e Política da Capitania de Rios de Senna', Tete, 20 May 1806, *A.C.U.*, p.n.o., I (1857), p. 411.
93. Rowley, *Story*, p. 206; *A.C.U.*, p. n.o.,III (1862), p. 87, being extracts from reports of the Governor of Quelimane District to the Secretariat of the Government-General.
94. Manuel Galvão da Silva, 'Diario das Viagens feitas pellas terras de Manica . . .', 14 November 1788, *A.C.U.*, p.n.o., I (1857), p. 244, also published in ibid., II

(1861), and Luíz Fernando de Carvalho Dias, 'Fontes para a História, Geografia e Comércio de Moçambique (Sec. XVIII)', Junta de Investigações das Colónias, Estudos da História da Geografia da Expansão Portuguesa, *Anais*, IX, 1 (Lisbon, 1954), p. 328; Alexandre Lobato, *História do Presídio de Lourenço Marques* (Lisbon, 1960), II, p. 360.

95. E. W. Chafulumira, *Mbiri ya Amang'anja* (Zomba, 1948), Ch. 20. I am grateful to Gomo Michongwe for translating relevant parts of this book for me.

96. Rowley, *Story*, p. 206; cf. Foskett, *Zambesi Journal*, I, pp. 236–7, with other brief descriptions of iron working at pp. 165, 178, and 196. For a more detailed account of Mang'anja smelting, see Stannus, 'Notes', p. 331.

97. Rowley, *Story*, pp. 194–5; also Foskett, *Zambesi Journal*, I, p. 192.

98. For the fish trade, see Livingstone, *Last Journals*, I, p. 91; Rowley, *Story*, p. 247.

99. For Chewa cotton production, see A. G. P. Gamitto, *King Kazembe and the Marave, Cheva, Bisa, Bemba, Lunda, and other peoples of Southern Africa being the Diary of the Portuguese Expedition to that Potentate in the Years 1831 and 1832* (Lisbon, 1960), I, pp. 80–5, and for the production of barkcloth, I, pp. 143–4, while noting that the people he calls Maravi were Chewa; cf. Rita-Ferreira, *Os Cheuas da Macanga*, Ch. 6, especially at p. 193, where he mentions communal farming under the direction of the territorial chief as a method of establishing a famine reserve.

100. See, e.g., Truão, 'Extracto', p. 411.

101. See Isaacman, *Mozambique*, pp. 69–71. That there was no gold in Yaoland was known to the Portuguese in the mid-eighteenth century: see Xavier, 'Noticias', p. 151.

102. Livingstone, *Narrative*, pp. 146, 109; see also Foskett, *Zambesi Journal*, I, p. 144.

103. Robert Codrington, 'The Central Angoniland District of the British Central African Protectorate', *The Geographical Jl.*, XI (1898), p. 510; Price, 'More about the Maravi', *African Studies*, XI (1952), p. 78.

104. Foskett, *Zambesi Journal*, I, pp. 145–7, also 152; Rowley, *Story*, p. 323; Stannus, 'Notes', p. 325; cf. Miranda, 'Memoria', p. 245.

105. Foskett, *Zambesi Journal*, I, pp. 117, 145, n. 8.

106. For the Mang'anja, see ibid., II, p. 357, and George Shepperson (ed.), *David Livingstone and the Rovuma: A Notebook* (Edinburgh, 1965), p. 143; for the Chewa, see Gamitto, *King Kazembe*, I, p. 127. 'The lands of each chief are very well defined, the boundaries being usually marked by rivulets', wrote Livingstone, 'and, if an elephant is wounded on one man's land and dies on that of another, the under half of the carcass is claimed by the lord of the soil; and so stringent is the law, that the hunter can not begin at once to cut up his own elephant, but must send notice to the lord of the soil on which it lies, and wait until that personage sends one authorized to see a fair partition made'. Livingstone, *Missionary Travels*, p. 642.

107. For a detailed reconstruction of Chewa political organization, see Harry Langworthy, 'Chewa or Malawi Political Organization in the Precolonial Era', in Pachai, *Early History*, pp. 104–22, and 'Conflict among rulers in the history of Undi's Chewa kingdom', *Transafrican Jl. of History*, I, 1 (1970), pp. 1–23; for village and family structure, see Rita-Ferreira, *Os Cheuas da Macanga*, Ch. 4, J. P. Bruwer, 'The composition of a Cewa village (mudzi)', *African Studies*, VIII, 4 (1949), pp. 191–7, and M. G. Marwick, 'The kinship basis of Cewa social structure', *South African Jl. of Science*, 48 (1952), pp. 258–62; for the Chipeta, see Gamitto, *King Kazembe*, I, p. 67; for the Mang'anja, see A. W. R. Duly, 'The Lower Shire District, Notes on Land Tenure and Individual Rights', *Nyasaland Jl.*, I, 2 (1948), pp. 11–44.

108. Walter Rodney, *How Europe Underdeveloped Africa* (London and Dar es Salaam, 1972), Ch. 2.

109. Chafulumira, *Mbiri ya Amang'anja*, Ch. 14. Again I am grateful to Gomo Michongwe for translating this passage for me.

110. In a comparable analysis concerning environmental potential and the development of labour-exporting peasantries, to whom both the ivory-hunting Makua and the caravaneering Yao bear such a striking resemblance, Saul and Woods argue that an important potential variable was 'the degree to which adult men were under-employed in the traditional agricultural system and hence the extent to which they could be absent without threatening the security of minimal subsistence production', John S. Saul and Roger Woods, 'African Peasantries', in Teodor Shanin (ed.), *Peasants and Peasant Societies* (Harmondsworth, 1971), pp. 108–9.

111. See Alpers, 'Trade, State, and Society'.

112. D. C. Scott and A. Hetherwick, *Dictionary of the Nyasa Language* (London, 1929), p. 267, second entry under *Manga*, 'riches', the first meaning of which is, significantly, 'the coast'. Cf. *A Standard Swahili-English Dictionary*, pp. 258–9, where *manga* is given only as a name for Arabia, especially for the region of Masqat, and for objects derived from it.

113. O'Neill, 'Journey from Mozambique', p. 639, italics in original.

CHAPTER TWO

The Impact of
Portuguese Intervention, 1498–1698

ะเฉะเฉะเฉะเฉะเฉะเฉะเฉะเฉะเฉะเฉะเฉะเฉะเฉะเฉะเฉะเฉะเฉะเฉะเฉ

Portugal's African Mission and its Muslim Antecedents
The intrusion of the Portuguese into the Indian Ocean after 1498 signalled the beginning of a new era throughout the East. The reasons for their presence there are well known and are usually grouped under the contrasting symbols of God and Mammon. Actually, both Portuguese economic expansion and Portuguese missionary activities overseas were but different aspects of the same imperial drive which was and remains one of the hallmarks of Western capitalism. In East Africa, although the Portuguese failed miserably in their early religious mission and ultimately in their attempt to export Lusitanian culture, their impact on trade and economy was immediate and lasting.

Taking the Orient as a whole, the main object of the Portuguese was to capture the vitally important Indian Ocean spice trade. This they soon accomplished by seizing control of the high seas and of a number of strategic ports. Several of these were located on the coast of East Africa, which the Portuguese passed as they made their way across to the Far East. But it was not long before they discovered that East Africa was peripheral to the spice trade as it was then operating. Soon their only reason for maintaining a presence in East Africa—and thereby badly straining Portugal's meagre financial and human resources—was to protect the entire basin against their imperial rivals. Initially, this meant the Ottoman Turks, for here the Portuguese represented all of Christendom in its struggle against the world of Islam. Indeed, the Portuguese episode in Ethiopia was simply one front of this battle, rather than an instance of early Portuguese attempts to engage Africans as racial and cultural equals. Later, of course, the Portuguese fought for and lost their control of the Indian Ocean to their more vigorously capitalistic Dutch and English rivals. If at first, however, the Portuguese maintained a foothold in East Africa for larger strategies of trade and empire, their local activities immediately crystallized around their desire to control the gold trade of the Zimbabwean plateau. And once the larger Portuguese empire in the Orient crumbled away in the seventeenth century, the secondary empire in East Africa became most important to them in that part of the world. For nearly five centuries, then, the heart of the Portuguese mission in East Africa has been to exploit its natural resources.[1]

In the sixteenth century the Portuguese first sought to achieve their ends by controlling the port of Sofala, which was the main coastal outlet for the ancient gold trade of the Zimbabwean plateau. Located well to the south of the Zambesi River delta, on the same natural harbour where the modern deep water port of Beira stands today, Sofala had only recently asserted its independence from the suzerainty of Kilwa when the Portuguese came into the picture. Indeed, Sofala had initially been established as an outpost of the more powerful city-states which dotted the coast to the north of Cape Delgado, for the Portuguese were by no means the first foreigners to attempt to exploit the wealth of East Africa, nor was the trade conducted by their Muslim predecessors any less extractive or more conducive to the economic development of East Africa. For the people of East Africa both the Muslims and the Portuguese posed the same economic threat to their independent development.[2]

Sofala was first dominated by merchants from Mogadishu, in southern Somalia, which before the rise of Kilwa to greatness under the Abu'l-Mawahib dynasty was the dominant commercial, as well as cultural, community on the entire coast. After Kilwa seized control of the Sofala trade from Mogadishu in the late thirteenth or early fourteenth century, Mogadishu remained the cultural capital, but Kilwa became the great centre of trade. Kilwa, like all the trading towns of the pre-Portuguese era, was oriented outwards to the sea, rather than inwards towards the continent. Established and invigorated by sea-faring Muslims from the Middle East, Kilwa was essentially an Islamic commercial outpost in another land. Over centuries, of course, the physical population was Africanized, thus laying the foundation for the development of Swahili society, but the world view of these coastal societies remained Islamic and outwardly directed. Relations with the Africans on the mainland, outside the local Islamic community, appear to have been marked more by hostility and aggression than by amity and cooperation. This was certainly the state of affairs when Ibn Battuta visited Kilwa at the height of its prosperity in 1332.[3] The only known point of significant interaction, economic or otherwise, with the people of the interior was at Sofala. Whoever controlled Sofala controlled the trade of East Africa. Kilwa's ancient greatness thus dates from its achievement of commercial domination of the gold of the Zimbabwean plateau. This domination was based on its control of the sea route to Sofala and of Sofala itself, as is recorded in the version of the *Kilwa Chronicle* which was collected by João de Barros in the sixteenth century, not on any trade that Kilwa carried on with the peoples of its own hinterland.[4]

There was, of course, an important overland trade route from the Zimbabwean goldfields to Sofala. There was surely also some limited trade in foodstuffs between the people of Kilwa Kisiwani and the people of the mainland opposite the island upon which the town was located. But there is no evidence for postulating the existence of any sort of overland trade route linking Kilwa Kisiwani and the gold-producing regions of southern Zambesia.[5] The argument against the existence of such a route finds support from the excavations at Ingombe Ilede, which suggest that the major alternative route to Sofala for exporting the gold of Zimbabwe was the Zambesi River. Ingombe Ilede is situated on a ridge lying just north of the Zambesi, in the Gwembe valley. For perhaps two generations after about 1400 this site was a trading centre of some importance, exhibiting obvious connections with the coast.[6] These were clearly maintained by means of contact down the Zambesi, which was the principal highway to the interior of Central Africa and the one by which the Portuguese moved inland in the sixteenth century. Indeed, early Portuguese intelligence reports concerning the gold trade from Zimbabwe noted that some five per cent of the total trade avoided paying taxes at Sofala by resorting to the Zambesi route.[7]

There are, then, neither archaeological nor documentary bases which would indicate that ancient Kilwa was in any overland commercial contact with the peoples of the far interior. Kilwa's monopoly of the sea route, if such it was, was surely challenged over the next two centuries by merchants from the other city-states of the coast. Internal dissensions also sapped Kilwa's vitality, and by the end of the fifteenth century Sofala was able to free itself from Kilwa's overlordship.[8] Nevertheless, until the arrival of the Portuguese in the Indian Ocean, Kilwa, despite its decline, continued to trade for the gold of Sofala by the familiar sea route, while contacts with the mainland behind Kilwa remained as tenuous as ever.

The Commercial Reorientation of Kilwa

Thus for the Portuguese Kilwa and Sofala became the main targets for their ambitious plans to capture the wealth of East Africa for themselves. In 1505 they attacked and razed Kilwa, after which they established a trading factory and built a fort. Later that year they founded another trading factory at Sofala, where news of Kilwa's fate obviated the use of force. The Portuguese rigorously pursued a policy of squeezing the Muslims out of the gold trade, and Kilwa, already in decline, became moribund. Firmly in control of Sofala, the Portuguese soon realized that the continued maintenance of their establishment at Kilwa was an unnecessary attentuation of their already over-extended resources. Kilwa's wealth had come from the duties that its Sultans had levied on the trade of Sofala and on the business of its merchants; deprived of these sources of income it was commercially impotent. Furthermore, Kilwa was a less convenient port of call for vessels sailing between Portugal and India than was Mozambique Island, where the Portuguese had established a settlement for this purpose in 1507. Accordingly, in 1512 the Portuguese withdrew their garrison from the fortress at Kilwa and left the island to its traditional rulers, who remained vassals of the Crown.[9]

After liberation from the commercial stranglehold which the Portuguese occupation had enforced, Kilwa's fortunes revived noticeably, as its merchants joined those from the other coastal towns in circumventing Portuguese control over the Zimbabwean gold trade. This they did by avoiding Sofala, where the Portuguese were masters, in favour of Angoche, itself a thriving Muslim town, or other points along the coast between Mozambique Island and the Zambesi delta. The Angoche coast quite probably had ancient ties with the Zambesi route to the interior, perhaps even serving as an embarkation point to Ingombe Ilede. During the second decade of the sixteenth century, Angoche and the Zambesi route became a much greater threat to the gold trade of Sofala than they had ever been to the rulers of Kilwa, as increasingly large numbers of Muslim traders sought to avoid Portuguese supervision of the trade. Traders from Kilwa, Mombasa and Malindi, some one hundred kilometres north of Mombasa, sailed past Mozambique Island to Angoche, where their merchandise was transported to the Cuama mouth of the Zambesi and landed some six leagues (perhaps thirty to forty kilometres) upstream at the town of a powerful chief named Mongualo, who in one source is identified as a Kaffir (African) and in another as a Moor (Swahili). Here the traders paid duties to Mongualo, who then supplied them with dugout canoes for carrying their goods farther up the Zambesi. After making a portage around some rapids, lying at an unspecified distance up-river, they continued a further twenty leagues (perhaps 100 to 135 kilometres) until they reached a mountain called Utonga, where a large settlement was situated. According to António de Saldanha, Captain of Sofala and Mozambique, it was there that 'all the Kaffir and Moorish merchants of the land gather together and where they sell and set up their markets'.[10] Having seen the Portuguese withdraw from Kilwa, it seems not unlikely that the Muslim traders hoped, by undermining the gold trade to Sofala, to force the Portuguese to retire from Sofala, as well.

Had there been any tradition of an overland route from Kilwa to Zimbabwe in the pre-Portuguese period, surely this would also have flourished and gained notoriety after the Portuguese withdrawal from Kilwa in 1512. The recourse which the Swahili traders of the East African coast, including those from Kilwa, had to the Angoche-Zambesi route in order to subvert the effectiveness of the Portuguese control of Sofala is yet another indication that there was no overland trade route connecting Kilwa with the Zambesi before the arrival of the Portuguese on the coast.

In the second and third decades of the sixteenth century it became apparent to the Portuguese that if this 'clandestine' trade were to be terminated, they would have to establish themselves in the interior.[11] They therefore began the gradual occupation of the area which was to become known as the Rivers of Sena by

43

ascending the Zambesi and establishing a fair on the right bank, at Sena, in 1531. Some time thereafter another Portuguese fair was founded farther upstream, on the same bank, at Tete; and in 1544 a trading factory was set up at Quelimane to supervise the entrance of vessels at the several mouths of the Zambesi. By 1560 both Sena and Tete had become important markets. Nine years later the ill-fated visionary, Dom Sebastião, King of Portugal, was persuaded to attempt to conquer the Zimbabwean mines for the Portuguese Crown. But the massacre in 1575 of some two hundred Portuguese troops who had been stationed at Chicoa, up the Zambesi beyond Tete, put an end to this unsuccessful episode.[12]

During this half-century, when the Portuguese were seeking to master the commerce of the Rivers of Sena, a major change had apparently taken place in the trade of Kilwa. Following the Portuguese withdrawal from Kilwa in 1512, the only Portuguese point of occupation along the coast of East Africa north of Cape Delgado was at Malindi. There, a Captain of the Malindi coast, operating from an unfortified base, did his best to safeguard Portuguese interests on that coast. At first, Kilwa clearly ignored any claim to authority by the Captain of Malindi over its trade.[13] Sometime after 1530, however, Kilwa began gradually to re-orient its external trade to the north and the Portuguese Captain of Malindi began to play a more important role in its commerce. Simultaneously, the merchants of Kilwa seem to have begun to carry on a more substantial trade with the Africans of the Kilwa hinterland than had ever been the case previously. Both these developments appear to have been caused by the Portuguese penetration inland up the Zambesi.

As the Portuguese gradually extended their influence in the Rivers of Sena and acquired a more secure control of the Zimbabwean gold trade, the 'contraband' gold and ivory trade on which Angoche had flourished since 1505 declined correspondingly. Throughout its history Kilwa had functioned exclusively as a commercial entrepôt, producing little locally for export. The gold and ivory of Zimbabwe had been the staples of Kilwa's commercial life for more than two centuries. Now these had been arrogated by the Portuguese, leaving Kilwa without a source for the raw materials of Africa which were so highly valued throughout the Indian Ocean basin. If Kilwa were not to decline into a small fishing village it was incumbent upon its merchants to develop another source for those materials. This they did by creating a demand for ivory from the mainland opposite their own island settlement.

Prior to the middle of the sixteenth century, both the ivory and gold which sustained the trade of Kilwa came from Sofala. In 1511, it was reported to King Manuel of Portugal 'that only a little ivory comes from Kilwa and that much comes from Sofala'.[14] Nor was Kilwa unique in its dependence on Sofala, which exported ivory to Malindi and even to Mozambique, where large elephant were known to abound.[15] The only exception to this situation may well have been Mombasa, whose rise to power and wealth in the late fifteenth century has previously gone without explanation.[16] The merchants of Mombasa also traded to the south, and were key figures in the business done through Angoche up the Zambesi. But it seems more likely that it was their early and successful cultivation of the trade with their own hinterland that may have provided the key to the remarkable and sudden rise of Mombasa, so that by the time the Portuguese came along it was the most powerful city-state on the coast. In the second decade of the sixteenth century, the most important early compendium of information about the East African world as it was known to the Portuguese noted specifically of the people of Mombasa that 'They are sometimes at war with those of the mainland, sometimes at peace, they trade with them and obtain quantities of honey and wax, and a lot of ivory'.[17] The absence of such evidence for Kilwa does not mean that similar interchange did not exist, but the fact that this was noteworthy for Mombasa alone suggests that it was an unusual situation among the coastal communities during this period. Indeed, unlike Kilwa, whose strength was sapped the moment that Sofala was severed from it, Mombasa weathered a succession of catastrophic Portuguese attacks in the sixteenth century (1505, 1528–29, 1589) without ever losing its enormous economic and political vitality. If this tentative reconstruction of Mombasa's emergence as the major East African coastal city-state is correct, then Mombasa's example may well have influenced or have been an earlier manifestation of the decisive reorientation of Kilwa's African trade which occurred after the Portuguese penetration of Zambesia from 1530.[18]

No specific piece of evidence has yet been found to document the process of reorientation for the African trade of Kilwa, but

Monclaro's description of Kilwa's trade in 1571 leaves little doubt that such a change had taken place:

> These Moors have some commerce with the islands of Comor, and in the interior in ivory, which they buy from the Kaffirs to sell to the Portuguese who are always on these parts, or to the factor of the captain of the said [Malindi] coast, whence there come also quantities of honey and wax.[19]

His remarks also indicate that the Portuguese at Malindi had assumed a more important role in the trade of Kilwa during the previous decades. They did not, however, have any political control over Kilwa at this time, although a nineteenth-century Governor-General of Mozambique claimed Kilwa as 'our land after 1529'.[20] To be sure, the Portuguese razed Mombasa in 1528–1529, but by 1541 it was able to repulse another Portuguese assault. Two decades later there is evidence that Kilwa was still very much independent of Portuguese control.[12] When Monclaro visited the coast, he noted that while all the local rulers were 'poor and without power', those of Kilwa and Malindi were the principal ones. It is likely that he was slighting the importance of Mombasa, and the Sultan of Kilwa was still in possession of Mafia Island, where a factor of the Captain of Malindi was stationed.[22]

So by the last quarter of the sixteenth century, Kilwa had already adjusted its commercial orientation from one which had previously been exclusively seaward, to one which now looked to its own hinterland for the majority of its raw trade goods, especially ivory. The initial impulse which instigated this reorientation came from the coast. Effectively cut off by the Portuguese from the gold of Zimbabwe after 1530, it was the Muslim traders of Kilwa who sought to develop the previously insignificant ivory trade with the hinterland of their own town. But the development of long-distance trade routes between the coast and the interior did not owe its genesis entirely to this impulse. In the interior different, but closely related, changes in the political economy of the Maravi, together with the gradual expansion of Yao regional trade, were equally important factors in this process.

The Zimba and the Maravi Empire

The Maravi kingdoms came into being as a result of the immigration of a group of chiefly invaders, the Phiri, who came from the

Congo Basin in the fourteenth century to settle in northern Zambesia.[23] Soon afterwards the Zambesi became an important channel of trade to the interior, as is clear from the findings at Ingombe Ilede. Although Ingombe Ilede itself seems to have developed independently of Phiri patronage, the new ruling class of the Maravi found themselves dominating a large area which had lucrative trading connections, based on ivory, with the Muslim traders from the coast who ventured up the Zambesi and the Shire River valley towards Lake Nyasa.[24] It seems probable that they ultimately gained control of much of that trade and that their stake in it had become a major variable in their internecine political struggles by the sixteenth century. Certainly the intensified use of the Angoche-Zambesi route by Muslim traders after 1505 increased the stakes of this business for the Phiri Maravi chiefs.

Eric Axelson has written that 'It was gold that lured the Portuguese into the interior. It was the absence of gold north of the Zambezi that rendered penetration in that direction unremunerative'.[25] But there appears to be still more to it. In their eagerness to exploit the Zimbabwean gold trade, the Portuguese ignored the ivory trade with the Maravi. Indeed, while the Portuguese were not adverse to dealing in ivory as a secondary item of trade in southern Zambesia, to the north of the river this general attitude endured until well into the eighteenth century, even after gold had been found in Chewa country. (See Chapter 4.) To a very considerable extent this negative Portuguese attitude to the northern Zambesia ivory trade was probably instrumental in straining the relations of power that existed between the two principal Maravi chiefs, thereby setting in train a series of conflicts and extensions of power that dramatically affected the history of East Central Africa for the next century.[26]

The Maravi chiefs in question were the Kalonga, whose ancestor had led the Phiri migration from Uluba, and the Lundu, who was by this time master of the lower Shire valley. By the mid-sixteenth century the actual political relationship between these two great chiefs is not discernible, but traditionally the Kalonga was paramount over all and was owed formal obeissance by the Lundu, who had succeeded in establishing his primacy among the Mang'anja by gaining control of the M'Bona rain cult. From his town at Mbewe-wa-Mitengo, below Chikwawa on the right bank of the Shire, he was in a better position than the

47

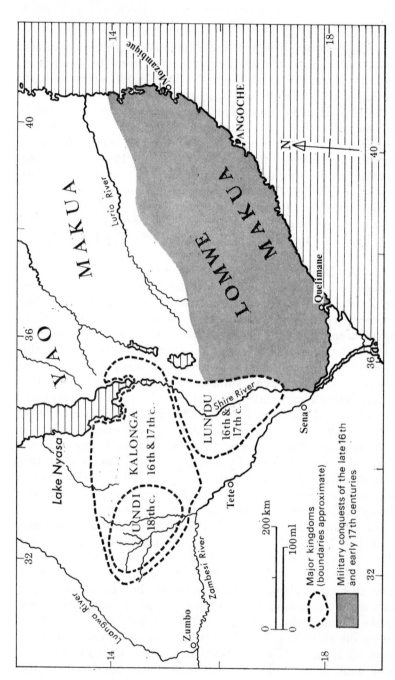

4   *The Maravi Empire*

Kalonga, whose centre of power was near the south-west corner of Lake Nyasa, to exploit the Zambesi trade and to control movement along the Shire.[27] I believe that this is what the Lundu actually did and that it was his attempt to dominate the ivory trade of northern Zambesia that led to his lengthy struggle with the Kalonga for supremacy there.

The first indication that this struggle may have been coming to a head is Santos' reference to the Portuguese defeat of a Mumbo chief named Quizura at Chicorongo (modern Chicorongue), some forty kilometres north-east of Tete.[28] This was sometime late in the sixteenth century. Mumbo could possibly be a reference to the Mbo, a Maravi group bordering on this vicinity, or else the fact that Quizura was a *mambo* or chief. Santos nowhere indicates what lay at the root of Quizura's dispute with the Portuguese, but in light of immediately succeeding events there is strong reason to believe that the issue at stake was control of the Zambesi trade. Another possibility that emerges from this line of argument is that Quizura was the Kalonga Muzura, the Lundu's great rival and nominal overlord during this period. Assuming these hypotheses to be tenable, then it follows that the Kalonga Muzura's concern might have had two immediate causes. First, Muzura was faced with increasing Portuguese control of the Zambesi valley from Sena to Tete, precisely that stretch of the river which immediately bordered his kingdom. Second, as Monclaro notes during the 1570s, Muslim traders were still able to circumvent Portuguese control at Quelimane and travel unimpeded up the Zambesi and the Shire in their quest for ivory from northern Zambesia.[29] In these circumstances, it appears that control of this trade fell to the Lundu, who then used it to deny the Kalonga Muzura contact with the Muslim traders operating in the Shire valley. Seeking a way to break through this enclosure, Muzura attacked the Portuguese, judging them to be a more vulnerable opponent than the Lundu. When he was defeated at Chicorongue, however, the Lundu decided that the moment had come for him to extend his challenge to his paramount chief. This he did by unleashing his army, the Zimba, a group who used to be dismissed as a wandering horde of cannibals.

The earliest known reference to any of the Maravi peoples is the inclusion of Zimba territory, stretching roughly from the Luangwa River to the Shire, on the world map executed by Bartolomeu Velho in 1561.[30] Contemporary Portuguese usage of this name was vague, to be sure, but there is strong evidence that the notorious Zimba horde who struck off to the east into northern Mozambique were the warriors of the Lundu. According to Santos, sometime in the 1580s a minor but ambitious Zimba chieftain is said to have set out to make a name for himself.[31] He and his followers abandoned their homeland and began warring with the peoples lying to their east. By killing and, allegedly, eating their way 'through all the places and kingdoms of Kaffraria', this Zimba band soon grew into a horde of some 15,000 individuals, relentlessly moving to the east. About 1588, having passed along the coast opposite the Kerimba Islands, the Zimba are said to have reached Kilwa, which they besieged for several months in an effort to take it. But they failed in all their attempts to cross the strait separating the mainland from the island and town of Kilwa, until a Muslim who lived there showed them a ford on the condition that he and his family be spared. The Zimba crossed to Kilwa by night, and in the ensuing massacre slaughtered and captured some three thousand inhabitants of the island. Only a handful managed to flee. After reportedly devouring their victims, the Zimba—leaving Kilwa a ghost town—continued to march northwards along the coast until they arrived opposite the island of Mombasa.

At Mombasa, Santos continues, the Zimba were prevented from crossing to the island by two Turkish galleys which were guarding the Makupa ford. The Turks, led by the energetic Mir Ali Bey, had set themselves up at Mombasa with a view to making it a permanent base from which to drive the Portuguese from East Africa. The Portuguese, having previously been caught off their guard by the same adventurer in 1585–6, were advised of his plans this time, and in January 1589 a large fleet sailed from Goa for East Africa. This fleet arrived at Mombasa on 5 March to find the Turks and the people of the town, who had always opposed the Portuguese, confronted by the Zimba. A few Portuguese sorties weakened the Turkish defence, and on 15 March the Zimba crossed over to Mombasa and laid waste the island. Before long the Zimba pressed on north to Malindi, where the Portuguese had their staunchest allies on the coast. Here the tables were turned on them. Aided by a small Portuguese garrison, the people of Malindi were able to keep the Zimba at bay for a while, Santos reporting that Portuguese gunfire took a heavy toll of the enemy. But the superior numbers of the Zimba eventually began to sway the battle and before long they were able to scale the low ramparts which surrounded the town. At this decisive moment, a force of three thousand Segeju, with whom the rulers of Malindi had apparently allied themselves, fell upon the Zimba from behind. The Zimba were all but annihilated. Only a hundred men and their once ambitious leader are said to have returned safely to their homeland north of the Zambesi.[32]

However melodramatically Santos' account of the Zimba reads, there is good reason to believe that his vivid impressions of their impact throughout much of East Central Africa are at least partially reflected in the traditions of the people with whom the Zimba came into contact. For example, the origin of the Chirima clan of the Makua-Lomwe would appear to date to the era of the Zimba invasions.[33] And according to traditions reported by Eduardo do Couto Lupi, a Portuguese colonial official at the beginning of the twentieth century, the ma-rúndu invaders of Angoche district—the Lundu's warriors—are to be identified as the Zimba. According to what he was told by 'the people who commit to memory the history of the region,' Lupi learned that many years before, the indigenous Makua of the Angoche hinterland were invaded by the ma-rúndu, who swept across the country, 'destroying everything, killing all, and even having cannibalistic habits.'[34] Moving relentlessly to the north-east, these invaders are said to have set in motion many people who lay in their path and on their flanks. Arriving at Mossuril, on the mainland opposite Mozambique Island, they allegedly killed 'all the whites and Arabs, as they had done in Sena', and 'they were only checked and repelled at a fortified village where the a-cunha (whites) had pieces of artillery'. Although he stated that there were other details to this body of tradition, Lupi did not recount them, as he felt no need for further evidence to substantiate his identification of the ma-rúndu with the Zimba, as described by Santos.[35]

The immediate parallel between the ma-rúndu invasion and that of the Zimba struck Lupi at once. But the specific point which confirmed his belief in this identification is a passage in which Santos describes his own personal experience of the Zimba. Santos relates that when he was returning from Sofala to Mozambique in April 1595, several years after the Zimba had marched eastwards, a storm forced his vessel to take port in the mouth of the Quizungo, or Tejungo, River, located at the southern limit of the former administrative division of Angoche. While stranded there for thirty-two days, he and his companions were unable to procure provisions from the mainland, not only because there was a great famine at the time, but also because the Zimba were in occupation of the country. Even the local Makua had fled to a deserted island lying off the coast.[36]

Between the arrival of the Portuguese in East Africa in 1498 and the crossing of the Zambesi by the Ngoni in 1835, there is no other known population movement to compare to that of the Zimba, save that of the *ma-rúndu*. Santos' testimony places the Zimba on the borders of *ma-rúndu* territory several years after the initial invasion had taken place. While there has not yet been reported any tradition that the Zimba, by that name, had ever been present in the Angoche district, Lupi records that the *ma-rúndu* consolidated their authority after passing through the area by installing true *ma-rúndu* as chiefs over the people who recognized their hegemony. So great was *ma-rúndu* prestige at the beginning of the twentieth century that virtually every chief of any consequence in the Captaincy of Angoche claimed *ma-rúndu* descent.[37] Another example of the enduring influence of the Lundu in this region is the fact that it is known today as Maganja da Costa, which implies that it is different from the Mang'anja homeland in the Shire valley. Of equal importance is the fact that although the Lundu's political influence east of the Shire has long since vanished, the cult of M'Bona, with which the Lundu maintains an intimate relationship, is still active in this part of Mozambique.[38] The existing evidence thus points to the conclusion that the Zimba and *ma-rúndu* invaders of northern Mozambique were one and the same, and that the Lundu's hegemony over to the coast dates from their conquest of this region. Furthermore, this bold move was arguably the fruit of an economic rivalry which was created, or at the very least heightened, by the Portuguese intrusion into East Central Africa.

If the foregoing reconstruction at first raises as many questions as it answers, Portuguese accounts concerning the Maravi after the Zimba/*ma-rúndu* movement had got under way, as well as Mang'anja traditions, tend to confirm it as being essentially valid. Santos indicates that from 1590 to 1593 the Zimba caused the Portuguese much concern to the west of the Shire. In 1592 detachments from both Sena and Tete were crushed in the field by the Zimba. A year later a special expedition led by the Captain of Mozambique, D. Pedro de Sousa, unsuccessfully besieged the stronghold of the Zimba, who remained undisputed masters of the north bank of the Zambesi. Another account of this trouble, based on Sousa's letters to the Portuguese Viceroy of India, notes that the specific aim of this expedition was 'to expel forcibly from those lands a Negro who was disturbing trade there', while in 1599 the new Captain, Nuno da Cunha de Ataide, urgently sought leave 'to be able to go castigate Tondo, because after he defeated Dom Pedro de Sousa he remained excessively insolent'.[39] This Tondo should be identified with Tundu, whom some Mang'anja traditions name both 'as a kinsman of Lundu and M'Bona and as ancestor of the Zimbas'. According to Schoffeleers, Tundu is also known as the spirit of destruction and is still called upon by the Mang'anja in times of violent calamity.[40] Tundu's belligerency and his traditional ties with the Lundu seem to indicate that during the last decade of the sixteenth century the Lundu was also extending his challenge to Muzura to the west of the Shire.

By threatening not only the weakened position of the Kalonga Muzura, but also that of the Portuguese, the Lundu made natural allies of once natural enemies. Both the Kalonga and the Portuguese hoped to eliminate a powerful antagonist while at the same time maintaining the upper hand with respect to their new allies. In 1608 the Portuguese sought and received military support in the persons of four thousand Maravi warriors from Muzura so that they might successfully pursue a campaign against rebellious chiefs who were seeking to overthrow Mwene Mutapa Gatsi Rusere (c. 1589–1623).[41] In 1620 Gatsi Rusere affirmed that a number of Maravi chiefs, including Muzura, were his military allies; but in the chaos which followed the Mwene Mutapa's death in 1623, Muzura led his forces south across the Zambesi together with another chief named Chombe. According to Miguel Ruiz, Muzura captured much booty in cattle and gold, but failed to seize the lands of the Mwene Mutapa. Another observer noted that the trade of Zambesia was completely at a standstill as a result of Muzura's war.[42] By late 1630 at least one official was recommending to the Crown that it was particularly important that the Portuguese seek to befriend Muzura, who for the first time was referred to as 'King of the Bororo,' which was the name by which the region east of the Shire and north of the Zambesi as far as Angoche was known to the Portuguese.[43]

Clearly Muzura benefited more from his alliance with the

Portuguese than they did, but the question remains of the fate of the Lundu, who only recently was himself the conqueror of Bororo. According to António Bocarro's *Livro do Estado da Índia Oriental*, which was written in 1635 and revised a year later by Pedro Barreto de Rezende,

> This King [Muzura] is at peace with the Portuguese, and he used to keep it better than today, before he was so powerful, because since he has defeated, with our help, a Kaffir king called Rundo [Lundu], with whom he was fighting, he thinks of making war against us; it is said that some Portuguese have been killed in his lands by his order, and he wrongs us at every occasion.

Muzura, with an army of ten to twelve thousand men at his disposal, controlled the mainland opposite Mozambique Island, having come 'from the Rivers of Cuama [Zambesia] to conquer the Makua who lived there'. To the south he ruled right up to Quelimane. The Portuguese considered him 'extremely cunning and very powerful', while Bocarro notes that he was no longer satisfied with the title of 'King', but wished to be addressed as 'Emperor', as was the Mwene Mutapa.[44] Bocarro's testimony is positive confirmation of the rivalry between Muzura and the Lundu. To the Portuguese, who did not realize that the Lundu was a Maravi chief, Muzura's triumph in 1622, the year before his southern Zambesia campaign, established the primacy of Maravi rule over all the lands which had already been subjugated by the Lundu's army at the end of the previous century.[45] Furthermore, Bocarro's account strongly points to the identification of Muzura as the Kalonga.[46]

Muzura's triumph imposed Maravi military domination over a vast portion of East Central Africa and for the first time made possible the establishment of a long-distance overland trade route from Zambesia to Mossuril, opposite Mozambique Island. According to a royal letter summarizing an otherwise unknown report from Cristovão de Brito de Vasconcelos, interim Captain of Mozambique in the early 1630s, the origins of this trade was in 'the proximity of the Maravi Kaffirs, who have conquered a great part of the mainland to Mozambique'. Trade was conducted on the mainland, where African goods were purchased with cloth, firearms, and gunpowder, which the Maravi carried back home. One Portuguese colonist went so far as to sell his land and houses, and then to employ all the proceeds in buying cloth for trading with the Maravi.[47] The main stock-in-trade of the Maravi was ivory. In Zambesia itself the Maravi also drove a considerable trade in *machilas*. Some of these may have been traded to Mozambique. Within the effective limits of Maravi hegemony, Muzura was said by Bocarro to be the only person who could conduct trade.

The creation of a rich new trade in Macuana, as the Portuguese called the coastal hinterland of northern Mozambique, led at once to a heated conflict over rights to trade with the Maravi between Brito de Vasconcelos and the Portuguese colonists of Mozambique. As interim Captain, Brito de Vasconcelos could claim that the external trade of the Rivers of Sena was by royal decree his monopoly, and that this new trade contravened the Crown's control.[48] Accordingly, he issued orders at the beginning of 1632 that no one from Mozambique was allowed to trade with the Maravi, emphasizing that transgressors would suffer heavy penalties.[49] After first upholding this decree, the Crown ordered that a *devassa* should be undertaken to determine the facts of the case. Although the Viceroy at Goa agreed to arrange the inquiry, he strongly defended the right of the colonists to continue this trade, as it was their sole means of earning a living. He also argued that they were especially due this right in gratitude for the valuable assistance which they had given to the Portuguese garrison in withstanding the three Dutch sieges of the fortress of São Sebastião, at Mozambique, earlier in the century. So persuasive was the Viceroy that the Crown acted in favour of the colonists, and the order for a *devassa* became a dead letter.[50]

By 1635, whatever misunderstandings might have arisen between the Maravi and the Portuguese of Mozambique as a result of Brito de Vasconcelos' prohibition of three years earlier had been resolved, and amicable relations prevailed. In that year it was reported that the Maravi had aided the Portuguese in a campaign against some local Swahili. This Maravi cooperation reinforced the Crown's previously expressed recommendations in favour of their trade with the colonists of Mozambique, which were duly repeated to the Viceroy in 1640.[51] Within a few years, however, reports reached Lisbon that the Captains of the colony sometimes seized the trading goods of the colonists by force, and that the greed of these officials was at the root of the state of destitution into which Mozambique and the Rivers of Sena had fallen.[52] Similar charges denouncing the Captain of Mozambique's violation of the trading rights of the colonists were lodged in 1663.[53] The most vivid protest against the repeated vexations which the colonists had to endure at the hands of successive Captains was made in 1667 by Manuel Barreto, who wrote of the Macuana ivory trade that

> the governors of Mozambique have prevented it under various pretexts, as they have other trade . . . and they usurp everything, so that now only one or two colonists have any capital, whereas in past years the town contained many rich merchants. If His Majesty does not put a stop to this, Mozambique will soon be deserted, and the Captain will be left alone with the keys of his fortress.[54]

But it is also Barreto who explains most trenchantly why, despite the continued problems of trading at Mozambique which were caused by the conflict within the Portuguese community there, African traders were nonetheless eager to cultivate that market.

> It is much easier for the [African] traders who go from Mozambique to Maravi, and there meet those of Tete, to bring their ivory to Tete, but they avoid coming to Tete in order not to be subjected to the monopoly of the governor of Mozambique.[55]

By trading their ivory in a competitive market—that which the Portuguese Crown had repeatedly asserted was the prerogative of the colonists of Mozambique—Africans could secure a far more favourable price for it than if they had to dispose of it at Tete, where the monopoly of the Captain of Mozambique enabled him to dictate his own terms of trade. In this price-conscious response by Africans to the trading conditions of seventeenth-century East Central Africa, as in the conflict over control of the trade of Macuana within the community of Mozambique Island, we find a major pattern of trade which endured into the nineteenth century. Keenly aware of the market in which they were operating, African traders suffered most through the fact that the market itself was not of their own making and that this luxury trade was in no way contributing to the economic development of their own societies. Their rapid mastery of entrepreneurial skills could not free them from the disadvantageous relations by which this trade linked them to the world economy.

In addition to his valuable notes on the ivory trade of East Central Africa, Barreto also provides the most complete contemporary description of the Maravi empire of the Kalonga, whose dominion extended from Maravi country right across to the coast just north of Mozambique Island. The ruler of Bororo was the Lundu, 'the second person in the Maravi empire'. This confirms the situation as it was reported by Bocarro three decades before, while suggesting that despite his defeat in 1622 the Lundu was far too important a chief to be dislodged from his own territory. Throughout the entire region the Maravi were dominant by virtue of their military superiority. The Makua near Mozambique Island and the Bororo admitted 'such obedienceas they are compelled to by violence'; elsewhere they were 'subjected by force to the Maravi'. The mainland opposite the Portuguese island-capital was 'infested by the Maravi', while Quelimane was occasionally raided by the Bororo 'under the name of Maravi'. Barreto also remarks revealingly that 'The Maravi are very warlike, and are feared among all the Kaffirs as the Bororo and Makua are despised, so that as any Kaffir is offended at being called a Bororo or Makua, so it is a great honour to be a Maravi'.[56] Additional testimony to the influence of the Maravi in northern Mozambique may also be found in the traditions of the Lomwe of Larde, near Angoche, and possibly those of Mihavani, farther inland. To the north, in the country around Fernão Veloso Bay, a number of Makua chiefs in the first half of the nineteenth century were reported to have been 'of the Maravi caste' or Maravi chiefs.[57]

But the Maravi empire of the Kalonga barely seems to have survived the seventeenth century. The principal reason for its decline was the inevitable fragmentation of an empire which was both decentralized and over-extended. The Phiri political tradition was not equipped to deal with this sort of situation and before long began to display the old problems of fragmentation which had beset it from the start. The Kalonga could expect no more, in the end, than the Lundu's recognition of his senior position in the Phiri hierarchy, while at the same time he was having to contend with the rise of the Undi's Chewa kingdom in the western reaches of Maravi territory.[58] On the economic front, the effects of this predicament were already visible to Barreto in 1667. 'The merchants of Mozambique trade in this kingdom with the Makua, those of Quelimane with the Bororo, those of Sena with the Rundo, and those of Tete with the said Maravi [i.e. the Kalonga] in his court.'[59]

Nearly thirty years later, in 1696, the Portuguese still complained that only the Kalonga and a few of his most important territorial chiefs were permitted to sell ivory.[60] But by this time the Maravi route from Zambesia through Bororo to Mozambique Island had become largely obsolete, and the Maravi no longer were to be found 'infesting' the coast, either as traders or as warriors. Instead, two new routes dominated by the Yao became the major arteries of trade from the interior of East Central Africa to the coast. One route led out of Yao country along the Lujenda River until it met the Ruvuma, whence an irregular path was pursued until the coast was reached at Kilwa. The other passed eastwards from the Lujenda into Meto Makua country and descended south-eastwards to Mossuril across the Lurio River and through a part of Macuana which was known as Uticulo. Both routes drew upon the country to the west of Yaoland.

The Emergence of Yao Trading Power and the Route to Kilwa

In contrast to the rise of the Maravi as traders in the early seventeenth century, a phenomenon which was linked intimately to the political and military rivalries of the two most powerful Maravi chiefs, the emergence of the Yao in the same capacity was the product of a much more specifically economic set of factors. From their key position as ironsmiths within Yao society, and their important role in local and regional trade, it was the Chisi who formed the vanguard of Yao expeditions to the coast. According to Abdallah,

> It happened that there was a certain district up-country, on the way to the coast, where there were no hoes, and the Achisi did not go there to sell theirs; . . . these people took foodstuffs and went to sell them to the people who lived near the Coast, and there they bought a piece of white calico. When they got this they took it to buy a hoe at a village visited by the Achisi. And they (the Achisi) carried word of it when trading to another village. In this manner the fame of this calico spread throughout Yao-land, disseminated by those who had seen it; and its fame extended also wherever the Yaos went. . . . That was when the Yaos first began to trade and to penetrate as far as the coast.

Eventually, small groups of Yao banded together to strike out for the coast themselves. Abdallah states that this trade was at first limited to hoes, tobacco, and animal skins. Carrying their produce across the Ruvuma, Yao adventurers travelled until they reached the coast 'at Mchiwi Mchilwa (Kilwa), and so that has always been the part of the coast most favoured by us Yaos, as being known to us from ancient times'.[61]

It is important to try to establish with greater certainty when the Yao began to trade to Kilwa. It seems very unlikely that there was any contact between the Yao and the Kilwa coast before Monclaro's initial reference to Swahili trade with the interior in 1571. After the devastation wrought at Kilwa in 1588, it must also have taken several years before more than a trifling trade of this sort could have been re-established. Besides the determination of the people of Kilwa, a principal element in the revival of this trade was the presence of the Portuguese at Kilwa. In 1592 the Portuguese seat of power was transferred from Malindi to Mombasa, where, in the following year, construction began on the monumental Fort Jesus. Within several years the Captain of Mombasa had his personal trading agent, or factor, established at Kilwa, among other places along the coast, for despite specific instructions not to monopolize trade, this is precisely what successive Captains usually strove to do.[62] When Gaspar Bocarro reached Kilwa from Tete in 1616, 'the factor and other Portuguese, who received him seem to have been in control of the place.[63] On the strength of this evidence concerning Kilwa's revival, the most likely dating of initial Yao contact with Kilwa is the quarter century from about 1590 to 1616.

This period coincides with the height of the struggle between the Kalonga Muzura and the Lundu for supremacy among the Maravi. And while the Maravi exercised no military domination over the regions through which the route to Kilwa ran, the description of Bocarro's march in 1616 from Muzura's town of Marauy to Kilwa clearly reveals that Muzura's influence extended along the entire route and that his interest there was to trade. The first part of Bocarro's trip was spent in the lands of the Kalonga Muzura. Five days after leaving his town, Bocarro reached 'the limits of the land of the son [Caromboe] of Muzura', which marked the border with the territory of Manguro. Manguro was subject to a chief named Chicoave, whose village was located two full days' march into Manguro, just south of the Ruambara [Luambala] River. A week later Bocarro arrived at the Rofuma

[Ruvuma], beyond which a chief named Manhanga is said to have ruled. His village was three days' journey beyond the Ruvuma, and it was there that Bocarro left his guides from Muzura. For seven days Bocarro marched through uninhabited country until he reached the village of Chiponda, which was also separated from the next villages of Ponde and Morengue by another long stretch of wilderness. From there to the Swahili settlement of Bucury, only a half-day's walk to the coast opposite Kilwa Kisiwani, Bocarro traversed a final tract of barren land.[64]

There have been a number of attempts to reconstruct Bocarro's route to Kilwa. Rangeley did so with the help of Yao informants who had participated in the nineteenth-century caravan trade from Malawi to Kilwa. If anything, his results match Bocarro's route too perfectly and must also be tempered by his own reservations about the accuracy of his informants' testimony. Similarly, his attempt to identify the Manguro people as Yao must be rejected on the basis that the name has no precise ethnographic meaning.[65] Hamilton's identification of Chicoave's people as Makua-Lomwe must also be rejected on the same grounds.[66] Nevertheless, there is reason to believe that the Manguro through which Bocarro passed in 1616 was inhabited by the Yao.

Bocarro's identification of the boundary between Muzura's lands and Manguro virtually tallies with the southern frontier of Yao occupation as described by Abdallah. Chicoave, the Manguro chief, seems also to have been independent of Muzura's control, if somewhat in awe of him, since it was necessary for the Maravi paramount chief to send him gifts in order to assure safe passage and to procure additional guides for Bocarro through Manguro. Nor were the chiefs beyond Chicoave subject to Muzura's authority, although both Bocarro and his chronicler believed otherwise. Bocarro's journey was facilitated by gifts of cloth, beads, and copper bracelets to the chief of each village at which he rested. In return he received the hospitality of his host and on several occasions was presented with a young slave. Chiefs Quitenga and Muangongo, whose villages were immediately to the south of the Ruvuma, merited greater gifts than did most of the chiefs of Manguro, but by this measure there is no doubt that Chicoave was the most important chief whom Bocarro encountered in Manguro. A likely reason for treating him with special respect was his commanding position at the frontier between the Maravi and Manguro, though which the trade route to Kilwa passed. His cooperation was probably of the utmost importance to the Kalonga Muzura.

Across the Ruvuma it is more difficult to determine if Manhanga should be identified as a Yao chief. Certainly his rule did not extend to the coast, as Bocarro seemed to think it did, and it is clear that Bocarro was equally mistaken in his belief that 'this Kaffir also obeys Muzura'. Chiponda was called 'brother of Manhanga' by Bocarro, but this identification could have been the result of cooperation in trading to the coast as much as it may have indicated a real or structural genealogical relationship. It is more likely that once Bocarro was beyond the realm of Muzura most of the chiefs were politically independent but economically linked through their common interest in the coastal trade. Indeed, the existence of chiefs and the absence of any centralized authority among them accords well with what little information exists on early Yao political structure. So while the evidence is less than conclusive, the indications of the available sources are that the Yao probably were the people who were known to Bocarro only as Manguro.

Once the Kilwa route was established by the Yao it more than held its own during the remainder of the seventeenth century, while Kilwa survived a variety of problems which reflected Portugal's critical role along the entire Swahili coast. At Kilwa itself political assassinations in 1614 and 1616 seem to have had their roots in the growth of pro- and anti-Portuguese parties within the ruling class.[67] A major uprising in 1631 at Mombasa threw the Portuguese out of their one coastal stronghold, but it was retaken in the following year. Matters were only slightly better at Kilwa in 1631, where the oppressive behaviour of successive Portuguese trading factors from Mombasa had created a state of near revolt among its inhabitants. It took the attentions of a visiting Portuguese judge, who investigated Portuguese affairs there, to appease the irate Sultan. It also seems likely that the decision of Francisco de Seixas Cabreira, who became Captain of Mombasa in 1635, to exercise his monopoly of the ivory trade at Kilwa through Sharif Alaum, a native of Kilwa, was intended to demonstrate the continued good faith of the Portuguese with respect to the people of Kilwa. If so, it was intelligently conceived, as Kilwa remained friendly and well within the commercial sphere of the Captain of Mombasa throughout the remainder of the century, even after 'Uman began to challenge Portuguese supremacy of the East African coast.

The rise of 'Uman under the new Ya'arubi dynasty after 1624 and the decline of Portuguese maritime domination in the Indian Ocean, which was largely the result of Dutch expansion, combined to result in the 'Umani capture of Masqat from the Portuguese in 1650. By being quick to adapt European ship design, the 'Umani were soon able to present the Portuguese with a formidable challenge in East Africa. In 1652 Arab raiders from 'Uman seriously threatened the Portuguese, and Kilwa was attacked by a fleet mounted by the pro-Arab ruler of Pemba. But Portuguese hegemony was shortly re-established on the coast, with Kilwa remaining far more securely within the fold than other towns. While the 'Umani continued to test Portuguese strength along the coast, even attempting unsuccessfully to seize Mozambique in 1670, Kilwa was largely untouched by these events until after the 'Umani capture of Mombasa in 1698.[68]

Until then the only additional information on Kilwa which has come to light is found in the *Journal* of William Alley, an Englishman who spent several months at Mombasa in 1667. Mombasa he described as 'a place of noe great traffiq', but what there was lay in the hands of the captain of the coast.

> Mombaza its selfe seldome sens anything considerable, their onely trade consisting in their small boates, with which the Governor sends down to Quilo, Pembah, and Zanzebar, and oft times to Musembeque. Their returnes are gould, amber, elevants teeth, and slaves, most of which commodity they purchase at very inconsiderable rates, and for which the Governor maintains continually a factory at Quilo att his own charge.[69]

While there must have been a certain amount of independent exporting done by the Muslim merchants of Kilwa, as well as the introduction of some Indian merchant capital (see Chapter 3), it seems likely that the most important buyer at Kilwa was the Captain of Mombasa. His prominence was established there at the very beginning of the seventeenth century, when Kilwa was at its weakest, and despite occasional set-backs he seems to have remained the most vital commercial force at Kilwa throughout that century.

Conclusion

There is no doubt that the long-distance overland trade which developed after 1505 in East Central Africa was based on ivory. Before the middle of the sixteenth century, there was virtually no call at Kilwa for ivory from the interior. The trade described by Monclaro does not appear to have been very considerable. While it is possible that the Yao may have begun trading some ivory at the coast at this time, it is more likely that this trade only became important after the disaster of 1588, when Kilwa's export trade came to be dominated by the Portuguese Captain of Mombasa. Certainly the transition to long-distance international trade between Yaoland and Kilwa was a gradual process, growing from a limited regional trade in hides, ironware, and agricultural products which were of secondary interest to the coastal merchants to a thriving, well-organized trade in ivory by the end of the seventeenth century. Equally, the joining of forces between the Maravi and the Yao in the ivory trade was probably gradually achieved, although the rise of the Maravi empire at the same time as the beginning of a steady demand for ivory at Kilwa, a relationship which may not have been entirely coincidental, surely combined to encourage this development.

According to Abdallah's version of Yao traditions, the transition from the earlier regional trade to that in ivory was a major watershed in Yao history. Through chronological telescoping this development is also linked in his account to the beginning of the slave trade. But if the ivory trade clearly preceded that in slaves in East Central Africa, the Yao were certainly correct in putting these two trades into the same category, as each represented but different manifestations of the penetration of the international market economy into their part of the world. Abdallah records that

> When they went to the coast they were told, 'Next year you must bring ivory and slaves from Yaoland, and you will make your fortune. You will get the powder you want so much, and *milandawala* (i.e. guns) you will also obtain. You will get anything you want if you bring these two things, ivory and slaves.'
> And it was those words which suggested a new idea to our fathers of old; when they got home they spread the word, 'A new business has arisen in ivory and slaves.'[70]

Abdallah has little to say on the subject of trading to Mozam-bique Island beyond noting that 'the Walolo [Makua-Lomwe] were neighbours and they [the Yao] used to trade with them too'.[71] Perhaps the role of Yao traders along the route to Mozam-bique Island was more important during the seventeenth century than presently available sources indicate, although there seems little doubt that the Maravi first put this community into direct contact with the far interior. By the end of the seventeenth century, or by the 1740s at the very latest, the Yao were recog-nized by the Portuguese as the principal traders to both Kilwa and Mozambique Island. Specific details are lacking here; perhaps they can be resolved by further research, particularly in the field, when that becomes possible. Meanwhile, we do know that by the end of the seventeenth century two long-distance overland trade routes were well established in East Central Africa. One led from northern Zambesia to Kilwa, the other to Mozam-bique Island. During the next two centuries a variety of factors operating on the coast affected the ivory market so as to cause two major redirections in the flow of ivory from the interior to the coast; others combined to increase the importance of the slave trade. Both of these phenomena reveal how closely linked and subordinated to international merchant capitalism the people of East Central Africa had become.

NOTES

1. See Charles R. Boxer, *The Portuguese Seaborne Empire: 1415–1825* (New York, 1969), Chs. 1–2, and his 'The Portuguese in the East, 1500–1800', in H. V. Livermore (ed.), *Portugal and Brazil* (Oxford, 1953), pp. 189–95.
2. Alpers, 'Re-thinking African Economic History', pp. 110–12; Abdul M. H. Sheriff, 'The Development of Underdevelopment: the role of international trade in the economic history of the East African coast before the sixteenth century', unpublished seminar paper, University of Dar es Salaam, 1972.
3. H. A. R. Gibb, *The Travels of Ibn Battuta* (Cambridge, 1962), II, pp. 379–80.
4. For the relevant passage, see G. S. P. Freeman-Grenville, *The East African Coast: Select Documents from the first century to the earlier nineteenth century* (Oxford, 1962), p. 91.
5. For several attempts to argue otherwise, see Roger Summers, *Inyanga-Prehistoric Settlements in Southern Rhodesia* (Cambridge, 1958), p. 263; Gervase Mathew, 'The East African Coast until the Coming of the Portuguese', in Oliver and Mathew, *History of East Africa*, I, pp. 112, 117; Freeman-Grenville, 'The Coast, 1498–1840', ibid., I, p. 147.
6. Brian M. Fagan, 'Excavations at Ingombe Ilede, 1960–62', in B. M. Fagan, D. W. Phillipson, and S. G. H. Daniels, *Iron Age Cultures in Zambia, II: Dambwa, Ingombe Ilede and the Tonga* (London, 1969), pp. 135–9, 142–9; Phillipson and Fagan, 'The date of the Ingombe Ilede Burials', *Jl. of African History,* X, 2 (1969), pp.

199–204. The earlier and much longer occupation of Ingombe Ilede spans the last third of the first millennium A.D. The site was abandoned for several centuries before its reoccupation in about 1400.

7. Diogo de Alcáçova to Crown, Cochin, 20 November 1506, in *Documentos sobre os Portugueses em Moçambique e na África Central/Documents on the Portuguese in Mozambique and Central Africa*, National Archives of Rhodesia and Centro de Estudos Históricos Ultramarinos (Lisbon, 1962), I, p. 395.

8. Freeman-Grenville, *The Medieval History of the Coast of Tanganyika* (London, 1962), pp. 111–40; Mathew, 'The East African Coast', pp. 119–25; H. N. Chittick, 'The "Shirazi" Colonization of East Africa', *Jl. of African History*, VI, 3 (1965), p. 293.

9. Lobato, *A Expansão Portuguesa em Moçambique de 1498 a 1530* (Lisbon, 1954), I, pp. 51–238, 262–5, and (Lisbon, 1960), II, pp. 13–31; Eric Axelson, *South-East Africa, 1488–1530* (London, 1940), pp. 64–97; Justus Strandes, *The Portuguese Period in East Africa*, trans. J. F. Wallwork, ed. J. S. Kirkman (Nairobi, 1961), pp. 38–81, 103–16; Boxer, 'Moçambique Island and the "carreira da India"', *Stvdia*, 8 (1961), pp. 95–132.

10. Strandes, *Portuguese Period*, p. 111; Lobato, *Expansão*, II, pp. 21–5, 34–5, 117–23, 128–9, 134–5, and (Lisbon, 1960), III, pp. 22–4, 103–18; Axelson, *South-East Africa*, pp. 109, 121–6, 145; António Carneiro, summary of letters from António de Saldanha to Crown, [1511], and Gaspar Veloso to Crown, [1512], in *Documentos* (Lisbon, 1964), III, pp. 15, 187; Cristovão de Távora to Crown, Moç., 20 September 1517, and 'Descrição da Situação, Costumes e Produtos de Alguns Lugares de África', [c. 1518], in *Documentos* (Lisbon, 1966), V, pp. 203, 363. Santos, 'Ethiopia Oriental', p. 304, also mentions a small Makua chiefdom named Mongallo near Quelimane. See M. D. D. Newitt, 'The Early History of the Sultanate of Angoche', *Jl. of African History*, XIII, 3 (1972), pp. 397–406.

11. Lobato, *Expansão*, II, pp. 44, 53–5, 62–3, 81–4, 95, 143–5, 151–2, and III, pp. 213–217, 236, 243–4, 317–18, 323–7, 356–8, 369–71, 375–6, 383–7; Axelson, *South-East Africa*, pp. 149–50, 154, 158–9.

12. José Justino Teixeira Botelho, *História Militar e Política dos Portugueses em Moçambique* (Lisbon, 1934), I, pp. 93–4, 146–7, 162–70, 175–207; James Duffy, *Portuguese Africa* (Cambridge, Mass., 1959), pp. 35–8, 107–8; Lobato, 'Para a História da Penetração Portuguesa na África Central', in his *Colonização Senhorial da Zambézia e Outros Estudos* (Lisbon, 1962), pp. 77–80; Lobato, *Evolução Administrativa e Económica de Moçambique, 1752–1763* (Lisbon, 1957), pp. 169–72.

13. In addition to its merchants' cultivation of the Angoche trade, Kilwa also furnished Mozambique with provisions and Portuguese vessels with coir, which was used for matting and for making rope. But relations with the Portuguese were not always cordial. In 1519 the crew of a shipwrecked Portuguese vessel were massacred by Swahili in the vicinity of Kilwa. Towards the end of the following decade several French ships are known to have spent some time at Kilwa without suffering attack. Lobato, *Expansão*, II, pp. 76–9, 89–90, 152, 154, 181, and III, pp. 285–7.

14. Carneiro, summary of letters from Afonso de Albuquerque to Crown, [1511], in *Documentos* (Lisbon, 1963), II, p. 7.

15. 'Descrição da Situação', in *Documentos*, V, pp. 365, 377; for examples of the export of ivory from Sofala to the northern ports, see Jorge de Figueiredo, [Moç.], 15 July 1518, ibid., p. 537; 'Regimentos de Sofala', Lisboa, 20 May 1530, and Jordão de Freitas to Crown, Goa, 17 September 1530, in *Documentos*, VI, pp. 389–91, 427–9.

16. See, e.g., Mathew, 'The East African Coast', p. 124. Dr. A. H. M. Sheriff informs me that Dr. B. A. Datoo (University of Dar es Salaam) has argued in his recent University of London Ph.D. thesis on the historical geography of the ports of East Africa, which I have been unable to consult, that the rise of Mombasa can be linked to the entry of Indian traders into East Africa. Dr. Sheriff agrees, however, that Mombasa's contact with the interior partly explains its rise and certainly its resilience.

17. 'Descrição da Situação', in *Documentos*, V, p. 369; cf. slightly different version of this document on p. 379.
18. A valid objection to this reconstruction is that it is based exclusively on Portuguese documentation and that the key passages relating to the ivory trade of the coastal towns must be read in light of the Portuguese preoccupation with Sofala and the gold trade of the Zimbabwean interior. But it must also be remembered that the Portuguese encountered a well established system of trade in East Africa and merely attempted to wrest control of it intact from its Muslim architects, to whom the Portuguese bore such a close resemblance in their seaward orientation. The combination of these factors leads me to believe that the early Portuguese writers saw the international trading system in East Africa essentially as it was seen by their Muslim predecessors. Cf. F. J. Berg, 'The Coast from the Portuguese Invasion to the Rise of the Zanzibar Sultanate', in Ogot and Kieran, *Zamani*, p. 125.
19. 'Relação da Viagem que fizeram os Padres da Companhia de Jesus com Francisco Barreto na conquista de Monomotapa no anno de 1569 feita pelo padre Monclaro da mesma companhia', in Theal, *Records* (London, 1899), III, p. 211, and reprinted in Freeman-Grenville, *Select Documents*, p. 138, where Monclaro's side trip to Kilwa is incorrectly dated to 1569.
20. Sebastião Xavier Botelho, *Resumo para servir de introducção a Memoria Estatistica sobre os dominios portuguezes na Africa Oriental* (Lisbon, 1834), p. 17.
21. Strandes, *Portuguese Period*, pp. 126–7, 132–3; Axelson, *South-East Africa*, pp. 154–8; Bernardo Gomes de Brito, *Historia Tragico-Maritima* (Lisbon, 1904), II, p. 69.
22. Monclaro, 'Relação da Viagem', pp. 211, 216.
23. Alpers, 'The Mutapa and Malawi Political Systems to the time of the Ngoni Invasion', in Ranger (ed.), *Aspects of Central African History* (London, 1968), pp. 18–19.
24. The earliest Portuguese indication of Muslim trading activity up the Shire River dates to the third decade of the sixteenth century. See Lobato, *Expansão*, III, p. 358.
25. Axelson, 'Portuguese settlement in the interior of south-east Africa in the seventeenth century', Congresso Internacional de História dos Descobrimentos, *Actas*, V, 2 (Lisbon, 1961), p. 3.
26. For a summary of the following interpretation of early Maravi history and the role of the Zimba in it, see Alpers and Christopher Ehret, 'Eastern Africa, 1600–1790', in R. Gray (ed.), *The Cambridge History of Africa*, IV (forthcoming).
27. Mathew Schoffeleers, 'The History and Political Role of the M'Bona Cult among the Mang'anja', in Ranger and Kimambo, *African Religion*, pp. 73–94; see also Rangeley, 'Two Nyasaland Rain Shrines: Makewana—The Mother of all People', *Nyasaland Jl.*, V, 2 (1952), pp. 31–2, and 'Mbona—the Rain Maker', *Nyasaland Jl.*, VI, 1 (1953), p. 8; Price, 'More about the Maravi', pp. 75–9.
28. Santos, 'Ethiopia Oriental', p. 292.
29. On this point, see Monclaro, 'Relação da Viagem', p. 226.
30. See W. G. L. Randles, 'South East Africa and the Empire of Monomotapa as shown on selected printed maps of the sixteenth century', *Stvdia*, 2 (1958), p. 159 and photographic reproduction of Velho's map. While there is, according to D. P. Abraham, a demonstrable ancestral relationship between the Zimba marauders of the late sixteenth century and the modern Zimba (Chewa of Makanga), I think it best not to confer any firm ethnic identification to the early Portuguese use of this term. D. P. Abraham, 'Tasks in the Field of Early History', in *Conference of the History of the Central African Peoples*, mimeographed (Lusaka, 1963), p. 3 and note 16. For the modern Zimba, see Rita-Ferreira, *Os Cheuas de Macanga*, a revised version of his 'Os "Azimba" (Monografia Etnográfica)', *Boletim da Sociedade de Estudos de Moçambique*, XXIV, 84–5 (1954), pp. 47–140, 5–116. Rita-Ferreira changed his nomenclature for these people in consideration of 'The pejorative character with which the epithet of Zimba has come to be associated for many

years, and, finally, the reluctance which our friends in Macanga demonstrated upon being designated in that manner'. Rita-Ferreira, *Os Cheuas de Macanga*, p. 4.

31. It is worth noting that Diogo de Couto, although a less reliable source of information for East Africa than Santos, assigns the beginning of this period of unrest in East Central Africa to about 1570. Couto, *Da Asia*, Década X (Lisbon, 1788), Livro 6, capítulo xiv, p. 98.

32. Santos, 'Ethiopia Oriental', pp. 299–302. For the Turkish raids along the East African coast and related events, see Strandes, *Portuguese Period*, pp. 145–63, 349–50; Boxer, 'The Portuguese on the Swahili Coast, 1593–1729', in Boxer and Carlos de Azevedo, *Fort Jesus and the Portuguese in Mombasa, 1593–1729* (London, 1960), pp. 19–25. It is very likely that the so-called Zimba who fought at Mombasa and Malindi were different from those in East Central Africa. Their real identity is not, however, of importance here. See Joseph C. Miller, 'Requiem for the "Jaga"', *Cahiers d'Études Africaines*, XIII, 49 (1973), pp. 124–5, including notes 1 and 2, for a sceptical evaluation of Santos' testimony and subsequent interpretations.

33. Santos Baptista, *Os Macuas*, pp. 16–20, although he himself believes that this invasion pre-dates that of the Zimba.

34. For a more recent reference to Makua belief in Maravi 'cannabalism', see António Pires Prata, 'Os Macuas Tem Outros Nomes', *O Missionário Católico*, XXIII, 260 (1946), p. 47, cited in José Júlio Gonçalves, *O Mundo Arabo-Islâmico e o Ultramar Português* (Lisbon, 1958), p. 222.

35. Lupi, *Angoche*, pp. 116, 119–23, 162–9. All italics are in the original text.

36. Santos, 'Ethiopia Oriental', pp. 368–9.

37. Lupi, *Angoche*, pp. 123–6.

38. Price, 'Malawi Rain-cults', in *Religion in Africa* (Edinburgh, 1964), pp. 114–24, and Schoffeleers, 'M'Bona Cult', pp. 80–1. As late as the eighteenth century the Portuguese reported that the Makua of this region had rebelled against the Sultan of Angoche and the 'Rundo or Maganja': see document cited in Rita-Ferreira, *Os Cheuas de Macanga*, p. 37. Perhaps less trustworthy confirmation of the identification of the Zimba with the *ma-rúndu* is the fact that Santos' descriptions of the Zimba-Portuguese hostilities near Sena and Tete, the Makua chief Mauruça's destruction of António Pinto's column in Macuana in 1585 (see Chapter 3), and the demise of the Zimba at Malindi in 1589 are all echoed in Lupi's version of *ma-rúndu* tradition. See Santos, 'Ethiopia Oriental', pp. 293–9, 302–3.

39. ibid., pp. 293–9; Joaquim Heliodoro da Cunha Rivara (ed.), *Archivo Portuguez-Oriental* (Nova–Goa, 1857–1876), III, pp. 583, 927. See also, N.A.I.P.G., L.M. 2-B, fl. 422, Crown to Viceroy, Lisboa, 21 November 1598.

40. Schoffeleers, 'M'Bona Cult', p. 93, n. 10. Fr. Schoffeleers collected these traditions in May 1967, when a sacrifice was made to Tundu at Khulubvi after rice fields in the neighbourhood had been ravaged by birds.

41. 'Viagem que fez o Padre Ant.º Gomes, da Comp.ª de Jesus, ao Imperio de de (*sic*) Manomotapa . . .', with notes by Axelson, *Stvdia*, 3 (1959), pp. 183–4. This is the earliest reference to Muzura's name, although the source itself dates from 1648: Axelson, *Portuguese in South-East Africa, 1600–1700* (Johannesburg, 1960), p. 32.

42. Archivum Romanum Societatis Jesu', Goa, 33 II, fl. 750–72, Sebastian Barreto to Vitelleschi, Goa, 15 December 1624, at paragraphs 40–2, 67. I am indebted to Professor Richard Gray for allowing me to utilize his notes. A.H.U., Moç., Cx. 1, Diogo de Sousa de Meneses, Moç., 1 April 1624.

43. Biblioteca Nacional de Madrid, Codice 2362, fl. 289–92, 'Copia da informação que deu Pero d'Allmeida Cabral dos Rejnos de Monomotapa, e Rios de Cuama por mandado de Sua Magestade em carta de 15 de Novembro de 1630'. Axelson, *Portuguese*, pp. 72–4, summarizes this report, but omits the reference to Muzura, for which I am again grateful to Professor Gray. For the use of Bororo, see Rita-Ferreira, *Agrupamento e Caracterização Étnica dos Indígenas de Moçambique* (Lisbon, 1958), pp. 53–4, 70.

44. A. B. de Bragança Pereira (ed.), *Arquivo Português Oriental*, nova edição, Tomo IV, Vol. II, Parte I (Bastorá, 1937), pp. 13–15, and B. M., Sloane Ms. 197, fl. 100. Muzura's request to be called 'Emperor' by the Portuguese is not surprising, since he was much more powerful than the Mwene Mutapa in 1635.

45. For the date of the Lundu's defeat, see Georg Schurhammer, 'Die Entdeckung des Nyassa-Sees', *Stimmen der Zeit* (1920), p. 349.

46. It is important to recognize that the Portuguese never made this connection for themselves. The last contemporary documentary reference that I have found to Muzura occurs in Gomes' report of 1648; the first mention of the Kalonga is made by one António Álvares Pereira, who wrote to the Crown in 1661 that 'he had been to the court of the Marave king, the Caronga . . .'. See Gomes, 'Viagem'; Pereira's letter is cited by A. Teixeira da Mota, *A Cartografia Antiga da África Central e a Travessia entre Angola e Moçambique, 1500–1860* (Lourenço Marques, 1964), p. 52.

47. N.A.I.P.G., L.M. 17, fl. 138, and L.M. 18, fl. 33, Crown to Viceroy, Lisboa, 27 February 1633; see also, Crown to Viceroy, Lisboa, 12 February 1636, in Theal, *Records*, IV, pp. 267–70.

48. Axelson, *Portuguese*, p. 76; José Joaquim Lopes de Lima and Francisco Maria Bordalo, *Ensaios sobre a Estatistica das Possessões Portuguezas . . .*, Segunda Serie, Livro Quarto, *Ensaio sobre a Estatistica de Moçambique . . .* (Lisbon, 1859), p. 113 (cited hereafter as Bordalo, *Ensaio*).

49. A.H.U., Moç., Cx. 1, Cristovão de Brito de Vasconcelos, *provisão*, Moç., 7 January 1632.

50. N.A.I.P.G., L.M. 17, fl. 138, and L.M. 18, fl. 33, Crown to Viceroy, Lisboa, 27 February 1633, and reply, Goa, 19 October, 1633; Crown to Viceroy, Lisboa, 28 March 1635 and 12 February 1636, in Theal, *Records*, IV, pp. 265–70. On the Dutch siege of Mozambique, see Axelson, *Portuguese*, pp. 15–29.

51. *Boletim da Filmoteca Ultramarina Portuguesa*, 14 (1960), pp. 85–6, no. 20; N.A.I.P.G., L.M. 21–A, fl. 90, Crown to Viceroy, Lisboa, 11 March 1640; see also, N.A.I.P.G., L.M. 21–B, fl. 503–4, 'Lista de 43 cartas de Sua Magestade, tocantes ao governo, que vão resondidas por este maço No. 1', no. 41, for a passing reference to this trade.

52. A.H.U., Moç., Cx. 2, anon., document beginning 'Em prezença do Conde da Torre . . .', n.d., but dating from the 1640s. The document is based on the testimony of two experienced men from Mozambique and the Rivers, Carlos Luís de Almeida, who had last served in East Africa as Captain of the Rivers, and Manuel da Silva Louzado. They had been summoned to give witness before the Count, who became a member of the *Conselho do Estado* in 1641, and died in 1651: *Grande Enciclopédia Portuguesa e Brasileira* (Lisbon and Rio de Janeiro, n.d.), XXXII, p. 203.

53. Axelson, *Portuguese*, p. 131.

54. Manuel Barreto, 'Informação do Estado e Conquista dos Rios de Cuama . . .', Goa, 11 December 1667, in Theal, *Records*, III, pp. 464–5. Barreto had resided in Zambesia for four years when he wrote this report.

55. ibid., pp. 476–7.

56. ibid., pp. 463–4, 470–1, 475, 480.

57. See Castro, 'Os Lómuès no Larde', pp. 41–3; O'Neill, 'Journey from Mozambique', pp. 645, 726. Although Maravi influence among the Mihavani was said to date from the Ngoni invasion of southern Malawi, the tone of O'Neill's passage suggests the possibility of telescoping here and the substitution of the Ngoni for the Zimba. Francisco Santana. *Documentação Avulsa Moçambicana do Arquivo Histórico Ultramarino* (Lisbon, 1967), II, p. 380; A.H.U., Cod. 1432, fl. 52–3, Manuel da Silva Gonçalves to José Joaquim Rodrigues, Moç., 7 April 1832.

58. For a broader overview of this period in the history of northern Zambesia, see Alpers and Ehret, 'Eastern Africa'.

59. Barreto, 'Informação,' p. 480.

60. Frei António Conceição, 'Tratados dos Rios de Cuama', Sena, 20 June 1696,

and Goa, 15 December 1696, in J. H. da Cunha Rivara (ed.), *O Chronista de Tissuary* (Nova-Goa, 1867), II, p. 42.

61. Abdallah, *The Yaos*, pp. 26–7. As late as the 1870s Yao tobacco was 'selling for three or four times the price of coast tobacco in Zanzibar'. U.S.P.G., U.M.C.A. A/I/iii/2, Steere to Heanley, London, 21 June 1877.

62. Boxer, 'Swahili Coast', pp. 25–9; Strandes, *Portuguese Period*, pp. 164–73, 241, 242.

63. Freeman-Grenville, *Select Documents*, pp. 168, 183–4.

64. ibid., pp. 166–8.

65. Rangeley, 'Bocarro's Journey', *Nyasaland Jl.*, VII, 2 (1954), pp. 15–23, especially pp. 22–3.

66. R. A. Hamilton, 'The Route of Gaspar Bocarro from Tete to Kilwa in 1616', *Nyasaland Jl.*, VII, 2 (1954), pp. 10–11. Other analyses of Bocarro's journey have been written by Ernesto Jardim de Vilhena, 'De Tete a Quiloa', *Revista Portugueza Colonial e Maritima*, 5.º ano, 2.º semestre (1901), pp. 1–14, 49–59, 97–107, and by John Milner Gray, 'A Journey by Land from Tete to Kilwa in 1616', *T.N.R.*, 25 (1948), pp. 37–47.

67. N.A.I.P.G., L.M. 12, fl. 161–7, D. Jerónimo de Azevedo to Crown, Parajem dos Queimados, 31 December 1614; B. G. Martin, 'Notes on Some Members of the Learned Classes of Zanzibar and East Africa in the Nineteenth Century', *African Historical Studies*, IV, 3 (1971), p. 529, and letter to the author dated Bloomington, 13 April 1972.

68. Strandes, *Portuguese Period*, pp. 178–240; Axelson, *Portuguese*, pp. 78–96, 127–8, 139–43, 151–3, 155–8; N.A.I.P.G., L.M. 22–B, fl. 388, Francisco de Seixas Cabreira, Mombasa, 30 August 1652; A.H.U., Cod. 211, fl. 305–6, Conselho Ultramarino, *consulta*, Lisboa, 9 October 1654.

69. Freeman-Grenville, *Select Documents*, p. 190. Alley was apparently ignorant of Portuguese trade with the Mombasa hinterland; see Chapter 3, p. 71.

70. Abdallah, *The Yaos*, p. 30. Santos' generalized description of elephant hunting at the end of the sixteenth century also has the merit of reminding the modern reader that the economic value of ivory was imposed on Africa from without. Before that development the main economic reasons for hunting elephant appear to have been quite different.

> Throughout this Kaffraria there are many very large and wild elephants, that cause great damage to the plantations of millet and rice, which they eat and tread under foot to the loss of the Kaffirs. Besides this they do much harm to the palm groves by pulling down the trees to eat the small leaves . . . . The principal reason why the Kaffirs hunt elephants and kill them is to obtain the flesh for food, and secondly to sell the tusks, that is the ivory from which all the articles of taste and trinkets are made which come to Portugal from India, and it forms the principal trade of this coast.

Santos, 'Ethiopia Oriental', pp. 321–2.

71. ibid., p. 28.

CHAPTER THREE

The Rise of the Ivory
Trade at Mozambique, 1698–1750

፠፠፠፠፠፠፠፠፠፠፠፠፠፠፠፠፠፠፠፠፠፠፠፠፠፠፠፠፠

The Failure of Early 'Umani Imperialism

The fall of Mombasa, and with it Kilwa, from Portuguese into 'Umani hands in December 1698 marks another important turning point in the economic history of East Africa. Until the 'Umani seizure of the Swahili coast a large part of the goods carried to Kilwa from the interior had been purchased by the factor of the Captain of Mombasa. There can be little doubt that with the Portuguese withdrawal from the coast north of Cape Delgado a considerable market was lost to those Africans who were in the habit of trading to Kilwa. Chief among these people were the Yao. In 1758 Inácio Caetano Xavier, the knowledgeable Secretary of the recently formed (1752) Government-General of Mozambique, wrote that the Yao ivory trade, which was by then the mainstay of the island-capital's economy, 'formerly was divided, part to Mombasa, and part to this Island, and since the former was lost, all goes to this market'. Later in the same account Xavier repeats that 'before our losing Mombasa the trade of it [Yaoland] went to that port'.[1] Xavier's sources for this extremely important and unique piece of evidence concerning the Yao shifting of markets are unknown, but Costa Mendes states that he utilized the records of the convent of the Hospitalers of São João de Deus at Mozambique.[2] As Secretary, Xavier undoubtedly had access to a wealth of information, much of which has likely been lost since the middle of the eighteenth century. Certainly, there is no reason to suppose that he fabricated these notes. Accepting him at his word, then, the problem at hand is to discover the factors which caused the shift to occur.

70

The re-direction of Yao trade in the early years of the eighteenth century was not simply a matter of the commercially minded Yao turning their efforts to the Mozambique route solely because the Portuguese had abandoned Kilwa. This is an important reason, but it does not tell the whole story. The commercial importance of Kilwa was based exclusively upon its position as an entrepôt for the trade of the hinterland. Without a steady demand from the outside, there was bound to be a consonant abatement in the supply from within. The prosperity of Kilwa, in common with all the commercially oriented towns of the coast, depended upon the interplay of these two factors. After the Portuguese flight from beyond Cape Delgado, 'Uman failed to fill successfully the economic role previously played at Kilwa by the Portuguese Captain of Mombasa.

In the first flush of triumph it seems that the 'Umani did trade with some success there. After Saif ibn Sultan, the reigning Imam of 'Uman, had taken possession of Mombasa at the end of the seventeenth century, he continued south along the coast, gaining recognition of his sovereignty at both Zanzibar and Kilwa, although it appears that he met with some resistance at Kilwa, which may have been sacked by the Arabs.[3] In November 1701 it was reported 'that they have profited from the factories which they have along the coast above [Mozambique] up to Kilwa'.[4] A year later, however, according to information forwarded by Swahili spies working for the Portuguese and reporting to the Captain of the Kerimba Islands, the Arabs had failed to come to trade at Kilwa because they were so strapped for funds at Mombasa. The same report indicates that no aid had come from Masqat for two years. The Mosungulos of the Mombasa coast, who had been the main trading partners of the Portuguese there, refused to deal with the Arabs. Like everyone else on the coast they were said to be awaiting Portuguese aid so that they could throw off the Arab yoke.[5] In the following years word continued to reach Goa that the 'Umani Arabs were generally abhorred and that their behaviour had seriously disrupted the trade of the entire coast.[6]

In 1708, the Mwenyi Mwanya (Mungumanha), chief of Mongalo (Mgau Mwania), a small port to the south of Kilwa killed the Arabs who came to trade and seized all their goods.[7] Rightly or wrongly, this action was seen by the Portuguese as signifying support for them as much as it was a manifestation of

71

simple anti-Arab sentiment. Similarly, when the Queen of Zanzibar died in 1709, she left a sealed letter for the Portuguese, whom she had always favoured, in the care of her daughter and successor, Mwana Mtoto. Elsewhere along the coast the Arabs were allegedly obeyed by the Swahili only in the absence of the Portuguese, while at Tanga they were actively opposed by one Mwinyi Chame or Chuma.[8] Before long he was killed by the Arabs.[9]

In 1710 the Portuguese sent a spy named Mwinyi Juma bin Mwinyi Kajo, a member of the Mombasa nobility, to gather information along the entire Swahili coast. According to his sources, the Arabs had a garrison of fifty men at Mombasa under one Muhammad Rasul; another of fifty at Zanzibar under Che Vaziri; a force of thirty men at Pemba; while at Kilwa there were fifty men under a man named Sa'id. Mwinyi Juma learned that at Mombasa the Arabs continued to be rebuffed by the Mosungulos in their efforts to trade, particularly by Mamolaia bin M[winyi] Mozunga, who had been the chief trader with the Captain of Mombasa. At Pate the Swahili had incited the Mosungulos against the Arabs as a result of the new restrictions on trade. For example, one of the most important Swahili traders of Pate, Mwinyi Aquile, had in the previous year been prevented by the Arabs from proceeding from Kilwa to Mozambique on business. In general, the Arabs were said to kill the Swahili whom they believed to trade with the Portuguese. When they intercepted a letter from the Queen of Zanzibar to Mozambique, they seized her son, Mfalme Hasan, a Prince Sagayo, and one Shariff Muhammad, and sent all three to Masqat to be imprisoned. Elsewhere, the Swahili of Faza, Malindi, and Mombasa had all been robbed by the Arabs and many had since moved to Zanzibar, where they apparently felt more secure, as did a colony from Kilifi; others from Oza and Shaka, at the mouth of the Tana River between Pate and Malindi, had fled to Pemba. Finally, Mwinyi Juma reported that the people say 'that the ['Umani] captain at Kilwa is very vigorous and violent'. He had occupied and fortified the house of a certain Mwana Bakari and when he went to trade along the coast he simply appropriated the latter's boats.[10]

If the 'Umani Arabs were making the normal conduct of trade increasingly hazardous as a result of their robberies and appropriations, they were apparently faring no better in maintaining normal supplies of trade goods for exchange along the coast. Mwinyi Juma also was told that in 1709 the Arabs managed to send only three small dhows from Masqat to East Africa. A year or two later, two sons of a former Sultan of Kilwa wrote to him in these terms:

> You may tell the Portuguese that it is they whom we want to free these lands; because all of us want the Portuguese and we are hoping that they will come from the sea [to fight] against the Arabs, and we will give land to the Portuguese; and all the coast does not want the Arabs. This year all the cloth which came from Masqat is on credit and none of it is black, which to us is a deceitful omission. Could you write to the Viceroy to send us some cloth secretly, so that no one will know our design, and we will give him as much in return in ivory, or in something else.[11]

The ruling dynasty of Kilwa had particular reason to hate the Arabs, as it happened. After the loss of Mombasa a handful of Portuguese fugitives had found temporary refuge at Kilwa on their way to Mozambique. The Arabs accused the regent, Queen Fatima binti Sultan Mfalme Muhammad, of harbouring other Portuguese, imprisoned her daughter, Mwana Nakisa, and released her only on ransom of one hundred slaves.[12] A decade later a captain named Ali bin Muhammad came from Masqat, together with a trading agent named Muhammad bin Mubarak Ribocar, bearing orders from the Imam to command the Queen to recall all of her subjects living in the Kerimba Islands, in nominal Portuguese jurisdiction, to return to Kilwa.[13] A letter from Mwana Nakisa from the same period clearly reveals her low opinion of the Arabs. 'This year the Arabs who came from Masqat are all scabs, striplings, and weaklings (*sarmentos, rapazes, e magros*), and many die every day; they do not have the kind of people they used to have in Masqat.' She urged the Portuguese to help liberate the coast and requested cloth from the Portuguese, again with the promise of ivory in return.[14] However biased this evidence may be, it is clear that if the Swahili did not necessarily want a renewal of Portuguese imperial rule, that of the 'Umani Arabs was viewed with even greater distaste.

From Mombasa it was learned that 'the Arabs swagger about saying that next year they will take Mozambique, but they are mistaken and we do not believe them'.[15] As it happened, the Portuguese were in such straits themselves that they took considerable stock in such rumours. But the 'Umani Arabs were entering upon an even more uncertain period in their history. The death in 1711 of Saif ibn Sultan plunged 'Uman into thirty years of civil strife which was only resolved by the replacement of the Ya'arubi dynasty by that of the Bu Sa'idi in 1741, and the election of Ahmad ibn Sa'id al Bu Sa'idi as Imam in 1744. Until then East Africa could only occasionally command more than passing attention from 'Uman, although in 1714 there were an unusual number of Arabs in East Africa as part of what appears to have been a show of force.[16]

In the second decade of the eighteenth century the 'Umani garrison apparently continued to hold sway at Kilwa. During these years a furtive diplomatic contact was maintained between Kilwa and Mozambique, each party aspiring to enlist the services of the other to achieve its own goals against the Arabs.[17] For the rulers of Kilwa the end was to regain full independence from foreign rule; for the Portuguese it was to recapture Mombasa and to re-establish its imperial hegemony over the Swahili coast. By the end of the decade the Portuguese ambassador to the new Sultan of Kilwa, Ibrahim bin Yusuf, was one Mwinyi Muhammad al-Malindi (Volay Mamede Malindane), who lived in the Kerimba Islands. With respect to the Sultan's disposition to Portugal, Mwinyi Muhammad wrote that he 'received me with great decorum, and honour, as being important and ambassador of Your Majesty, always proclaiming his good friendship'. Nor was he contradicted by the Sultan's personal recommendation to the Portuguese monarch, which noted that during Mwinyi Muhammad's second appearance at his court 'I conceded him the liberty to enter my royal chamber dressed in his *kanzu* and *kofia*, as he was a vassal of my brother, the King of Portugal'.[18]

Eventually it must have become impossible for the Swahili rulers of Kilwa to conceal their contempt from the Arabs, who in about 1725 forced the Sultan and his immediate followers to flee to safety on Vamizi (Amiza) Island, under protection of the Portuguese. His initial reception there was cool, but this affront was rapidly rectified by the astute Governor of Mozambique Island, António Cardim Fróis, who seems to have provided the Sultan with both moral and material support in his efforts to regain control of his state from the 'Umani Arabs. This was achieved sometime in 1726 or 1727, the Sultan's men having first re-established his authority at Mongalo. Fróis received enthusiastic support from the Viceroy, who saw the drama at Kilwa as part of the general effort to regain the entire coast for Portugal, and authorized Fróis' expenditure of 500 *cruzados* to the Sultan. If necessary, Fróis was even authorized to sell or rent property to raise funds in order to maintain the Sultan's position against the Arabs.[19]

The following few years on the Swahili coast were occupied with the Portuguese recapture of Fort Jesus, Mombasa, in 1728, and their loss of it a year later when the local population became so outraged at the heavy-handed behaviour of their 'liberators' that they unceremoniously turned them out for good.[20] During this turbulent period conditions did not permit any regular trade to be conducted, and by the early 1730s the ruling dynasty of Kilwa found itself unable to keep its trading economy from faltering seriously. Once again it had become clear that if Kilwa were to survive with even a shadow of its old prosperity remaining it was absolutely necessary for it to be linked to an external market economy which could create the demand and supply the trade goods that would encourage the people of the interior to bring their merchandise to Kilwa. 'Uman seems to have been singularly incapable of doing this, either in its own right or by providing stable conditions for the operation of Indian merchant capitalism on the Swahili coast, as will be seen later in this chapter. So it was to this end that in the late 1730s negotiations were conducted between the Governor of Mozambique, Nicolau Tolentino de Almeida, and the son of the Sultan of Kilwa for the purpose of establishing 'a new Trade' between the two islands. The creation of officially sanctioned and regularized trading links between Kilwa and Mozambique was not achieved, however, as negotiations soon broke down in an atmosphere of what seems to have been mutual suspicion. Almeida blamed 'the inconstancy, and the little faith of these barbarians' for the failure to achieve this end; no doubt the representatives of Kilwa had a similar explanation to give to the Sultan.[21] Of necessity, the merchants of Kilwa were reduced to carrying on an insignificant trade with the smaller towns dotting the coast between the Rufiji River delta and Cape Delgado, and with the Mafia, Kerimba, and Comoro Island groups. As a result, it seems reasonable to assume that the attraction of Kilwa for the Yao and for other people of the interior declined accordingly. There was little reason for them to spend up to three months making the return journey to Kilwa when there was small hope of receiving the goods which they sought.

The most probable explanation, then, for the important early eighteenth-century change in the direction of Yao trade, which is so briefly noted by Xavier, is that a combination of three factors caused most of the Yao trading to Kilwa to transfer their business to Mozambique Island, a market which was already known to them and which remained stable and free of major disruptions during these years. These factors were: (1) the loss to Kilwa of the Portuguese market at Mombasa after 1698; (2) the subsequent failure of 'Uman both to provide Kilwa with a steady demand for its goods and to maintain a regular supply of cloth and beads with which to purchase these goods; and (3) the active disruption of the pattern of trade at Kilwa by the 'Umani garrison established there during the first quarter of the eighteenth century.

The Yao and the Macuana Ivory Trade

While it is possible that the change in the direction of Yao trade to the coast was only gradually realized, Portuguese sources concerning the ivory trade from Macuana during these years suggest that it was achieved rather quickly. The first documentary reference to the Yao adds support to this interpretation. Describing the coast north of Mozambique in 1736, a Sieur Vigoureux, Captain of the *Légère*, observed that a river flowing into Fernão Veloso Bay was 'on the way of the Yao Negroes, who are those who come thence to trade at Mozambique'.[22] This casual observation, by a man who was making his first voyage to Mozambique, seems to indicate that the shift in the direction of the Yao-controlled trade had occurred well before the 1730s.

Similar references to the Yao in the late 1730s are included in the investigation of the corrupt Governor Almeida. These, too, strongly suggest that the Yao had been trading regularly and in considerable strength to Mozambique for many years. Among numerous charges levied against him (most of which concerned his illegal dealings with French slave traders from the Mascarene Islands), it was alleged, and proved, that Almeida had obstructed the ivory trade carried on by the inhabitants of the mainland with the Yao. Interference of this sort by a governor in the trade of

Macuana was a problem which had plagued the colonists of Mozambique intermittently since the inception of this traffic a century before. In Almeida's case it was specifically charged that he had declared that the trade should be the prerogative of several of his cronies, and that he had ordered soldiers from the fortress to act as his personal trading agents on the mainland when the Yao descended from the interior to the coast during the dry season.[23] Almeida, for his part, sought to justify his reasons for allowing the French to trade for slaves at Mozambique by arguing that since the Yao had not brought their ivory to Mossuril, the local traders could earn money with which to pay their creditors only if this otherwise illegal situation was condoned.[24] Almeida's explanation was clearly an attempt to throw a cloak over his own greedy motives in promoting this trade, but even if his story about the Yao not coming had been false, the context in which he cited it clearly indicates the importance of Yao trade to the economy of Mozambique by the late 1730s.

It is one thing to demonstrate the factors underlying the decline of trade at Kilwa in the first decades of the eighteenth century and the new importance which the trade of the Yao had assumed at Mozambique by the 1730s. It is quite another to integrate this knowledge with what little and confusing evidence exists about the trade of Macuana before the administration of Almeida. To do so it is first imperative to understand the peculiar nature of the economic administration of the Portuguese regime in East Africa, as much of the relevant documentation is intelligible only in the context of the conflicts which existed within the system. In particular, the historic preoccupation with the area south of the Zambesi River meant that the Rivers of Sena continued to be central to all administrative plans to make the colony pay, while Macuana and its hinterland remained a peripheral area. In 1674 the Captains of Mozambique were deprived by the Crown of the former trading monopoly; but after a quarter century of varying commercial regimes, including ten years of free trading and several forms of control from Goa, the administration of the trade of the Rivers of Sena was delegated to a *Junta do Comércio* of Mozambique, which maintained a monopoly of certain trade cloths and *velório*, the basic Venetian trade beads. The *Junta* had its seat at Goa, the capital of the Portuguese *Estado da Índia*, of which Portuguese East Africa still formed a part, while its affairs were handled locally by a Superintendent, who was often the

Captain of Mozambique. In the midst of these changes, however, the trade of Macuana remained the perquisite of the colonists of Mozambique and the mainland opposite the island. After its reformulation in 1739, the *Junta* remained the sole legitimate authority for the trade of the rest of the colony until its dissolution in 1755.[25]

From the point of view of the Portuguese colonists in East Africa, the *Junta* presided over no less restrictive a trading monopoly than had earlier captains of Mozambique. Certainly during the early years of its tenure complaints against its practices were most eloquently expressed by colonists in the Rivers of Sena, rather than by those at Mozambique. In 1711 seven residents of Sena complained bitterly to the Viceroy that they had almost no share at all in the allegedly huge profits which the *Junta* gained from its control of trade. Indeed, the truly desperate nature of their struggle is sarcastically expressed in their concluding statement to the Viceroy that the *Junta* so severely restricted their liberty 'that it would be easier on us to be captives in Algeria.'[26] A year later the *Junta* began to make its move against the colonists of Mozambique.

The principal bone of contention between the *Junta* and the colonists was the question of whether or not the trade of Macuana was illegitimately siphoning off trade which fell within the jurisdiction of the Rivers of Sena. This, too, was not a new dispute, having been commented upon by Barreto half a century earlier; but in this context it reveals even more about the mentality of Portuguese mercantile imperialism, which liked to divide up vague areas of economic influence into neat spheres of trading jurisdiction, without any reference to the commercial predilections of the local inhabitants. Accordingly, during the tenure of the *Junta* all references to the trade of Macuana are couched in these terms, without any notice being taken of the possible role of African traders. In 1712 the *Junta* requested a *devassa* into the irregularities which it claimed were taking place in the trade of Mozambique and the Rivers of Sena. This the Viceroy approved immediately, and a series of twenty-two questions were incorporated into the charge of the *devassa*. Among these are three which deal specifically with the trade of Macuana. Since the implementation of this *devassa* did not occur until a decade later, it is useful to repeat the questions as they were originally formulated in order to gain some idea of what the grounds of the dispute were, if only from the perspective of the *Junta*. The Crown sought to know:

> 5. If the ivory which is cleared in Mozambique on pretence of the lands of Macuana is from the prohibited ports [i.e. those under the *Junta's* monopoly] and with consent and authorization of the officials of the *Junta* is transported by sea or by land through the port of Sanculo [just south of Mozambique Island] or some other in order to clear it under the aforementioned pretence of being from Macuana.
> 6. If any of the officials of the *Junta* gave authorization or consent that Kaffirs or any other person should go from Mozambique to Sena by land, and carry cloths or any other trade goods.
> 8. If the individuals who go to trade in Macuana spread themselves out to trade ivory up to the lands adjacent to Sena, and who are these individuals, and if they conducted the aforementioned trade with authorization or with consent of the officials of the *Junta*.[27]

Four years later the *Junta* again appears to have gained the ear of the Viceroy, who reported to the Crown that the ivory trade of Macuana was a growing danger to that of the Rivers of Sena, and wondered about the possibility of withdrawing the colonists' established rights to that trade.[28] Before the Crown came to a decision on this matter, however, a new Viceroy had taken office at Goa. In 1718 he advised the Crown against the need for taking such a drastic measure. Not only was the ivory trade of Macuana the only source of income for the colonists of Mozambique, but it was also said to be so limited that it caused no harm to the *Junta do Comércio*, even though it did serve as a cover for maritime smuggling from the Rivers of Sena.[29] Two years later, the *Junta* fell into temporary disfavour and was suspended by the Viceroy, who empowered the new Governor of Mozambique to exercise once again a monopoly of the trade which had been under the jurisdiction of the *Junta* for the past two decades. In view of the seventeenth-century conflicts over the ivory trade of Macuana between the colonists and the Captains of Mozambique, there were understandable fears that this freedom would be abrogated in the process. In fact, the new Governor's orders specifically protected the colonists' trade with Macuana, which was equally preserved when the *Junta* was reinstated as the Crown agency for trade in East Africa in 1722.[30]

None of this provides any indication that the trade of the Yao was in the process of being re-channelled from Kilwa to Mozambique. That conclusion remains founded exclusively upon Xavier's testimony and the clear evidence of a striking economic decline at Kilwa during this period. For the trade of Mozambique during the first three decades and more of the eighteenth century about all that can be claimed is that the trade of Macuana continued to draw upon the far interior of Zambesia at least as much as it did when Barreto made his observations on the same phenomenon in 1667. In consideration of the decline of Maravi trade and the rise of the Yao, it seems reasonable to suggest that the Yao were very much involved in this long distance carrying trade. In any case, by Almeida's time the Yao were evidently in command of supplying ivory to the market at Mozambique.

The quantity of evidence is no greater for the 1740s, but its character is better. By this time the Portuguese were feeling especially sensitive to the vulnerability of their position in East Africa. They had long since lost the initiative in the wider Indian Ocean trade to the Dutch and the English. Now their familiarity with the energetic French plantation colonies on the Mascarene Islands put them in immediate fear for the prosperity of their East African colony, a spectre which was exacerbated by two formal French requests, lodged in 1739 and 1744, that Portugal relinquish her territorial claims to the coast north of Cape Delgado. Both were denied by D. José V, the Portuguese monarch, but the Portuguese remained apprehensive as to French designs on East Africa.[31] It was in this context that the Governor of Mozambique, Pedro de Rego Barreto, warned late in 1745 that both the French and the English sought to take control of Mombasa. Even if the Portuguese maintained their position south of Cape Delgado, he feared, the establishment of another European power at Mombasa would be ruinous for the Portuguese at Mozambique. Indeed, Rego Barreto predicted that

> all the Kaffirs of Macuana, and of the Yao provinces . . . will carry the ivory and other goods there which they now bring to us at these shores; and if these traders are lacking, the patrimonies of these inhabitants [of Mozambique], who maintain themselves on the Trade, will be ended.[32]

Rego Barreto's testimony as to the importance of the Makua and Yao ivory trade is the only reference which survives from this decade, but in consideration of the wealth of information that exists for the second half of the century, all of which supports his impression, there is no reason to doubt its accuracy. By 1745, at the very latest, and very probably from a decade earlier, the ivory trade carried on at Mozambique by the Makua and the Yao was considered to be an essential component of its economic life. Furthermore, Rego Barreto's expressed fear of the crippling damage to this trade which would result from the revitalization of commercial activity along the coast north of Cape Delgado supports the interpretation that the bulk of Yao trade flowed to Kilwa before Portugal lost Mombasa in 1698. His prognostication seems to show that the Portuguese knew full well that the growth of Yao trade to Mozambique was the result of a combination of unusual factors operating at the coast which had caused the Yao to abandon their principal route to the coast—a preference which is also noted by Abdallah—in favour of a previously less frequented market. It also reveals that the ability of the Mozambique route to maintain its dominance for the Yao depended largely upon the continued depression of Kilwa.[33]

Rego Barreto's fears were entirely justified, as developments over the next four decades were to prove, but it was mainly the combined forces of Indian merchant capitalists and the 'Umani imperialists, rather than either the French or the British, who were to engineer the economic resuscitation of the Swahili coast. Indeed, even as Rego Barreto was making his analysis the foundation of Kilwa's commercial revival was already being laid. After his proclamation as Imam of 'Uman in 1744, Ahmad ibn Sa'id al Bu Sa'idi ordered several ships to East Africa to receive the recognition of those towns which were nominally under 'Umani suzerainty. At Mombasa he was denounced as a usurper by the 'Umani-derived Mazrui family, who had recently achieved recognition as the ruling dynasty by all of the *Thenashara Taifa* (Twelve Tribes) of the Swahili community of Mombasa. This action marked the beginning of a long and bitter struggle between the houses of the Mazrui and the Bu Sa'idi for control of the trade and politics of the northern Swahili coast.[34] At Kilwa there was no possibility of sustaining such defiance and the suzerainty of the new Imam was apparently recognized without opposition. It is doubtful, in view of the enormous problems facing the Imam at home, whether he was able to impose a governor on Kilwa at so early a date, as Miles implies.[35] Nevertheless, by mid-century Kilwa was already poised to begin a gradual revival of its trade to the north.

Luso-Makua Relations

Notwithstanding the central importance of Kilwa in the pattern of trade in East Central Africa during the earlier eighteenth century, there were factors coming into play to the south of Cape Delgado at this time which would take on equal importance later in the century. Foremost among these were (1) the hostility between the Portuguese and the Makua, (2) the emergence of Indian traders as the principal merchants of Mozambique and the attempts of the Portuguese to restrict Indian economic dominance of that market, and (3) the growth of French slave trading at Mozambique and the Kerimba Islands.

The significance of the Makua lay both in their proximity to the Portuguese settlements on the mainland of Mozambique where the Yao transacted their business with the merchants of the island-capital, and in their position astride the route of the Yao from the interior to the coast. In particular it was the Makua of Macuana, as the Portuguese called the coastal hinterland, and Uticulo, to the north-west of Mozambique Island, who were at the centre of this problem. The Makua had first posed a serious challenge to the security and welfare of the Portuguese at Mozambique late in the sixteenth century, when the Portuguese garrison at Mozambique suffered an ignominious rout at the hands of the powerful chief of Uticulo, the eponymous Mauruça, whose successors plagued the Portuguese well into the nineteenth century. Mauruça and his followers had only recently swept into Uticulo, very likely forced out of their own country farther inland by repercussions that were themselves set in motion by the first stirrings of the Zimba outburst. So while Mauruça was a Makua chief, he was an invader in Uticulo and had to conquer the Makua who were already living there in order to establish his political authority over the region.

According to Santos, Mauruça's people were fearsome cannibals who scourged the immediate coastal hinterland for several years without disturbing the Portuguese. But in 1585, when Nuno Velho Pereira was Captain of Mozambique, they began regularly to terrorize the Portuguese settlements on the coast itself.[36] Pereira decided to punish Mauruça for his audacity and mounted an expedition of nearly four hundred men, including forty Portuguese soldiers and colonists, to destroy Mauruça's main village, which was situated some three or four leagues (perhaps fifteen to twenty-five kilometres) inland. Commanded by António Pinto, the column marched to their destination by night and attacked Mauruça's village at dawn. The raid was a complete success and the settlement was destroyed. The ease of the victory lulled the Portuguese into a false sense of security; as they made their separate ways back to the coast—some of them being carried in litters by their slaves—they were attacked by the Makua, who had fled from Mauruça's village and had concealed themselves in the bush. Almost the entire Portuguese force was annihilated, and only two or three Portuguese and a few slaves reached the coast some three days later. 'Many other similar catastrophes have befallen the Portuguese', wrote Santos sardonically, 'because of the great confidence they have in themselves in these lands, and the contempt with which they look upon the Kaffirs.' Mauruça remained unpunished and his Makua continued to plunder the mainland at will for some time thereafter. Eventually, Mauruça realized that it was to his advantage that there be peace in his lands, and an agreement was struck with the Portuguese so that there might be trade with them. Nevertheless, Santos makes it quite clear that there were many instances of violence by the Makua against the Portuguese in the succeeding years.[37]

During the seventeenth century the Mauruça seems to have maintained his sway over the other chiefs of the Mozambique hinterland. According to Barreto, the Makua in the 1660s were ruled by a number of petty chiefs, 'who all obey in the first place the great emperor of the entire nation of the Makua'.[38] This 'emperor' would appear to have been the Mauruça, who was undeniably the most powerful Makua chief in the neighbourhood of Mozambique and who probably dominated the sort of confederation that later observers also noted among the Makua (see Chapter 1). But the Makua, like the other peoples of the interior during most of the century, were thoroughly dominated by the Kalonga, who when necessary could apparently bring far greater military forces into action away from the centre of his political authority than could even the Mauruça in his own immediate area of influence (see Chapter 2). Earlier in the century, when the Maravi were first making their presence felt at the very doorstep of Mozambique, Brito de Vasconcelos tried to induce the coastal Makua, who were characterized as the 'enemies of the Maravi', to take up arms against them. Although he went so far as to offer to build the Makua a wooden fortress on the mainland at Cabaceira, they refused to be drawn into a conflict with the Maravi.[39] It would appear, then, that so long as Maravi military power remained effective, neither the Mauruça nor any other Makua chief was willing to risk invoking their wrath. On the other hand, the decline of Maravi power not only enabled the Makua to assert themselves militarily again, but also raised the consequent possibility for the Makua to emerge as principal middlemen for the trade of the interior, since Maravi trading hegemony depended entirely on Maravi military domination. At the same time, however, this new situation argued for the maintenance of peaceful relations between the Makua and the Portuguese, as the first Mauruça recognized after achieving his stunning victory over the Portuguese in 1585.

Perhaps for economic reasons of this kind, perhaps for other reasons which are not known, relations between the Portuguese and the Makua were apparently peaceful for most of the early eighteenth century, as there are no references in the extant documentation to any conflicts between them. In both 1721 and 1722, however, there were reports of a few skirmishes with the Makua, some of whom raided one of the small Portuguese settlements on the mainland opposite the island. These skirmishes were soon resolved in favour of the Portuguese. In 1727 Macuana was reported to be at peace, which suggests by implication that it had not been at peace fairly recently. This impression is borne out two years later by the Viceroy's agreement to finance 'the war to castigate Chief Maia' which had been waged by Governor Fróis in 1728.[40] These references are so spare as to give absolutely no indication why relations with the Makua should have begun to sour again during the 1720s. In general, it can be argued that Luso-Makua relations were more naturally antagonistic than amicable, with peace existing only when the Makua had good reason to maintain it, or during those less frequent periods when the Portuguese had the upper hand over the Makua. Failing these conditions, the Makua were able to pose a serious challenge to Portuguese security on the mainland whenever they wished to do so. More particularly, in the 1720s a possible reason for resumption of intermittent hostilities with the Portuguese may well have been the emergence of the Yao as a serious trading threat to the position of the Makua as major middlemen in the trade with the interior. This is a highly speculative argument, but it has the virtue of conforming to what we know about Makua relations with the Portuguese and the Yao later, in the second half of the eighteenth century. Whatever the situation may have been in the 1720s, no further references to the Makua, in any capacity, occur until the next known resumption of hostilities in 1749.

Indian Merchant Capitalism and the Ivory Trade

Within the community of Mozambique, competition and conflict over the trade of Macuana had traditionally focused on the captains and colonists. Similarly, when the *Junta do Comércio* made its move in the 1720s to restrict the trade of Macuana, the object of their attack was the colonists of Mozambique. As late as 1728 the Governor of Mozambique, most likely in his role as Superintendent of the *Junta* in East Africa, was still promulgating decrees which were designed to prohibit the trade of the colonists to Macuana.[41] But by this time it was becoming increasingly evident that the colonists were no longer the only or, indeed, the principal traders and merchants at Mozambique. Instead, this role was rapidly being taken over by a growing community of Indian traders, both Hindu (Banyan) and, to a lesser extent, Muslim.

The origins of the domination of Indian merchant capitalism in East Africa at this time have never been properly examined. The presence of Indian, as opposed to Arab, traders in East Africa has been noted in all the usual sources for the pre-Portuguese period, while it has been assumed all along that their domination of trade at Zanzibar during the nineteenth century was the result of Seyyid Sa'id ibn Sultan's conscious policy of welcoming them in his dominions. This latter point has recently been challenged by Sheriff, who argues that it was Indian merchants who opened the East African market and Seyyid Sa'id who followed their lead and merely formalized the situation under the aegis of 'Umani imperial rule.[42] But to appreciate the roots of Indian mercantile activity in East Africa during this period, and the complex inter-relationship between 'Umani imperialism and Indian merchant capitalism, necessarily involves returning to the intrusion of the Portuguese into the Indian Ocean at the beginning of the sixteenth century and exploring the growth of Indian merchant capital under the Mughal Empire in the seventeenth century. In view of the critical importance of Indian capital at Mozambique during the eighteenth century and later at

85

Zanzibar, it seems valuable to try to understand how this situation evolved.

Before the sixteenth century Indian Ocean trade was controlled by Muslims, as was noted in the previous chapter. On the Indian sub-continent their activities were dominant along the Malabar coast down to Calicut. The arrival of the Portuguese transformed this situation as they seized control of the high seas by sheer force. This struggle did not, however, involve the major Indian states, who as land powers were willing to trade with all parties.[43] Despite the disastrous impact on Muslim shipping after 1500, at least one Indian economic historian argues that the coming of the Portuguese led to an expansion of the Indian export market and especially to an intensification of inter-Asian trade, although there was no net capital increase involved in overseas trade.[44] So long as they obtained passports from the Portuguese, Indian traders could still carry on a limited amount of business, and by 1600 it was the Cambay ports from Diu to Daman, at the extreme north-west coast of modern India, which were the most important for India's external trade. Goa, as Moreland points out, was exclusively an entrepôt, and had its closest ties with Balaghat, in Madhya Pradesh.[45] In 1600 the African trade, which rested largely upon the Portuguese gold trade at Sofala, represented no more than four per cent of the total trade of Western India, if Moreland's figures are accepted. Goldsmiths and craftsmen in ivory, another major import from Africa, catered exclusively to a small and extravagant ruling class and were not economically significant in the total Indian economy. The dominant industry in India was cotton-weaving, the aggregate production of which, argues Moreland, 'was one of the great facts of the industrial world of the year 1600'. Yet it is clear that the East African market for Indian cotton textiles was very small indeed when compared to the domestic market and to those of Arabia, Burma, and Malacca.[46] However important the gold and ivory trade may have become in certain sectors of East Central Africa by this time, in the context of Indian economic history it represented only a small part of India's total overseas trade.

At this point it is worth considering why there was a demand for East African ivory in India, which had a large elephant population of its own. The basic demand for ivory was for the manufacture of the marriage bangles which were an integral part of Hindu and Indian Muslim wedding ceremonies.[47] Indian ivory was unsuitable for this purpose, as indeed for any fine carving that was required to satisfy the luxury trade for the Indian ruling classes, because of its brittle texture, its opaqueness, and its tendency to discolour. The finest grain ivory is said to have come from Sri Lanka, although supplies to India appear to have declined after the Dutch captured the island from the Portuguese in 1656, thereby necessitating a greater dependency on the ivory of East Africa.[48]

Ivory also reached India from West Africa and South-East Asia, but the best white ivory came from East Africa. According to an early nineteenth-century Indian commercial guide, 'In Europe, the African teeth are the most esteemed, as being of a closer texture, and less liable to turn yellow than those from India', an important opinion which was echoed in a similar volume at the end of the century.[49] Eventually, the Indian market for East African ivory became intertwined with that of Europe, which expanded enormously with the rise of industrial capitalism. Indeed, during the nineteenth century the European market not only consumed about half of East Africa's annual ivory exports directly from Zanzibar (see Chapter 7), but also accepted about half of the annual export to India, which was re-exported to Europe.[50] Before about 1800, however, the main market for the ivory of East Africa remained the traditional demand from India.

During the seventeenth century there was, in fact, a marked expansion of India's export trade. Part of this phenomenon can be accounted for by the steady growth of European, particularly English, trade, and the collapse of Portuguese hegemony in the Indian Ocean. This is by no means, however, a complete explanation for the growth of Indian overseas trade and certainly does not directly concern East Africa. According to Irfan Habib, it was, rather, the policy of intensive agricultural exploitation pursued by the Mughal rulers of northern India which provided the basis for the revival of India's overseas trade in the seventeenth century.

Habib demonstrates that the rural peasantry surrendered between one-quarter and one-third of their total agricultural produce to the Mughal hierarchy, who used it both to support vast numbers of non-productive dependants and to finance lavish display. This system of exploitation necessarily called into being a complex rural market system, the development of a money economy, and cash cropping. As the market system grew so did money-lending and peasant debts, and profiting from all of these new developments were an increasingly prosperous number of Indian merchants. The extent to which they became involved in the Mughal system of agricultural exploitation may be judged by the fact that during this period people began to use the term *baqqal* or grain-merchant as the name for the traditional merchant or *banyan*. Each year hundreds of thousands of tons of grain were transported across the Mughal Empire. Vast sums of capital were involved in this business, much of which found its way into overseas trade as well. The most important single seat of Indian merchant capitalism was the Cambay port of Surat, although it was in no way unique. In the early 1660s Surat merchants had fifty ships trading overseas and the wealthiest of these, Virji Vora, had an estate valued at perhaps eight million rupees (each rupee being 178 grains of nearly pure silver). At the end of the century another Surat merchant, Abdul Ghafur, had amassed a similar fortune and possessed a trading fleet of some twenty ships of between three and eight hundred tons each. 'He alone conducted trade equal to that of the whole English East India Company.'[51] An integral part of this mercantile system was a well-developed system of credit and banking. Virtually every village of any consequence had its *sarrafs*, who lent money locally, issued their own bills of credit (*hundis*), and arranged insurance for the inland trade. As Habib points out, the *sarrafs* essentially acted as deposit bankers and at the major commercial centres of Mughal India financial obligations were negotiated almost entirely through the exchange of paper notes. Indian international trade was conducted similarly.[52]

During the seventeenth century, then, the growth of European trade and the Mughal system of agricultural exploitation joined forces to expand India's export trade to a marked extent. Indeed, before the English established their monopoly over the export trade of the Mughal Empire in 1717, Indian merchant capitalists very often profited by serving both systems.[53] During the second half of the seventeenth century Indian merchant capitalists began to exploit the weaknesses in the highly competitive European system and to strengthen their own position overseas. Raychaudhuri suggests that this new-found commercial vigour was expressed in two ways: 'First, Indian participation in trade with the regions already familiar increased substantially. Secondly, Indian merchants opened trade with new markets previously unknown to them: their growing trade with the Philippines was the most striking instance of this development.'[54] Wherever possible the great Indian merchants tried to protect markets against the intrusion of European capital, as in the Red Sea. How this affected Indian trade to East Africa is uncertain, but it is very possible that the economic revival of the Swahili coast during this century was as much the work of Indian merchants as of Portuguese officialdom, under whose protection they would have been able to work in reasonable security.[55]

Certainly the roots of Indian domination of the trade of Mozambique date to this period, when a tax-free monopoly of the trade between the Portuguese colony of Diu and Mozambique Island was granted in 1686 by the Viceroy of India to the Banyan Company of Mazanes.[56] The East African trade was clearly a high-risk business and depended heavily on the availability of generous credit for those who did the actual trading. It required both large liquid assets for the payment of immediate expenses and the security of considerable capital resources in order to absorb the many individual reverses which regularly plagued the entire business. At no point in time did the Portuguese colonists of Mozambique possess any of these assets to a significant degree. They were always acting at a local level, as middlemen, and the fortunes which Barreto ascribes to some of them in 1667 were very probably only local fortunes. More generally, the Portuguese in the East were capable of such capitalization only through the offices of the Crown, as in the case of the *Junta do Comércio*, and even there they did not possess the commercial acumen to make it a genuinely successful economic proposition. But Indian merchant capitalists, most notably the Hindu trading caste of Banyans, were capable of precisely such capitalization and mercantile organization. Indeed, by the fourth decade of the eighteenth century, when the Portuguese presence in India was being severely tested by the same Maratha kingdom which was also dismantling the southern reaches of the Mughal Empire, it became necessary to float a million *xerafim* loan to make the government solvent. Among the main subscribers were the Catholic Church, local municipalities, and Indian merchants.[57]

Despite its vigour, Indian merchant capitalism remained outside the system of production and did not lead to the rise of industrial capitalism. Habib argues that the failure of industrial capitalist development in Mughal India can be traced to the fact that the entire commercial structure was basically parasitical. The fortunes of merchant capitalism, he asserts, lay with the Mughal ruling class and when the Mughal Empire collapsed in the eighteenth century as a result of severe agrarian crisis and external attacks, Indian merchant capitalists had necessarily to attach themselves to its imitators. 'Denied during the eighteenth century the large market that it had been provided with by the Mughal Empire, merchant capital had no choice but to atrophy.'[58]

Given the atrophy of Indian merchant capital during the eighteenth century, how are we to explain the expansion of Indian merchant capitalism in East Africa during this and the following century?[59] One possibility is that despite the decline in Indian participation in overseas trade and shipping, those surviving Indian merchant capitalists sought new outlets in East Africa, much as they had done previously in the Philippines, under rather different circumstances. This possibility would have been especially attractive during this period since the major European powers were not yet interested in the East African market. Another factor at play may have been that those Indian merchant capitalists who enjoyed Portuguese or 'Umani protection in Western Asia were better able to weather the prevailing economic trends of the times. Later in the eighteenth century the interweaving of Indian merchant capitalism and British industrial capitalism also probably began to revitalize the former so that it could play an intermediary role in East Africa until such time as the British and other Western capitalists should decide to take control of that market for themselves.

Less tentatively, the emigration of Indian merchant capital to East Africa during this period might have been at least partially governed by the existence of a fairly stable imperial government first at Mozambique and later at Zanzibar. This factor would also help to explain any putative withdrawal of Indian traders from the Swahili coast after 1698, when conditions for successful business were clearly unstable, until after mid-century, when 'Uman began slowly to impose a new imperial order along the coast. That some Indian merchants were probably interested in the re-establishment of a stable political situation along the Swahili coast at this time may be inferred from the fact that three of the dhows which were used to carry 'Umani reinforcements to East Africa in the late 1720s were borrowed from Banyans.[60] More positive evidence of the desire of Indian merchant capitalists for a secure market may be found in a contemporary report from the Sultan of Pate to the Portuguese Viceroy, which noted the annual arrival of three ships from Surat at Barawa, to the north of Pate, where they could operate without 'Umani interference or restrictions, and were able to offer a much better price for ivory than prevailed at Pate. As a result of this, the Sultan complained, the Galla no longer brought much ivory to Pate, going in preference to Barawa.[61] It seems valid, then, to suggest that the Swahili coast was regarded by at least some Indian merchants as a potential, but difficult, area for commercial involvement in the first half of the eighteenth century.

Whatever the reasons, Indian merchant capitalism undeniably did experience a pronounced growth in East Africa during the eighteenth and nineteenth centuries. To the north of Cape Delgado, under the protection of 'Umani imperialism, it nurtured the rich trade that ultimately made East Africa a more attractive province to the Bu Sa'idi rulers of 'Uman than their Persian Gulf homeland. To the south of Cape Delgado, in an analogous situation, it provided a struggling Portuguese administration with most of its local revenue, through taxation, during the entire eighteenth century.

Once the Indian traders gained a foothold at Mozambique, they were able to achieve a gradual mastery over the colonists through their control of the supply of those trade goods which remained outside the control of the *Junta do Comércio*. Owing to an appreciable lack of currency at Mozambique, the colonists who wanted to engage in trade with Macuana inevitably had to buy their trading cloth and beads on credit from the local Indian traders, who usually acted as agents or as independent associates of their counterparts in the Cambay cities, as was clearly the case with the Company of Mazanes. Even in the case of the cloths and beads which were under the monopoly of the *Junta do Comércio* it was necessary to raise sufficient capital to purchase enough of these to make one's trading a meaningful enterprise, and capital was increasingly in Indian hands. The Indian merchants had no assurance that an individual colonist would succeed in his trading; often, he lost all his goods to plundering Makua, or to his African or mulatto agent in the hinterland. These agents, called *patamares*, itself a term that derived from the Indian coastal 'country' trade, occasionally returned empty-handed from the interior, claiming to have been robbed, when in fact they may actually have been trading on their own account with their master's goods.[62] To protect themselves against these not infrequent losses the Indian merchants of Mozambique charged very high rates of interest on the merchandise which they sold on credit to the colonists, many of whom were constantly deep in debt to their creditors. Furthermore, the Banyans, although apparently not the Muslim Indians, were allowed to trade freely in competition with the colonists in Macuana.

The greater efficiency which the Indians could bring to the trade of Mozambique no doubt accounted for the general vice-regal support which they enjoyed in East Africa, not to mention their financial support of the *Estado da Índia* itself. But it is easy to see that their developing monopoly of its trade and of the trade of Macuana put them into potential conflict with the colonists of the capital settlements. From this time on trading conflicts within the community of Mozambique focused on the Indian merchants and the colonists.

Although the Banyans from Diu enjoyed the protection of the Jesuit College at Mozambique, neither they nor the other Indians established there, both Hindu and Muslim, were accepted as equals by the Portuguese, especially the colonists. As a rule, they were disliked intensely for their economic power and were looked upon with much suspicion. They also suffered from the general prejudice, both official and popular, against non-European peoples that riddled all official Portuguese attempts to utilize them in the development of their seaborne empire.[63] The Muslim Indian community was the first to experience this racial, cultural, and economic antipathy at Mozambique. Influenced by pressure exerted from Goa by the Holy Office of the Inquisition, in 1720 the Crown ordered that Muslims should no longer be allowed to act as captains, pilots, and sailors on vessels sent from Asia to Mozambique. Three years later the King repeated this command, which was designed 'to avoid the very considerable evils' which might otherwise afflict Mozambique. The King also instructed the Viceroy to remove the Indian Muslim who was currently the paymaster at Mozambique and to replace him with a Christian, 'because of the evil results of his residence in that fort, employing the profits which he obtains in the worship of his false prophet and for other lamentable and perverse purposes, moved thereunto by the error of his religion'.[64] It is an apt comment upon the economic situation of the Portuguese at Mozambique that the removal of the paymaster, Basire Mocali, was never carried out because only he could afford the post.[65]

Early in 1727 the Viceroy granted a special licence in response to a petition from several exceptional men of the Muslim community which allowed them to trade to the mainland of Macuana, a privilege which was forbidden to them otherwise. Although the licence was permanent, it carried the restriction that each time any of these men, or their relatives, wanted to exercise this concession, he was obliged to inform the local Commission of the Holy Office. An extremely interesting fact which emerges from this document is that the prohibition against the Indian Muslims was definitely not extended to East African Muslims, so that the Swahili who lived within the jurisdiction of Mozambique were free to trade without restrictions of any sort.[66] It is important to remember, however, that the local Swahili did not pose a significant economic threat to the local Portuguese community, whose unseen hand surely was busily influencing official opinion against the Indian traders. Less than a week later, however, the Viceroy issued a further writ which expressly forbade 'the Muslim inhabitants' of Mozambique, the subordinate mainland, and the Rivers of Sena from owning slaves. This seriously hurt their trading, as slaves were used for transporting the heavy goods in which they dealt, and were also employed as *patamares*. The Muslims were permitted to continue to trade for slaves in the interior, but once they brought them to the coast they were required to register them immediately with the Holy Office and then to sell them within six months to Christians. Failing compliance with these regulations, the slaves were to be confiscated and the trader punished. It is not made clear in this decree, as it was in the granting of the petition earlier in that week, if the Swahili were to be included in this restriction, but it does seem incontestable that it was the Indian Muslims who were the particular targets of the Inquisition. A year later the Muslims were prohibited from trading 'any slave already baptized', and orders were given that they must not try to convert heathen slaves to Islam.[67] Regarding the Swahili, the Viceroy made it absolutely clear in 1730 that the religious zeal of the Holy Office in maintaining control of the Muslims of Mozambique should not be extended to include them.[68]

At the end of 1729 the Viceroy observed that as all the traders of Mozambique were Muslims and Gentiles (i.e. Banyans), their great fear of the Holy Office had caused the commerce of that place to decline. The Muslims had complained to him that the Governor of Mozambique had issued independent orders which further restricted their activities. These appear to have been lost. Nor were the Banyans free from harassment. In August 1729 they complained to the Viceroy that the *Ouvidor* (Crown Judge) of Mozambique, Francisco Gonzalez Pinheiro, had caused them considerable difficulties. For his part, the Viceroy promised them a just investigation into Pinheiro's activities.[69] The outcome of the investigation is unknown, but the situation provides a perfect example of the characteristic dichotomy between royal policy and local practice in the Portuguese empire.

In 1730, with the approval of the Holy Office, the Viceroy allowed that the Muslims might keep slaves whose parents and grandparents were Muslim, while stipulating that any heathen slaves whom they wished to retain had to be converted to Christianity within six months.[70] Despite the problems of the 1720s, however, harassment of the Indian merchants of Mozambique was not severe during the first half of the eighteenth century, particularly when compared to the situation after 1750. Indeed, the scattered notices of a French trader who was at Mozambique in 1733 suggest that during the crucial years of Kilwa's economic decadence the Indians were relatively free to pursue their business as they wished at Mozambique.[71]

France, the Mascarenes, and the Slave Trade

While the earliest notices of East Africa in the international commerce of the Western Indian Ocean make it abundantly clear that the staple item of trade was the ivory of the African elephant, the fact remains that the notoriety of the Yao in contemporary and modern European accounts arises from their having been the greatest African slave traders in East Africa during the second half of the nineteenth century.[72] Similarly, what little was known of the Makua by Europeans of the age primarily concerned the debilitating internecine struggles which were an outgrowth of their involvement in the late nineteenth-century slave trade to Madagascar (see Chapter 7). But despite the promulgation of an imperial interpretation of East African history which argued that the slave trade in its nineteenth-century proportions had its origins at the beginning of the Christian era and 'ran like a scarlet thread through all the subsequent history of East Africa until our own day',[73] more recent research has established conclusively that the rise of extensive slave trading in East Africa had its roots only in the eighteenth century. For all their slaving in the South Atlantic, however, the Portuguese in the East did not require any major supply of slave labour from East Africa, rarely taking more than five hundred slaves each year for sale in Portuguese India, where cheap labour was abundant. Rather, it was the French and to a lesser extent the 'Umani Arabs who initially generated this greater demand. The Portuguese in Brazil later followed suit.

French slaving in East Africa dated from their development after 1735 of the long neglected Mascarene Islands—Ile de France (Mauritius) and Ile Bourbon (Réunion), which were situated some 1,300 kilometres to the east of Madagascar—as major plantation colonies on a scale to rival the more notorious prototypes in the Caribbean.[74] Until the 1770s the total volume of this trade at Mozambique and the Kerimba Islands, which represented a last, tenuous vestige of Portuguese authority on the coast north of Mozambique, was quite small. It had virtually no direct impact on the Yao during the second quarter of the eighteenth century. But for the Makua of Macuana even the small numbers of individuals traded into bondage to supply the French colonies with manual labour to work their fields of sugar, cotton, coffee, and indigo, set the stage for significant changes after mid-century. Indirectly, these changes would also come to affect the trade of the Yao to Mozambique.

The basic reasons for the French turning to East Africa for their supply of slaves were both their dissatisfaction with slaves from Madagascar, who were thought to be 'insolent and idle, and consequently of little reliance', and the fact that during the eighteenth century it became increasingly difficult to persuade the Malagasy with whom they had once dealt for slaves at Madagascar to do business with them.[75] Despite the petty vexations involved in trading with the Portuguese, all of which derived from the fact that foreign trade was explicitly forbidden by a series of royal decrees dating most importantly from 1720, it was during this formative period that the French became convinced of the potential of Mozambique and the Kerimba Islands as major providers of slaves. Prices were reasonable and early French emissaries to Mozambique were impressed with the number and quality of slaves available there. As for the Portuguese, the opening of trade, illegal or not, with the French was welcomed by all but the most scrupulous of the Crown's subjects in East Africa. The French were in a position to provide the barren island with a regular supply of grains, and thereby to free the Portuguese somewhat from relying for foodstuffs exclusively upon their mainland holdings, which were always vulnerable to attack from the Makua. The fact that the French also traded in specie was equally important in view of the endemic shortage of coinage in Portuguese East Africa. Finally, trading with the French provided successive Governors and all other officials at Mozambique and the Kerimba Islands with an unrivalled—and usually irresistible—opportunity for turning a handsome profit out of otherwise unremunerative appointments.

What particularly struck fear into the hearts of those at court in Lisbon was the possible establishment of a French imperial presence in what was nominally assumed to be Portuguese-controlled East Africa. In the late 1720s Governor Fróis was instructed that he 'must not allow any European nation whatever to hold trade or commerce with the Negroes of that coast' nor 'any of the said nations to establish themselves in the land, employing every possible means to prevent them from doing so, for which it is very necessary that no offence should be given to the Kaffirs inhabiting the said shores'.[76] In fact, the bulk of French trade at Mozambique and the Kerimba Islands was tightly controlled by the responsible Portuguese officials, who simply wished to monopolize this trade for themselves and to prevent the French from trading directly with the Makua and Swahili of the coast. But by 1741 at least a few bold French slavers had apparently managed to do just that. According to a certain Captain Saveille,

the island of Mozambique furnishes better slaves than the island of Madagascar and . . . it is from the former that the French take their good slaves. The price there is 40 Spanish *piastres* per head, men and women alike, but it is necessary to act with much circumspection and with prudence, because the South-Africans are great thieves and blood-thirsty people.[77]

To make sense of this passage requires an interpretation which suggests that although most trade was carried on with the official Portuguese establishment at Mozambique, there had already been sufficient direct contact with the local Makua and Swahili (the 'South-Africans' of this account) to give the French a healthy respect for them. The importance of this 'contraband' trade is

that it enabled the French to trade firearms to the Makua in exchange for slaves. Portuguese Crown regulations expressly forbade such trade between Portuguese and Africans, and this was
one order which only the most thoughtless Portuguese local official
would knowingly contravene. By the 1750s, however, the Makua
of Macuana were well supplied with firearms and consequently
posed an even greater threat to the security of the Portuguese on
the mainland than ever before.

During the first half of the eighteenth century, then, both the
Yao and the Makua were forced to come to grips with two major
changes in the pattern of international trade in order to retain a
significant role in that trade. For the Yao the adjustment involved
making an abrupt shift in the routing of their trade to the coast
in response to the economic decline into which Kilwa plummeted
after the replacement of the Portuguese by the 'Umani Arabs as
the major imperial power along the Swahili coast. The Yao
channelled most of their trade during this period to the previously known, but less frequented market of Mozambique, which
enjoyed a half century of relative stability that was conducive
to its emergence as a major centre of the ivory trade.[78] By mid-
century, the ivory trade of the Yao was fundamental to the
prosperity of the Portuguese empire in East Africa.

Perhaps the clearest index of the rising demand for ivory at
Mozambique is the rising price which ivory fetched. Up to 1710
the free market price of ivory at Mozambique—what was known
locally as the 'price of the land'—ranged between 600 and 700
cruzados per *bar*, but in response to factors unknown it surged to
800 *cruzados* per *bar* in that year. In an attempt to control what
was seen to be an inflated price, a problem which would vex the
Mozambique ivory market a century later, the Crown ordered an
official price ceiling of 550 *cruzados* per *bar* to be put into effect,
except when prices of cloth in India rose unexpectedly and a more
flexible policy seemed advisable.[79] Three decades later, the accounting of officially controlled beads used in the purchase of
ivory at Mozambique reveals that the official price of ivory had
increased all the way up to 1000 *cruzados* per *bar*, a price that prevailed until the early 1760s.[80]

For the Makua the process of readjustment in their international trading hinged on the arrival of the French slavers from the
Mascarene Islands along the Mozambique coast. The Makua had
carried on only a limited trade in slaves with the Portuguese in

previous years, so that the creation of even so small a demand as was generated by the French at this time would have brought about a commensurate change in attitude towards slave trading among the Makua of Macuana. The slave trade also enabled the Makua to hold their own as traders on the international market at Mozambique against the increasingly aggressive Yao ivory traders. At the same time, the fact that the French were willing to exchange firearms in payment for slaves enabled the Makua to build up their military strength during the second quarter of the century. After 1750, the external economic forces which had brought about these changes in the pattern of the East African export trade would come to bear even more insistently upon all its participants. And the tensions produced by their competition for its profits would lead to a long series of bitter confrontations.

NOTES

1. Xavier, 'Notícias', pp. 153, 159. See Chapter 4, p. 104, and Table 2.
2. F. da Costa Mendes, *Catalogo Chronologico e Historico dos Capitães Generaes e Governadores da Provincia de Moçambique desde 1752 . . . ate 1849* (Mozambique, 1892), p. viii; see Andrade, 'Fundação do Hospital Militar de S. João de Deus, em Moçambique', *Stvdia*, 1 (1958), pp. 77–89.
3. Boxer, 'Swahili Coast', pp. 57–74; Strandes, *Portuguese Period*, pp. 245–73; Guillain, *Documents*, I, p. 522; J. M. Gray, 'A History of Kilwa: Part II', *T.N.R.*, 32 (1952), p. 27.
4. P. S. S. Pissurlencar, *Assentos do Canselho do Estado [da Índia] (1698–1750)* (Bastorá-Goa, 1957), V, p. 123.
5. N.A.I.P.G., L.M. 71, fl. 310, João Roiz da Costa to Viceroy, Caza [Goa], 7 January 1708. Costa was former Castellan and Governor of Mozambique Island and his report specifically relates to 1702, drawing upon his letter of 26 January 1702 to the Governing Triumvirate of India.
6. N.A.I.P.G., L.M. 70, fl. 3, Viceroy to Crown, Goa, 27 December 1705, and L.M. 69, fl. 108–109, same to same, Goa, 15 January 1707.
7. N.A.I.P.G., L.M. 73, fl. 49, Fr. Manuel de Santo Alberto to Cristovão de Melo de Castro, Amiza, 22 May 1708. It appears that the chief of Mongalo was wounded in this skirmish; see N.A.I.P.G., L.M. 77, fl. 87, Mwinyi Juma bin Mwinyi Kajo to Bwana Dau bin Bwana Sheikh, Moç., 15 August 1711.
8. N.A.I.P.G., L.M. 74–A, fl. 270–1, Fr. Manuel to Melo de Castro, Amiza, 18 May 1709; ibid., fl. 265, Francisco de Melo e Sousa to same, Ibo, 30 June 1709.
9. N.A.I.P.G., L.M. 77, fl. 93, same to same, Ibo, 6 July 1711.
10. N.A.I.P.G., L.M. 75, fl. 174–5, Luís Gonçalves da Camara e Coutinho to Viceroy, Moç., 10 August 1710.
11. N.A.I.P.G., L.M. 77, fl. 95, Muhammad bin Yusuf and Ibrahim bin Yusuf to Mwinyi Juma bin Mwinyi Kajo, trans. Bwana Dau bin Bwana Sheikh, Goa, 25 January 1711. This is one of a series of fourteen letters in the original Swahili in Arabic script with facing Portuguese translation. The original texts still await linguistic analysis and translation, but a hasty reading of some of them by Muhammad Abdulaziz, University of Nairobi, and M. H. H. Alidina, University of Dar

es Salaam, indicates that the essential content is represented in the Portuguese translations, which I have used. The translator was a pro-Portuguese exile from Faza, in the Lamu archipelago, living at Goa.

12. ibid., fl. 88, Mwinyi Juma bin Mwinyi Kajo to Bwana Dau bin Bwana Sheikh, Moç., 15 August 1711.

13. ibid., fl. 101, Queen of Kilwa to Mwinyi Juma bin Mwinyi Kajo, trans. Goa, 25 September 1711.

14. ibid., fl. 104, Mwana Nakisa to same, trans. Goa, 25 September 1711.

15. ibid., fl. 107, anonymous to same, trans. Goa, 25 September 1711.

16. N.A.I.P.G., L.M. 80, fl. 48, Viceroy to Crown, Goa, 10 January 1715.

17. B.M., Add. Mss. 20, 906, fl. 211, D. Luís de Meneses, Conde de Ericeira, to King of Kilwa, Goa, 27 January 1719.

18. N.A.I.P.G., L.M. 93–A, fl. 2–3, Vollay Momade to Crown, Goa, 15 January 1724; ibid., fl. 4, King of Kilwa to Crown, n.d. Mwinyi Muhammad nevertheless had to struggle to obtain some sort of recompense from the Portuguese for his services, eventually securing in 1729 a place as a soldier in the fortress at Mozambique and reimbursement for expenses incurred during his trips to Kilwa. See ibid., fl. 3–4, certification from Manuel Pais de Morais, Bringano, 8 May 1721; ibid., fl. 1, Crown to Viceroy, Lisboa occidental, 8 October 1725; ibid., fl. 6, Viceroy to Crown, Goa, 12 December 1726; N.A.I.P.G., Cod. 2323, fl. 16, same to António Cardim Fróis, Goa, 13 January 1727; ibid., fl. 23, same to same, Goa, 15 January 1728; ibid., fl. 25, same to Volay Mamede, Goa, 15 January 1728; ibid., fl. 31, same to same, Goa, 15 January 1729. See also N.A.I.P.G., L.M. 92, fl. 251, Vollay Mamade to Viceroy, Goa, 13 January 1724. *Kanzu* is a full length cotton garment worn over other clothes; *kofia* is a Muslim cap, now usually decorated with fine stitching.

19. N.A.I.P.G., Cod. 2323, fl. 16, Viceroy to King of Kilwa, Goa, 14 January 1727; ibid., fl. 22, same to Fróis, Goa, 15 January 1728; ibid., fl. 23, same to same, Goa, 15 January 1728; ibid., fl. 26, same to King of Kilwa, Goa, 16 January 1728; ibid., fl. 27, same to same, Goa, 16 January 1728; ibid., fl. 30, same to Fróis, Goa, 15 January 1729; ibid., fl. 43, same to same, Goa, 16 January 1730; N.A.I.P.G., L.M. 94–A, fl. 46, same to Crown, Goa, 15 January 1728; N.A.I.P.G., Cod. 2323, fl. 74, same to same, Goa, 20 January 1736; N.A.I.P.G., L.M. 105, fl. 140, petition of Fróis to Crown, n.d., enclosed in Crown to Viceroy, Lisboa occidental, 14 April 1736.

20. See Boxer, 'Swahili Coast', pp. 75–84, and Strandes, *Portuguese Period*, pp. 273–98, for details.

21. A.H.U., Moç., Cx. 3, Nicolau Tolentino de Almeida to Crown, n.d., but probably *c.* 1741–2.

22. Albert Lougnon, *Receuil Trimestriel de Documents et Travaux inédits pour servir à l'histoire des Mascareignes françaises* (Tananarive, 1939), IV, p. 394. The original French text gives the name for the Yao as *mongeaux*, which clearly derives from the Portuguese *mujao* and recalls later English renderings of *monjou*.

23. A.H.U., Moç., Cx. 3, Crown to Marquês de Louriçal, Lisboa, 28 April 1740, and António da Silva to same, São Pedro, 22 and 26 December 1741. Copies of these documents are also be to found in N.A.I.P.G., L.M. 111–A, fl. 3–7, while another of the first alone is in B.M., Add. Ms. 20, 890, fl. 38. Almeida was by no means the first Governor of Mozambique to abuse his official position by employing royal troops to conduct his illegal trading for him. For an earlier royal admonition against this practice, see N.A.I.P.G., L.M. 9, fl. 2, Crown to Viceroy, Valledolid, 23 March 1604.

24. A.H.U., Moç., Cx. 3, Almeida to Crown, n.d., but probably *c.* 1741–1742.

25. Teixeira Botelho, *História*, I, pp. 346–51, 406–7; Axelson, *Portuguese*, pp. 145–6, 176–7, 181–2, 186–7; Alcântara Guerreiro, *Quadros da História de Moçambique* (Lourenço Marques, 1954), II, pp. 248–9, 189–93; Fritz Hoppe, *A África Oriental*

Portuguesa no tempo do Marquês de Pombal (1750–77) (Lisbon, 1970; original edition, Berlin, 1965), p. 139.

26. N.A.I.P.G., Cod. 832, fl. 10, Manuel Soares and others to Viceroy, Sena, 22 May 1711.

27. ibid., fl. 12, *Junta do Comércio* to Viceroy, [Goa], 21 January 1712; fl. 12, Viceroy to *Junta*, Panelim, 22 January 1712; fl. 13–15, royal *despacho*, 22 January 1712; and fl. 69–72, royal *despacho*, Goa, 15 January 1723, for the orders given to the Juiz Sindicante, Duarte Salter de Mendonça, who was in charge of the *devassa*.

28. N.A.I.P.G., L.M. 81, fl. 258, Viceroy to Crown, Goa, 16 January 1716.

29. B.N.L., F.G., Cod. 4408, pp. 66–9, Crown to Viceroy, Lisboa, 8 February 1717, and pp. 69–72, Viceroy to Crown, Goa, 15 January 1718; the second letter is also in N.A.I.P.G., L.M. 83, fl. 88.

30. A.H.U., India, maço 18, Viceroy to *Junta do Comércio*, Panelim, 2 and 3 January 1720; other copies are in B.N.L., F.G., Cod. 4406, fl. 99; Huntington Library, Boxer Collection, Indiana University, Bloomington, Castello-Novo Codex, no. 63, fl. 190–3; and B.M., Add. Ms. 20,906, fl. 38, published in Theal, *Records*, V, pp. 74–5. See also A.H.U., India, maço 18, *Junta do Comércio* to Viceroy, [Goa], 9 November 1720. I am grateful to Professor Boxer for allowing me to use the Castello-Novo Codex when it was in his private library.

31. Strandes, *Portuguese Period*, pp. 300–4.

32. A.H.U., Moç., Cx. 3, Pedro de Rego Barreto to Crown, Moç., 10 November 1745.

33. For an early, more general expression of the fear that Arab control of Mombasa would divert business from Zambesia to that part of the coast, see N.A.I.P.G., Cod. 832, fl. 1–4, André Lopes de Laura and João Roiz Machado, undated report on Rivers of Sena, enclosed in Viceroy to Crown, Panelim, 5 November 1709.

34. See Berg, 'The Swahili Community of Mombasa, 1500–1900', *Jl. of African History*, IX, 1 (1968), pp. 35–56.

35. S. B. Miles, *The Countries and Tribes of the Persian Gulf* (London, 1919), II, p. 266; R. F. Burton, *Zanzibar: City, Island, and Coast* (London, 1872), II, p. 366; Guillain, *Documents*, I, pp. 547, 555.

36. For this date, see Z. Sarmento, 'Um santareno no Oriente: Nuno Velho Pereira—Notas biográficas', Congresso Internacional da História dos Descobrimentos, *Actas*, V, 1 (Lisbon, 1961), pp. 263–75.

37. Santos, 'Ethiopia Oriental', pp. 309–14. Cf. Couto, *Da Asia*, Década X, Livro 6, capítulo xiv, pp. 98–105. For the reaction in Portugal to this massacre, see N.A.I.P.G., L.M. 3-A, fl. 162–6, Crown to Meneses, Lisboa, 22 January 1587, also published in Cunha Rivara, *Archivo Portuguez Oriental*, III, p. 84, where it is misdated to 21 January.

38. Barreto, 'Informação', p. 463.

39. N.A.I.P.G., L.M. 17, fl. 138, and L.M. 18, fl. 33, Crown to Viceroy, Lisboa, 27 February 1633; see also, same to same, Lisboa, 12 February 1636, in Theal, *Records*, IV, pp. 267–70.

40. A.H.U., India, maço 23, *requerimento*, Bernardo de Távora, n.d., but post-30 November 1723, enclosing supporting testimony of Álvaro Caetano de Melo e Castro, Moç., 15 November 1721; ibid., *Conselho Ultramarino*, 'Nomeaçaõ de pessoas p.ª o posto de Capp.ᵐ da Seg.ᵈᵃ Companhia de Infantario, q̃ na prezente monçaõ passa de Socorro a O Estado da India', Lisboa, 27 March 1726; A.H.U., Moç., Cx. 3, Fróis to Crown, Moç., 11 August 1727; N.A.I.P.G., Cod. 2323, fl. 30, Viceroy to Fróis, Goa, 15 January 1729.

41. ibid.

42. Sheriff, 'The Rise of a Commercial Empire: An Aspect of the Economic History of Zanzibar, 1770–1873', Ph.D. thesis, University of London, School of Oriental and African Studies, 1971, especially p. 181. For Indians in pre-Portuguese East Africa, see Strandes, *Portuguese Period*, pp. 92–3.

43. W. H. Moreland, *India at the Death of Akbar—An Economic Study* (London, 1920,) pp. 200–3.
44. Tapan Raychaudhuri, 'European Commercial Activity and the Organization of India's Commerce and Industrial Production, 1500–1750', in B.N. Ganguli (ed.), *Readings in Indian Economic History* (London, 1964), p. 67. See Strandes, *Portuguese Period*, p. 131.
45. Moreland, *Akbar*, pp. 203–12.
46. ibid., pp. 209, 216, 234–5, 179–81; the quotation comes from p. 179.
47. For details, see Sheriff, 'The Rise of a Commercial Empire', pp. 118–20, and Free-man–Grenville, *Medieval History*, p. 25.
48. Hoppe, *África Oriental Portuguesa*, p. 219.
49. William Milburn and Thomas Thornton, *Oriental Commerce; or the East India Trader's Complete Guide* . . . (London, 1825), p. 39; George Watt, *A Dictionary of the Economic Products of India* (London and Calcutta, 1890), III, p. 227. The information on other types of ivory also comes from these two sources.
50. ibid., III, p. 226.
51. Irfan Habib, 'Potentialities of Capitalistic Development in the Economy of Mughal India', *Jl. of Economic History*, XXIX, 1 (1969), pp. 38–44, 71–2; see also his *Agrarian Systems of Mughal India* (Bombay, 1963), and 'Usury in Medieval India', *Comparative Studies in Society and History*, VI, 4 (1963–1964), pp. 393–423. For shipbuilding at Surat, see A. Jan Qaisar, 'Shipbuilding in the Mughal Empire during the Seventeenth Century', *The Indian Economic and Social History Review*, V, 2 (1968), pp. 149–70.
52. Habib, 'Potentialities', pp. 73–4.
53. See, e.g., Ishwar Prakash, 'Organization of Industrial Production in Urban Centres in India during the 17th Century with special reference to textile', in Ganguli, *Readings*, pp. 48–9.
54. Raychaudhuri, 'European Commercial Activity', p. 74.
55. Strandes, *Portuguese Period*, p. 174.
56. Viceregal *álvara*, Diu, 27 March 1686, in *A.C.*, I (1917), pp. 281–6; cf. A.H.U., Moç., Cx. 19, Jerónimo José Nogueira de Andrade, Moç., 8 July 1783, for a slightly different copy. For the conditions under which this organization operated, see Hoppe, *África Oriental Portuguesa*, pp. 176–8. It would be most valuable to have a full history of this company, as it appears to form a distinct exception to Ray-chaudhuri's statement that 'companies' brought into existence by European stimulus concerned themselves exclusively with supplying orders for the European factories. 'The possibility of setting up similar organizations for overseas trade or at least for controlling the supplies in order to increase the bargaining power vis-a-vis the Europeans does not appear to have occurred to anybody'. The Portuguese, of course, ran their Indian operations quite differently from other European establishments, which may account for the formation of the Company of Mazanes. Raychaudhuri, 'European Commercial Activity', p. 75.
57. Holden Furber, *Bombay Presidency in the Mid-Eighteenth Century* (London, 1965), p. 42.
58. Habib, 'Potentialities', pp. 77–8.
59. Very little work has been done on Indian trade in the eighteenth century, particularly with reference to the critical Gulf of Cambay area. A major study is under way by Ashin Das Gupta, who has written a general overview of this period, 'Trade and Politics in 18th Century India', in D. S. Richards (ed.), *Islam and the Trade of Asia* (Oxford, 1970), pp. 181–214, especially pp. 187–95.
60. N.A.I.P.G., L.M. 97–B, fl. 610–11, Faquy Abedu buno mwenha Saveia of Kilwa to Frois , n.d., but clearly *c.* 1728–1729; fl. 614–15, Secu Vegy to Álvaro Caetano, n.d., but from the same period.
61. N.A.I.P.G., L.M. 95–B, fl. 585, Sultan Babucar Bun Sultano Umar Bun Dhau and his brother Bana Mucu Bun Sultano Babucar Fumovay, King of Jagaya, to Viceroy,

10 October 1728. The *maund* was a weight of wide local variation in India and was finally standardized under the British Empire at about 32 kg. The *doti* was a common measure of cloth on the East African coast, generally two metres of full width or four metres of narrow width.

62. For the hazards of depending upon *patamares*, see A.H.U., Moç., Cx. 21, António Manuel de Melo e Castro to Martinho de Melo e Castro, Tete, 1 June 1784. Cf. Speke, *Journal*, p. 40, on the same system along the Swahili coast in 1860. This practice has been confirmed in interviews conducted in eastern Tanzania in 1972–1973.

63. See Boxer, *Race Relations in the Portuguese Colonial Empire, 1415–1825* (Oxford, 1963), pp. 53–4.

64. A.H.U., Moç., Cx. 17, Crown to Viceroy, Lisboa, 21 April 1720; same to same, Lisboa, 7 April 1723, in Theal, *Records*, V, pp. 124–6.

65. A.H.U., India, maço 19, Prov. Govt. to Crown, Goa, 17 December 1724, enclosing Paulo da Costa to Prov. Govt., Moç., 10 August 1724; A.H.U., India, maço 31, *Junta do Comércio* to Crown, Goa, 27 January 1731, enclosing same to Viceroy, [Goa], 2 December 1730, and Crown to Viceroy, Lisboa, 6 April 1729; cf. Andrade, *Relações*, p. 100.

66. A.H.U., Moç., Cx. 3 and Cod. 1317, fl. 251–3, *provisão*, João de Saldanha da Gama, Goa, 10 January 1727; see also A.H.U., Moç., Cx. 3, Fróis, Moç., 10 March 1727.

67. *Provisões*, Saldanha da Gama, Goa, 18 January 1727 and 9 January 1728, in Cunha Rivara, *Archivo Portuguez Oriental*, VI, pp. 286–7, and Theal, *Records*, V, pp. 143–145, 155–8.

68. N.A.I.P.G., Cod. 2323, fl. 43, Viceroy to Fróis, Goa, 16 January 1730.

69. ibid., fl. 40, Viceroy to the Banyan traders of Mozambique, Goa, 13 January 1730, and Viceroy to Canogy Guca, Goa, 18 January 1730.

70. Saldanha da Gama to Crown, 19 December 1729, in J. F. J. Biker, *Collecção de Tratados . . . nas partes da Asia e Africa Oriental* (Lisbon, 1885), X, pp. 172–5; *provisão*, Saldanha da Gama, Goa, 14 January 1730, in Cunha Rivara, *Archivo Portuguez Oriental*, VI, pp. 301–3, and Theal, *Records*, V, pp. 163–7.

71. Lougnon, *Receuil trimestriel*, IV, pp. 345, 349, 359. See N.A.I.P.G., Cod. 2323, fl. 63, Viceroy to José Barbosa Leal, Goa, 29 January 1735, for an inconclusive reiteration of the problem regarding the slaves of Indians at Mozambique.

72. See, e.g., Livingstone, *Last Journals*, I, p. 78; Oliver, 'Discernible Developments in the Interior, *c.* 1500–1840', in Oliver and Mathew, *History*, I, p. 208; and J. M. Gray, 'Zanzibar and the Coastal Belt, 1840–1884', ibid., I, p. 227.

73. Reginald Coupland, *East Africa and its Invaders, from the earliest times to the Death of Seyyid Said in 1856* (Oxford, 1938), pp. 31–5.

74. For a full analysis of the history of French slaving in East Africa, see Alpers, 'The French Slave Trade'. Unless otherwise noted, the sources for my discussion of this trade in succeeding chapters can be found in this essay. For a more inclusive treatment of this topic at its source, see J. M. Filliot, *La traite des esclaves vers les Mascareignes au XVIIIe siècle*, ORSTOM, Tananarive: Section Historique, roneograph, 1970.

75. Charles Grant, *The History of Mauritius* (London, 1801), p. 297.

76. Crown to Viceroy, Lisboa occidental, 2 April 1723 and 7 April 1727, in Theal, *Records*, V, pp. 122–4, 151–5; A.H.U., India, maço 29, Crown to Saldanha da Gama, Lisboa, 28 August 1729, with reply, Goa, 11 October 1730, on opposite column.

77. O.L. Hommy, report of the voyage of the *De Brack*, 9 November 1741, in Alfred Grandidier *et al*, *Collection des Ouvrages anciens concernant Madagascar*, (Paris, 1913), VI, p. 195.

78. The assertion of the Count of Ericeira in 1730 that the ivory trade of Macuana was not at all considerable was emphatically disputed in 1753 by the Governor-General of Mozambique, who cited the records of the local *Santa Casa da Misericórdia*. A.H.U.,

Moç., Cx. 3, Meneses to Crown, Lisboa, 4 November 1730, paragraph 17; A.N.T.T., M.R., maço 603, Francisco de Melo e Castro to Crown, Moç., 20 November 1753, enclosed in same to same, Moç., 28 December 1753.

79. N.A.I.P.G., L.M. 78, fl. 13, Crown to Viceroy, Lisboa, 17 September 1711.
80. B.N.L., F.G., Cod. 1603, Marco António d'Azevedo Coutinho to António de Brito Freire, Lisboa, 1 April 1749; ibid., João Machado Borges, 'Entrada da Carregação . . . que chegarão aeste Estado em Setembro de 1744 . . .', n.d., but attached to preceeding document. Brito Freire was *Vedor Geral da Fazenda da Índia*, so he was at the very centre of the commercial affairs of Mozambique. The transaction concerned here involved 2,568 *maços* of *missanga*, a variety of trade bead, sent aboard the *Nossa Senhora Madre de Deus*, which were sold at Mozambique for 15,807 *cruzados*, which in turn paid for the purchase of 152 tusks of ivory. These tusks, according to the second document, weighed 15 *bares*: 1 *faraçola*: 6 *mainas*: 3 *rubos*, therefore yielding a price of about 1,000 *cruzados* per *bar*, assuming that all the tusks were large ivory (see Chapter 4, pp. 118–20).

CHAPTER FOUR

Trade and Conflict
at Mozambique, 1750-1770

❦❦❦❦❦❦❦❦❦❦❦❦❦❦❦❦❦❦❦❦❦❦❦❦❦❦❦❦❦

The Ivory Trade: Yao Domination and Makua Obstruction

By the middle of the eighteenth century the Yao trade in ivory
to Mozambique was at its height, constituting the very backbone
of the economy of both the island and its dependent settlements
on the mainland. The Makua also continued to trade ivory to this
market, but contemporary sources make a clear distinction between the importance of this business and of that done with the
Yao, all stressing the fundamental importance of the latter. Both
Inácio Caetano Xavier and Francisco de Melo e Castro estimated
that the Yao alone carried approximately 400 to 500 *bares* of
ivory to Mozambique each year, a figure which is supported by
other knowledgeable members of the Portuguese community
there.[1] The official figures for the years 1759–1761 of the total
exportation of ivory from Mozambique to Portuguese India, which
imported virtually all the ivory embarked from that port, lend
further credence to these opinions.[2] In fact, a close reading of these
sources suggests that the ivory which the Yao carried to Mozambique constituted more than 90 per cent of that traded overland
to Mossuril and the Cabaceiras, and about 65 per cent to 70 per
cent of all the ivory which entered the island itself, including that
which came from the Rivers of Sena, Sofala, Inhambane, and the
Kerimba Islands.[3]

Nevertheless, the duties collected on this ivory, including those
levied on the cloth and beads for which it was traded, were not
sufficient to remedy all the financial ills of the Portuguese
East African administration. By 1752 the Portuguese Crown
realized that a drastic solution was required in order to improve

the sorry state of its empire there. So long as it remained sub-ordinate to the Viceroyalty of Goa, which was preoccupied in Asia with protecting its own solvency and territorial integrity, it seemed hopeless to expect a revival in Portuguese East Africa.[4]

TABLE I

Ivory Exported from Mozambique, 1759–1761

Classifications of ivory[a]	Weights 1759	Weights 1760	Weights 1761	Three year total
Large and average made large	588:10:7:0	519:6:0:1	473:15:7:1	1,581:12:2:2
Small made large	41:2:0:2½	32:1:7:1½	36:19:11:1	110:3:7:1
Cera made large	8:2:5:½	10:9:2:3½	10:7:1:1	28:18:9:1
Annual total	637:15:0:3	561:16:10:2	521:2:7:3	1,720:14:7:0

Source: A.H.U., Moç., Cx. 9, António Francisco Xavier, 'Extracto do todo o Marfim que foy extrahido deste Porto para o de Goa, e Norte no tempo dos Rendeiros actuaes desta Alfandega da Ilha e Fortz.ᵃ de Moss.ᵉ, tirado pellos livros dos despachos da mesma Alf.ᵃ', Alfândega de Moç., 15 December 1761.

ᵃFor the system of calculating ivory for export, see pp. 118–120.

Note: Weights are given in *bares; faraçolas; mainas* and *rubos*.

TABLE 2

Approximate Annual Distribution of Ivory for Export at Mozambique, 1762

Source	Quantity in *bares* of 4 *quintais*	Percentage of total
Rivers of Sena	40	6·7–5·7
Sofala	40	6·7–5·7
Inhambane	50	8·3–7·2
Kerimba Islands	40	6·7–5·7
Macuana[a]	430–530	71·6–75·7
Total	600–700	100–100

Source: Anonymous, 'Memorias da Costa d'Africa Oriental e algumas reflexões uteis para estabelecer e fazer mais florente o seu comercio', Sena, 21 May 1762, in Andrade, *Relações*, pp. 219–20.

ᵃMacuana is not specifically named, but is clearly the source of the remainder.

Thus, on 19 April 1752 the King of Portugal, D. José (1750–1777), decreed that in view of the 'decadency of the Government of Mozambique, . . . it will be more convenient to separate it from that of Goa for its restoration'.[5] Francisco de Melo e Castro, who had been serving as Governor of the colony since January 1750, was appointed as the first Governor-General of Mozambique. But while these decisions were hopefully being made at Lisbon, another change of significance to the internal trade of East Central Africa was already taking place at Mozambique.

The resumption of hostilities between the Makua and the Portuguese, whose relations seem to have been at least tolerable for nearly two decades after the skirmishes of the 1720s, marked the beginning of more or less endemic warfare until the final colonial conquest of the twentieth century. By 1749 the Portuguese had taken up arms against a number of belligerent Makua chieftains.[6] But peace was not restored and Portuguese relations with the Makua, especially with the important chief Murimuno, whose main village lay some eight to ten leagues (perhaps forty-five to sixty kilometres) inland from the coast, deteriorated further. The disturbances caused by the Murimuno, whom Xavier tagged 'the most arrogant of all', were serious. According to the new Governor-General, the Murimuno was 'making an asylum in his main village for all the slaves who fled from the inhabitants of this island, and from the other side, robbing our merchants, and severely abusing people from our lands who go to his'. Furthermore, wrote Brigadier David Marques Pereira, the Murimuno 'impeded the inhabitants of his continent from carrying provisions, and ivory to this fortress, and did the same to his neighbours, seizing from them what they carried'.[7] Unsettling as these local disorders were, however, the most critical result of the Murimuno's hostility was the ruinous effect which it had on the trade of the Yao to Mozambique. In view of what is known about the volume of trade of the Makua and the Yao, this is surely the only interpretation to give to the observation that the Makua were also obstructing the 'trading and commerce of their nation which comes from three or four months' away', and that 'this trade with us consists of the quantity of more than a thousand negroes loaded with ivory, from which this fortress derives great profits'.[8]

The different trading habits of the Makua of Macuana and the Yao with the people of Mozambique also attest to the validity of the interpretation that the anonymous writer of these lines was mistaken in his belief that the traders from the far interior were of the same nation as the Makua who were disrupting the trading economy of the island. Being closer to the Portuguese mainland settlements of Mossuril and the Cabaceiras, in peacetime the Makua traded with them throughout the year. The Yao, whose country lay beyond the Lujenda River, could only travel to the coast during the dry season, from May through October. The observation made by Luís Antonio Figueiredo, who served as Chief Justice of Mozambique, that *patamares* were not necessary for trading with the Makua substantiates the conclusion that those Makua who traded to Mozambique throughout the year did not come from a great distance inland. It also carries the implication that these Makua lived close enough to the Portuguese settlements so as not to be apprehensive about bringing their merchandise directly to them. By contrast, the remark made by João Baptista de Montaury, long a resident of Mozambique, that *patamares* were sent into the interior 'to call together the bands of the Makua and Yao, who do not come without the assurance that the *patamares* are waiting for them beforehand', confirms the belief that there were also some Makua who came from the far interior to trade to Mozambique.[9] In general, however, the volume of their trade was not comparable to that of the Yao. More specific evidence that the traders in question were more likely Yao than Makua comes from Melo e Castro, who was the first of several writers to state plainly that the Yao came to the coast of Mozambique from some two to four months' journey distant.[10] Thus it was not primarily the more localized attacks of the Murimuno's Makua against the Portuguese which caused the latter to declare open war against that chief, but rather the ruin which he was causing to their vitally important trade with the Yao. As Xavier put it:

> The dependency which we have of these Chieftains is of neighbourliness, and trade of some ivory, slaves, provisions, and above all that of free passage to the Yao, who cannot come to the coast with their ivory, without passing through their lands.[11]

Whatever Melo e Castro's pleasure at receiving on 4 June 1753 the King's instructions regarding the new composition of the administration of Portuguese East Africa, he must have been particularly grateful that the military expedition which had been fitted out in Lisbon in the previous year 'to repress the chiefs and to terrorize Kaffraria' was also safely arrived at Mozambique.[12] On either 10 or 14 September, it is not clear which, Melo e Castro sent these troops into battle against the Murimuno. This force, numbering over one hundred regular soldiers, and augmented by some 600 to 1,000 auxiliaries, most of whom were supplied by the allied Sheikhs of Sanculo and Quitangonha, advanced directly into the Murimuno's territory. In a campaign reminiscent of that against the first Mauruça in 1585, several deserted villages were burned to the ground without resistance being encountered. The Portuguese impetus then seems to have spent its force, and in the following hours any cohesion which remained was thoroughly dissipated by senseless quarrelling within the Portuguese camp. For reasons known only to himself, a certain Diogo Martins first charged the Sheikh of Sanculo with being a traitor and then, in full view of his retainers, shot him dead. The contingent from Sanculo immediately withdrew from the field, although that from Quitangonha remained, but the Portuguese position was no longer tenable. With a decision to retire the expedition all discipline was lost, and the retreat turned into a disorderly flight of individuals to the coast. Once this disarray became known to the Makua, who were hidden in the bush, they seized upon the opportunity without hesitation and inflicted heavy casualties on the fleeing Portuguese. The bitterly disappointed Melo e Castro reported to Lisbon that 'this action was one of the most tragic, and unhappy which has been seen in this Conquest', a sentiment which was borne out by the fact that at least half of the regular troops were lost in the rout.[13]

The need to put down the Murimuno was thereafter complicated by the fact that the new Sheikh of Sanculo had stopped supplying Mozambique with cattle and provisions in retribution for the murder of his father.[14] At first Melo e Castro sought the services of the powerful Makua chief Micieyra, who was the nearest neighbour of the Portuguese. The Micieyra agreed to attack the Murimuno, but his continual procrastination frustrated the Governor-General, who consequently turned for aid again to the Sheikh of Quitangonha. Without further delay, the Sheikh's forces penetrated Macuana up to the main village of the Murimuno and routed his followers, killing and imprisoning many of them. The Murimuno sought revenge for this bold attack and prepared to attack the Portuguese mainland, but the Sheikh of

Quitangonha got wind of the Murimuno's intentions and pre-pared an ambush for his army. The Makua fell into the trap and were caught in a crossfire, from which they fled into the interior. The Sheikh's men pursued them ruthlessly for three days and in-flicted heavy losses on them, as well as taking many prisoners. By late 1754, the Murimuno had removed the centre of his operations farther into the hinterland of Mozambique and was seeking an *entente* with the Portuguese. These informal overtures were snubbed by Melo e Castro, who wished the Murimuno to send personal emissaries to negotiate with the Captain-Major of the Cabaceiras and Mainland, but it did not really matter. The mainland was at peace and there was again freedom of movement and trade between Macuana and the Portuguese settlements.[15]

Before long, however, the Murimuno was waging war again, very much to the detriment of the economy of Mozambique. From late September 1756 until February 1758 (i.e. from the last month of one dry season on throughout all of the next), the Yao were un-able to come to trade with the Portuguese as a result of war with the Makua, who refused to let them pass through Macuana to the coast. 'Consequently', Xavier recorded, 'this land, and the Treasury of His Majesty, suffered irremediable damage in re-spect to the duties of the customs-house, as well as to the *velório* of the [Royal] Monopoly which was not sold, because they [the Yao] consume more of it than do the rest.'[16] The Royal Monopoly over the vital importation and sale of *velório* at Mozambique had been retained by the Royal Decree of 29 March 1755, which abolished the supervision of all the remaining trade of Mozam-bique by Goa and entrusted it to the new Government of Mozam-bique.[17] In most years, between 20,000 and 30,000 packets of *velório* could be expended in Portuguese East Africa, mostly in trading with the Yao. Official requisitions for shipments of Vene-tian *velório* from Lisbon to Mozambique show that in 1758, 20,000 out of 32,000 packets (62·5 per cent) were specifically to be of that sort 'which serves for the Yao', while in the following year, 16,000 out of 25,200 (63·5 per cent) were similarly earmarked for the Yao market. In the period during which the Makua were warring with the Yao, only 9,295 packets of *velório* were sold by the Royal Monopoly. From the cessation of these hostilities until October 1758, a total of 36,592 packets were sold. Most of these went for trading with the Yao, who had a two years' backlog of ivory which they brought to the coast in the course of that season.[18]

These figures on the *velório* trade, together with those concerning the ivory trade, eloquently bear witness to the undisputed primacy in the economy of Mozambique which the trade of the Yao had attained by the middle of the eighteenth century. It was, simply, 'the principal application' and 'the unique commerce' by which the people of that island and the mainland sustained themselves.[19]

During the 1760s, Macuana continued to be a restless and potentially explosive area, but there were no further dramatic clashes between the Makua and the Portuguese, or the Makua and the Yao, during this decade. A close watch was kept by the Portuguese on the movements of the Murimuno and the Mauruça, the great chief of Uticulo, and in 1761 some undefined warring took place in Macuana. Five years later things were more threatening to the Portuguese, but the Governor-General feared to mount a campaign against the Makua lest it should suffer the same fate as that of 1753. By late October 1766, however, their raiding of both the Portuguese and the Yao finally provoked a reaction from Mozambique. With the help of warriors from Quitangonha and friendly Makua, the Portuguese carried out some indeterminate operations against several Makua chieftains of Uticulo and Cambira, which lay to the south-west of Mozambique. Their main antongonists were named as Corripe Muno, nephew of Muzama Muno; Emtutte Muno, nephew of Maurussa Muno (the Mauruça); and Helimue Muno, nephew of Muere Muno (the Murimuno).[20] Information is scarce for these years, but this pattern of desultory Makua raiding, with occasional Portuguese reprisals along similar lines, seems to have characterized the fluid state of affairs in Macuana right into the next decade.

While the Makua had always been a dangerous adversary, there is no doubt that their acquisition of firearms vastly increased their striking power. By 1754 it was possible for one man to write that 'thirty years ago none of the Makua knew the use of firearms, and they used only weapons of their own creation, which are arrows, or spears; it is not thus today'.[21] Indeed, their readiness to take up arms against the Portuguese from the middle of the eighteenth century may partly have its origins in this development. Certainly one of the reasons for the defeat of the Portuguese by the Murimuno, wrote the Governor-General late in 1758, was their possession of firearms.[22] Following the French lead, which dated back to 1735, Brazilian traders became particularly ardent gun-runners in the second half of the century, as did individuals operating from aboard the annual vessel which was sent from Portugal to trade at Mozambique. Of necessity this trade was carried on surreptitiously by these people, who—much to the consternation of the Government—found their chief accomplices in the Portuguese inhabitants of the mainland.

A typical example of local Portuguese participation in this trade concerns the problem of gun-running at the mainland village of Mutomunho, located below Sanculo on the coast south of Mozambique. Mutomunho was the village of the Makua chief Mavere and was one of the principal mainland markets supplying provisions for the island-capital. Portuguese colonists maintained houses there in which they conducted their trade in foodstuffs with the friendly Makua. According to the answers made by Chief Mavere to the questions posed by the Governor-General's investigating officer, the contraband trade in firearms, ball, and powder, was conducted by people with Portuguese names or by their African agents, presumably from the privacy of their houses under the guise of the legitimate trade in provisions.[23] But despite the potentially dangerous consequences of this trade with the Makua, at whose hands these mainlanders suffered in particular when the Makua turned their guns against the Portuguese, it continued unabated. It seems likely that their willingness to run this risk can be traced to the fact that they were otherwise only very marginal participants in the dominant ivory trade of Mozambique. In the illegal trade in firearms they could turn a handsome profit.

Following the upheavals caused by the Makua in the 1750s, Pedro de Saldanha de Albuquerque. who had taken over the government of the colony on 5 August 1758, issued a proclamation strictly prohibiting anyone from trading arms and ammunition to all the Africans of the continent. In 1760 the King consequently ordered that the right to do business in firearms and gunpowder would henceforth be the sole monopoly of the Royal Treasury, and that these goods were to be sold only by individuals selected by the Governor-General. Yet despite these orders the trade continued to flourish, and the Makua, according to the knowledgeable mainlander, Francisco Pereira Henriques, refused to sell slaves to the Portuguese if they did not receive gunpowder in return.[24]

The colonists of Mossuril and the Cabacieras were also responsible for other disorders which hampered the smooth operation of trade there. Their competition for the trade of the Yao and the Makua was so great, that during the dry season the colonists sustained a continual state of petty war. One result of this vicious competition was that the Africans were able to get a much higher price for their goods, especially ivory, as each trader offered another length of cloth and a few more strings of beads for them. Thus the margin of profit for the Portuguese was considerably lowered in this trade. Furthermore, at least some of the Portuguese traders seem to have pursued a policy of setting the Makua and Yao traders against each other, as well as against other Portuguese, each in the hope of making the greatest profit from the ensuing turmoil. Not surprisingly, these efforts only led to greater chaos, and Montaury believed that they were the cause of the havoc often wreaked on the Portuguese lands by the disgruntled African traders as they withdrew to the interior from the coast. While this situation may not have precipitated the resumption of Makua-Portuguese hostilities, it could only have aggravated matters during the 1760s.[25]

Seeking to minimize the disturbances which occurred in the trade with the Makua, in 1760 Saldanha de Albuquerque pro-hibited the people of Mozambique from going themselves, or from sending their slaves, into the interior of Macuana to procure provisions. Instead, he ordered that foodstuffs should be obtained only in the old bazaar, the location of which is unknown. In the same vein, his successor as Governor-General forbade anyone from 'sending *Patamares* to Macuana in search of the Yao'.[26] A more striking attempt to prevent these disorders and to regulate the vital trade with the Yao was Saldanha de Albuquerque's proposal to the Portuguese inhabitants of Mozambique that they form a company in order to achieve this end. He envisioned a company embracing rich and poor alike, and left it to them to decide among themselves what form the corporation should take. Not surprisingly, they were unable to respond coherently to the Governor-General, and the many divergent replies obliged him against his will to drop the project.[27] A possible reason for their failure to act on this proposal, which was so obviously intended for their own benefit, as well as for that of the Crown, may have been the continued applicability of Barreto's caustic observation of a century earlier:

> That all outside Mozambique is better than Mozambique is a
> proverbial saying in the mouths of the inhabitants and persons

acquainted with those parts, but in our nation to endeavour to improve a place is considered a metaphysical exercise and a loss of time in discussion.[28]

Another factor may have been the inability of the Portuguese colonists to admit that these disorders were of their own making, and not due to the connivance of the Indian traders at Mozambique, whose continued domination of all aspects of trade there obviously embittered them.

The Ivory Trade: Indian Domination and Portuguese Obstruction

During the administration of Melo e Castro, Indian traders were spared the sort of harassment which they had experienced in the 1720s and 1740s, although Indian Muslims still needed licences from the Holy Office of the Inquisition in order to cross over to the mainland.[29] In 1749 the Church threatened Portuguese who sold Christian slaves to Muslims with excommunication and in 1750 the Marquis of Távora forbade Muslims to own any such slaves, but this restriction was abrogated by the Crown in 1752. Melo e Castro, by contrast, was interested in revitalizing the economy of Mozambique and must have realized that to persecute these traders could only defeat his purpose. Nevertheless, he did oppose proposals from Lisbon and Goa to open the trade of the entire colony directly to all citizens of Portuguese India, which he felt was detrimental to the economy of Portuguese East Africa. But in granting administrative independence to Mozambique, the Portuguese Crown had also to bear in mind the economic health of Goa. Thus when these proposals became law in 1755, Melo e Castro's continued vigorous opposition led to his dismissal by the Crown in 1757. On 29 July 1757, Melo e Castro finally promulgated the laws of 29 March and 10 June 1755 which granted the liberty of all trade in Portuguese East Africa, except for the Royal Monopoly of *velório*, 'to all the inhabitants of Goa, and of the other parts and lands of Asia, subject to my Royal Dominion'.[30] In the months before his successor's arrival the Indian traders of Mozambique proceeded to take complete command of the entire trade of the colony, something which had been denied to them previously by the continued existence of the now defunct *Junta do Comércio*. In no time at all a great deal of resentment built up against them among the Portuguese colonists, as well as in the Church, with which Melo e Castro bitterly clashed throughout this tenure of office. Following the suicide of his successor only three weeks after taking office in March 1758, the government was entrusted to David Marques Pereira who was not one to protect the interests of the Indian traders.[31]

On 9 May 1758, the Brothers of the *Santa Casa da Misericrâdia*, acting together as the *Senado da Câmara* (Municipal Council) of Mozambique, submitted a lengthy proposal to Pereira which violently attacked the position of the Indians at Mozambique and on the mainland. Only two days later it was completely incorporated in a decree issued by the Governor-General.[32] This decree ordered that Banyans who owned any property on Mozambique or the mainland, or who possessed any boats, had to sell these within three months or else have them sequestered by the Crown; that no Banyan or Indian Muslim could go or send anyone on his account to Macuana or Mutomunho for provisions; that trading firearms and gunpowder was a treasonable offence; that Banyans, as well as Muslims, required licences from the Holy Office for passing over to the mainland; and that except for the twelve most important Banyan merchants, each of whom was allowed to maintain two other Banyans and four slaves as assistants, all other Indians at Mozambique, who numbered more than 200 individuals, would be sent back to their own countries in the next monsoon. The attempt of the Brothers to blame the Indians for the economic ills of the colony was clearly a sham. The ultimate purpose of their proposal and the resultant decree was not to improve the state of the Royal Treasury, but rather to ameliorate that of the economically impotent Portuguese settlers at the expense of the Indian trading class. About the only accurate charge levelled against the Banyans was that those who maintained residences on the mainland sold their cloth to the Makua at half the prices that they charged the Portuguese.

Even so, neither the Brothers nor the obliging Governor-General were so blinded to the facts of life by their rhetoric that they did not provide for what they believed would be enough prosperous Banyan merchants 'to make the trade of this land run'. But the decree was patently unacceptable to the Indian community, who shortly petitioned for its reversal. Pereira, who seems to have been little more than the tool of the Brothers in this affair, took their advice and refused to rescind the order. Further pleas from the Muslims went unheeded until the arrival at Mozambique on 14 July of Manuel de Saldanha de Albuquerque, Count of Ega, who was en route to Goa as the new Viceroy.[33] Within a week the Count had received petitions from both the Banyans and the Indian Muslims. Theirs is hardly an unbiased view, but it is surely more accurate than that of the Brothers of the *Santa Casa da Misericórdia*. Exposing the speciousness of the colonists' charges against them, the Banyans argued cogently that their trading constituted the main support of the economy and thus of the Royal Treasury, and specifically contended that the recent proclamation contravened the King's decree of 29 March 1755. Persuaded by this logic, the Viceroy issued a decree on 25 July 1758 which rescinded both of Pereira's odious proclamations and re-established the will of the Crown.[34]

The Count of Ega then swept Pereira out of office and replaced him with his own brother, Pedro de Saldanha de Albuquerque, a move which could only have further frustrated the local colonists and clergy.[35] During the next two years, the Church, led by the Episcopal Administrator, Fr. João de Nossa Senhora, hammered away at the position of the Indians at Mozambique, but to no avail. Saldanha de Albuquerque upheld the rights of Indians to seek provisions on the mainland, prohibited the Chief Justice from making inventories of the possessions of deceased Indians, and declared his belief that 'up to now it has not seemed convenient for me to prohibit the Trade, which the Muslims and Gentiles [Banyans] have with the Kaffirs of the Interior', because of its importance to the colony. His only concession to the Church, which was strictly in accordance with royal orders, was that the Muslims' slaves regularly had to be taken by their masters to the See for instruction in Christianity.[36] In all this the new Governor-General received the backing of the Crown, which commented that Indians had always resided and traded at Mozambique without harm to the Crown's interests, and emphasized that the problem had to be judged fairly.[37]

The departure of Saldanha de Albuquerque as Governor-General early in 1763 brought an abrupt end to the protection which the Indian traders had enjoyed under his administration. Almost immediately upon assuming office, João Pereira da Silva Barba issued a proclamation embodying several of the 1758 proposals made by the Brothers of the *Santa Casa*. Indians were restricted to selling their goods 'on this Island to the Portuguese inhabitants of these Captaincies', while non-resident Muslims were to be remanded home. All slaves were to be sold within three months. But provision was made for travelling to the other parts of the colony by licence of the Governor-General, and this Silva Barba was apparently prepared to grant to the Banyans.[38] Resigned to their fate, and still able to carry on with their business at a handsome profit, the Indian trading community decided not to protest against these orders and attempted to live with them. Two years later Silva Barba issued another proclamation which was designed to curb the Indians' practice of selling their cloth to the Portuguese at high rates while trading it to the Yao at cost value. His order specified that 'the Gentile [Banyan] traders of this City . . . cannot personally, or through another, trade with the same Yao, as a result of this trade remaining solely reserved for the Vassals of His Majesty established in these Dominions, being, however, obliged to obtain my Licence in order to be able to do so, which will be conceded to them'.[39] By the ambiguous wording of the proclamation, however, Silva Barba again revealed his ability to satisfy the anti-Indian agitation of the Church and the colonists without completely disabling the operation of trade at Mozambique.

Yao ivory continued to dominate the internal trade of Mozambique throughout the 1760s. A census taken in 1766 reveals that fifty-two of the 181 Portuguese colonists of the island and mainland settlements listed as their 'way of life', in part or in whole, 'Neg.° de Mojao', or 'trade with the Yao'.[40] For Baltasar Manuel Pereira do Lago, who began an unprecedented fourteen-year tenure as Governor-General in 1765—apparently his fate as a political exile from Portugal—the immediate problem facing him was to organize this trade more efficiently.[41] Taking up Saldanha de Albuquerque's project of 1759, several of the more prosperous colonists proposed on 4 March 1766 the establishment of a company for trading with the Yao and the Makua. Unlike the earlier plan, however, this one was not intended to include both rich and poor among its correspondents, but only the 'experienced inhabitants of credit'. The others they dismissed as 'vagrants' who had caused great disorders by sending their *patamares* into the interior to trade with poor quality beads and cloth on which no duties had been paid. This practice, they complained, had deprived the legitimate traders, themselves, of the profits of this trade, and was generally causing the ruin of the entire colony.[42] In support of the company, Pereira do Lago described the fighting which took place among these petty traders and between them and the Yao. He also charged them with avoiding the taxes payable on the export of slaves by spiriting them away at night directly to a waiting ship. The Banyans he decried for having corrupted the Africans so thoroughly in their trade that the Africans had become 'exceedingly artful' in their negotiations with the Portuguese, which had also resulted in declining profits for the colonists. With the full concurrence of the principal civil, ecclesiastical, and military officers of the capital, on 11 March 1766 Pereira do Lago confirmed the incorporation of the *Companhia dos Mujaos, e Macuas,* which was empowered to exercise a complete monopoly over the trade in ivory, slaves, and rhinoceros horn with the Makua and the Yao. To the impoverished majority of colonists only the trade in provisions was permitted.[43]

Opposition to the Company was mounted from several quarters. The Viceroy at Goa protested that its monopoly caused great damage to the welfare of both Diu and Daman, since the Indian merchants from those Portuguese centres were at the mercy of the new Company which had suddenly become their principal buyer of cloth. Nor was the Crown pleased with the monopoly, since the instructions of organization which had been sent out to Mozambique in 1763 had expressly abolished even the Royal Monopoly of *velório,* thereby liberating the trade of Portuguese East Africa from the hold of any official monopolies.[44] At another level it is clear that the Company cannot have been warmly received by most of the common colonists of Mozambique. Speaking at Court on their behalf, Figueiredo argued that the proposed monopoly would further reduce the capital's already miserable population, and attacked Pereira do Lago's conception of the public interest by accurately accusing him of consorting with French slave-traders to the detriment of the Royal Treasury. D. José quashed the Company and ordered Pereira do Lago to reopen the trade of Mozambique to the traders of Portuguese India.[45] While he pleaded for a reversal of this decision, the Governor-General executed the order and abolished the Company in 1768.[46]

The only permanent contribution which Pereira do Lago made in these years to the stabilization of trading practices on the mainland was the establishment of two public fairs, one in the district of Mossuril and the other in that of Sanculo, for the purchasing of provisions for the island. The fair at Mossuril probably formed the basis of what was to become known in the 1780s as the *feira dos Mujaos* (Yao fair), and represented a step forward in the struggle to induce the Yao and Makua to bring their goods to the shores opposite the capital itself. Not everyone was willing to abandon the practice of sending *patamares* after the Makua and Yao, but Pereira do Lago's measure may have helped to reduce the frequency of conflicts arising from it.[47]

Despite his transparent hostility to the Indian traders of Mozambique, whom he attacked bitterly for their concerted opposition to the defunct Company, Pereira do Lago imposed no limitations on their freedom beyond those already established by Silva Barba.[48] But he strongly opposed their attempts to have the obligation to obtain travel licences rescinded by the Crown, commenting that they were tolerated at Mozambique only so that the duties of the Royal Treasury should not suffer.[49] By virtue of their being the only reliable source of merchant capital at Mozambique, and therefore the principal financiers of its administration, the Indians were able to pursue their business there so long as the Crown was willing to protect them against the attacks launched periodically by the colonists, churchmen, and civil administrators.

In view of the importance that rising prices were to play in the collapse of the Mozambique ivory market at the beginning of the nineteenth century, it is useful to examine the price structure existing at this time. But for this to be intelligible, it is also necessary to understand the prevailing method of weighing and evaluating ivory at Mozambique. In the 1750s ivory was divided into four classes according to the weight of the individual tusk: *grosso* or large (over 18 *arráteis*); *meão* or average (over 13½ *arráteis*); *miudo* or small (over 3¾ *arráteis*); and *cera* (under 3¾ *arráteis*).[50] For the purpose of exportation and taxation these different-sized tusks were then grouped together in units of *bares*. Final evaluation of ivory for export was not, however, simply calculated on real weight, but converted to what was known as a standard *bar* of ivory, which was taken to be the equivalent of one real *bar* of large ivory comprised of 20 *faraçolas*. Obviously, the most desirable quality of ivory was the largest, and the fact that greater real weights were needed to comprise one standard *bar* of average, small, and *cera* ivory reflects this. Thus, a standard *bar* of large ivory weighed 20 *faraçolas* and was sold at the official price of 1,000 *cruzados* per *bar*; a standard *bar* of average ivory

TABLE 3

Ivory Prices at Mozambique, 1754–1777

Classification / Date	Large ivory		Average ivory		Small ivory		Cera ivory	
	Price of the land	Official evaluation	Price of the land	Official evaluation	Price of the land	Official evaluation	Price of the land	Official evaluation
1754	1,000$000a per bar of 20 farazolas	1,000$000b per bar of 20 farazolas	1,000$000a per bar of 30 farazolas	1,000$000b per bar of 30 farazolas	700$000a per bar of 40 farazolas	700$000b per bar of 40 farazolas	400$000a per bar of 60 farazolas	400$000b per bar of 60 farazolas
1757	960$000 per bar of 20 farazolas	1,000$000c per bar of 20 farazolas	960$000 per bar of 30 farazolas	1,000$000c per bar of 30 farazolas	672$000 per bar of 40 farazolas	700$000c per bar of 40 farazolas	384$000 per bar of 60 farazolas	400$000c per bar of 60 farazolas
1763–1767 and	56$000 per arroba equivalent to	59$096c per bar of 20 farazolas	36$000 per arroba equivalent to	39$192c per bar of 30 farazolas	19$080 per arroba equivalent to	20$288c per bar of 40 farazolas	7 or 8$000 per arroba equivalent to	7$264c per bar of 60 farazolas
1777	945$000 per bar of 20 farazolas	999$270 per bar of 20 farazolas	911$000 per bar of 30 farazolas	999$234 per bar of 30 farazolas	647$000 per bar of 40 farazolas	699$120 per bar of 40 farazolas	354 or 405$000 per bar of 60 farazolas	387$305 per bar of 60 farazolas

Sources: A.N.T.T., M.R., maço 603, 'Contas do Feytor de Mossambique, Ignacio de Mello Alvim, e dos Administradores do Real Estanco do Vellorio = M.^{el} Domingues = Pedro da Costa Soares . . '; 1 March 1758–28 February 1761; A.H.U., Moç., Cx. 12, *caderno* of Fran.^{co} Antonio Xavier, Moç., 1767; A.H.U., Moç., Cx. 14, João Vito da Silva, 'Memoria A respeito da Correspondencia de Comercio de Goa, Dio e Damão com Moçambique', including a 'Pauta das Avaliaçoens na Alfandega de Moçambique', post–1777; B.N.L., F.G., Cod. 2320, fl. 107–8, 'Guia para o Negocio da India e Africa Oriental, e uzo de todos os que uzo o frequentarão', *c.* 1777.

ᵃ2 per cent import duty payable at Mozambique. ᵇ 2 per cent export duty payable at Mozambique. ᶜ4½ per cent export duty payable at Mozambique.

Note: Prices are given in *cruzados* and *réis.*

weighed 30 *faraçolas* and was also sold for 1,000 *cruzados* per *bar*; small ivory 'made large', as the process was known at Mozambique, weighed 40 *faraçolas* and sold for only 700 *cruzados* per standard *bar*; and a standard *bar* of *cera* weighed 60 *faraçolas* and sold for only 400 *cruzados* per *bar*.[51] This complex system directly mirrored the way in which ivory was sold at Surat and Cutch, where most of the ivory of Diu and Daman eventually found its way, and where most of the trade cloths for East Africa were manufactured.[52]

Before 1753 all ivory exported from Macuana to Mozambique, except for that handled by the Company of Mazanes of Diu, paid a 2 per cent *ad valorem* tax on entering the island and another 2 per cent *ad valorem* tax on leaving. Under Melo e Castro this became a standard 4 per cent *ad valorem* tax on ivory exports from the island-capital only, and when free trade was instituted for the subjects of Portuguese India a $\frac{1}{2}$ per cent charge was added to cover the costs of collecting this tariff.[53] It must be noted, however, that the posted 'price of the land' paid for a standard *bar* of ivory at Mossuril or Mozambique was actually 4 per cent lower than the official evaluation, which was calculated only for the purpose of taxation. The original purpose of this arrangement was to shift the burden of the export tax from the Portuguese suppliers on the mainland to the Indian merchants who controlled exports, but even after the beginning of free trade the system remained in force.

In 1763 a new system of weights was introduced at Mozambique by royal decree, so that henceforth ivory was evaluated in terms of *cruzados* per *arroba*, a smaller unit of real weight. Accordingly, nearly equivalent prices were established for each category of ivory, while upward adjustments were made in their minimum weight requirements, the most significant of which was a doubling of that for small ivory: large (above 18 *arráteis* and 9 *onças*); average (14 *arráteis* and 4 *onças* to 18 *arráteis* and 9 *onças*); small (7 *arráteis* to 14 *arráteis* and 4 *onças*).[54] The reason for this standardization was that the *bar* varied so widely from place to place in Portuguese East Africa that the interests of the Crown would be better served by the implementation of a single system of measurement. But except for a slight reduction in the price of the land for the larger categories of ivory, no major changes in the price structure of the ivory market at Mozambique took place at this time.

The Ivory Trade in the Interior

We have so far examined the ivory trade of Mozambique mainly from only one vantage-point, that of the island itself. But the ivory which the Yao and Makua carried to the coast came from the interior, often the far interior. A full appreciation of the ivory trade on the coast cannot be achieved without some knowledge of the African end of the trade. The ivory which the Makua brought to the coast probably came from their own country, but their trade was not important enough to have moved any contemporary observer to leave a single word on the subject. Their nineteenth-century reputation as great elephant hunters suggests that they probably did most of their own procurement of ivory, rather than trading with other Africans for it. Quite the reverse may well have been the case of the Yao, whose reputation was that of traders, not hunters. And for the Yao there is clear evidence that they had major sources of ivory outside their own lands. A considerable amount of trading must have been done with the people of the upper Shire River valley, but the Shire was not the limit of Yao penetration of the interior. In 1753 Melo e Castro observed that 'the Kaffirs whom they call Yao' carried ivory to the mainland opposite Mozambique from the

> Lands of the Marave, Bive, Caronga, and of various other potentates in those hinterlands bordering the Lands of our Jurisdiction of the Rivers of Sena of the other [northern] side of the Zambezi, where our traders would acquire it if their goods did not cost so very much, which causes those Kaffirs to come to the mainland of Mossuril, opposite this Fortress, where they find them [the cloths] cheaper by one hundred per cent, and of better quality than are introduced to them there, in those territories, by our traders.[55]

Cloths were cheaper at Mossuril than in the Rivers for two principal reasons, different in detail but similar in effect to those factors which had operated in the Rivers of Sena in the seventeenth century. First, the cost of transporting cloths from Mozambique to Quelimane, and then up the Zambesi, was very high and the risk of loss great. Second, the prices of cloths going for sale to any of the subordinate ports of Portuguese East Africa were regularly raised by 30 per cent over the prevailing rate at Mozambique. Furthermore, the monopoly which until 1755 was exercised by Goa over the sale of the principal items of trade was limited to the external trade of the Rivers, Sofala, and Inhambane. North of the Zambesi both internal and external trade were free of its control, so that while the prosperity of those areas subject to its supervision steadily declined, the overland ivory trade to Mozambique flourished. Moreover, the fierce competition for this trade must have resulted in the Africans' being able to secure a continuously better price for their ivory at Mossuril.[56] After 1755 the inauguration of a system of free trade in Portuguese East Africa, except for *velório*, might have enabled the colonists of Sena, Tete, and Zumbo to recapture at least part of the Maravi ivory market from the Yao, but the simultaneous imposition of a crippling 41 per cent tariff on all trade goods going there from the capital only aggravated the situation. This tax was extended to *velório* after the abolishment of the Royal Monopoly in 1763, but Macuana remained, as before, a tax-free area. By trading with the Yao, rather than with the local Portuguese, the Maravi could obtain a much more favourable exchange value for their ivory. In view of these circumstances, then, it is not at all surprising to find the petitioners for the formation of the *Companhia dos Mujaos, e Macuas* complaining that the Yao were carrying the duty-free cloths of Mozambique hundreds of leagues inland and selling them to chiefs 'in order to introduce them into our fair of Zumbo'.[57]

In any case, after about 1750 the trade of the Rivers was largely in the hands of Banyans, whose links with their compatriots at Mozambique enabled them to squeeze most of the local Portuguese out of effective competition. Like everyone else in Zambesia, however, the Banyans were preoccupied with the trade of Zimbabwe and were not especially involved in that of Maravi country.[58] Even in southern Zambesia, however, the effect of Yao commercial influence was discernible in their successful penetration of Abutua, where the Changamire held sway. As Pereira do Lago put it in his preface to the statutes of the *Companhia dos Mujaos, e Macuas*, the freedom of trade which the Yao enjoyed and the effect of the 41 per cent impost were combining to make them masters of the gold trade with the Changamire.[59]

It is very likely that by the 1760s the Yao were trading in northern Zambesia not only with the Maravi, but also with the Lenje and the Bisa, from across the Luangwa River, and possibly even with the eastern Lunda state which was established by the Mwata Kazembe in the Luapula River valley in about 1740.

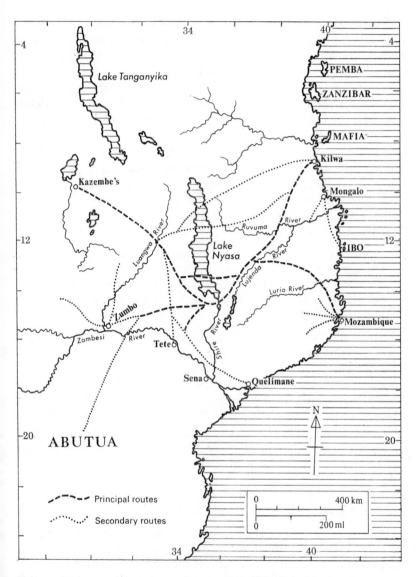

5 *Eighteenth-Century Trade Routes in East Central Africa*

The principal elephant-hunting ground of the western Maravi, the Chewa (one of whose chiefs, Biwi [Bive], is mentioned specifically by Melo e Castro), was known as the Malambo and was located around the middle and lower reaches of the Luangwa. As early as 1723, the Portuguese had become aware of the 'great lands of Uringi', which lay beyond the Luangwa and bordered on Maravi territory, but it was only in the second half of the century that the potential of these lands became known to them. Four decades later, another observer recorded that 'the great hinterland of Orange [is] situated forty days' journey to the north-west of Zumbo', although another unidentified writer stated in 1788 that it was only a fortnight's march from the same fair to Orange.[60] Of the trade of Urenje [Orange, Uringi] the earlier source explained that

> neither *Canarins* [a pejorative term for Goans], nor negro traders go to this hinterland, but those of that country come to Zumbo every year to trade in exchange for ivory, and copper, which they carry already cast in large bars, and of which there is a great abundancy.[61]

These traders should probably be identified as Lenje, who emerged as important traders to Zumbo during the eighteenth century. But the extension of the term Urenje by the Portuguese to include a much more general area beyond the Luangwa raises the possibility that some of the traders of this wider area may have been Bisa,[62] as from the accession of Kazembe III in about 1760, the western Bisa, occupying an ecological borderland and already actively engaged in local trade, became the principal carriers of ivory and copper from his domain to the Rivers of Sena and the East African coast.[63]

There was certainly plenty of opportunity for the Yao to trade with the people of Urenje. It was reported in 1762 that:

> The greater part of the ivory which goes to Sena comes from this hinterland; and because gold does not come from it, the [Portuguese] traders never exert themselves for these two commodities [ivory and copper] . . . as a result of which the negroes have on many occasions gone back carrying the goods which they had brought, through there not being anybody who would buy these from them.[64]

If the Portuguese traders of the Rivers of Sena were not interested in this ivory from Urenje, the Yao certainly were, as were the merchants of Mozambique, Portuguese and Indian alike. The wealth of the Luangwa hunting ground must have been known to the Yao through dealing with the Chewa. Once this connection with Urenje was made in about 1760, an important and regular trade, based upon ivory and involving the Yao, the Maravi, the Lenje, and probably the Bisa, began to flourish between the coast of East Africa and the Luangwa watershed, possibly extending even to the Luapula valley. The operation of this interior trade between different African peoples remains obscure, regrettably, until later in the nineteenth century (see chapters 6 and 7).

At the coast, however, this trade debouched at two main points, Mozambique and Kilwa. For the moment it is only the route taken to Mozambique by the Yao, who commanded the eastern half of the trade, that concerns us; the Kilwa route will be taken up again in the following chapter. The Yao probably crossed into Maravi country over the Mandimba hills, which appear to have marked the southern limits of Yaoland, proceeding around the southern toe of Lake Nyasa and thence across the Shire. Alternatively, they may have been ferried across the narrower southern end of the lake by Maravi canoeists.[65] At the coastal end of the route the Yao approached Mossuril from the north-west, through Uticulo, as we have already seen. In between these ends of the route only speculation is possible, but it seems most likely that the Yao avoided the hilly country of the Lomwe, which lay athwart a direct route from the southern end of Lake Nyasa to Mozambique. Besides, the Lomwe were said to be hostile to outsiders and their country was difficult to traverse even in the late nineteenth century.[66] That a route avoiding the Lomwe was, in fact, followed between these two points by about 1850 is demonstrated by the thirty-three day itinerary given to Dr. Heinrich Barth at Yola, in present-day Nigeria, by Sherif Mohammed ben Ahmedu, an Arab from Moka, who had travelled it himself. According to Sherif Mohammed (who offered to guide Barth across the continent for the sum of 300 dollars, to be paid at Zanzibar), from Mozambique the route progressed north-west, through the flat country behind the coast. Thereafter it crossed the Lurio River into Meto, reaching the town of the Mwalia, the Makua chief of Meto, on the fifteenth day out. From Mwalia the route continued west through Meto until it reached the Lujenda River, which marked the beginning of Yao territory, and followed this river to the environs of Lake Chilwa.

From there it finally led along the Mandimba hills until it descended to Lake Nyasa at the market town of Mwala, three days to the south of Ng'ombo, the most important nineteenth-century eastern lakeshore trading settlement. Thence a traveller could cross the lake.[67]

The Slave Trade in Transition

While it is clear that ivory continued to dominate the trade of East Central Africa in the 1760s, the slave trade was already beginning to make an impression, however slight, on the trade of the Yao. After the halcyon days of Almeida a quarter-century earlier, the slave trade with the French at Mozambique had not grown appreciably in the 1740s and 1750s. Most of those slaves supplied from Macuana were undoubtedly Makua. But at least some Yao slaves were taken to the slave market at Mozambique, where Melo e Castro described them in 1753 as being 'of such delicate endurance, through their being subject to diseases while they are otherwise getting adjusted to the climate, that of those who are brought, ordinarily half survive, and often fewer'.[68] Perhaps the main indication of the level of Makua slave trading with the French is the frequency of references to the allied trade in firearms to the Makua, which was discussed earlier with respect to the role of the Portuguese colonists in it. Both of these trades began to pick up again in the 1760s under the tutelage of Pereira do Lago.

In addition to encouraging the French to trade at Mozambique, Pereira do Lago, inspired by Saldanha de Albuquerque, nurtured the slave trade from East Central Africa to the Mascarene Islands in Portuguese and Brazilian vessels. In 1760 and 1763 extraordinary trading expeditions which included traffic in slaves, were made by Portuguese ships to the French colonies. All the local authorities agreed that while it was clearly illegal for foreigners to trade for slaves in the Portuguese dominions, it was nowhere stated that Portuguese subjects could not trade from the dominions to foreign lands.[69] Despite a lukewarm response from the Crown to his argument that this trade was both profitable and preferable to the illicit trade carried on by French vessels in the Kerimba Islands and with the mainland of Macuana, Pereira do Lago continued to foster this policy.[70] Besides sending local vessels from Mozambique to Ile de France and Bourbon, he apparently encouraged Brazilian traders from Bahia and Rio de Janeiro to ship slaves there from Mozambique. Figueiredo wrote that the Brazilians set up trading houses there, from which they dispatched these slaves to the French islands, as well as ivory, gold, and cowries to Portuguese India. Certainly some slaves were also taken from Mozambique to Brazil, but a decade earlier Melo e Castro wrote that they had a bad reputation there. Accordingly, the Crown's tentative sponsorship of this trade in 1753 seems to have produced few results.[71] Nevertheless, the attitude of Pereira do Lago towards the trade in Portuguese and Brazilian vessels to the French islands marked the beginning of serious slave trading at Mozambique on a regular basis as did also his French policy.

Dynastic Change in 'Uman and the Roots of Kilwa's Revival

Although the peak years of Yao trading at Mozambique appear to have come during the middle decades of the eighteenth century, the seeds of decline there were already being sown during the 1750s in the disturbances which have been examined above. Figueiredo, Montaury, and others specifically mentioned the decline of the Yao ivory trade at Mozambique, despite its continued pre-eminence there, and prescribed various remedies for its rejuvenation. As important as the unstable conditions of trade at Mozambique, however, was the fact that its dominance of Yao trade was being threatened by the gradual commercial revival of Kilwa. This was initially the result of increased Arab trading activity along the Swahili coast following the stabilization of political affairs in 'Uman under the new Bu Sa'idi dynasty. Less clearly but almost certainly an underlying factor was the corresponding growth of Indian merchant capital at Zanzibar under the aegis of a more effective 'Umani imperial order. Indeed, the apparently close relations between 'Uman and the British at Surat and Bombay can only have encouraged the expansion of Indian merchant capitalism at Masqat at this time.[72] Information on the Swahili coast was difficult for the Portuguese to obtain, and what they received was often no more than baseless rumour, especially where it concerned alleged European threats to Mozambique. But the increased pace of Arab and Swahili commercial activity along that coast was a fact which was vividly perceived by the Portuguese in the Kerimba Islands.

Portugal's hegemony over these islands and the Cape Delgado coast was tenuous, at best, and her sovereignty there was made a mockery of by virtually all its inhabitants. The islands were totally defenceless, with only a handful of soldiers stationed at Ibo, the administrative headquarters, where there were no fortifications whatever until 1760. Had any other power wished to command them, it could have done so at will.[73] In addition even the commercial ties between Mozambique and the islands had dwindled to a minimum, despite the fact that up to 1765 no taxes were levied on the cloths which were sent there from the capital. Taxes on trade by the islanders to Mozambique were often avoided by disembarking the cargoes at Quitangonha or Savasava, on the coast immediately north of the capital. All attempts to regulate this trade proved to be futile in these years.[74]

Although virtually all were involved in one form of proscribed activity or another, the principal Portuguese renegades were those who inhabited the island of Vamizi and its mainland. The security of this island was particularly important to the administration, as it physically commanded the coast below Cape Delgado and was the most northerly outpost of Portuguese settlement in East Africa. But Vamizi was about 150 kilometres distant from Ibo, and its residents obeyed only their own instincts, trading with whom they pleased and generally ignoring all directives from Mozambique. In 1765 it was reported that the Portuguese of Vamizi, all of whom had acquired their land by virtue of royal grants, had not paid the Crown its due tithe for the past three years. In the following year, some of these people, together with local Africans and some Swahili from Tungui, looted the annual vessel from Daman, which was grounded on the coast opposite Rongui Island, near Funji [Cape Afungi]. Auxiliary troops led by the Sergeant-Major of Vamizi, a post which was created in 1762, sought out the looters at Funji, where a heated battle occurred with the combined forces of one Simão Leite and an allied Makonde chieftain, who were routed. Soon afterwards, an appeal was made by some of the Vamizi rebels to the Sultan of Kilwa, Hasan b. Ibrahim, under whose protection they wished to render the island. But the Sultan was on good terms with the Portuguese, who had given aid and comfort to his father when he was a refugee at Vamizi nearly forty years before, and he refused their request. Rebuffed and defeated, the Portuguese colonists of Vamizi made their peace with the Commander of the Kerimba

Islands, Caetano Alberto Judice, and returned in a fashion to the official fold.[75]

Portuguese control of the islands was also threatened by harassment from the local Africans. In the late 1750s and early 1760s, there were sporadic conflicts with the Makua opposite Querimba Island. By 1765, Judice was reporting 'the great thefts' which the chiefs of the Makua were committing against people from the islands who traded for ivory in the hinterland. These were so serious that he was obliged to put a large force in the field in order to control the situation. While the effectiveness of this measure is not known, relations with the Makua appear to have remained strained. At the end of the decade the appointment of João Baptista as Commandant of the Mainland of Cape Delgado was recommended by his experience in dealing with the Makua, and thus by the hope that he would be able to improve trade there.[76] In the vicinity of Vamizi Island and Tungui there was a great deal of trouble in the 1760s with the Makonde, who regularly attacked the island and terrorized the mainland. About 1763, in reprisal for recent outrages, Portuguese forces from Vamizi successfully attacked the settlement of Pangani, burning it and capturing two chieftains; but nothing seems to have been settled by this action.[77] Notwithstanding imagined external threats to their claim to rule the Kerimba Islands, the Portuguese were hard pressed to maintain even the vaguest semblance of order there.

Such threats as existed were limited to contraband trading, in which nearly everyone was involved. The French dominated this trade, but at least a few British vessels also visited the area, perhaps to trade for cowry shells.[78] Rigorous enforcement of the prohibition of foreign trade at Mozambique in the 1750s, and the ease of trade in the Kerimba Islands, made them a favourite haunt for the French in this decade. So great was official participation in this trade that the inhabitants of Matemo Island, immediately north of Ibo, were moved to complain about the Commander's excesses to the Viceroy of Portuguese India.[79] All efforts to control this trade were futile.

Whatever their concern about the French in the Kerimba Islands, the Portuguese were far more disturbed at the prospect of any European power seizing Mombasa and, by promoting commerce along that coast, causing the Yao to re-route their trade back to Kilwa. At the end of 1758, Saldanha de Albuquerque repeated the groundless fear that the British were planning to

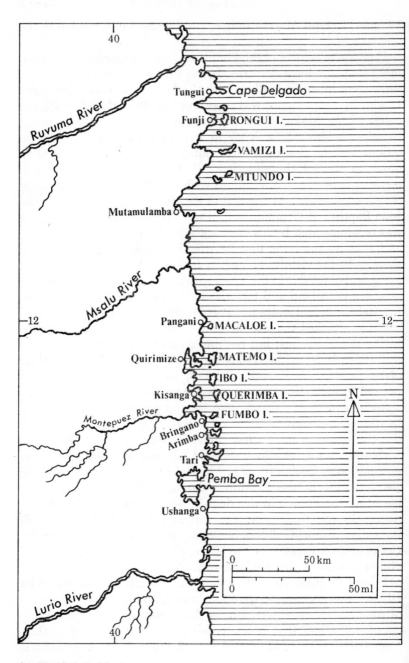

6   *The Kerimba Islands*

occupy Mombasa. It is indicative of the role of the Yao in the trade of Mozambique that the gravest consequence which he could imagine resulting from such a development was that 'the propensity which Foreigners have for trade' would cause the Yao to gravitate to Mombasa once again.[80] The shipment in 1759 of beads which were unsuitable for trading with the Yao again provoked his warning that if such mistakes continued, the Yao would surely go to Mombasa for their needs.[81] In his own way, then, Saldanha de Albuquerque had recognized the two elements which were steadily to attract the trade of the Yao back to the Kilwa coast to the detriment of trade at Mozambique: the renewal of an active commerce along the Swahili coast, and the continuing problems which plagued the smooth operation of trade at Mozambique. Saldanha de Albuquerque was mistaken only in his persistent belief that other Europeans, rather than the 'Umani Arabs and Indian merchant capitalists, would be at the root of the revival of that coast, which would bring with it a renewed demand for ivory, the staple of Yao trade.

Zanzibar Town was the foremost 'Umani stronghold in East Africa. Despite the continued Bu Sa'idi conflict with Mazrui Mombasa, Zanzibar's commercial strength was considerable, for in 1754 it was reported that there were nearly four hundred Arab merchants on the island.[82] Much of their trading was undoubtedly done at Kilwa, which had accepted 'Umani overrule under the new dynasty in the 1740s. In 1758 the Imam dispatched seven ships to fight against Mombasa and Pate. The outcome of this expedition is unknown, but it would appear that it strengthened 'Umani control of Zanzibar and consequently stimulated trade along the Kilwa coast.[83] The increased pace of Arab trade there is indicated by a marked expansion of their activity along the coast south of Kilwa and opposite the Kerimba Islands during the 1760s. In common with the rest of East Africa, however, the trade goods of Zanzibar were primarily of Indian derivation, and it seems clear that the main capitalization of this trade was in Indian hands, the Arabs and Swahili acting principally as middle-men. According to the French adventurer, Jean-Vincent Morice, writing in 1776, the trade from Zanzibar to the coast followed this pattern:

When the ships from India arrive in December, January, or February, all the Moors from Kilwa, Mafia, Mombasa, Pate, &c., go to Zanzibar to buy cargoes and distribute them subsequently in their districts in exchange for ivory tusks, provisions and slaves, &c. In March and April all the Moors and Arabs come to the Kingdom of Kilwa to trade there for slaves, for Kilwa is the assembly point for all the slaves who come from the mainland.[84]

On the assumption that this pattern of trade was operating before Morice's time, it is possible that by the 1750s Kilwa may already have been a place of considerable commercial activity at the beginning of the dry season, when all these traders were gathered there to bargain for the ivory and slaves with which the Africans of the interior began to arrive in June.

A limited trade in provisions and cattle had been carried on throughout the first half of the eighteenth century between the Kilwa coast and the Portuguese settlements of the Mozambique coast. But the Portuguese Crown specifically did not allow the Swahili to trade cloth and beads in their territories, strictly limiting this cabotage to foodstuffs. This is documented by official agreements negotiated with the Sultan of Kilwa in 1760, and with the Mwenyi Mkuu of Zanzibar in 1768, both of which permitted certified vessels sent by these rulers to enter Mozambique for trading within this limitation.[85] The threat of traders from the Swahili coast seeking to introduce the prohibited goods into Portuguese lands was first noticed only in 1754, when several small boats from Mombasa and Pate, whose owners had come to trade at the rising small town of Mongalo, passed south to the Kerimba Islands in search of slaves.[86] A decade later there is a solid body of evidence which reveals the increasing activity of Arab and Swahili traders along both the Kilwa and the Cape Delgado coasts.

In July 1762, the Commander of the Kerimba Islands reported that there were seven Arab ships trading there. Together they had more than 50,000 *cruzados*' worth of cloth in exchange for which he feared that they would carry off all the ivory in the district. He had also received information that there were 4,000 Arabs at Mombasa, where a three-masted ship was being constructed by them, and suggested that the Arabs might be considering an attack on the islands, such as those which had occurred in the late seventeenth century.[87] The tenuousness of the Portuguese hold on the islands caused them to react violently to such rumours. Saldanha de Albuquerque at once issued a proclamation prohibiting Arab vessels from entering the islands, but it is obvious that the Portuguese did not possess the means to enforce it. The Governor-General sent a detachment of twenty-two soldiers, with two pieces of artillery, to be stationed at Vamizi Island for this purpose, but contrary winds forced their boat ashore before reaching Vamizi, and they were set upon by the Makonde.[88] Silva Barba followed his predecessor's lead and sought to have all Swahili resident in the Kerimba Islands and the Cape Delgado mainland recalled to Mozambique, but this was little more than wishful thinking. Further exhortations to local officials to put an end to Swahili trading there were equally futile.[89] Indeed, the difficulty of preventing this trade was intensified by the imposition of a 20½ per cent duty on all goods sent to the islands from Mozambique. Rather than buy cloth from the capital, the Portuguese islanders preferred to obtain it illegally, and less expensively, from the Arabs and Swahili.

Further pressure from the north was felt when in 1766 the Arabs succeeded in establishing their rule over Mongalo by seizing it 'almost violently' from its Makonde chief, Moanha (Mwenyi Mwanya), and placing a governor there.[90] In June, Judice warned that 'the Arabs will come with cloth to distribute them in Mongalo, as well as throughout these Islands, especially in the district of Vamizi, because of the certainty they have that cloth no longer comes from Mozambique due to the great duties which it pays in that customs-house'. Two months later he reported that, so far as he could learn from his 'trustworthy spies', the Arabs intended only to trade at Mongalo, and not to utilize it as a base from which to launch an attack on the Portuguese. But he confirmed his previous fears that the Arabs 'have spread, and continue to send, to Macuana cloth, which has already reached our territory, and which causes considerable damage to His Majesty's vassals through their not being able to procure any ivory, since the Arabs sell their cloth at a lower price'.[91] In 1769 the new Commander of the Kerimba Islands tried to enforce several drastic measures designed to control the trade of the Swahili, whom he accused of depriving the Portuguese of their ivory trade, God of the souls of Africans who were being enslaved by Muslims, and the King of his taxes.[92] These efforts seem to have been no more successful than those of his forerunners.

Frightened by the growing strength of 'Uman and encouraged by reports of dissatisfaction with their domination along the Swahili coast, not to mention the arrival at Mozambique in 1765 of a pro-Portuguese pretender to the leadership of Mombasa, the Portuguese launched a farcical expedition to regain supremacy there. The Sultan of Kilwa, who had encouraged the Portuguese and whose military aid they had hoped to enlist in this cause, apparently had little need for their support, however, for in about 1770 Kilwa reasserted its independence from 'Uman. At the beginning of that year, we are told by Morice, when the 'Umani Arabs, including the governor, made their customary exodus for Zanzibar in order to procure trade goods,

> the Kilwa people took advantage of this absence to signify to them that they would not return to their island and that they no longer wished for a governor—in a word, that if they repre-sented themselves under any name other than traders they would be given no quarter.[93]

Caught off guard and faced with the united opposition of the coast from Mafia to Cape Delgado, the 'Umani were unable to do anything except comply with this demand. There can be no doubt that 'Uman's political and military position in East Africa, outside Zanzibar, was considerably weaker than it had been a decade previously.

Kilwa's action did not, however, in any way adversely affect the steady progress of trade along that coast. The 'Umani were still established at Zanzibar and able to trade freely at Kilwa and along its coast. Indian merchants were thus able to invest securely there and were not yet concerned to trade outside the 'Umani East African capital. The revival which the Portuguese at Mo-zambique had feared for so many years was in progress. That it was beginning to have the effect on the trade of the Yao to Mozambique which Rego Barreto, Xavier, and Saldanha de Albuquerque had predicted it would, is indicated by Pereira do Lago's appraisal of the situation along the Swahili coast, which was written just after the return to the capital of the unsuccessful Mombasa expedition in 1770 and was based upon news which it had gathered there. The Swahili coast, the Governor-General wrote,

> has many valuable goods, but above all a greater quantity of ivory than is brought to this Capital by the Yao and the Makua, all running to that Coast, as the goods which the Arabs and Foreign Nations introduce there are one hundred per cent cheaper.[94]

Pereira do Lago's analysis of what was taking place verifies what we already know about the more localized effects of competitive Arab prices on the ivory trade of the Cape Delgado coast. After nearly three-quarters of a century, the position of Mozambique as the principal coastal outlet for the ivory trade of the Yao, which was increasingly that of all of East Central Africa, was being whittled away. The dominance of the Mozambique route, which had been achieved by a depressed market along the Swahili coast, was being undermined both by its gradual revival and by the conflicts which were adversely affecting the normal operation of trade at Mozambique. Both of these situations were to continue for the next fifteen years, and the result was to be no different.

NOTES

1. Xavier, 'Notícias', p. 153; A.N.T.T., M.R., maço 603, Melo e Castro to Crown, Moç., 20 November 1753; anonymous, 'Memorias da Costa d'Africa Oriental, e algumas reflexões uteis para estabelecer e fazer mais florente o seu comercio', Sena, 21 May 1762, in Andrade, *Relações*, p. 215 (original copy in A.N.T.T., M.R., maço 604); Luís António de Figueiredo, 'Noticia do Continente de Mossambique e abreviada Relação do seo Comercio', Lisboa, 1 December 1773, in Carvalho Dias, 'Fontes', pp. 264-5 (original copy in A.N.T.T., M.R., maço 604).

2. About 59 per cent of these exports went to Daman, 23 per cent to Goa, and 18 per cent to Diu: A.H.U., Moç., Cx. 9, A. F. Xavier, 'Extracto', Moç., 15 December 1761.

3. Using the sources and figures cited in this paragraph and in Tables 1 and 2, I have arrived at these percentages in the following manner:

    (a) *Yao percentage of Macuana trade*
(lower figures) Macuana: 430 *bares*; Yao: 400 *bares* = 93 per cent
(higher figures) Macuana: 530 *bares*; Yao: 500 *bares* = 94 per cent

    (b) *Yao percentage of exports from Mozambique*
(lower figures) Mozambique: 600 *bares*; Yao: 400 *bares* = 67·7 per cent
(higher figures) Mozambique: 700 *bares*; Yao: 500 *bares* = 71·4 per cent

Finally, as a check, I compared the 1762 estimated total of exports with the three-year average of official ivory exportations at Mozambique, 1759-1761:

(1762) 600-700 *bares* of 4 *quintais* each = 140,940—164,430 kg
(1759-1761) 573 *bares* of 20 *faraçolas* = 141,025 kg

Within the limits of the documentation, and allowing for the annual fluctuation of 100 *bares* in the 1762 figures to be accounted for mostly by the Yao (cf. the estimates of Melo e Castro and I. C. Xavier), the percentages arrived at in the text are about as precise as can be expected.

4. See Boxer, *Portuguese Seaborne Empire*, pp. 136-7.

5. Lobato, *Evolução*, p. 283, quotes the decree of 19 April 1752 in its entirety, and on pp. 272-307 gives a masterly analysis of the events leading to the establishment of an independent administration of Mozambique.

6. Teixeira Botelho, *História*, I, p. 436.
7. Xavier, 'Notícias', p. 152; Melo e Castro to Sebastião José de Carvalho e Melo, Moç., 28 December 1753, in *A.C.*, IV (1919), p. 55; A.H.U., Moç., Cx. 4, Pereira to Diogo de Mendonça Corte Real, Moç., 15 November 1753; cf. ibid., Melo e Castro to Crown, Moç., 27 November 1753.
8. Anonymous, 'Breve Noticia Da infelicidade que teve a nossa Expedição de Monçambique primeira que fez El Rey N. Señor D. José I.º destruida pello Rey dos Macuas em que deram fim a maior parte della com a relação dos que morrerão, e da cause que noveu esta guerra hindo na Nau Nossa Senhora da Piedade e o Corsario N. Senhora de Atalaya, que entrarão neste Porto, 8 de Maio de 1754 hindo de Ryo de Janeyro', n.d., but obviously composed in Lisbon, in *A.C.*, II, 9 (1918), p. 106.
9. Figueiredo, 'Noticia', p. 264; João Baptista de Montaury, 'Moçambique, Ilhas Querimbas, Rios de Sena, Ville de Tete, Villa de Zumbo, Manica, Villa de Luabo, Inhambane,' *c.* 1778, in Andrade, *Relações*, p. 349.
10. A.N.T.T., M.R., maço 603, Melo e Castro to Crown, Moç., 20 November 1753.
11. Xavier, 'Notícias', pp. 152–3; cf. Lobato, *Evolução*, pp. 110–11.
12. A.H.U., Cod. 1310, p. 10; A.H.U., Moç., Cx. 6, Saldanha de Albuquerque to Sec. St., Moç., 28 December 1758, quoted in Andrade, *Relações*, p. 56.
13. *A.C.*, II, 9 (1918), pp. 106–11; *A.C.*, IV (1919), pp. 54, 56–7; A.H.U., Moç., Cx. 4, Pereira to Corte Real, Moç., 15 November 1753.
14. *A.C.*, II, 9 (1918), p. 112.
15. A.H.U., Moç., Cx. 4, Melo e Castro to Crown, Moç., 16 November 1754; A.H.U., Moç., Cx. 5, same to same, Moç., 18 August 1755.
16. Xavier, 'Notícias', p. 153; cf. Melo e Castro to Crown, Moç., 8 August 1751, in *A.C.*, III, 16 (1918), p. 166.
17. A.H.U., Moç., Cx. 5, royal decree, Lisboa, 29 March 1755; Crown to Conde de Alva, Lisboa, 4 April 1755, in Theal, *Records*, V, pp. 220–2.
18. A.H.U., Moç., Cx. 6, Saldanha de Albuquerque to Crown, Moç., 10 December 1758, with enclosure, 'Distinção de Vellorio que vay de amostra, e a qualidade, que delle deve vir na monção de *1760*', Moç., 31 December 1758; another copy in A.N.T.T., M.R., maço 603; A.H.U., Cod. 1317, fl. 8–9, anonymous, 'Copia da Rellação sobre qualid.ᵉ de vellorio que deve vir para o Estanque Real de Moss.ᵉ', Moç., 18 August 1759; see Caetano Montez, 'Inventário do Fundo do Seculo XVIII', *Moçambique*, 72 (1952), Document 24, p. 139, for the inflationary effect of these events on the price of *velório* at Mozambique.
19. Xavier, 'Notícias', p. 141; A.H.U., Cod. 1313, fl. 47, Pereira to Crown, Moç., 10 July 1758.
20. A.H.U., Moc., Cx. 8, [Saldanha de Albuquerque] to P.ᵉ M. Dg.ᵉˢ, Moç., 24 January 1760; A.H.U., Moç., Cx. 9, *carta patente*, Saldanha de Albuquerque, naming Inácio de Melo Alvim as Commandant of the Cabaceiras, Moç., 3 March 1761; A.H.U., Moç., Cx. 12, Pereira do Lago to Crown, Moç., 20 August 1766; ibid., Francisco Pereira Henriques to Pereira do Lago, Cabaceira, 23 October 1766.
21. A.H.U., Moç., Cx. 4, Brito Freire to Crown, Lisboa, 8 November 1754, paragraphs 92–3.
22. A.H.U., Moç., Cx. 6, Saldanha de Albuquerque to Crown, Moç., 28 December 1758, also in *A.C.*, IV (1919), p. 215.
23. A.H.U., Moç., Cx. 7, *bando*, Saldanha de Albuquerque, Moç., 14 January 1759; ibid., report of Gregório Taumaturgo de Brito to Governor, with Mavere's mark and Arabic signature of the interpreter, Motomonho, 16 January 1759; A.H.U., Cod. 1317, fl. 105–6, 'Registo de Outra Ordem sobre devassar do incendio succedido em Mutomonho', Saldanha de Albuquerque, Moç., 9 September 1759.
24. A.H.U., Moç., Cx. 6, *bando*, Saldanha de Albuquerque, Moç., 5 September 1758; A.H.U., Cod. 1317, fl. 245 and Cod. 1320, no. 166, Tomé Joaquim da Costa Corte Real to Saldanha de Albuquerque, Ajuda, 5 April 1760; A.H.U., Moç., Cx. 8

and Cx. 9, and Cod. 1317, fl. 247, royal *bando*, Ajuda, 5 April 1760, published at Mozambique on 1 August 1760; A.H.U., Moç., Cx. 12, Henriques to Pereira do Lago, Cabaceira, 23 October 1766.

25. A.H.U., Moç., Cx. 4, Brito Freire to Crown, Lisboa, 8 November 1754, paragraph 30; Figueiredo, 'Noticia', pp. 263–4; Montaury, 'Moçambique', pp. 349–50.

26. A.H.U., Cod. 1317, fl. 216–17, *bando*, Saldanha de Albuquerque, Moç., 1 May 1760; A.H.U., Moç., Cx. 11, João Pereira da Silva Barba, Moç., 23 June 1764.

27. A.H.U., Moç., Cx. 7 and Cod. 1317, fl. 73–4, 'Proposta aos Moradores, e habitantes desta Praça de Mossambique, Portuguezes, Naturaes de Goa, e Nacionaes desta Terra', Saldanha de Albuquerque, Moç., 14 July 1759; ibid., fl. 71, Saldanha de Albuquerque to Sec. St., Moç., 16 August 1759.

28. Barreto, 'Supplimento da Informação do Estado e Conquista dos Rios de Cuama', in Theal, *Records*, III, p. 502.

29. Crown to Marques de Leurical, Lisboa occidental, 3 May 1741, in ibid., V, pp. 190–2; Cunha Rivara, *Archivo Portuguez Oriental*, VI, pp. 467–9.

30. A.H.U., Moç., Cx. 5, royal decree, Lisboa, 29 March 1755; cf. B.M., Add. Ms. 28,163, fl. 466–7, royal *alvará*, Lisboa, 10 June 1755, also in Theal, *Records*, V, pp. 226–30; A.N.T.T., M.R., maço 603, 'Copia de Alvará porq̃ se faz publica a ordem de S. Mag.ᵉ, pella qual manda, que os Portos de Senna, Sofalla, e Inhambane sejão Livres para todos os seus Vassalos, mor.ᵉˢ de Goa, e das mais partes, e terras de Azia, sugeitas ao Seu Real Dominio', 29 July 1757. For a full discussion of this controversy, see Hoppe, *África Oriental Portuguesa*, Ch. 2, especially pp. 139–44.

31. Andrade, *Relações*, pp. 68, 79, 88–9, 96, 98; B.N.L., Pombalina 742, fl. 8–9, *bando*, Távora, Moç., 4 August 1750; A.H.U., Moç., Cx. 6, Conde de Ega to Crown, Moç., 16 August 1758; for more about the administration of Melo e Castro, see Lobato, 'A Ditadura do Primeiro Governador-Geral, em 1753', in his *Colonização*, pp. 139–61.

32. A.H.U., Moç., Cx. 6, proposal of the *Senado da Câmara* to Pereira, Moç., 9 May 1758; ibid., *bando*, Pereira, Moç., 11 May 1758.

33. A.H.U., Moç., Cx. 6, petition presented by forty Gentiles and fourteen Muslims to Pereira, Moç., 22 May 1758; ibid., *Senado da Câmara* to same, Moç., 4 June 1758; ibid., representation of Muslims to same, Moç., 7 June 1758; ibid., same to same, n.d. (the last two documents are enclosed in ibid., representation of Muslim traders to Conde de Ega, Moç., 25 July 1758); ibid., Ega to Crown, Moç., 18 August 1758.

34. A.H.U., Moç., Cx. 6, representation of 'Baneanes, Guzerates, e Bangaçães, Mercadores todos', to Ega, Moç., 20 July 1758; ibid., representation of Muslim traders to same, Moç., 25 July 1758; ibid., *alvará*, Ega, Moç., 25 July 1758. In this *alvará*, the Viceroy also condemns an otherwise unknown proclamation by Pereira dated 8 April 1758 which specifically reversed the royal decree of 29 July 1757 as implemented by Melo e Castro.

35. A.H.U., Moç., Cx. 6, Ega to Crown, Moç., 18 August 1758; ibid., Pereira to Costa Corte Real, Moç., 10 August 1758.

36. A.H.U., Moç., Cx. 6, representation of Fr. João de Nossa Senhora, Moç., 8 August 1758; A.H.U., Moç., Cx. 7, Saldanha de Albuquerque to Crown, Moç., 2 January 1759, enclosing representation of 'Baneanes, Mouros e mais gentios habitantes desta Praça', to Gov., 1758; A.H.U., Cod. 1320, no 174, Costa Corte Real to same, Ajuda, 5 April 1760, enclosing latter's reply to same, Moç., 9 August 1760; A.H.U., Cod. 1317, fl. 146–8, Saldanha de Albuquerque to Episcopal Administrator, Moç., 10 September 1759; ibid., fl. 148–51, further correspondence and orders, dated 5, 10, and 11 September 1759, all relating to licensing Muslims to cross over from Mozambique to the mainland to trade; ibid., fl. 310–13, same to Crown, Moç., 5 August 1760; ibid., fl. 247–8, same to Costa Corte Real, Moç., 14 August 1760, enclosing, fl. 248–51, his *bando* of 10 August 1760 concerning the instruction of Christian slaves, the Episcopal Administrator's letter to him of 24

July 1760, 'Sobre a extirpação da Seita dos Mouros', and related documents; cf. Andrade, *Relações*, pp. 67–102, for a decidedly pro-Church account of the preceding and related events.

37. A.H.U., Cod. 1323, fl. 56, Francisco Xavier de Mendonça Furtado to Governor, Ajuda, 27 May 1761; cf. A.H.U., Cod. 1332, fl. 121–6.

38. A.H.U., Moç., Cx. 6 and Cod. 1324, fl. 69–70, *bando*, Silva Barba, Moç., 31 January 1763.

39. ibid., fl. 287–8, *bando*, Silva Barba, Moç., 7 March 1765. Silva Barba also sought initially to appease anti-Indian sentiment at Mozambique by Lusitanizing the post of *tareiro* or ivory evaluator. Each tusk of ivory had to be examined for flaws (*taras*), caused by age and weathering, before final classification by weight. The *tareiro* estimated the weight loss which would result from cleaning. This estimate, also called the *tara*, was usually more than five *arráteis* and was written inside the base of the tusk of ivory and subtracted from its gross weight. Lobato claims that the *tara* was always exorbitant as a result of a mutual understanding between the Indian *tareiros* and the Indian merchants, as a result of which the Crown lost revenue in the export tax on ivory. By 1765, however, this experiment had failed, and Silva Barba again appointed an Indian as a *tareiro*. See ibid., fl. 76–7, *bando*, Silva Barba, Moç., 1 March 1763; ibid., fl. 80–1, *provisão*, Silva Barba, appointing Miguel Machado and António da Costa as *tareiros*, both dated 9 March 1763; ibid., fl. 316, *portaria*, Silva Barba, nominating Anagy Monagy as a *tareiro*, Moç., 9 August 1765.

40. A.H.U., Moç., Cx. 12, 'Mapa dado . . . pello Juiz, e Ver.es da Camr.ª, dos Mor.es, e habit.es Nesta mesma Cap.tal, e terras firmas . . .', Moç., 30 May 1766, enclosed in Pereira do Lago to Crown, Moç., 20 August 1766.

41. Costa Mendes, *Catalogo*, p. 17.

42. A.H.U., Moç., Cx. 12 and Cod. 1325, fl. 20–31, petition presented by 'os homens de negocio, moradores nesta Capital, e Terra firma', to Pereira do Lago, Moç., 4 March 1766.

43. ibid., testimonies from various officials, confirmation of the company on 11 March 1766, and terms of office for its administrators, 3 May 1766; A.H.U., Moç., Cx. 12 and Cx. 33, Cod. 1321, fl. 168–9, and Cod. 1325, fl. 149–51, Pereira do Lago to Mendonça Furtado, Moç., 15 August 1766; A.H.U., Cod. 1322, pp. 185–8, same to *Conselho Ultramarino*, Moç., 15 August 1766; A.H.U., Moç., Cx. 12, same to Crown, Moç., 24 August 1766; see also A.H.U., Cod. 1321, fl. 200–1, and Cod. 1325, fl. 48–9, 'os Deputados da Comp.ª do Mujaos' to Pereira do Lago, Moç., 24 May 1766, and his reply, Moç., 30 May 1766. The statutes of the company as approved by Pereira do Lago on 11 March 1766 are also published in Hoppe, *África Oriental Portuguesa*, pp. 353–61.

44. A.H.U., Cod. 1322, fl. 40, *auto da posse*, Silva Barba, Moç., 6 January 1763; A.H.U., Moç., Cx. 9, Crown to Calisto Rangel Pereira de Sá, Ajuda, 7 May 1761; cf. A.H.U., Cod. 1322, fl. 75–95; Teixeira Botelho, *História*, I, pp. 360–66, for a summary of the instructions of organization; A.H.U., Cod. 1327, fl. 22, Crown to Governor, Lisboa, 24 March 1763, being orders concerning the abolition of the Royal Monopoly of *velório*. Calisto Rangel had been nominated to succeed Saldanha de Albuquerque, but died en route to Mozambique.

45. A.H.U., Cod. 1321, fl. 242–3, Pereira do Lago to Sec. St., Moç., 20 August 1767; Montaury, 'Moçambique', p. 350; A.H.U., Moç., Cx. 12, Benevides Cirne, 'Narração . . .', Moç., post-August 1766; A.H.U., Moç., Cx. 15, Pereira do Lago to Crown, Moç., 25 November 1775, enclosing Figueiredo, 'Narração dos descaminhos da Fazenda Real', Ajuda, 21 March 1768, with Pereira's answers to the charges therein, Moç., 20 November 1775; A.H.U., Cod. 1333, no. 337, Mendonça Furtado to Pereira do Lago, Ajuda, 18 March 1768.

46. A.H.U., Cod. 1332, fl. 35–6 and 45–6, Pereira do Lago to Sec. St., Moç., 20 September 1768.

47. A.H.U., Cod. 1329, fl. 236–7, *bando*, Pereira do Lago, Moç., 13 January 1768.
48. A.H.U., Cod. 1325, fl. 163–91, and B.N.L., F.G., Cx. 12, Document 25, Pereira do Lago, instructions to his successor, Moç., 20 August 1768; a bowdlerized version of these instructions, omitting the references cited in the text, is in Andrade, *Relações*, pp. 317–38.
49. A.H.U., Cod. 1322, pp. 251–3, two letters of Pereira do Lago to Crown, Moç., both dated 14 August 1769.
50. Lobato, *Evolução*, p. 270. Lobato's source is the anonymous 'Noticias de Moçambique e Suas Conquistas', which is in his own library. He dates the manuscript to 'a little later' than 11 November 1754 and states that it was written at the request of the ambassador extraordinary Francisco Xavier da Assis Pacheco de Sampaio, who was then at Mozambique on his way back to Portugal from China. See Lobato, *Colonização*, pp. 139–40. *Cera* is the Portuguese word for wax. A former meaning was 'the weight of 3½, or 3¼ *arráteis*, of wax,' and the term came to be applied to ivory of about the same weight. When the official weight limit of this category of ivory was later doubled, the term continued to be used. *Grande Dicionário da Lingua Portuguesa*, 10th edition, II, p. 1094.
51. Lobato, *Evolução*, p. 270; A.H.U., Moç., Cx. 6, 'Extracto do Rendim.to da Alfandega desta Ilha e Fortaleza de Monss.e de tempo de 3 annos comesiados no de 1754, e acabados no de 1756', António Francisco Xavier, Moç., 18 August 1758 (an incomplete copy also in A.H.U., Moç., Cx. 5).
52. Milburn and Thornton, *Oriental Commerce*, p. 39, where they give the following information on sales of ivory tusks from Mozambique: 'those above 16 seers' weight, by the maund of 40 seers; under 16, and not under 10, by that of 60 seers; under 10, and not under 5, by that of 80 seers; under 5, by that of 160 seers'; Hoppe, *África Oriental Portuguesa*, pp. 216–17.
53. A.H.U., Moç., Cx. 4, *provisão*, Melo e Castro, Moç., 20 June 1753; Hoppe, *África Oriental Portuguesa*, p. 143.
54. A.H.U., Moç., Cx. 12, *caderno* of Francisco António Xavier, Moç., 1767.
55. A.N.T.T., M.R., maço 603, Melo e Castro to Crown, Moç., 20 November 1753. A decade later it was charged that Swahili traders from Sanculo were also siphoning off the trade of the Rivers, as a result of the same conditions, as well as introducing Islam to the Africans. They were said to be operating at Murrambala, near Sena. See A.H.U., Moç., Cx. 9, Marco António Azevedo Coutinho de Montaury to Crown, Sena, 19 July 1762.
56. Anonymous, 'Memorias da Costa d'Africa Oriental', p. 218; Lobato, *Evolução*, pp. 270–1.
57. For Xavier's opinion on the 41 per cent tax as applied to cloths, see Xavier, 'Notícias', pp. 179–81; A.H.U., Cod. 1321, fl. 72–3, Mendonça Furtado to Saldanha de Albuquerque, Ajuda, 25 May 1761, and reply, Moç., 19 August 1762; A.H.U., Moç., Cx. 10, Silva Barba to Mendonça Furtado, Moç., 15 August 1763.
58. Isaacman, *Mozambique*, p. 84.
59. In Hoppe, *África Oriental Portuguesa*, p. 354.
60. Price, 'More about the Maravi', p. 78; Cunha Rivara, *O Chronista de Tissuary*, IV, p. 61; anonymous, 'Memorias da Costa d'Africa Oriental', p. 204; Varella, 'Descrição', p. 402.
61. Anonymous, 'Memorias da Costa d'Africa Oriental', p. 204. See also N.A.I.P.G., L.M. 103-A, fl. 13–16, Fróis to Viceroy, Goa, 28 December 1734, where Fróis refers to 'the Provinces of the Oranjes, and Anvuas', beyond Zumbo; cf. Barreto, 'Informação', p. 481, on the Amvuas.
62. Nicola Sutherland-Harris, 'Zambian Trade with Zumbo in the Eighteenth Century', in Gray and Birmingham, *Pre-Colonial African Trade*, pp. 233–5.
63. Ian Cunnison, *The Luapula Peoples of Northern Rhodesia* (Manchester, 1959), pp. 39–53; Roberts, 'Pre-Colonial Trade in Zambia', *African Social Research*, 10 (1970), p. 729. For a description of modern Bisa local trade, see Bruce Kapferer, *Co-*

operation, Leadership and Village Structure: a preliminary economic and political study of ten Bisa villages in the Northern Province of Zambia, Zambian Paper No. 1 (Manchester, 1967).

64. Anonymous, 'Memorias da Costa d'Africa Oriental', p. 204.

65. Abdallah, *The Yaos*, p. 28.

66. O'Neill, 'Three Months' Journey', p. 203, and 'Journey from Mozambique', pp. 644, 730–2, 739–40.

67. Heinrich Barth, 'Routes from Kano to Nyffe, and from Mozambique to Lake Nyassi. Extracted from letters from Dr. Barth, dated Kano, March 4th, and Luka, July 25th, 1851', *Jl. of the Royal Geographical Society*, XXIV (1854), pp. 285–8. There is no mention of this meeting with Sherif Mohammed in Barth's *Travels*. Cf. the misleading suggestions concerning routes to the coast in Rangeley, 'The Ayao', *Nyasaland Jl.*, XVI, 1 (1963), pp. 7–27, and 'The Arabs', *Nyasaland Jl.*, XVI, 2 (1963), p. 22.

68. A.H.U., Moç., Cx. 4, Melo e Castro to Crown, Moç., 27 December 1753, also enclosed in A.H.U., Moç., Cx. 5, *parecer, Conselho Ultramarino*, Lisboa, 26 March 1755; cf. ibid., Melo e Castro to Costa Corte Real, Moç., 29 November 1753.

69. A.H.U., Cod. 1317, fl. 185–94, 'Sobre a perda da Navio Francez no dentro da Fortaleza', Saldanha de Albuquerque to Sec. St., Moç., 15 August 1760, followed by seven documents relating to same subject, dated between 5 January–8 August 1760; A.H.U., Moç., Cx. 10, 'Rezumo da Receita da Alfandega desde 1.º de Janeiro, the fim de Dezembro de 1763', and similar, undated fragment, but probably from the same year.

70. A.H.U., Cod. 1321, fl. 191–92, Pereira do Lago to Sec. St., Moç., 20 August 1766; see A.H.U., Cod. 1324, fl. 330–1, passport issued by Pereira do Lago to Francisco Bertrand, captain of the corvette *Nossa Senhora da Conceição, e Pérola*, Moç., 16 October 1765; A.H.U., Cod. 1329, fl. 69–70, passport issued by same to Francisco dos Santos e Silva, captain of the ship *Nossa Senhora do Rosário, Santo António, e Almas*, Moç., 6 September 1766.

71. A.H.U., Cod. 1333, no. 350, Mendonça Furtado to Pereira do Lago, Ajuda, 29 March 1768; Montaury, 'Moçambique', p. 351; Figueiredo, 'Noticia', p. 254; A.H.U., Moç., Cx. 5, Melo e Castro to Crown, Moç., 18 August 1755; A.H.U., Moç., Cx. 4, same to same, Moç., 27 December 1753, enclosing 'Carregação dos Escravos . . . p.ª serem vendidos no Rio de Janeiro', Caetano da Silva e Savdra, 1 January 1754.

72. Xavier, 'Notícias', pp. 153–4.

73. A.N.T.T., M.R., maço 603, Melo e Castro to Crown, Moç., 20 November 1753; same to same, Moç., 10 August 1756, in *A.C.*, III, 16 (1918), p. 161; Teixeira Botelho, *História*, I, pp. 427, 434, 458. A great many of the Portuguese inhabitants of the Kerimba Islands appear to have been mulattoes.

74. A.H.U., Moç., Cx. 9, Saldanha de Albuquerque to Crown, Moç., 28 November 1762; A.H.U., Cod. 1324, fl. 21–2, *bando*, Saldanha de Albuquerque, Moç., 5 May 1762; ibid., fl. 26–7, registration of this *bando*, João de Meneses, Ibo, 25 May 1762; ibid., fl. 232, *bando*, Silva Barba, Moç., 26 May 1764; A.H.U., Cod. 1325, fl. 44–5, and Cod. 1329, fl. 172, *bando*, Pereira do Lago, Moç., 12 May 1767. Today what was formerly known as Ibo Island is called Queramba Island, of which the town of São João de Ibo is the capital. What is now designated as Ibo Island is a tiny islet lying to the east and in the shadow of Queramba Island. Querimba Island has maintained its name without change since the eighteenth century.

75. A.H.U., Moç., Cx. 11, Caetano Alberto Judice to Pereira do Lago, Ibo, 15 December 1765; A.H.U., Moç., Cx. 12, same to same, Ibo, 20 April 1766; ibid., João Baptista to Judice, Bringano, 3 May 1766; ibid., Judice to Pereira do Lago, Bringano, 26 June 1766; ibid., Baptista to Judice, Bringano, 28 June 1766; ibid., Judice to Pereira do Lago, Ibo, 1 September 1766; ibid., same to same, Ibo, 27 October 1766; ibid., Fr. Domingos de Deus to Judice (?), Vamizi, 8 April 1766;

A.H.U., Cod. 1324, fl. 35, *provisão* naming João Baptista to be Sergeant-Major of Vamizi Island, Saldanha de Albuquerque, Moç., 7 December 1762; cf. Teixeira Botelho, *História*, I, pp. 377–80.

76. A.H.U., Moç., Cx. 6, João da Costa to Governor (?), Querimba, 5 May 1758; A.H.U., Moç., Cx. 9, Vitório Vasconcelos da Silva to João de Morais, Querimba, 14 April 1761, mentioning a chieftain named Mutubulla; A.H.U., Moç., Cx. 11, Judice to Pereira do Lago, Ibo, 15 December 1765; A.H.U., Cod. 1331, fl. 181–2, *carta patente*, naming João Baptista as Commandant, Pereira do Lago, Moç., 17 April 1769.

77. A.H.U., Moç., Cx. 11, Baptista to Judice (?), Vamizi, 19 October 1764; A.H.U., Cod. 1324, fl. 300–1, *carta patente*, naming João da Silva Ferreira as Sergeant-Major of the Auxiliary Troops of Cape Delgado, Silva Barba, Moç., 29 April 1765; A.H.U., Moç., Cx. 12, Baptista to Judice, Vamizi (?), April 1766.

78. Alexander Dalrymple, *Plan of Querimboo and the Adjacent Islands, From a Portuguese MS. supposed by Capt.ⁿ Bento de Almedoe*, 1 November 1779, including a note explaining how to identify the islands of Querimba and Ibo by a Mr. Alexander Sibbald, 'who was on this coast about 1753'; A.H.U., Moç., Cx. 11, Baptista to Judice (?), Vamizi, 19 October 1764.

79. A.N.F., Colonies C⁴7, pp. 3, 4, 12, 15, De Lozier Bouvet to Syndics and Directors of the *Compagnie des Indes*, 31 August and 31 December 1753; A.H.U., Moç., Cx. 4, Brito Freire to Crown, Lisboa, 8 November 1754, paragraph 90; A.H.U., Cod. 1310, fl. 4–5, Melo e Castro to Manuel de Sousa e Brito, Moç., 22 July 1753; A.H.U., Cod. 1307, p. 291, royal *alvará*, Lisboa, 10 April 1756.

80. A.H.U., Cod. 1313, fl. 73–4, Saldanha de Albuquerque to Crown, Moç., 27 December 1758, also in Andrade, *Relações*, pp. 591–2; cf. Xavier, 'Notícias', p. 153.

81. A.H.U., Moç., Cx. 6, Saldanha de Albuquerque to Crown, Moç., 30 December 1758, also in *A.C.*, IV (1919), pp. 76–9; A.H.U., Moç., Cx. 7, same to same, Moç., 1 January 1759; A.H.U., Cod. 1317, fl. 8, same to Costa Corte Real, Moç., 4 August 1759; A.H.U., Moç., Cx. 8, same to Crown, Moç., 18 August 1760; see also A.H.U., Cod. 1317, fl. 257–8, Costa Corte Real to Saldanha de Albuquerque, Ajuda, 5 April 1760.

82. A.H.U., Moç., Cx. 5, Melo e Castro to Crown, Moç., 27 November 1754, enclosing report from the sailors of the *Santa Ana e São Francisco de Paula*, who had gone to Ibo to build a fort there, Querimba, 1 November 1754.

83. A.H.U., Moç., Cx. 7 and Cod. 1317, fl. 72–3, King of Kilwa to Governor of Mozambique, n.d. This letter was received at Mozambique on either 20 or 24 April 1759. Cf. Guillain, *Documents*, I, p. 555.

84. Freeman-Grenville, *The French at Kilwa Island—An Episode in Eighteenth-Century East African History* (Oxford, 1965), p. 82.

85. A.H.U., Cod. 1317, fl. 215, Saldanha de Albuquerque to King of Kilwa, Moç., 12 May 1760; A.H.U., Cod. 1329, fl. 225, *alvará*, Pereira do Lago, Moç., 11 January 1768.

86. A.H.U., Cod. 1310, fl. 53–4, Melo e Castro to Sousa e Brito, Moç., 19 May 1754.

87. For references to these raids, see Alpers, 'French Slave Trade', p. 95, n. 1.

88. A.H.U., Moç., Cx. 10, José Rodrigo Barros to Saldanha de Albuquerque, Ibo, 24 July 1762; A.H.U., Cod. 1324, fl. 27–8, *bando*, Saldanha de Albuquerque, Moç., 16 August 1762; A.H.U., Moç., Cx. 10, *Conselho Ultramarino* to Saldanha de Albuquerque, Lisboa, 25 June 1763, enclosing Saldanha de Albuquerque to Crown, Moç., 25 November 1762; A.H.U., Cod. 1324, fl. 300–1, *carta patente* of Silva Ferreira, Silva Barba, Moç., 29 April 1765.

89. A.H.U., Cod. 1328, fl. 322, *bando*, Silva Barba, Moç., 9 (?) May 1763; A.H.U., Moç., Cx. 11, Judice to Silva Barba, Ibo, 17 July 1765; ibid., same to Pereira do Lago, Ibo, 11 October and 15 December 1765; A.H.U., Cod. 1328, fl. 321–39, various letters from Mozambique to Portuguese officials in the Kerimba Islands, 26 April 1763–21 April 1769.

90. The Swahili *History of Sudi* states that it was the capital of Mwanya (Moanha) and that the first Sultan of Sudi was a Shirazi named Mwenyi Mwanya. The Makonde are only spoken of as being up-country folk, distinct from the coastal inhabitants of Sudi, but this is not surprising in a late nineteenth-century Swahili document. Freeman-Grenville, *Select Documents*, pp. 230–2. The name of the town and its chief are virtually identical: Mongalo/Mungumanha/Mwenyi Mwanya/Mgau Mwania.
91. A.H.U., Moç., Cx. 12, Judice to Pereira do Lago, Bringano, 26 June 1766, and Ibo, 1 September 1766.
92. A.H.U., Moç., Cx. 13, João Ferreira da Cruz to Pereira do Lago, Ibo, 8 July 1769.
93. Strandes, *Portuguese Period*, pp. 302–4; A.H.U., Cod. 1328, fl. 330–1, Pereira do Lago to Judice, Moç., 26 January 1766; Freeman–Grenville, *French at Kilwa*, pp. 151–2.
94. A.H.U., Moç., Cx. 14, Pereira do Lago to Crown, Moç., 21 January 1770; cf. A.H.U., Cod. 1332, fl. 48–51, 53–4, same to Sec. St., Moç., 20 January 1770; A.H.U., Moç., Cx. 14, same to Crown, Moç., 20 January 1770, enclosing Judice to Pereira do Lago, Moç., 15 January 1770.

CHAPTER FIVE

The Undermining of the Mozambique Ivory Market, 1770–1785

The prosperity of Mozambique during the eighteenth century had been built upon the ivory trade of East Central Africa, but its future wealth was to derive increasingly from the slave trade. Although there is no reason why these two trades could not co-exist, as they did from this period at Kilwa, at Mozambique a unique combination of factors brought them directly into conflict with each other. Specifically, whereas the ivory trade was almost exclusively capitalized by Indian merchants, the slave trade was largely capitalized by Europeans; and whereas the ivory trade was largely in the hands of the Yao, the slave trade became mainly an affair of the Makua. During the fifteen years after 1770 the complex interweaving of elements involving both of these trades and their major participants affected adversely the operation of the ivory trade at Mozambique. In the early 1780s these various processes, together with the continued resuscitation of the Zanzibar-Kilwa market, combined to cause such severe disruption in the normal operation of trade there that it is possible to date the demise of Mozambique's domination of the ivory trade of East Central Africa from 1785, although the process was not completed until about 1810.

The Official Attack on Indian Control of the Ivory Trade

Perhaps more than anything else, Portuguese efforts to restrict the commercial power of the Banyan traders of Mozambique served to depress the ivory market there. Pereira do Lago maintained Silva Barba's position on controlling the Banyans' access to the mainland and subordinate ports, but beyond this restriction he would not commit himself, despite unremitting pressure from the colonists, and his own inclinations.[1] He understood far too well the pivotal role which the Banyans played in the economy of the capital to risk undermining its entire structure. One week after his death, however, public sentiment again unleashed its frustration as it had during the brief administration of David Marques Pereira in 1758, blaming all the commercial ills of Mozambique on the Banyans in a petition dated 10 June 1779.[2]

In the two decades since the 1750s the Indian resident community at Mozambique had increased its population by half to some three hundred persons, nearly all of them male adults, while their holdings on the mainland also appear to have increased. By 1781, there were about two dozen Banyan trading houses established at Mossuril and the Cabaceiras.[3] Compared to the situation in the middle of the century, when the Indian community was apparently larger than that of the colonists, however, the increase in the Portuguese population of the island and the mainland settlements to more than four hundred Portuguese by the late 1770s meant that Indians were now a minority of the total population of the capital of Portuguese East Africa.[4] But their continued monopoly of the supply of Indian trading cloths made it virtually impossible for any colonist to compete with them in trading for ivory with the Yao and the Makua. In addition, whereas in the 1750s it was rare for more than one ship to come from Diu and one from Daman each year to Mozambique, twenty years later it was normal for five to arrive there from Diu alone in a single monsoon.[5] This increase was a direct consequence of the termination in 1777 of the monopoly of the Mozambique trade from Diu by the Company of the Mazanes, which had been established in 1686. Freed from this restriction, the energetic Banyan traders of Diu thereafter converged on Mozambique in unprecedented numbers. That there was a proportionate seasonal increase in the Indian population of the island is attested to by the fact that Saldanha de Albuquerque was greeted by more than three hundred Banyans upon his arrival there in 1782.[6] Coinciding as it did with the height of the Yao trading season, this increase in the Indian population of Mozambique probably exacerbated what were already very strained relations with the Portuguese population, although it must be recognized that many of these were engaged in trading to the Rivers of Sena, Inhambane, and Delagoa Bay, rather than Macuana.[7]

The accusatory petition of the colonists of Mozambique received no official response until the arrival at the year's end of the new Governor-General, Fr. José de Vasconcelos de Almeida.[8] Eager to enrich himself, Vasconcelos de Almeida was only too willing to attack the commercial monopoly of the Banyans. On 27 May 1780, in response to the wishes of the *Senado da Câmara* and the colonists at large, he issued a proclamation which prohibited the trade of the Yao and all the mainland to 'all those who are not nationals of this Continent, and Portuguese'. He also formed an exclusive company of twelve men, with himself at its head, to trade with the Yao. The effect of these two measures was completely to eliminate the Banyans from trading on the Mozambique mainland.[9] Few details are known about this new *Sociedade de Mujao* (Yao Society), but the Governor-General's measures against the Banyans were later spoken of as being unusually harsh. Seeing no other way to prosecute their case at Mozambique, the Banyans retaliated by not ordering any trade cloths to come from Diu in the south-west monsoon of 1780-1, as a result of which the revenue from importation duties fell by some 35,000 *cruzados* in the latter year.[10] But this was scarcely of any concern to Vasconcelos de Almeida, who died with a fortune of more than 90,000 *cruzados* on 7 May 1781.[11]

The measures taken against the Indians of Mozambique Island by Vasconcelos de Almeida affected the Yao and Makua ivory traders at Mossuril no less disastrously. In the early 1780s the *feira de Mujaos* at Mossuril, where all commercial transactions with the Yao and Makua were now negotiated, still handled 'the best trade of all others that are lauded in this [part of] Africa', as the Banyans themselves attested.[12] The Banyans had gained a monopoly of this trade both by giving the Yao and the Makua a better price for their ivory and by using considerably more acumen in their personal, as well as commercial, relations with them than did the Portuguese. For their part, the Portuguese looked upon the Africans merely as 'barbarians', and saw no reason to trade intelligently with them. Mozambique being their colony, they believed that the Africans should naturally come to trade with them, at whatever price they chose. The Banyans were neither so myopic nor so naive. According to a petition from the Portuguese colonists, the Banyans

> through their slaves, make themselves known to the various [Makua] chiefs at the price of large presents, so that these

chiefs should direct to them not only the produce of their own lands, but also the Yao, who pass through their territory, and resorting to these subtleties in this manner, they make the chiefs believe that only they themselves are masters of the shipments of cloths, and that they alone order these to come to their country.[13]

That the last part of the colonists' indictment of the Banyans was more truth than subtlety is evident, but the whole statement does serve to illustrate the way in which the Banyans carefully wooed the cooperation of the Makua chiefs.

In another tirade against the trading practices of the Banyans, the *Senado da Câmara* complained that whereas the Portuguese had formerly bought ivory 'with the usual cloths', they were no longer able to do so, because the Banyans had

insinuated themselves into, and corrupted, the Yao and Makua, solely to attract their trade, by cleverly giving them fashionable wide-sleeved tunics, caps, and shoes, with new colours, which they especially order to come from Diu . . . the negroes, seeing these strange painted cloths to be to their liking every year, hasten to the Banyans, and not to any Christian trader, and when one accidently does so, he leaves disconsolate, and certainly does not return again. And the rest is that when it is time for the Yao to come, the Banyans immediately send their *patamares* half way out along the route, only in order to induce and forestall them from going to the colonists.[14]

Finally, the Banyans realised that to conduct business profitably it was essential to deal reasonably with their African suppliers on a personal level, for Pereira do Lago observed with a certain lack of comprehension that 'the Kaffirs respect them'. The only Portuguese colonist of whom this was said to be true was João de Morais, who was widely respected by the Africans of the Cape Delgado mainland.[15]

In view of these conditions, and of the fact that the Banyans gave the Yao a consistently better price for their ivory,[16] it seems beyond dispute that any measures which prevented the Banyans from trading on the mainland with the Yao would have discouraged many of them from trading with the Portuguese at Mossuril. In addition to the various restrictions which were imposed on their freedom to trade, Vasconcelos de Almeida's regulations lowering the official price of ivory can only have had a similar effect. Incorporated in his 1780 proclamation against the

Banyans, this measure established that ivory could not be purchased from the Yao and Makua at a price greater than 40 *cruzados* per *arroba*, which was considerably less than the official 'price of the land' of 56 *cruzados* per *arroba* which had prevailed at the *feira de Mujaos* since the 1760s.[17] The Yao and Makua, who were famous for 'the excessive price for which they reckoned ivory', must have been greatly angered by such high-handed measures.[18] Nor was the corporation of merchants known for its generosity, but rather for 'selling the cloths which they carried to the Negroes at very high prices, and buying very cheaply the goods which they received from them; which is precisely the way to ruin at its foundations all the Portuguese business [and] to make ourselves odious to the Negroes'.[19]

Following the death of Vasconcelos de Almeida, the *Senado da Câmara* elected the senior military officer of the colony, Vicente Caetano da Maia e Vasconcelos, to succeed as Governor-General. Although he had been an intimate councillor of his predecessor, as well as a member of his exclusive trading society, he did not seek to propagate that monopoly under his own tutelage. But he did press the assault against the Banyans in other ways, in an effort to throw open the trade with the Yao and the Makua to the entire local Portuguese community.[20] On 1 June 1781, Maia e Vasconcelos promulgated yet another decree which specifically and absolutely forbade all Banyans from going to trade at Mossuril with the Yao. According to its terms, they were only to sell their cloth to colonists on the island, and only at prices established by the officials of the customs-house. As a palliative, he made provisions facilitating the collection of their debts from the colonists, who always bought on credit, but this was scarcely a satisfactory substitute for the right to trade for themselves, at prices responsive to the home market.[21] The ensuing conflict which raged over the legality of this decree mimicked those which had preceded it. In the end, the outcome was determined not by legalities, but by economics. Faced with the practical impossibility of breaking the Banyans' monopoly over the supply of Indian trade cloths to Mozambique, and fearful that the customs-house would suffer another crushing loss of revenue in the coming year, the *Senado da Câmara* and Maia e Vasconcelos reluctantly bowed before the economic pressure which the Banyans were able to exert if they so chose. It also appears that another form of economic pressure, the crossed palm, was influential in convincing the Governor-

General and the *Senado* to tolerate the Banyans. On 7 August both agreed to the granting of licences which would allow individual Banyans 'to go to the mainland of Mossuril to trade for ivory with the Yao, Makua, and other Kaffir nations', notwithstanding the decree of 1 June 1781, from which the licensees would be excepted. Licences were immediately granted to seventeen Banyans.[22] Nevertheless, the effect of these measures scarcely alleviated the main problem confronting the Yao and Makua, as the artificially depressed evaluation of ivory continued to remain in force.

As a parting shot, Maia e Vasconcelos dispatched a scathing letter denouncing the Banyans to the Crown.[23] Together with Pereira do Lago's retrospective condemnation, it now fell on more sympathetic ears in Lisbon, where the fanatically devout Queen Maria I (1777–1816) was much less inclined to protect enemies of the faith than any previous monarch. Finally, the complete reversal of Saldanha de Albuquerque's attitude, when he resumed the governorship in late August 1782, transformed him from the Indians' champion into their most bitterly prejudiced adversary, and signalled yet another major assault on the position of the Indian trading community of Mozambique.

The new Governor-General's orders not only specifically disapproved of the licensing arrangement of his predecessor, but also provided that he was 'under no circumstances, to grant the trade of the continent to the Banyans and Moors'.[24] Saldanha de Albuquerque immediately ordered the withdrawal of all Indians to the island-capital. The effectiveness of this measure seems to have been minimal. Far more drastically for the trade of Macuana, he ordered that all those Banyans who owned property, including slaves, on the mainland, must sell all to Christian colonists within a month.[25] This order was not implemented at once, but the compilation in December of a list of all the property owned by Banyans at Mozambique and on the mainland indicates that Saldanha de Albuquerque had certainly not abandoned the idea. At the same time, the *Senado da Câmara* was taking other steps to break the commercial power of the Banyans on the mainland. These means included the forcible eviction of the local Swahili and Makua, whom the *Senado* regarded as agents of the Banyans in their trading with the Yao, from the settlements of Nandoa, Mutamulamba, and Savasava.[26]

By the following dry season, the cumulative effect of these

measures had led to their logical conclusion: the virtual suspension of trade.[27] Saldanha de Albuquerque's solution to the problem of invigorating and Lusitanizing the trade of the colony was to propose the formation of a new monopolistic trading company, despite his earlier condemnation of Almeida de Vansconcelos's company.[28] At first, Saldanha de Albuquerque, the *Senado da Câmara*, and the principal Portuguese merchants were strongly inclined towards making it an exclusively Portuguese concern. In the end, however, the reasoning of António de Morais Durão, Chief Justice of the colony, persuaded them that unless the principal Banyan merchants of the island were admitted into the company, not only would it be doomed to financial failure, but it would certainly be rejected by the Crown, as the Banyans were 'Vassals of the Sovereign, like the rest'. In its final form, the corporation had a monopoly of all trade in common cloths, beads, ivory, rhinoceros horn, hippopotamus teeth, and cashew wine, although significantly the buying of slaves remained outside its provenance. The trade of these items was to be controlled throughout Portuguese East Africa, except for Delagoa Bay, which was controlled by a separate society of traders.[29] Standard prices were to be fixed for all cloths and for ivory, which were the most important of all articles of trade. The numerous conditions for the establishment of the company were subscribed to by eighteen colonists and thirteen Banyans.[30]

The new corporation was not without its opponents, mainly those disgruntled Portuguese who were excluded from it. It was also attacked by the merchants of Daman. Not least of all, it failed to fulfill its purpose, as trade and revenue plummeted. Besides, as Alexandre Lobato has so rightly observed, it was customary 'to undo, before long, all the works of any governor'.[31] Thus, Saldanha de Albuquerque's corporation shortly came to the same end, after his death on 24 November 1783, as had that of Vasconcelos de Almeida. Sometime thereafter the ceiling on ivory prices also seems to have been removed, and the pre-1780 prices re-established.[32] But while the Crown ordered on 2 March 1785 'that trade should continue to be carried on with the same Freedom which formerly was practised', it equally stipulated 'that the prohibition of the Banyans trading personally on the mainland should remain in effect, until her Majesty, being better informed, should determine what seems fitting in this matter'.[33]

The Promotion of the Slave Trade and the Deterioration of Luso-Makua Relations

While the ivory trade at Mozambique was being racked by the uninhibited official Portuguese assault on the commercial position of the Indian community, the slave trade was encouraged by considerable, though illicit, support. At the international level, this increase in the demand for slaves from this part of the continent was brought about by the French plantation colonies on the Mascarene Islands. Peace with England in Europe, and thus in the Indian Ocean, was one factor making for greater movement of trade from the Mascarenes. More important, though, was the abolition of the trading monopoly which the French *Compagnie des Indes* exercised over the islands, and the inauguration of free trade. These factors, together with the increasing hazards of slave trading at Madagascar, caused the French to turn increasingly to Portuguese East Africa, and eventually to the Swahili coast. At Mozambique French trading was carefully nurtured by Pereira do Lago, who built himself a massive fortune by local standards through patronage of the slave trade. By the time of his death in June 1779 the slave trade at Mozambique was an ingrained institution in the economic life of the Portuguese capital. The same held true for the Kerimba Islands, where Pereira do Lago's example and his ransoming of the office of Captain-General to the highest bidder encouraged a mirror situation. In both districts, virtually all the local colonists were involved in one capacity or another in this trade.

Although prices were reasonable at both Mozambique and Ibo, the nuisance of having to pay for each individual service there eventually caused the French to explore the possibility of trading along the Swahili coast. The opportunistic Jean-Vincent Morice pioneered this trade and in 1776 concluded his well-known one hundred year treaty for principal rights in the European slave trade at Kilwa with Sultan Hasan bin Ibrahim.[34] Most of his trade was for the supply of the Mascarenes, but Morice was also involved in the opening up of slave trading from East Africa to the French Antilles, a trade which briefly exploded later in the 1780s. Kilwa was also the principal entrepôt for the 'Umani slave market at Zanzibar, which is where Morice learned about it in the first place. Beyond the French and the Arabs, then, there were no other major slavers operating in East African waters until the Brazilians became more aggressive in the late eighteenth century.

It is very difficult to gauge the volume of this augmented slave trade, so much of which was carried out beyond the reach of European documentation. Contemporary figures and generalizations suggest that perhaps 1,500 slaves were exported annually from Mozambique during the 1770s, this figure rising somewhat in the early years of the following decade. At Ibo the figure of 1,500 annual exportations seems to have held steady throughout this period, while at Kilwa the French slave trade maintained about this same level from about 1775. As for the 'Umani slave trade, of which we are woefully ignorant until the nineteenth century, a crude guess based upon Morice's generalized comments suggests that possibly 1,500 to 2,000 individuals were exported annually from the Swahili coast. The majority of these slaves were probably re-exported from Zanzibar to 'Uman, where they were employed in domestic service and on date plantations, or transported elsewhere in the Persian Gulf for the markets of the Muslim world. With respect to the prices paid for slaves in East Africa at this time, the French found those purchased at Kilwa to be considerably less expensive than those coming from the Mozambique coast. Of greater significance for African traders supplying these growing slave markets, however, is the fact that during the course of a decade the price which the French paid for slaves at both Kilwa and Mozambique had doubled. Although most of this increase was absorbed by the middlemen in the slave trade—Portuguese officialdom and the Sultan of Kilwa—at least some of these profits were also passed on to the African providers of slaves, if only as a necessary inducement to their bringing ever increasing numbers of men, women, and children to the coast for sale into bondage.

Where did the brunt of this trade fall? Morice's initiative at Kilwa tapped a valuable new source of slaves for the French colonists of the Mascarenes. But despite the lower cost of the slaves at Kilwa, Morice concluded that slaves from Mozambique 'are preferred to those from Kilwa and are sold for a higher price in Ile de France', an observation which is substantiated by the comment of Joseph-François Charpentier de Cossigny, Morice's correspondent on the island, that 'the Makua slaves they bring to Ile de France are the most esteemed of all the Mozambique people'.[35] Undoubtedly, the great majority of slaves exported from Ibo were Makua, the remainder being Makonde, but it is more difficult to determine the ethnic origin of those embarked at Mozambique, which drew on the resources of the entire colony. Pereira do Lago's remark that 'the Yao introduce infinite numbers of slaves here, and Macuana has no other commerce', helps but little. According to one authority, however, of every 1,000 slaves exported from Mozambique by the French, 150 came from Yao and 370 from the Makua, with the remainder coming from Sofala (80), Inhambane (150), and Sena (250). But while Portuguese sources confirm the popularity of the Makua, as slaves, with the French, they themselves viewed the situation rather differently. As José Joaquim de Segreira Magalhães Lançous wrote, the French 'bring the best merchandise, which is money, and take away the worst commodities, which are Makua slaves'.[36] This sentiment, which probably was shared by all the Portuguese of Mozambique, was a reflection of the radically deteriorated state of relations between the Makua and the Portuguese, a situation which was a direct result of the increased tempo of the French slave trade at that port.

Ever since its beginnings in the 1730s the slave trade had been an important factor in the political economy of Macuana. In particular, it enabled Makua chiefs to increase their military power, partly through the acquisition of firearms and partly through the accumulation of cloth and beads with which to attract and reward their followers. Their aggressiveness since mid-century was probably not, however, simply a reflection of their increased striking power. More likely, it was a reflection of their increasingly sensitive links to the market for slaves at Mozambique. According to Pereira do Lago, relations with the Makua had been tense since 1772.[37] But according to another well-informed authority, there were other, more specific factors which led to the resumption of open warfare between the Makua and the Portuguese in the mid-1770s. In 1774, during the height of Pereira do Lago's slave trading with the French, one of the most active local participants was João Francisco Delgado, the Captain-Major of the Mainland. Unsatisfied with the profit that he was making by trading openly, he is said to have begun secretly to seize free Africans who were residents of Voacella, a small settlement situated two leagues from Mossuril on the route to Uticulo. These he also sold to the French. Delgado was soon joined by Mateus Coelho de Castro, and the two kidnappers applied themselves diligently to this profitable but risky business. Within a very short time, 'Voacella was depopulated, as it is still found today'. The Murimuno, who exercised political authority over Voacella, naturally sought satisfaction from the Portuguese, but neither his solicitations nor his threats evoked any response from Delgado. Thus, on 6 January 1776, the Murimuno swept over Mossuril at the head of more than 8,000 'well armed Kaffirs', burning and looting everything at hand. More than one hundred Portuguese, or their followers, were killed, and many captives, including Portuguese, were seized. Both the fortress and the church were robbed, and the Makua returned to their settlements, leaving the field 'full of truncated bodies, and the survivors filled with such a fear that they never more will lose it'.[38]

Pereira do Lago's initial efforts to punish the Murimuno failed completely, and eight months later the Makua were still terrorizing the Portuguese mainland. Food supplies were low at Mozambique because the Makua had prohibited all trade with the Portuguese. By August 1776, however, Pereira do Lago had enlisted the aid of more than twenty Makua chieftains from Cambira, 'who always were useful due to their farming and their good friendship with the Portuguese'. These Makua had long been anxious to establish their domination over Uticulo, so they willingly took up the Portuguese cause as a cover for their own ambitions. As such, their accommodation with the Portuguese was a typical instance of differently motivated African and European self-interests intersecting at a point in time for the achievement of a common goal, in this case the conquest of the powerful Makua chiefs of Uticulo. The Mocutoamuno, one of the most powerful of the Cambira chieftains and a long-standing ally of the Portuguese, commanded this force, which soon drove the Murimuno's people out of their villages and farther into the hinterland.[39] Nevertheless, two years later Portuguese holdings on the mainland were still largely abandoned, and their owners were ever fearful of 'the continual threat of those indomitable Kaffirs', a situation which was unchanged at the time of Pereira do Lago's death in 1779.[40] His policy of setting rival Makua groups against each other for the benefit of the Mozambique colony eventually backfired, however, for in the early 1780s the Mocutoamuno was numbered among the enemies of the Portuguese, as an ally of the Murimuno and the other important chieftains of Uticulo.[41]

7   *Mozambique and Macuana*

The unsettled conditions at Mossuril and in Uticulo in the later 1770s could only have prejudiced long-distance trading to Mozambique, as they had in previous years. The Yao route to Mozambique took them through Uticulo, and there is no evidence that they ever reached Mozambique by detouring through Cambira. Certainly their trade to Mossuril must have been severely disturbed during the chaotic year of 1776. That nothing further is heard of the Yao until 1778, however, and then only very little, is partially due to the sparseness of documentation for the entire decade; but it also seems to be indicative of a decline in the volume of trade being driven by the Yao to Mozambique, a conclusion which is attested to by the events of the succeeding years.

Pereira do Lago's successors in the government of Mozambique had no more success than he in dealing with the belligerent Makua of Uticulo. Indeed, until the return of Saldanha de Albuquerque as Governor-General in 1782, they seem to have had little interest in restoring order to the mainland. At the end of 1779, the Portuguese mainland remained in a state of total confusion as a result of the constant raiding of the Makua. What trade was still carried on was subjected to the robberies of the Makua of Uticulo. Half a year later, Makua incursions appear to have been less frequent and less serious, but the situation on the mainland was still precarious.[42] When Saldanha de Albuquerque arrived at Mozambique, he found that the general terror of a Makua raid was so pronounced that a single shout announcing their approach could send all the Portuguese on the mainland fleeing to their boats. In order to give himself time to formulate a plan of action, Saldanha de Albuquerque conveyed his wishes for peace to the Makua, together with presents for the chiefs, as had been the custom of each government since January 1776. As usual, the chiefs agreed, but within two months the Makua had resumed their raiding of the Portuguese mainland settlements. After consulting with the ranking officials of the capital, the Governor-General opted for a new war against the Makua of Uticulo.

It was decided to attack Uticulo in a pincer movement employing the regular and auxiliary troops of Mozambique, the combined forces of numerous 'friendly' Makua chieftains, those of the Sheikhs of Sanculo and Quitangonha, and a special force coming overland from the Cape Delgado mainland. These were all to go into action at the beginning of October 1783, on the arrival of the Cape Delgado force. But its commander, Joaquim José da Costa Portugal, who was also Governor of that district, fell seriously ill on the banks of the Lurio River, and the expedition was detained there into November. The Murimuno took advantage of this delay and launched a quick, effective attack on Matibane, in the jurisdiction of the Sheikh of Quitangonha. By the end of the month, Saldanha de Albuquerque had died. As specified by law, the colony was then entrusted to a provisional government consisting of the senior military, judicial, and clerical officials at Mozambique until a new Governor-General was nominated by the Crown.[43] At first, the new government was divided on the issue of whether or not to pursue the war, which had begun so inauspiciously, but the repeated and increasingly bold sweeps of the Makua soon determined them to persist in that effort.[44]

On 8 January 1784, the Cape Delgado force, less than 200 men strong, but supported by the powerful Makua chief Inhamacomu, who was also known as Comalla, attacked Uticulo. This foray produced no permanent results, however, and a fortnight later the Portuguese again struck at Uticulo, concentrating on the Murimuno's own village of Mutipa. This time they met with greater success. With the tide of battle running their way now, the Portuguese pressed their advantage and on 11 February launched an even more successful attack against the enemy. This initiative was followed by independent assaults made by the Sheikhs of Quitangonha and Sanculo. By this time the Makua had suffered considerable losses, and many had fled from Uticulo. Weary of fighting, their chiefs sent five ambassadors to Cabaceira Grande with orders to make peace with the Portuguese.[45]

Before they would agree to call off hostilities, the Portuguese required the fulfilment of certain conditions of peace by the Makua. These included a call for the cessation of all hostilities among themselves, as well as with the Portuguese, support against foreign threats, and the return of fugitive slaves. More important for the economic history of Mozambique is the inclusion of an article which states: 'That they [the Makua] must allow the Yao, or any other Kaffirs who should come to trade with the Portuguese, to pass freely through their territory'.[46] The Murimuno, whose territory was nearest to the Portuguese mainland settlements and who had suffered the greatest losses, was willing to accept peace on these terms, but the other chiefs of Uticulo— the Mauruça, the Maviamuno, and the Mevorimuno, as well as the Mocutoamuno of Cambira—refused to abide by them. The Murimuno accordingly came to the coast to make his peace with the Portuguese, but his arrival was almost immediately followed on 8 June by another concerted Makua attack on Mossuril and the Cabaceiras, causing considerable damage and resulting in the capture of many prisoners of war. Nine days later, preparations were completed for the departure of a major expedition to crush the Mauruça. Portuguese forces were again joined by large contingents supplied by the Sheikhs of Quitangonha and Sanculo, so that the army numbered some 3,000 men. Seeing an ideal opportunity to increase his own authority, the Comalla independently declared war on the Mocutoamuno from his stronghold in Cambira. By 15 July the Portuguese force had returned to the coast, largely successful in its appointed mission. All the chiefs of Uticulo, save only the powerful Mauruça, now sued for peace.[47]

On 24 July 1784, the Murimuno formally ceded his country and its government to the Queen of Portugal, declaring himself to be her vassal. For their part, the Portuguese allowed him to continue as chief under their protection, which was their way of admitting that they were in no position to do otherwise, so long as he remained faithful and obedient. Formal possession of this newest conquest, which included the villages of Mutipa, Namuxixi, Greja, Namusupe, and their districts, was taken for the Portuguese Crown by Rodrigo da Fonseca, the Sergeant-Major of the Mainland, on 13 September 1784, in the presence of the Murimuno and his people's elders. Things were not so neatly concluded with the other Makua chiefs of Uticulo, whose greater distance from the coast made their professions of peace rather less certain. Although the Comalla was trying to establish one of his nephews as chief of Uticulo, it was feared that if Comalla's plan succeeded, the Portuguese might one day be faced with a more powerful enemy than those whom they had just defeated. But the Comalla had again shown his good faith by refusing to ally himself with some of the Mauruça's followers, so that nothing seems to have been done to discourage him from pursuing his design. For a while, at least, their faith in the Comalla was rewarded. Peace reigned, and after nearly a decade of devastating hostilities, relations between the Portuguese and the Makua were again free of open strife.[48]

Kilwa's Revival and the Penetration of Coastal Influence in the Interior

The combined effect on the trade of the Yao to Mossuril of these turbulent years of Portuguese conflict with the Makua in Macuana and with the Indian traders at Mozambique was striking. According to João Ferreira Nobre, an important colonist at Mozambique, during the war of 1783–4 the Makua so destroyed everything, disrupting both the trade and the agriculture of the mainland,

> that great famines have been experienced, all through their hindering the trade which they used to have with the inhabitants of the mainland, as it was also customary for large groups

of the Yao Kaffirs, traders from the far interior of the hinterland, to come to these shores every year with their merchandise, such as ivory, slaves, rice, and other goods which their lands yield; these, as soon as they had reports of the new campaign from the first who arrived here, turned around and took the route to Mombasa, and Mafia, and went there to trade, and up to the present there has been no news of them.[49]

Certainly, the fighting in Macuana made Mossuril a less attractive port of trade for the Yao than it had been in mid-century, but perhaps even more damaging to the position of Mozambique as a major outlet for the ivory of East Central Africa was the artificially depressed price which the Portuguese hierarchy imposed on the market from 1781 until about 1784.[50] Indeed, Sheriff has suggested that the war of 1783–1784 'may have been triggered by the price ceiling and what the Makua may have interpreted as a Portuguese attempt to cheat them'.[51] It must be remembered, however, that by this time the main staple of Makua trade in Macuana was slaves, and the slave trade was specifically excluded from the purview of the trading company organized by Saldanha de Albuquerque in 1782–1783. Moreover, prices in the slave market had doubled over the course of this decade. But in view of the fact that the Makua still traded some ivory to Mossuril, Makua objections to the price ceiling on ivory in the early 1780s were very likely a contributing factor to the general deterioration of their relations with the Portuguese. If the Makua were perturbed by Portuguese meddling in the ivory market, surely the Yao were even more affected by it. Indeed, by the 1780s the Yao were bringing no more than 100 to 130 *bares* of ivory to Mozambique annually, and the sum of all of their seasonal trading, which also included slaves, iron, provisions, fowl, and tobacco, was calculated at being worth no more than 300,000 *cruzados*[52] This was still a considerable volume of business, as the Indian traders pointed out at this time, but it was much reduced from the peak years of the 1750s, when the Yao traded 400 to 500 *bares* of ivory, which alone was worth 400,000 to 500,000 *cruzados*, to Mozambique in each trading season.[53]

It is typical of Portuguese officialdom that they rarely saw the flight of African trade from Mozambique as at least partly the result of their own damaging policies. As they had been doing for four decades now, most Portuguese persisted in the belief that the sole cause of this important change in the routing of Yao trade to the coast was the establishment of other Europeans—in this instance, the French at Kilwa—on the Swahili coast.

> From it unerringly follows a great deterioration of the trade of this Captaincy, because all of the Yao who carry their slaves, ivory, and other goods here, making our trade flourish, will necessarily bear them to Kilwa, not only because it is a shorter journey, but also, and principally, because they receive all the Kaffir cloth which they come to seek here at very moderate prices from the French; and besides this, they receive all the supply of powder, and arms, which is denied to them here, and these will pass easily to the Makua, our ancient enemy; already the customs-house duties are diminished, and all will shortly fall into total ruin.[54]

Yet even the Portuguese, while they remained preoccupied with illusory European imperial threats along the Swahili coast, also realized that 'it is true that in Kilwa, and on the island of Zanzibar (principally the latter), the Arabs of Masqat carry on a considerable trade'.[55] Chief among these was the Imam of 'Uman, who during the 1770s dispatched each year a large shipment of trading goods destined exclusively to purchase ivory.[56]

The key to this reinvigorated Arab trade in East Africa was the close relations between Masqat and Surat. Morice specifically commented on the Imam's intimate links with Surat and the British, thus confirming Xavier's impressions of two decades previously. All the trade cloths coming to Zanzibar and then Kilwa were supplied from Surat, usually by Banyan merchants, and all of the ivory bought with them was sold there. Finally, in addition to the Imam's personal trading vessel, each year the Muslim Indians of Surat sent two vessels of three to four hundred tons each to Zanzibar to trade salt and cloth in exchange for slaves, most of whom came from Kilwa.[57] Taken together with the vigorous new French demand for slaves along the Swahili coast, the steady growth of Indo-'Umani trade at Kilwa undoubtedly made it an increasingly attractive destination for the Yao. It follows, too, that from about this time the Yao must have been increasingly involved in trading slaves, as well as ivory, to Kilwa.

It is one thing to assert that the Yao were affected at this time by the growing demand for slaves at Kilwa; it is quite another to determine the extent of that influence. According to Morice, slaves reached Kilwa from the interior by means of a relay system. A few years later, another French slave trader wrote vaguely that 'the slaves caught in the neighbourhood are of very good quality'. But he also noted that the Swahili and Arabs acquired slaves at Mongalo, where they

> take from it a prodigious number of blacks [*in margin:* inferior to those of Kilwa but which they bring there to sell to us], particularly from the river Mongallo, a little known river which flows through fertile and thickly populated country stretching a long way inland.[58]

The provenance of slaves at Mongalo becomes a bit more precise in a report made by Saulnier de Mondevit, a French commercial agent, in 1785.

> Mongalo is the part of the African coast most sunken in the continent; consequently, it is nearer to the mountains inhabited by the Makua, the Makonde, the Ndonde, and the Yao, all different people, continually at war, solely to make each other prisoners, whom they sell. The bands of slaves from this part would come out of preference to Mongalo if there were a European establishment there.[59]

While it was surely an exaggeration to state that these peoples were constantly raiding each other for slaves to be sold at the coast, Saulnier's evidence suggests strongly that the principal source of slaves along the Kilwa coast was the more thickly populated country to the south of Kilwa, including the Makonde plateau and the well-watered country towards (and probably including) the Ruvuma River valley. Whether his inclusion of the Yao in this context indicates that Yao from farther up-country were not yet involved in slave-trading cannot be determined. The one certainty is that Kilwa was experiencing a definite commercial revival, based upon the reinvigorated 'Umani ivory trade and the French slave trade, and that the market-conscious Yao cannot have escaped the influence of either.

Had conditions been more favourable in Macuana, at Mossuril, and on Mozambique Island, the revival of Kilwa might not have so adversely affected the Yao trade to the south. But this was not the case, as we have seen. The high price of trade cloths, Portuguese interference in the operation of the ivory market, and hostilities in Macuana were scarcely conducive to stable market conditions. When order was restored in Macuana, and the price ceiling on ivory lifted, the ivory trade of the Yao to Mozambique would resume, but it was never again to approach the level of the 1750s.

Kilwa, by contrast, was entering a new era of stability in its economic history, and its merchants could afford to offer African traders a better price for their ivory. One of the most striking measures of the renewed vitality of Kilwa's economy is the beginning of Swahili penetration and influence in the interior. Before the second half of the eighteenth century a few adventurous souls from Kilwa undoubtedly travelled inland to trade, but these would have been isolated cases. By the 1780s, more meaningful contact between the coast and interior was established through the activities of Swahili and of superficially acculturated Yao traders. Morice made several references to Swahili traders travelling inland and crossing the continent to the coast of Angola. In view of the developing links between the coast of East Africa and the Mwata Kazembe's capital on the Luapula River, and of the intimate commercial relations between Kazembe and the Angolan coast, these references, however vague and garbled, cannot be dismissed merely as something Morice invented.[60] More open to challenge is Morice's belief that organized caravans departed on this transcontinental journey every year. Nevertheless, there are several independent African sources which confirm the opening of trading connections across Lake Nyasa and thence to the coast during this period.

According to the traditions of the Tumbuka people of northern Malawi, at about this time there arrived an immigrant group called the Balowoka, meaning 'those who have crossed over' from the east side of Lake Nyasa. Led by the eponymous Mlowoka, these men were traders who came dressed 'as Arabs', attracted to the country by rumours of rich sources of ivory. They were not disappointed, for 'the locals were found using tusks as seats, bedprops and so forth without any idea of trading value'.[61] While it is not possible to date the coming of the Balowoka precisely, Tumbuka traditions and Morice's evidence from the coast suggest a date of about 1770–1780, a date upon which students of Tumbuka history are in accord. Less certainty exists for the identification of the Balowoka, but the prime candidates are the Yao, perhaps intermingled with Swahili or Swahili-influenced people from the coast.[62] Whoever they were before reaching Tumbuka country, the Balowoka moved inland up the Henga River valley and rapidly established themselves as valued purveyors of the previously unknown cloths and beads which were used in trading for ivory.

The Balowoka were not content to leave this valuable trade exposed to the good-neighbourliness of the loosely organized Tumbuka. Spreading themselves out across the country, they settled among the Tumbuka as a group of trading chiefs, exercising a very loose hegemony over the people as a whole. Mlowoka made several strategic marriages and established for himself a local economic and political base at Nkhamanga, a pattern which was emulated by his followers. As their leader, he was able to coordinate the placement of his companions, so that within their lifetimes a genuine system of trade was created. By presenting the pre-existing Tumbuka chiefs with turbans of dark blue or black cloth—another obvious sign of coastal influence—Mlowoka both recognized their political authority and bound them to his side in recognition of his superior economic skills, with which most of them were quite happy to be identified. At no time during his own lifetime, however, did Mlowoka attempt to exercise political influence over the Tumbuka. Rather, as Leroy Vail has recently argued,

> the area organized by Mlowoka and ruled over by his successors was a trade route, with lieutenants placed along the route at strategic points on an East-West line to protect the ivory trade and its Lake Shore embarkation points. What Mlowoka organized and his successors 'ruled over' was less a state than a trade route for ivory.[63]

Eventually, this route linked up with the Bisa in the west, so that by the end of the eighteenth century, at the very latest, it is likely that the Balowoka were able to tap some of the same general sources of ivory as the Yao trading farther to the south.

To the north of the Tumbuka, evidence of coastal penetration into the interior is also found among the Ngonde. In contrast to the situation among the Tumbuka, however, the Ngonde are said to have recognized a central monarch under the Kyungu dynasty, which was linked closely to the Nyakyusa and Kinga chiefs around the north end of the lake. Royal traditions of the Ngonde state explicitly that although the authority of all the early kings was primarily ritual, with the kings themselves living in religious seclusion, the first Kyungu also established a profitable trade to the north, 'over the hills of the Ndali', in ivory and cloth, which he distributed to the indigenous chiefs as recognition of their position.[64] All of this accords well with what is known about the development of trade in the interior of East Central Africa during the late eighteenth and nineteenth centuries, but it rings a very false note when it is applied to the earliest period (*c.* 1400) of Ngonde history.[65] A developed ivory trade following a northern route from Ngonde country is quite out of step with the whole context of East African economic history in the fifteenth century. What seems far more likely is that we are here faced with a vivid example of the telescoping of events from one period back into another. Perhaps, too, the Kyungu dynasty did not exercise anything more than local control until a much later period, and the claims for royal control of the Ngonde before that time only reflect a typical attempt at political legitimization.

More plausibly, it is recalled that during the reign of Kyungu X Mwangende, in about the last quarter of the eighteenth century, a new trade route was opened across the north end of the lake with people called the Marabi, who were rowed across by the Mwela. 'These traders brought cloths, red and white and dark cloths'.[66] These cloths they traded for ivory. Dynastic tradition claims that the previously secluded Kyungu now emerged to take control of this new ivory trade, thereby increasing his secular control and limiting that of the hereditary nobility. Whether it is as received tradition would have it, or whether it is a case of the Kyungu dynasty only asserting its control over all the Ngonde as a result of its control of the new ivory trade across the lake, cannot be settled without further examination of a wider spectrum of Ngonde traditions. What counts here is that among the Ngonde, as in the case of the Tumbuka, there exists striking evidence of the varying impact of the opening of the far interior in the last decades of the eighteenth century.

By this time, then, there appear to have been three basic water routes across Lake Nyasa. One linked the extreme northern shores of the lake, joining Mwelya country to Ngonde. A second crossed the lake eastwards from Manda, or thereabouts, to the west shore, probably between Deep Bay and Mwamlowe, where the Balowoka were developing their control over the trade of Nkhamanga and the Henga valley.[67] The third, and earliest lake crossing, joined the southernmost shores, as we have already seen. Each of these routes would appear to have met, finally, at the Kilwa coast, although the two northern routes may also have carried trade to the Mrima coast around Bagamoyo, just as the route from Ng'ombo and Mwala, on the south-eastern lakeshore, could lead to Mozambique. Certainly the opening of the two northern routes reflects the revitalization of the trading economy of the Swahili coast during the second half of the eighteenth century.

On the Kilwa coast itself, there are traditions dating from this period which parallel those of the Ngonde and, in particular, the Tumbuka. According to the severely truncated and often inaccurate Swahili *Ancient History of Kilwa Kivinje*, trade between the lake and this still unimportant town was inaugurated by a man named Mkwinda.[68] Mkwinda originally hailed from around the lake and had lived at Machinga, in the Kilwa hinterland, for some years before settling at Kivinje. Surprisingly enough, this Mkwinda seems to have been an historical person and not merely an archetypal founding figure. According to Abdallah bin Hemedi 'lAjjemy, the author of the official history of the Kilindi dynasty of the Shambaa of north-eastern Tanzania, the paternal grandfather of his mother was Mwinyi Mkwinda of Kilwa Kivinje, 'who came from the Masaninga tribe in Nyasaland'. So Mkwinda came apparently from that section of the Yao-speaking people who are known to have been the undisputed leaders in trade and state-building during the nineteenth century.[69] Together with his kinsman Mroka, who also moved from the lake to settle at Kivinje, they plied their wares far inland, because 'at this time trade was very profitable, because the people of the hinterland were stupid, not knowing the value of things of this coast'.[70] Disregarding the ethnocentricity of this statement, it seems very likely that Mkwinda and Mroka were involved in the opening up of the west side of the lake to trade, since there can have been few people fitting their description among the Yao or their neighbours to the east of the lake.[71]

The northern routes from Lake Nyasa to Kilwa can only be vaguely reconstructed. These were little used in the nineteenth century, owing to the presence of the Ngoni in Songea, but the route from Manda probably followed the valley of the Ruhuhu River up onto the plateau before heading off towards the coast. The northern route more likely ascended the mountains of southern Tanzania before following the valleys of either the Great Ruaha or Kilombero Rivers, both of which ultimately feed the Rufiji River, to the coast.[72] For the Yao, however, there is a very precise route of march which has been recorded by Abdallah.

For the most part, this route followed that taken by Gaspar Bocarro in 1616. In addition to Ng'ombo, Abdallah names Likowe and the site by Fort Johnston which was later to become the town of the major chief of the Machinga Yao, Mponda, as important lakeshore termini of this route. From the lake, according to an itinerary provided for Abdallah by Che Nalelo, the route progressed through the heart of Yaoland, well to the west of the Lujenda River. Following a general north-easterly direction, it crossed the Lusanyando River, which arises to the east of the Lucheringo River, and crossed the Ruvuma to the south-west of Tunduru, the modern centre of Yao concentration in Tanzania. From there it passed through Chisyungule, Tunduru, and Mang'wang'wa until it reached the Mbwemkuru River. The route ran parallel to the river northwards until it turned sharply north-north-eastwards beyond the confluence of the Nakiu River. The route finally descended the coast to Kilwa Kivinje, passing on the way through the long-established villages at Migeregere and Singino Hill.[73]

It is important to emphasize at this point that the trade along this route still remained firmly in African hands. Arabs did not travel along the Yao route until well into the nineteenth century, and the Swahili who seem to have been doing so in the late eighteenth century were most probably men like Mkwinda and Mroka, men whose connections were still as much with the far interior as with the coast. Their actions in opening up the country to the north-west of Lake Nyasa to the ivory trade are noteworthy not only for the important impact which they had on the history of peoples like the Tumbuka and Ngonde, but also for the strong inferential evidence they provide for the growth of the ivory market at Kilwa.

By early 1785, however, just as these pioneering traders were edging across the lake, Kilwa Kisiwani was losing its embattled independence for the last time to the Bu Sa'idi rulers of 'Uman.[74] In 1783, Ahmad ibn Sa'id, Imam of 'Uman and founder of the Bu Sa'idi dynasty, died. He was succeeded by his son, Sa'id ibn Ahmad. A younger son, Saif, disputed his brother's claim to the Imamate, but realizing that there was no hope of his gaining support at home, he set out for East Africa with his followers in an attempt to create his own dominion there. At first, Saif sought supporters along the coast, primarily at Kilwa, where he met the French slaver Crassons, who was then engaged in negotiating a new trading agreement with the Sultan. Crassons obligingly offered armaments and money to Saif, but he was refused. Early in 1784, Saif landed at Zanzibar. Unsuccessful in his attempt to storm the fortress there, he began a leisurely siege. Before long, however, a substantial expedition arrived from Masqat to press the Imam's claims along the coast. Saif was persuaded to relinquish his bid for the throne and was permitted to retire to Lamu, where he died shortly thereafter.

After strengthening 'Umani control of Zanzibar, one ship from the squadron was sent to Mombasa, which was taken without a struggle in late January 1785. Other vessels were sent south along the coast with instructions to receive the obeisance of the Swahili towns, in particular of Kilwa. At Kilwa the Arabs met with some resistance, as the Sultan of Kilwa, who may still have been an aging Hasan bin Ibrahim, cannot have been anxious to share the revenue from the once more prospering trade of his state with the Imam. But the Arabs soon won the day, under the leadership of a man named Masudi. Peace terms were negotiated by a certain Monsieur Sausse, whose ship was then anchored in the harbour. The Sultan was allowed to keep his title, but sovereignty, as well as between one-half and four-fifths of the customs dues paid at Kilwa, passed to the Imam of 'Uman.[75] Later in that same year, an Ali bin Saif, who may have been the son of the thwarted usurper, was appointed 'Umani governor of Kilwa and Mafia.

With an 'Umani governor to supervise its trade and an 'Umani garrison in the old Portuguese fort of São Tiago, Kilwa had indeed lost its independence. But the imposition of 'Umani rule in 1785 in no way inhibited the continued commercial growth of Kilwa. On the contrary, the reaffirmation of 'Umani involvement in East Africa, with secure bases at Zanzibar and Kilwa, created more stable conditions for trading than before, a fact which undoubtedly encouraged the further investment of Indian merchant capital there. During the next quarter century, the Yao and other peoples of the interior continued gradually to transfer most of their trade to the Kilwa coast.

NOTES

1. A.H.U., Moç., Cx. 19, Saldanha de Albuquerque to Crown, Moç., 12 August 1783, enclosing Pereira do Lago to Crown, Moç., 10 August 1772.
2. A.H.U., Moç., Cx. 17, *Senado da Câmara* to Prov. Govt., Moç., 10 June 1779, enclosing *requerimento dos moradores* to *Senado da Câmara*, n.d., both included among

documents pertaining to the *residência* of Fr. José de Vasconcelos e Almeida, conducted by João Nogueira da Cruz in 1781.

3. ibid., Maia e Vasconcelos to Crown, Moç., 18 August 1781; ibid., *residência* of Vasconcelos e Almeida, 1781; A.H.U., Moç., Cx. 19, 'Mappa daz Cazas, Palmares, Chãos, Negros, Negras, Gados, Navios, Bateis, e mais Embarcaçoens, q̃ possuem nesta Villa Cap.ᵃˡ de Moçambique os Banianes existente nella, e nas Terras firmes feito em o Mez de Dezembro de 1782 . . .', summarized in Teixeira Botelho *História*, I, p. 597, and Hoppe, *África Oriental Portuguesa*, pp. 182–3.

4. In 1776 the total number of Portuguese colonists of all ages was, in Mozambique, 270; in Mossuril, 71; in the Cabaceiras, 79; in 1778, the figures for each of these places were 271, 68, and 72, respectively: A.H.U., Moç., Cx. 15, anonymous, *mapas* of population of *moradores*, 21 May 1776, and 1778. Cf. Hoppe, *África Oriental Portuguesa*, p. 113, where the temporarily enlarged population figures of 1780 should be balanced against those for the following two decades.

5. A.C.L., Vermelho Ms 273, 'Noticias que da João Vitto das Ilhas de Cabo Delgado', n.d., published in Carvalho Dias, 'Fontes', p. 269; A.H.U., Moç., Cx. 17 and Cod. 1345, fl. 95–6, Maia e Vasconcelos to Crown, Moç., 18 August 1781; A.H.U., Moç., Cx. 19, Pereira do Lago to Crown. Moç., 10 August 1772; ibid., Saldanha de Albuquerque to Sec. St., Moç., 12 August 1783, also in *A.C.*, 1 (1917), p. 235.

6. ibid., p. 235.

7. For Indian traders in the Rivers of Sena, see Chapter 4, p. 122; for the ivory trade of southern Mozambique, see Alan K. Smith, 'The Struggle for Control of Southern Mozambique, 1720–1835', Ph.D. thesis, University of California, Los Angeles, 1970, especially pp. 149–50, 192–5, 235–41.

8. At the request of sixteen local merchants, however, among whom were included both Banyans and Muslim Indians, a plan was formulated by Diogo Guerreiro de Aboim, who as Chief Justice was a member of the provisional government, to organize a new company of trade for Mozambique which would end the disorders which free trade had brought to the colony. The plan was never implemented, nor did it make mention at all of the trade of Macuana or of the Yao, which presumably was intended to remain free. A.H.U., Moç., Cx. 16, two attestations that Aboim met with sixteen merchants to discuss the organization of trade at Mozambique, one initiated by Aboim, the other signed by the merchants, both dated Moç., 6 August 1779; A.N.T.T., M.R., maço 604, Aboim to Crown, Moç., 27 August 1779, enclosing his *Plano da Companhia*, Moç., 24 August 1779; A.H.U., Cod. 1472, fl. 3–4, Crown to Governor of Mozambique, Lisboa, 23 February 1781; see also A.H.U., India, maço 18, Aboim, 'Memoria rellativa ao decadente Estado, e interesses da Capitania de Mossambique', Lisboa, 24 Lanuary 1782; Lobato, *Lourenço Marques*, I, pp. 115–16. For still another proposal for curing the commerical ills of Mozambique, see A.N.T.T., M.R., maço 602, José Joaquim de Segreira Magalhães Lançous, 'Memorias sobre Mossambique', Goa, 5 August 1779, enclosed in same to Visconde da Vila Nova de Cerveira, Goa, 12 January 1780. Lançous was *Chancelor do Reino* at Goa and passed through Mozambique in 1778.

9. A.H.U., Moç., Cx. 16, *bando*, Vasconcelos de Almeida, Mossuril, 27 May 1780; A.N.T.T., M.R., maço 604, *residência* of Aboim, 27 November 1780 to 4 January 1781; A.H.U., Moç., Cx. 18, Ricardo José de Lima, 'Relaçam dos descaminhos, Gravames da Faz. ᵈᵃ Real, e Ruinas do Comercio no Governo de Monsambique', n.d., articles 15–16, enclosed in Raimundo Luís de Lima to Crown, Goa, 24 January 1781. Ricardo de Lima was *Procurador da Coroa* (Special Crown agent) at Mozambique and was imprisoned by Vasconcelos de Almeida for his diligence; the document was part of his *residência*. For orders to release Lima, see A.H.U., Cod. 1472, fl. 10, Crown to Saldanha de Albuquerque, Lisboa, 6 March 1782. See also ibid., fl. 13–14, and Cod. 1340, no. 448, Saldanha de Albuquerque to Crown, Junqueira, 15 October 1781; A.H.U., Moç., Cx. 16, Vasconcelos de Almeida to M. de Melo e Castro, Moç., 20 August 1780.

10. A.H.U., Moç., Cx. 17, Maia e Vasconcelos to Sec. St., Moç., 25 September 1781; ibid., *Senado da Câmara* to Governor, [Moç], 7 August 1781; ibid., A.H.U., Cod. 1345, fl. 95–6, and Cod. 1344, fl. 2–3, Maia e Vasconcelos to Crown, Moç., 18 August 1781.

11. A.H.U., Cod. 1472, fl. 38–39, Crown to Custódio Dias de Sousa, Ajuda, 7 March 1785, gives the official figure of 37:135/200 *réis*, or 92,838 *cruzados*; cf. Alcântara Guerreiro, 'Episódios', p. 97, paragraph 15, where a figure of over 100,000 *cruzados* is given.

12. A.H.U., Moç., Cx. 17 and Cod. 1345, fl. 52–5, 'Registo de Requerimento dos Baneanes mercadores existentes nesta Capital, sobre o Comercio da Terra firme de Mossuril', Moç., probably 28 June 1781.

13. A.H.U., Moç., Cx. 17, *requerimento dos moradores* to *Senado da Câmara*, n.d., enclosed in *Senado da Câmara* to Prov. Govt., Moç., 10 June 1779.

14. ibid., and Cod. 1345, fl. 62–7, 'Reposta da Camara', Moç., 14 July 1781, paragraph 6.

15. A.H.U., Moç., Cx. 19, Pereira do Lago to Crown, Moç., 10 August 1772; Vito, 'Noticias', p. 279; A.H.U., Moç., Cx. 17, Maia e Vasconcelos to Crown, Moç., 25 September 1781, and enclosures.

16. A.H.U., Moç., Cx. 19, Pereira do Lago to Crown, Moç., 10 August 1772; A.H.U., Moç., Cx. 17 and Cod. 1345, fl. 95–6, Maia e Vasconcelos to Crown, Moç., 18 August 1781; A.H.U., Moç., Cx. 18 and Cx. 19, *bando*, Saldanha de Albuquerque, Moç., 16 October 1782, and *alvará*, Saldanha de Albuquerque, Moç., 7 June 1783.

17. A.H.U., Moç., Cx. 16, *bando*, Vasconcelos de Almeida, Moç., 27 May 1780. For ivory prices, see Table 3, Chapter 4, p. 119.

18. A.H.U., Moç., Cx. 19, 'Condiçoens com que se fundou a Corporação', Moç., 5 June 1783, article 7.

19. A.H.U., Cod. 1472, fl. 47–9, M. de Melo e Castro to A. M. de Melo e Castro, Ajuda, 5 April 1785, paragraph 9, also in Lobato, *Lourenço Marques*, I, p. 135. Cf. A.H.U., Cod. 1472, fl. 43–4, Crown to Dias de Sousa, Ajuda, 30 March 1785.

20. ibid., fl. 40–3, same to same, Ajuda, 21 March 1785. Maia e Vasconcelos began by ordering that all Banyans living in the Kerímba Islands should be dispossessed and resettled at Mozambique, but he was unable to effect this directive. See A.H.U., Cod. 1345, fl. 12, Maia e Vascondelos to Governor of Cape Delgado Islands, Moç., 14 May 1781.

21. ibid., fl. 17–18, *bando*, Maia e Vasconcelos, Moç., 1 June 1781, and fl. 32–3, 9 June 1781.

22. A.H.U., Moç., Cx. 17, Maia e Vasconcelos to Sec. St., Moç., 25 September 1781, enclosing 'Requirimento dos Banianes mercadores existentes nesta Capital, sobre o Comercio da Terra firme de Mossuril', [Moç.], n.d., but probably 28 June 1781, and 'Reposta da Camara', Moç., 14 July 1781; copies of these and related documents also in A.H.U., Cod. 1345, fl. 52–67. A.H.U., Moç., Cx. 17, testimonies supporting the Banyans' case, Caetano de Quadros and José Francisco de Segreira e Pires, both dated Moç., 21 July 1781, and Inácio de Melo Alvim, Moç., 22 July 1781; A.H.U., Cod. 1345, fl. 68–80, 'Reposta dos mercadores Banianes', Moç., 3 August 1781; A.H.U., Moç., Cx. 17, *Senado da Câmara* to Governor, Moç., 7 August 1781; A.H.U., Cod. 1471, fl. 40–3, Crown to Dias de Sousa, Ajuda, 21 March 1785; A.H.U., Moç., Cx. 24, *devassa* of Maia e Vasconcelos, 1787; A.H.U., Cod. 1345, fl. 87, 'Registo da Licença se passou ao Baniane . . . Punja Velgy, p.ᵃ hir comerciar as terras firmes de Mossuril, e aos mais Banianes abaixo declarados', Moç., 2 August 1781, and *bando*, Maia e Vasconcelos, Moç., 7 August 1781.

23. A.H.U., Moç., Cx. 17 and Cod. 1345, fl. 95–6, same to Crown, Moç., 18 August 1781; see also A.H.U., Cod. 1340, no. 465, *Conselho Ultramarino* to Governor of Mozambique, Lisboa, 29 January 1782.

24. A.H.U., Cod. 1472, fl. 12–13, M. de Melo e Castro to Saldanha de Albuquerque, Ajuda, 8 March 1782; see *A.C.*, I (1917), pp. 213–5, 275–80, for the latter's most

vituperative anti-Banyan tirade (12 August 1783); see also, Boxer, *Race Relations*, pp. 83–4.

25. A.H.U., Moç., Cx. 18 and Cx. 19, and Cod. 1355, fl. 233, *bando*, Saldanha de Albuquerque, Moç., 16 October 1782; A.H.U., Moç., Cx. 17, same, fragment concerning his orders to the *Senado da Câmara* and their surveillance of the selling of Banyan's *patamares*, n.d.

26. A.H.U., Moc., Cx. 19, 'Mappa das Cazas ... q̃ possuem ... os Banianes', Moç., December 1782; A.H.U., Moç., Cx. 18, Caetano de Quadros to Saldanha de Albuquerque, Cabaceira, 24 December 1782; ibid., *Senado da Câmara* to António de Morais Durão, Moç., 15 January 1783; ibid., Morais Durão to Quadros, Moç., 18 January 1783.

27. A.H.U., Moç., Cx. 19, Saldanha de Albuquerque to M. de Melo e Castro, Moç., 1 August 1783.

28. See A.H.U., Cod, 1340, no. 448, and Cod. 1472, fl. 13–14, Saldanha de Albuquerque to Crown, Junqueira, 15 October 1781.

29. See Lobato, *Lourenço Marques*, I, pp. 124–6, 130, 132–3.

30. A.H.U., Moç., Cx. 19, Saldanha de Albuquerque to M. de Melo e Castro, Moç., 1 August 1783, enclosing copies of (a) Morais Durão to Saldanha de Albuquerque, Moç., 22 April 1783; (b) twelve Portuguese merchants to same, Moç., 29 April 1783; (c) Morais Durão to same, Moç., 2 May 1783; (d) eleven Portuguese Traders to same, Moç., 6 May 1783; (e) 'Condiçoens com que se fundou a Corporação', Moç., 5 June 1783; (f) *alvará*, Saldanha de Albuquerque, Moç., 7 June 1783. For details of the administration of the corporation, see Lobato, *Lourenço Marques*, I, pp. 117–20.

31. ibid., I, pp. 121–4, 134–5, 151.

32. A.H.U., Moç., Cx. 21, Maia e Vasconcelos to Fr. Amaro José de São Tomas and Morais Durão, Moç., 21 July 1784.

33. A.H.U., Cod. 1472, fl. 23–4, and Cod. 1357, no. 520, M. de Melo e Castro to A. M. de Melo e Castro, Samora Correa, 2 March 1785; see also A.H.U., Moç., Cx. 19, Maia e Vasconcelos to M. de Melo e Castro, Moç., 15 October 1783; ibid., Manuel da Costa to Crown, Moç., 10 November 1783; A.H.U., Moç., Cx. 21, Prov. Govt. to M. de Melo e Castro, Moç., 6 August 1784; A.H.U., Moç., Cx. 22, *bando*, Morais Durão and Maia e Vasconcelos, Moç., 22 August 1785. Cf. Teixeira Botelho, *História*, I, pp. 516–17.

34. See Freeman-Grenville, *French at Kilwa*, p. 71. For a full exposition of prices and gratuities in the slave trade at Mozambique, Ibo, and Kilwa, and for volume at Kilwa, see Alpers, 'French Slave Trade'.

35. Freeman-Grenville, *French at Kilwa*, pp. 183, 189.

36. A.H.U., Moç., Cx. 15, Pereira do Lago to Crown, Moç., 15 August 1778; A.H.U., Moç., Cx. 13, anonymous, 'Os Francezes extraem ...', n.d.; A.N.T.T., M.R., maço 602, Lançous, 'Memorias', Goa, 5 August 1779.

37. A.H.U., Moç., Cx. 15, Pereira do Lago to Crown, Moç., 15 August 1778.

38. Alcântara Guerreiro, 'Episódios', pp. 79–109.

39. A.H.U., Moç., Cx. 15 and Cod. 1332, fl. 236–8, Pereira do Lago to Crown, Moç., 15 August 1776; A.H.U., Moç., Cx. 15, same to Viceroy, Moç., 15 August 1776.

40. ibid., same to Crown, Moç., 15 August 1778; cf. ibid., Lançous to M. de Melo e Castro, Moç., 17 October 1778, mentioning a Makua raid on Sanculo.

41. Alcântara Guerreiro, 'Episódios', pp. 93, 103.

42. A.N.T.T., M.R., maço 604, Aboim to Crown, Moç,. 27 August 1779; A.H.U., Moç., Cx. 16, Fr. Francisco de Santa Teresa to Governor, Moç., 21 December 1779; ibid., Maia e Vasconcelos to M. de Melo e Castro, Moç., 18 August 1780; A.H.U., Moç., Cx. 17, same to same, Moç., 25 September 1781.

43. See A.H.U., Cod. 1472, fl. 14–15, royal *alvará*, Ajuda, 11 February 1782; cf. Lobato, *Lourenço Marques*, I, p. 69.

44. Alcântara Guerreiro, 'Episódios', pp. 98–100; A.H.U., Moç., Cx. 19, Saldanha de

Albuquerque to M. de Melo e Castro, Mossuril, 9 November 1783; ibid., Maia e Vasconcelos to same, Moç., 12 November 1783; A.H.U., Moç., Cx. 21, Prov. Govt. to same, Moç., 7 August 1784. Each of the first three sources presents a different version of how the war was conducted, as each author had his own case to argue. For details of the organization of the force from Ibo, see A.H.U., Moç., Cx. 20, Costa Portugal to Saldanha de Albuquerque, Ibo, 27 and 28 September 1783, and Alagoa de Cagavero, 3 October 1783; A.H.U., Moç., Cx. 21, João de Morais to Prov. Govt., Arimba, 22 July 1784.

45. Alcântara Guerreiro, 'Episódios', pp. 100–02; A.H.U., Moç., Cx. 21, Maia e Vasconcelos to M. de Melo e Castro, Moç., 18 August 1784; ibid., Francisco de Freitas, Moç., 23 February 1784.

46. Alcântara Guerreiro, 'Episódios', pp. 102–3; see A.H.U., Moç., Cx. 19, Maia e Vasconcelos to M. de Melo e Castro, Moç., 12 November 1783.

47. Alcântara Guerreiro, 'Episódios', pp. 103–9; A.H.U., Moç., Cx. 21, Maia e Vasconcelos to M. de Melo e Castro, Moç., 18 August 1784; ibid., same to Marquês de Angonja, Moç., 18 August 1784.

48. ibid., Prov. Govt. to M. de Melo e Castro, Moç., 6 August 1784, and enclosure, anonymous, Moç., 24 July 1784, describing the Murimuno's vassalage; A.H.U., Cod. 1355, fl. 55, portaria, Prov. Govt. to Rodrigo da Fonseca, Moç., 30 July 1784; ibid., fl. 55, Bernardo da Silva, 'Autto da Posse tomada das Povoaçoens abaixo declarada, e Seus destrictos por vertude da Portaria supra', 13 September 1784; A.H.U., Moç., Cx. 21, João Vicente de Cardenas e Mira to Senado da Câmara, Mossuril, 6 October 1784; ibid., reply, Moç., 7 October 1784; A.H.U., Moç., Cx. 23, Maia e Vasconcelos to M. de Melo e Castro, Moç., 20 August 1785.

49. A.H.U., Moç., Cx. 21, Nobre to Sec. St., Moç., 18 August 1784.

50. See A.H.U., Moç., Cx. 19, Maia e Vasconcelos to São Tomas and Morais Durão, Moç., 21 July 1784, in which he attributes the absence of the Yao to the effect of Saldanha de Albuquerque's corporation of merchants, which he bitterly opposed.

51. Sheriff, 'Rise of a Commerical Empire', p. 95.

52. A.H.U., Moç., Cx. 21, Maia e Vasconcelos to São Tomas and Morais Durão, Moç., 21 July 1784; see A.H.U., Moç., Cx. 19, José Ferreira Nobre to Saldanha de Albuquerque, Inhambane, 11 June 1783; A.H.U., Moç., Cx. 18, Lima, 'Relaçam dos descaminhos', article 15.

53. See A.H.U., Moç., Cx. 23, Maia e Vasconcelos to M. de Melo e Castro, Moç., 20 August 1785, noting the arrival of the Yao at Mossuril in 1785.

54. A.H.U., Moç., Cx. 21, Prov. Govt. to same, Moç., 7 August 1784.

55. ibid.

56. Freeman-Grenville, French at Kilwa, p. 172.

57. ibid., pp. 107, 112, 114, 138, 161–3, 172, 184, 187.

58. ibid., pp. 119–20, 215; Freeman-Grenville, Select Documents, pp. 192–3.

59. A.N.F., Colonies C⁴80, Saulnier de Mondevit, 'Memoire sur la necessité & de les Moyens de former un Etablissement françois á Mongalo sur la Côte Orientale d'Affrique', n.d., but c. 1786.

60. See Cunnison, 'Kazembe and the Portuguese, 1798–1832', Jl. of African History, II, 1 (1961), pp. 61–76, and Luapula Peoples, pp. 39, n. 4, 151; Freeman-Grenville, French at Kilwa, pp. 48–9, 76, 102, 105–6, 112, 118–19, 136–7.

61. T. C. Young, Notes on the History of the Tumbuka-Kamanga Peoples of the Northern Province of Nyasaland (London, 1932), pp. 27–36.

62. See ibid., p. 37.

63. Leroy Vail, 'Suggestions towards a reinterpreted Tumbuka history', in Pachai, Early History, p. 156.

64. Godfrey Wilson, The Constitution of Ngonde, Rhodes-Livingstone Papers No. 3 (Livingstone, 1939), pp. 10–19.

65. Cf. Monica Wilson, 'Reflections on the Early History of Northern Malawi', in Pachai, Early History, pp. 140–2, and Alpers and Ehret, 'Eastern Africa'.

66. G. Wilson, *Constitution*, p. 44, citing Peter the Kyungu in 1937. The identity of the Marabi remains obscure; perhaps they were like the Balowoka, who came 'as Arabs'.
67. For information on the crossing at Manda during this period I am grateful to Professor Ronald E. Gregson, who gathered it in an interview with G. Tadeyu Harawa, Mhuju, Malawi, in 1968.
68. For early references to Kivinje, the nineteenth-century mainland successor to Kilwa Kisiwani, see Freeman-Grenville, *French at Kilwa*, pp. 104, 202, 206 (maps 2 and 4); J. B. Lislet Geoffrey, *Memoir and Notice Explanatory of a Chart of Madagascar* . . . (London, 1819), p. 39, where he is translating 'Observations on the Coast of Africa by Lieut. the Chevalier Saulnier de Mondevit, of the Royal French Marine'; Dalrymple, *Plan of Quiloa and Its Environs on the East Coast of Africa from the Observations of the Sieur Morice*, 9 May 1784; Freeman-Grenville, 'The Coast', pp. 152–4.
69. Abdallah bin Hemedi 'lAjjemy, *The Kilindi*, trans. and ed. J. W. T. Allen and William Kimweri (Nairobi, 1963), p. 9; on the Masaninga Yao, see Alpers, 'Trade, State, and Society'.
70. Carl Velten, *Prosa und Poesie der Suaheli* (Berlin, 1907), pp. 254–5.
71. There are a number of other supposed connections between the Yao and the founders of Kilwa, but these are far too vague or mythic to bear close examination at present. See Burton, *Zanzibar*, II, pp. 357–8, 361; Freeman-Grenville, *Select Documents*, pp. 221–2; W. H. Ingrams, *Zanzibar: Its History and its People* (London, 1930), pp. 144–5.
72. For the Ruaha route, see Alpers, 'The Coast and the Development of Caravan Trade', in Kimambo and A. J. Temu (eds.), *A History of Tanzania* (Nairobi, 1969), p. 52.
73. Abdallah, *The Yaos*, pp. 26–8. In reconstructing the route from the Ruvuma to Mang'wang'wa, I have been guided by the *Carta de Moçambique 1889* which was compiled by the Commisão de Cartografia. For the route between the Mbwemkuru River and the coast, I am indebted to the Rev. Canon R. G. P. Lamburn, who provided me with a reconstruction based upon early colonial maps and his own intimate knowledge of that area, in a letter dated Mohoro, 22 June 1967.
74. The following two paragraphs are based on J. M. Gray, 'The Recovery of Kilwa by the Arabs in 1785', *T.N.R.*, 62 (1964), pp. 20–4, and 'A French Account of Kilwa at the end of the Eighteenth Century', *T.N.R.*, 63 (1964), p. 224; Freeman-Grenville, *French at Kilwa*, pp. 53–4, 56; Strandes, *Portuguese Period*, p. 338.
75. News of the reassertion of 'Umani rule at Kilwa seems not to have reached the Portuguese until 1788. See A.H.U., Moç., Cx. 25, Manuel António Correira to A. M. de Melo e Castro, Ibo, 13 February 1788.

CHAPTER SIX

The Resurgence of
the Kilwa Route, 1785–1810

❧❧❧❧❧❧❧❧❧❧❧❧❧❧❧❧❧❧❧❧❧❧❧❧❧❧

The Waning of the Macuana Ivory Trade

In the trading season of 1795, D. Diogo de Sousa Coutinho, the Governor-General of Portuguese East Africa, informed Lisbon that the introduction of better-quality trading cloths at Zanzibar, as well as of European goods, was 'diverting from us the concourse of the Yao, who, in the time of my predecessors, used to convey from two hundred to three hundred *bares* of ivory to Mossuril, now, since that of the government of my predecessor, [i.e., since 1786] and during mine, bring scarcely thirty to forty'.[1] Sousa's striking testimony to the diminished importance of the Yao ivory trade to Mozambique is particularly revealing in that it comes at the end of a decade in which there were no unusual disturbances on the mainland of Mozambique which might have inhibited the Yao from trading there. Similarly, the Banyans of Mozambique appear to have been allowed to carry on their business with a minimum of interference during these years. Although the royal orders of 1785 advised António Manuel de Melo e Castro to continue the prohibition against their 'trading personally on the mainland', the Governor-General apparently reinstated the granting of passports to individual merchants. Besides, the Banyans had already learned that they could circumvent this restriction by consigning merchandise to Swahili agents who lived on the mainland and thereby introducing it tax free at Quitangonha and Cabaceira Pequena.[2]

Although relations with the people of Macuana again deteriorated after 1795 (see below, p. 195), the Banyans continued to receive licences for trading personally on the mainland and maintained a large stake in the financing of trade in the colony through the first decade of the new century. Epidariste Colin, a French slave trader, remarked in 1804 that not only their persons and property, but also their religion appeared to be respected by the Portuguese, although he suggests that they came by these liberties at a considerable price.[3] Towards the end of 1805, however, complaints were lodged against a new Governor-General, Francisco de Paula e Albuquerque do Amaral Cardoso, for his outrageous extortions and threats of deportation. This affair dragged on for the next several years and had some small repercussions in British India, with claims for compensation being lodged against the estate of Cardoso after his death in 1807. There is no indication that it was ever resolved.[4] What is most significant about this particular clash between the Indian merchants of Mozambique and Portuguese officialdom is that it had nothing to do with their trading to the mainland. That the Indians were still immensely wealthy is attested to by their ability to bribe Cardoso to the tune of 50,000 *cruzados,* but their fortunes seem now to have derived more from the trade with the rest of the colony, as well as from the general import trade, than from the trade of Macuana. That they were envied for their wealth is not surprising; that they were not bothered in their business on the mainland of Mozambique may well reflect the declining importance of the Yao ivory trade to Mossuril and the pre-eminent position which the European-financed slave trade had assumed at the capital by 1810.

Before the domination of the slave trade had become a fact of life at Mozambique, there were some significant changes in the commercial tax structure of the colony which bear examination in view of the decline in the Yao ivory trade to Mossuril. The end of the eighteenth century was a time of experimentation for the commercial administration of Portuguese East Africa. Beginning in 1787 and ending in 1801, after which date they remained unaltered until 1846, the customs-house duties in force at Mozambique were repeatedly altered in a futile attempt to stimulate regional trade and to get the colony on its feet financially. Those of importance to the trade of the Yao were the taxes levied on the importation of trading cloths and beads, and on their re-exportation to the Rivers of Sena. Before 1787, imports of *velório*, the basic trade beads, were taxed at a rate of 20 per cent on their value, while all re-exports going to the Zambesi paid a 40 per cent duty.

G

From 1787 to 1793, the tax on *velório* was reduced to 15 per cent and the re-exportation tax was lowered to 30 per cent. In 1793 both were further lowered to 10 per cent, but the measure was soon attacked from several quarters as being detrimental to both trade and the Royal Treasury. The re-export tax was raised up to 40 per cent by 1800, but in the next year it was finally established at the 1787 rate of 30 per cent. At the same time, however, the import tariff on *velório* was re-set at 20 per cent, while merchandise arriving from Diu and Daman, the chief sources of trade cloths at Mozambique, was taxed at 10 per cent *ad valorem*. It is not clear whether goods entering Mozambique on foreign vessels paid 15 per cent or 20 per cent of their value at the customs-house.[5]

The results of the policy of lowering re-export duties from Mozambique were immediate and salutary. In 1793 ivory exportations from Mozambique reached an eighteenth-century peak of about 12,885 *arrobas*, but they were not quite half this figure in 1801 and rose to only about 7300 *arrobas* in 1809.[6] Most of this ivory seems to have come from the subordinate ports, such as Inhambane, which accounted for exports of at least 1391 *arrobas* in 1802, and Quelimane, where duties were collected on the export of 4,375 *arrobas* of ivory in 1806. Nor is it likely that the Yao were diverting their ivory trade to Quelimane, which in spite of the reduced tariffs in force could still not compete with duty-free Macuana.[7] For the Yao, in fact, after the brief period of lower import duties on *velório* from 1787 to 1801, they were faced with a situation in which the staple trading cloths from India were now taxed at more than twice the rate which had prevailed for the past five decades (10 per cent as opposed to $4\frac{1}{2}$ per cent). A vivid measure of the effect which this increase had on the ivory market of Mozambique is that in 1801 a *bar* of Indian cloth, which formerly bought 10 to 11 *arrobas* of ivory, could purchase no more than $4\frac{1}{2}$ *arrobas*.[8] Given the normal trading practices of the land, it is very likely that the Yao were forced to bear a large part of this burden by reducing their demands for cloth in exchange accordingly. (See below, p. 181, for this practice in the Rivers of Sena.) Finally, although it seems that the dramatic decline in ivory exports from Mozambique after 1793 was partly the result of the threat of French corsairs in the waters of the Mozambique Channel, it is more probable that it reflects the return to high re-export duties in Portuguese

East Africa. It is all the more remarkable, then, that such a high proportion of Mozambique's total ivory exports during this decade seems still to have come from the subordinate ports of Inhambane and Quelimane.

Another feature of this transitional period in the ivory trade of Mozambique was the sharp rise in both its official evaluation and the market price paid for it there. In 1787, the official price for large ivory, which had remained unchanged for nearly a quarter century, was raised from just under 60 *cruzados* to 80 *cruzados* per *arroba*. But when Henry Salt visited Mozambique in 1809 he noted that the merchants there demanded from 104 to 128 *cruzados* for their best ivory, as much as 60 per cent more than the official price ceiling theoretically allowed. It is probably in response to this inflationary pressure that the official evaluation of large ivory was raised to 100 *cruzados* per *arroba* in the following year.[9] In view of Salt's observations the effectiveness of even this higher price restraint on the Mozambique ivory market seems questionable. Taken together with the increased level of taxation on Indian trade cloths, the effect of this inflation was to price Mozambique ivory right out of the Indian ivory market.

During the first decade of the nineteenth century the mean price of ivory in the Gulf of Cambay ports more than doubled in response to rising prices at Mozambique, and by 1809 the local price of ivory at Mozambique was equal to that of the London market of 1808.[10] To be sure, the ivory trade of the Cambay cities and Cutch in the eighteenth and nineteenth centuries still awaits its historian. But the weight of the present evidence suggests that although Mozambique ivory was still preferred to all others at Surat and Cutch, where it had been obtained in previous years through Diu and Daman, it was no longer as profitable a business in which to invest for the merchant capitalists of those places.[11] In succeeding years the Indian traders of the Cambay ports and Cutch turned increasingly to the Swahili coast as their major source of ivory, while those of Mozambique tried to sustain the decline in the ivory trade by channelling more of their capital into the trade in slaves.

Kilwa and the Ivory Trade of the Interior

In view of this interpretation of the changing international ivory market and its impact on the trading economies of East Africa,

GRAPH: *Prices of Large Ivory at Mozambique in the Eighteenth Century*

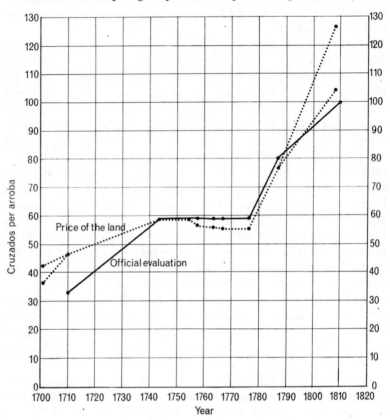

Sources: Chapter 3, notes 78–9; p. 119, Table 3; Chapter 6, note 9.

it is regrettable that our precise knowledge of the ivory trade on the Kilwa coast and of the ivory market at Zanzibar is no greater for this period than it is for the middle of the eighteenth century. In general, there is no doubt that Zanzibar increasingly was consolidating its position as the greatest commercial entrepôt in East Africa, and that Kilwa's ties to Zanzibar were becoming progressively more intimate. After 1785 there were no major challenges to Bu Sa'idi hegemony over Zanzibar. Peaceful conditions reigned for three decades both there and at Kilwa. In 1802–1804, Zanzibar already yielded the Seyyid of Masqat, who had replaced the Imam of 'Uman as the dominant political authority in 'Uman in 1796, no less than 40,000 *piastres* in customs rental, and by 1811 perhaps as much as 60,000 *piastres* revenue. As for Kilwa, in 1804 the customs rental there was 6000 *piastres* and in 1810 it was at least double that figure. Customs collection at Kilwa seems to have remained distinct from Zanzibar at this time. The large part of this revenue, which could be paid in ivory was raised from the collection of a 5 per cent duty on all imports to Zanzibar. Exports were not taxed. The import tariff had been only 3 per cent in the 1770s, but it was still considerably less than the tariffs imposed on both imports and exports at Mozambique, where all ivory leaving the custom-house for India still paid a $4\frac{1}{2}$ per cent *ad valorem* duty. The growing commercial strength of Zanzibar is further illustrated by the fact that by about 1810 between sixty and one hundred sailing vessels may have arrived at Zanzibar Town from Arabia, the Persian Gulf, and western India in each trading season.[12]

The French and British visitors who have left descriptions of Zanzibar at this time stress the importance of the slave trade and say very little about the ivory trade. However, the British were preoccupied with suppressing the slave trade, while the French were eager to promote it. Neither was much concerned with anything else in East Africa. Consequently, it has been commonplace to believe that slaves were already the most important item of export at Zanzibar at the beginning of the nineteenth century.[13] There are firm grounds for challenging the reliability of these indications in the reasons cited by the Portuguese in Zambesia for the removal of Yao trade away from Tete and Mozambique to Kilwa and Zanzibar. But even in the Zanzibar context the fact that the Imam's yearly revenue could be paid in ivory argues strongly for the greater importance of this product.

Lacking substantial figures for the ivory trade of Zanzibar, there is little hope for establishing definitely the priority of either item, ivory or slaves, in this period. It seems more likely, however, that ivory was still pre-eminent in the trade of both Kilwa and Zanzibar at the end of the first decade of the nineteenth century.

Immediately upon turning from the coast to the interior, there is no doubt that ivory still dominated the long-distance international trade of East Central Africa, and that it was the concentration of most Yao on ivory which continued to draw them to Kilwa. The sources for this period strikingly bear out the reconstruction of trading operations for the middle of the eighteenth century, but they also add important details and variations to it. In 1798, the Governor of the Rivers of Sena, Dr. Francisco José de Lacerda e Almeida, led a major expedition to the court of the Mwata Kazembe for the purpose of establishing regular trade with the state of the eastern Lunda. For the Portuguese, one of the reasons for mounting this venture was to re-channel the ivory trade of northern Zambesia back to themselves. Echoing the remarks of D. Diogo de Sousa in 1795, Lacerda wrote before setting out from Tete to the Luapula River that the ivory trade of the Yao to Mozambique 'had diminished considerably, because those Kaffirs had shifted their trade to Zanzibar and other neighbouring ports'. It also appears that the Kazembe was interested in seeking an alternative route for the export of his ivory in order to circumvent the monopoly of the Yao.[14]

Although they dominated his export trade, the Yao did not normally trade directly to the Mwata Kazembe's capital. Generally, the Yao are said to have received their ivory from the Bisa, with whom they were known to have been trading 'for a long time', according to the testimony of Manuel Caetano Pereira, who had already visited Kazembe and whose father, Gonçalo, had first begun to trade with the Bisa in 1793. The Bisa, in turn, received most of their ivory by trading with the Kazembe, who is said to have rendered the western Bisa tributary after a series of campaigns in the last decades of the eighteenth century. Lacerda probably over-emphasizes the Kazembe's dominance of the Bisa, but it is undeniable that their commercial ties with his court were most intimate and that their importance as ivory traders far outstripped their significance as elephant hunters.[15] According to the diary kept by Pedro João Baptista, one of two mulatto *pombeiros* (the Angolan equivalent of *patamares*) who reached Kazembe's town in 1806 and were detained there to 1810, the Bisa were 'the first travellers who ever traded with Kazembe'.[16] The goods with which the Bisa purchased ivory from the Kazembe came to them from the Yao, and Lacerda strongly suspected that the Yao were receiving them from the Swahili traders of Zanzibar and the Kilwa coast, because, as Manuel Caetano Pereira had told him,

> the great quantity of ivory, which every year leaves the kingdom of Kazembe, and those kingdoms or lands which he has conquered . . . ends in the hands of the Yao, their [the Bisa's] neighbours, and these do not sell it all in Mozambique, for there is a notorious difference between the quantity of ivory which the Yao formerly brought to Mozambique, and that which they presently introduce, to the advantage of the trade which the people of Zanzibar have carried on in that commodity since then.[17]

From the younger Pereira, Lacerda also learned that Bisa traders occasionally carried their ivory directly to Quelimane.[18] This extension of Bisa trading was probably in response to the Portuguese movement to lower re-export tariffs to the subordinate ports, and it supports the suggestion that the Kazembe may have been anxious to diminish his exclusive reliance on the Yao for his ivory exports and cloth and bead imports. But it is unlikely that this new Bisa route continued for long after the return to a 30 per cent duty in 1801. It was also believed in some quarters among the Portuguese that the Kerimba Islands were becoming a major terminus for the trade to the far interior at this time. As early as 1790, Nogueira de Andrade, in a confusing passage, reports the Yao and Maravi as trading there beside the Makua and Makonde. A decade later the Governor-General of Mozambique wrote in his report on the expedition to Kazembe's that 'the Negroes who usually go from Kazembe's to Tete are the same who usually come each year to Mozambique and to the islands of Cape Delgado'.[19] This is nowhere stated in Lacerda's diary, nor in that of Fr. Francisco João Pinto, who assumed command of the expedition after Lacerda's death at Kazembe's capital in October 1798. Presumably, it is simply an inaccurate interpolation on the part of the Governor-General. Indeed, the trade of the Kerimba Islands was moribund. Like the route to Quelimane, in fact, that to Kisanga, opposite Ibo, did not become significant until its rise to notoriety as a slaving centre, which did not occur until later in the nineteenth century.

While the Yao and the Bisa indisputably dominated the carrying trade of the interior of East Central Africa, the Maravi continued to participate in a limited way. A Bisa chief told Lacerda that he sold his ivory to the Manguro, who lived along the Shire River, and that the Yao received it from the Manguro. Considering the ethnographic vagueness of the name 'Manguro', it seems most likely that in some cases Mang'anja and Nyanja acted as short-haul intermediaries between the Bisa and the Yao, possibly ferrying ivory across the river, as the Nyasa and the Nyanja also controlled the canoe traffic on Lake Nyasa. Generally, however, the Maravi appear to have played no part in most of the long-distance trade, surrounded as they were by two peoples both of whom were extremely active and determined traders. This factor certainly was a cause of Chewa attacks on trading caravans travelling through their lands.[20] At Mossuril in 1809, Henry Salt learned something which adds a new dimension to the wider setting of trade in East Central Africa. The Yao 'told me themselves', he wrote, 'that they were acquainted with other traders called Eveezi [Nyamwezi] and Maravi, who had travelled far enough inland to see large waters, white people (this must be taken comparatively) and horses'.[21] Yao traders could have encountered Nyamwezi traders at either border of East Central Africa by the early 1800s. The two *pombeiros* from Angola found companies of Galagansa from western Unyamwezi at Kazembe's in 1806–1810, while other Nyamwezi may have been trading to the Kilwa coast along a route following the Ruaha River valley, which branched off from the better known, but still secondary, central Tanzanian route to the Mrima coast.[22] As for Salt's scepticism about African traders having met whites, the strong links between Kazembe's kingdom and the Angolan coast make it entirely possible that a few East Africans had travelled to the Atlantic coast, as Morice indicated some three decades earlier.[23]

Another aspect of trade in the interior concerns the distances which the Yao had to travel in order to bring their goods to the coast, a problem which again emphasises our inability to distinguish one group of Yao from another. As early as 1784 some Portuguese became convinced that a reason for the Yao trading to Kilwa in preference to Mozambique was that Kilwa was closer to their country than the Portuguese island.[24] Lacerda also suggested that the ivory which once had gone to Mozambique, but in his day passed to Zanzibar, did so 'not only because they evaluate it better there, but also because this country is closer to Zanzibar than to Mozambique'. In this matter, if not in that of Yao trading to the Kerimba Islands, Governor-General Francisco Guedes de Carvalho e Meneses da Costa was more close to truth in his observation that when the Kazembe was questioned as to the source of his standard trade beads and the destination of his merchandise, he replied that the beads 'came to him from Mozambique, and from the Zanzibar coast, where they also sent their ivory and slaves to be sold, since the distances were equal'. Several years later, Meneses da Coasta noted to the same effect that 'those chiefs and Negroes of the interior attribute little importance to distance, be it longer or shorter, in sending their caravans and their trade to more distant places, when the profits of trade pay them for their extra trouble'.[25] Additional substantiation of this point of view is provided by Dr. António Norberto de Vilasboas Truão, whose observations on the trade of the interior are the most sophisticated to have survived since the days of Francisco de Melo e Castro in the middle of the eighteenth century.

Truão was Lacerda's successor as Governor of the Rivers of Sena. In 1806 he wrote an important report on the state of his province, including a separate section which vividly reveals the effect on African trade of the high tariffs imposed on the trade of the Rivers by the Mozambique government. Truão argued that taxing the trade goods desired by Africans in this way required

> that the Kaffir traders of the interior should diminish in equal proportion the value of their gold and ivory, in order that such duties should not damage our trade. Ordinarily it is the buyer who pays this increase in price, but this is not what happens in this part of Africa.

Continuing his attack on the effect of these duties on trade, he explained that

> The Kaffirs who sell us gold and ivory, after establishing a certain price, and being used to it, by principle never pay more than that for trade goods, and are able to carry their ivory on a journey of two months longer, in hope of seeing if they get a small rise in price.

Truão added that the Swahili traders of the Zanzibar coast, including Kilwa, exported much of the gold and ivory taken by those Africans to that coast. Since Lacerda's expedition, the trade of the Rivers with the Kazembe, with the Bisa, and with the Maravi region had been interrupted. But these same Africans, he stressed, had not given up 'selling their ivory to the Yao Kaffirs, who have carried it to the ports of the coast of Zanzibar, as is known from certain information; and some of these Kaffirs still continue that trade because it is more important to them, as they have told our traders'.[26] There is no reason to believe that the proximity of Kilwa to the Yao was an important factor in influencing the shift of their ivory trade back to Kilwa from Mozambique. The operative factors were economic, not geographical.

Because of its proximity to both Mozambique and Kilwa, the Cape Delgado hinterland provides another interesting study of African responsiveness to coastal market factors during this period of transition. Whatever hopes the Portuguese may have entertained in the mid-1790s for a revival of this important frontier with the Muslim north were crushed by a series of blows struck at these settlements in the following years. In 1794, prospects were bleak enough, with the islands 'totally uninhabited' except for the poor and miserable denizens, almost no troops, provisions scarce, and the fortifications in disrepair.[27] Throughout that same year there were also numerous petty conflicts with the Makua, who had risen in 'a great revolution' on the death of João de Morais, long the only bastion of Portuguese authority on the Cape Delgado mainland. During the next year it became increasingly difficult to prevent French corsairs from slaving along that coast, and in 1796, despite official French protestations of peace, French vessels attacked both Ibo and Pangani, a mainland settlement located opposite the island of Macaloe (now known as Mahato), to the north of Ibo.[28] The end of the century saw a continuation of Makua harassment, a severe famine and an epidemic of an unidentified fever in 1798, and a move towards the closing of the customs-house at Ibo. Except for the Swahili slave trade from around Vamizi to the Kilwa coast, trade was at a standstill.[29]

After 1800 the Kerimba Islands were also subjected to a series of increasingly devastating raids launched from north-western Madagascar by the Sakalava. The express purpose of these raids was to capture slaves, both for employment at home as agricultural labour and for selling to European traders at Madagascar.[30] During the next two decades these maritime raiders caused extensive damage along the East African coast from Ibo to Mafia, where the presence of their fleets of *lakas*, single-sail and single-outrigger canoes, in the Mozambique Channel was a threat to all other shipping. Although they never actually attacked Mozambique Island, they were regarded as a menace to its safety throughout this period. The Sakalava raid of 1800 was a small affair, involving only three boats and some sixty men in the neighbourhood of Vamizi, but despite superior numbers the local inhabitants panicked in the face of these hit-and-run attacks.[31] The first major attack did not come until September 1808, when a force of perhaps 8,000 Sakalava raked the coast between Vamizi and Ushanga, at the south side of Pemba Bay, just north of the Lurio River mouth. Moving virtually at will up and down the coast, the Sakalava terrorized Portuguese and Africans alike for more than three months before sailing back to Madagascar in the first week of the new year. For their troubles they captured about 800 prisoners who were known to the Portuguese, and they must have seized a good many others, as well. Only Ibo, with its fortress, weathered the onslaught, and it was said to be 'in a miserable state'.[32] The fear which was inspired by the Sakalava raid of 1808 made the Portuguese in the Kerimba Islands every bit as apprehensive as those of the Mozambique mainland had been after the Makua had driven them to the sea in 1776. It demonstrated very clearly the total ineffectuality of Portuguese claims to sovereignty to the north of Mozambique Island at the beginning of the nineteenth century.

Throughout most of this decade the Makua, and sometimes the Makonde, continued to harass the coastal settlements of the Portuguese. Fighting extended along the length of the Cape Delgado coast, and the Portuguese lived in considerable fear of attack from the Africans. The chief aggressors were the Makua chiefs Mugabo and Mutuga, who should probably be identified as Mutica, a chief who by the middle of the nineteenth century was subordinate to Mugabo.[33] The Mutuga's town was then situated near the mouth of the Tari River, just north of Pemba Bay, while the Mugabo's stood inland from the coast between the bay and the Lurio River. The Mutuga dominated both the coast and the immediate hinterland from the mouth of the Lurio north to Kisanga, the most important Swahili settlement on that part of the coast. Mutuga was especially odious to the Portuguese administration because he encouraged Swahili traders from the Kilwa coast to trade in his territory, welcoming them especially at the Tari. The Portuguese feared to attack his town there because they believed themselves to be incapable of sustaining a major war with the Mutuga. From Kisanga to Vamizi district the Makua and Makonde limited themselves to small raids, which Governor Pereira admitted were usually 'caused by our people, who capture and sell any Kaffir still free', so that there was no end to these reprisals. Agriculture was crippled by the fact that many Africans had fled the immediate coast for the interior in order to escape being enslaved.[34] Lacking the military power to deal with the Africans as he would have liked, the Governor-General could only advise the continuation of a policy of conciliation and amity.[35]

Significant external trade was virtually impossible in such conditions. Makua and Makonde hostility made travel through the interior extremely treacherous for either Portuguese traders or their *patamares*.[36] Only the Swahili slave trade to the north sustained itself in these years, although even it became more uncertain after the Sakalava raid of 1808. The Mutuga's town was the Swahili's main port of call, but wherever they dropped anchor in the Kerimba Islands or offshore they could expect full cooperation from the Portuguese colonists, for whom this trade was almost their only means of maintaining themselves above a level of subsistence. Accordingly, at the end of 1810 the local Governor at last relented and began to issue licences for Swahili boats wishing to trade legally for non-Christian slaves in the islands.[37]

The decline of trade along this stretch of the coast had the same effect on the trade of the interior as did the depression of the Mozambique ivory trade on the routing of Yao trade. According to António da Silva Pinto, Governor of the islands at the beginning of the nineteenth century:

> All these lands are surrounded by the Makua Kaffirs, and through theirs run trails, some which go to Mozambique, and others to Zanzibar.
> There used to be a considerable trade in ivory, rice, maize, and oils which were exported every year in great quantities to Mozambique. This [trade] is extinct as a result of the Kaffirs of the interior going to Zanzibar, for they find there greater profit and better cloths than ours.[38]

Fears of this re-direction of the more localized trade of the Cape Delgado hinterland had been expressed as early as 1766. Silva Pinto's evidence demonstrates once again the impact which changes in political and economic conditions on the coast could work on the trading habits of African peoples whose trading economies were linked to the international trade of the Indian Ocean.

The Expansion of the Slave Trade: the Problem of Quantification

If ivory continued to dominate the international trade of East Central Africa during this quarter century, the foundations upon which the slave trade would come to challenge its primacy were being laid at the same time. This process was effected initially and most completely at Mozambique, but at Kilwa, too, there were signs of the expanded role which slaves were to play in the foreign trade of the region after 1810.

The sudden growth of the slave trade in the decade after 1785 was almost wholly the work of the French. The European peace between the end of the American War of Independence and the commencement of the Napoleonic Wars brought a spurt of unprecedented French slaving in East Africa, involving not only the Mascarene Islands, but also the most notorious of the Caribbean sugar colonies, San Domingo. Inflated slave prices at West African markets favoured by the French served as a stimulus to their seeking new sources of supply in East Africa, where men like Morice had already pointed the way for the trans-Atlantic traffic. By West African standards slaves were still a bargain in East Africa, so that neither the higher price of shipping nor the greater rate of mortality aboard ship, and presumably upon landing, deterred profit-minded Frenchmen who could expect a return of up to 500 per cent on each slave who was safely landed at San Domingo.[39] Some of these slaving ventures were directed at the Kilwa coast, but most of them were concentrated at Mozambique, where they were shortly to work a startling effect on the trading economy of that port.

From an estimated total average of rather more than 1,500 slaves exported from Mozambique during the first few years of the decade, official customs-house figures for the period 1786–1794 reveal that a total of 5,400 slaves were exported each year during this decade. Of these, an average of about 3,770 were embarked by French vessels, while the remaining 1,630 were shipped aboard Portuguese ships. These figures do not, of course, take account of the increasing numbers of slaves who were smuggled aboard ship directly from the mainland so as to avoid paying the capitation tax which was levied by the Portuguese government at Mozambique Island. It is also worth noting that a good many of the Portuguese vessels involved in this greatly expanded trade were Portuguese in name only, as the taxation rate for exports shipped aboard national vessels was lower than that for foreign ships. In any case, nearly all of these Portuguese slavers were involved in the trade to the Mascarene Islands, so that virtually the entire slave trade of the Mozambique market was directed toward the satisfaction of French demands for manual labour in the Indian Ocean and the Caribbean Sea.

There are several indicators of the impact of the increased volume of the slave trade on the economy of Mozambique. The Governor-General, António Manuel de Melo e Castro, son of Francisco, reported to Lisbon that 'the great exportation of slaves, the most flourishing branch of trade in this Captaincy' had caused a commensurate increase in the importation of both specie and trading cloths. Ivory and gold, which were the traditional mainstays of the colony's exports, he described as being 'faded, and in precipitate decadency', now accounting for less than one-third of the importations to Mozambique from India and Portugal. But Melo e Castro was not describing the mere substitution of slaves for ivory and gold, in a market with a stable ceiling of imports. Imports had increased, and, as the Governor-General observed, the only cause of this remarkable growth in the colonial economy was the French slave trade.[40] For his part, Nogueira de Andrade, who had served at Mozambique throughout the 1780s, strongly supported Melo e Castro's interpretation of the factors underlying this new development in the trade of Mozambique.[41] On the strength of these recommendations, trade with foreigners at Mozambique now became officially acceptable to the Crown. No longer did the French have to resort to a variety of ruses and bribes in order to make up their cargoes of slaves. From this period forward, the official structure of trade at Mozambique was to be efficiently directed towards the provision of slaves for export.

After 1794, however, the slave trade at Mozambique experienced a temporary slowdown until the second decade of the

TABLE 4

Slaves Exported from Mozambique, c. 1770–1803

Year	Number of slaves
c. 1770–1779	9,158[a]
1781	315[b]
1782	1,045[b]
1783	1,765[b]
1784	2,313[b]
1785	2,352[b]
1786	2,847[b]
1787	8,213[c]
1788	11,016[c]
1789	6,724[d] (9,674[c])
1790	7,145[d] (7,353[c])
1791	5,523[d]
1792	4,944[d]
1793	4,273[d]
1794	2,340[d]
1803	5,239[d]
Total	75,212 (78,370)

Sources: A.H.U., Moç., Cx. 16, Diogo Guerreiro de Aboim to Clerk of the alfândega, Moç., 23 August 1779; ibid., certidão, Joaquim Jorge, Moç., 24 August 1779; A.H.U., Moç., Cx. 33, anonymous, 'Mappa da Importancia das fazendas, marfim, ouro, escravos, e patacas . . .' (1781–1790), Moç., September 1796; A.H.U., Moç., Cx. 25, João da Silva Guedes, 'Resumo de Rendimento da Alfandiga no anno preterito de 1789', Moç., 11 August 1790; A.H.U., Moç., Cx. 27, A. M. de Melo e Castro to M. de Melo e Castro, Moç., 24 August 1790; ibid., same to same, Moç., 28 August 1791, enclosing Silva Guedes, alfândega figures for previous year, Moç., 15 March 1791; A.H.U., Moç., Cx. 33, anonymous, 'Mapa dos Rendimentos Reais da Capitania de 1788 a 1793', Moç., August 1794; ibid., anonymous, 'Mapa dos rendimentos de 1791 a 1795', n.d.; A.H.U., Moç., Cx. 44, Silva Guedes, 'Mapa do rendimento que houve na Alfândega no anno proximo passado de 1803 . . .', Moç., 1804.

[a]Aboard thirty-two French and two Portuguese ships, licensed by Pereira do Lago to carry slaves to the Mascarene Islands.
[b]Aboard Portuguese ships only.
[c]Aboard Portuguese and foreign ships.
[d]Based on customs-house duties collected on slaves exported aboard Portuguese and foreign ships.

nineteenth century, First, the Atlantic slave trade from East Africa was brought to an abrupt halt for the French in 1791 by the slave risings at San Domingo, which culminated in the independence of what was to be called Haiti on New Year's Day 1804. Next, the resumption of hostilities between France and Great Britain in 1794 impeded the free flow of trade between the Mascarenes and Mozambique, since Portugal was an ally of Great Britain in Europe and technically at war with the French. Nevertheless, except for a two-year period after March 1794 and the extension of the European conflict into the Indian Ocean in 1808, common need and mutual profit bound the French islanders and the Portuguese officials together in a still active, but diminished trade in slaves. Despite this turn of events, it appears that by this time the corner had been turned for the Portuguese and that the slave trade was not to be dislodged from its premier position in the trading economy of the Portuguese East African capital. Official figures are scarce for this important period of transition, but customs-house statistics for January 1805 to October 1806, after the return to high re-export duties, indicate that taxation on the exportation of slaves produced nearly twice as much revenue as that accruing from ivory and gold combined.[42] Besides, what slack there existed in the total volume of the slave trade at Mozambique as a result of the limitations on French slaving was already in the process of being taken up gradually by the promotion of the traffic to Brazil.

The Brazilian trade had attracted a certain amount of support from individuals at Mozambique, Rio de Janeiro, and Lisbon, for about a century and a half, but it was never allowed to take root until the very end of the eighteenth century. So far as the Portuguese Crown had been concerned, supplying slaves to Brazil was the business of its colony in Angola. In the past, each time some individual proposed establishing a regular slave trade between Brazil and Mozambique there were more powerful voices raised in opposition. But by the 1790s, when Governor-General Sousa actively encouraged the development of this trade, no opposition was encountered.[43] Indeed, in 1795 the Crown gave its blessing to a slaving venture from Mozambique to Brazil.[44] What ultimately sustained the trade was the increased demand for labour which followed the revival of sugar production in north-eastern Brazil and the development of coffee plantations in the Parahíba Valley.[45] A rather different, but not unimportant factor, which encouraged this traffic was the removal of the Portuguese Court to Rio de Janeiro in 1807–1808, which shifted the focus of the Portuguese empire from Portugal to Brazil and legitimized direct trade of all sorts between Mozambique and Brazil. About all that is known about the trade to Brazil in these years, however, is that in 1802 nearly five-sixths of a shipment of 620 slaves destined for Rio de Janeiro aboard the *Castelão* were lost in a violent storm.[46] But by August 1809, at a time when the total traffic at the port of Mozambique was severely restricted by the presence of French corsairs in the Mozambique Channel, Henry Salt was able to observe that 'five ships loaded with slaves went this year to the Brazils, each vessel carrying from three to four hundred'.[47] That this traffic was being pursued with equal vigour a year later was an indication of the importance which the Brazilian slave trade would assume in the economic life of Mozambique in the nineteenth century.[48]

Scarcely more is known about the slave trade carried on at Kilwa during this period, but clear evidence of its vitality is found in the increased pace of Swahili slaving in the Kerimba Islands. The coasting trade between the Kilwa coast and the Cape Delgado coast had always frustrated the Portuguese. Increased Portuguese vigilance against French trading in the Kerimba Islands, however, drove those French slavers who preferred not to trade at Mozambique to Kilwa. Their presence along that coast, together with the renewed 'Umani involvement at Kilwa, encouraged Swahili traders to try their luck at dealing with the frustrated Portuguese colonists who lived beyond the normal limits of Crown control at Ibo. In 1787, a number of slaves were seized from Swahili ships in the Islands.[49] Two years later, some thirty-five Swahili boats were registered by the Portuguese as having taken port at Ibo in pursuance of the legal trade in provisions to the Portuguese settlements.[50] But it was felt that many of these were also carrying on a clandestine trade in slaves. A petition by some colonists to trade slaves to the Swahili for the French at Kilwa brought a series of strong condemnations against the evils of this commerce from the Governor-General at Mozambique. On 18 April 1789, the Governor of the Kerimba Islands, António José Teixeira Tigre, issued a proclamation on behalf of the Governor-General 'absolutely forbidding the clandestine trade of the Swahili of the coast of Zanzibar, Pate, Mafia, Kilwa, Mombasa, &ª', and threatening contrabanders with heavy fines, imprisonment, and ultimately with banishment from Portuguese territory. Copies of this decree were sent to the rulers of Kilwa, Pate, Zanzibar, and Mombasa.[51]

All was to no avail. In the following year, Tigre reported with alarm that the Swahili from Pate 'travel through the lands of the jurisdiction of this Command, establishing themselves almost as masters of them, and fortifying themselves in Quirimize', on the mainland about twenty miles north of Kisanga. From Quirimize, he complained, they dispatched their boats to trade along the coast and to all the islands without regard for the Portuguese. Some of the colonists on the mainland, most notably (until his death) João de Morais, even protected them, in return for assistance in their own settlements. In September a large boatload of slaves from the interior had set sail from Quirimize to be sold to the French at Kilwa.[52]

It is, however, impossible to gauge the volume of the slave trade at Kilwa after 1785. At the end of 1788, Tigre was informed that seven French vessels were taking on slaves at Kilwa, while two more were anchored at Mongalo. Three weeks later, Governor-General Melo e Castro advised Lisbon that a total of eleven French ships were doing business at these ports and at Mikindani, to the south of Mongalo. Corroboration of continued French slaving activity at Kilwa during these years is also provided by the testimony of a certain Captain Le Maitre, who was engaged in the American trade. During his residence of nine months at Kilwa, Le Maitre informed Nogueira de Andrade, there were five other French slavers making up cargoes at that port.[53] This scarcely constitutes definitive evidence, but it does suggest that the French were driving a brisk trade in slaves at Kilwa during the late 1780s. Of the Arab trade there nothing is known.

Both the French and the Arabs of Mombasa entertained ideas of by-passing the 'Umani control of trade at Kilwa during this period. In each case the focus of their efforts fell upon the mixed Swahili and Makonde settlement of Mongalo. The position of towns like Mongalo, Lindi, and Mikindani is difficult to determine in the late eighteenth and early nineteenth centuries. Nominally, all were subject to the Imam of 'Uman. In practice, each was independent, although there seems to have been some sort of traditional recognition that the Sultan of Kilwa still had claim to a very loose overlordship of the coast down to Cape Delgado. At Mongalo, for example, which is best known to us because of the abortive French effort to establish an outpost there in 1786–89,[54] the Imam's claim to authority was acknowledged by the Swahili on the basis of his religious leadership, but it was rejected by the Makonde of the town, even though they were largely Islamized. At the same time, however, no tribute was rendered to the Imam by the political leadership of Mongalo, which was headed by the Mwenyi Mwanya. Lindi was described in 1786 by Saulnier, who was intimately involved in the Mongalo venture, as being 'under the domination of the King of Kilwa'.[55] Two decades later, the Portuguese Governor of the Kerimba Islands reported Mikindani as 'presently belonging to the King of Kilwa, with a population of three thousand Swahili capable of bearing arms'.[56] Neither of these accounts of Kilwa's imperial rule need to be taken too seriously, as Kilwa itself was indisputably under the thumb of its 'Umani governor and garrison. Mongalo, by contrast, appears to have conducted much of its trade with Arabs from Mombasa, who presumably were ready to seize any opportunity which allowed them to outflank 'Umani control of the coast. According to Saulnier, however, the Mombasa Arabs tyrannized the people of Mongalo, and gave them uncompetitive prices and cheap quality goods for their ivory and slaves. 'If the Arabs are contrary, they burn the villages,' he added.[57] These last details seem unlikely in view of the competition for trade which was being waged along the coast between Mombasa and the Bu Sa'idi dynasty at Zanzibar. More probably they represent part of Saulnier's propaganda for persuading his government to make a major commitment at Mongalo. But taken together with the fleeting references to Lindi and Mikindani in this quarter century, they underscore the tenuousness of 'Umani claims to authority beyond Kilwa.

After 1795 there are few references to French slave trading at Kilwa. Whatever business they conducted along the Swahili coast was gradually shifted to the principal 'Umani market at Zanzibar Town.[58] Kilwa continued to supply most of the slaves for the Zanzibar market, but it appears that as 'Umani strength grew in East Africa there was less opportunity for direct trading by foreigners at the mainland ports which were under effective 'Umani domination.

It remains to deal with the problem of quantifying the slave trade of the Swahili coast during this era. I have already suggested that the tendency of contemporary observers was to overestimate the volume of this trade for their own purposes. At best the European trade remained steady during these years, and Nicholls' estimate of 2,500 slaves exported annually before the Moresby Treaty of

1822, which specifically prohibited the trade to Europeans, is probably not far from the mark.[59] This figure is consonant with those from Kilwa and Zanzibar from the 1770s and allows both for a transfer of some traffic from Mozambique after 1794 and for the impossibility of European trade at the Kerimba Islands throughout this period. What presently defies all attempts at quantification is the non-European slave trade to the Persian Gulf and from it to the larger Muslim world. European estimates range wildly about this largely Arab trade, whose historical importance has been overemphasized by most European writers since the nineteenth century.[60] Even Nicholls, who lays particular emphasis on the catalytic importance of the European slave trade in attracting 'Umani attention to the economic potential of the Swahili coast, infers a much larger Arab slave trade during this same formative period. By relying on what appear to be inflated European estimates from the 1840s and 1850s, she unaccountably deduces an equivalent volume of trade for the years before 1822, when there are absolutely no estimates available. Thus, when she suggests an annual turnover of possibly 20,000 slaves on the Swahili coast before 1822, she is implicitly accepting a figure of at least 15,000 for the Arab trade (the remaining 2,500 being accounted for by the small Indian trade, the pre-plantation trade to Zanzibar and Mombasa, and smuggling).[61]

Sheriff, working independently on the same topic, arrives at a diametrically opposed conclusion. Owing to the absence of contemporary and local documentation, he, too, is forced to rely upon later and external sources of information, but finds support for his position in the low importation figures at Masqat in 1830 (1,200 slaves) and at Kharaq, on the route to Basra, in 1841 (about 1,200 slaves). He accordingly arrives at a figure of no more than 2,500 slaves traded to the Persian Gulf in the 1830s and would certainly not see this figure as being higher in the first decade of the nineteenth century.[62] If we accept Sheriff's calculations for the Arab trade, add to it the 400 to 500 slaves traded each year to India, a figure which seems to have remained stable, and accept a figure of about 2,500 slaves annually for the European trade at this time, the total of the slave trade on the Swahili coast in about 1810 was about 6,000 individuals. This is considerably higher than Sheriff's original estimate of 2,000 for 1810, but it is also much lower than that arrived at by Nicholls.

Not only does the lack of reliable figures for the slave trade of the Swahili coast bedevil attempts to determine its relationship to the equally obscure ivory trade during this very important period, and therefore to determine the impact of any changes on the peoples of the interior, but it also obscures the importance of the market for slaves that was created by the rise of the colonial plantation economies of Zanzibar and Pemba in the decades after 1820. Nicholls suggests a return in the 1840s to a trade of about 20,000 slaves annually along the coast after a decrease in the previous two decades which was caused by the demise of the European trade. But she also accepts a figure of perhaps 10,000 slaves for the internal market of the islands and the northern Swahili coast.[63] If the northern trade took about 15,000 slaves each year in the 1840s, again as she claims, then the total trade was at least 25,000 slaves annually; if not, then either the figure for the trade of Zanzibar and Pemba or that for the northern trade is seriously inflated. Sheriff's argument for a much smaller northern trade and for the critical importance of the plantation economy of the East African islands in generating the great mid-century demand for slaves at the coast (see Chapter 7) can now be seen to have two advantages over Nicholls' interpretation of the evidence. First, it is logically more consistent; and second, it provides an economic explanation for a rising demand for slaves from the continent. By contrast, Nicholls' conflicting figures clearly raise questions of their own, while there is nowhere any explanation how so high a demand for slaves in the Arab world was sustained throughout the first half of the nineteenth century. Nicholls does demonstrate, however, that there was an impressive general expansion of 'Umani commerce and shipping at the end of the eighteenth century.[64] Although she does not connect this directly to the Persian Gulf slave trade, the notion that the increased 'Umani carrying trade gave rise to an expanded northern slave trade remains an unsatisfactory explanation.[65] Until we know more about the sources of and changes in the demand for slaves in the countries which were being serviced by the Persian Gulf trade, it is more prudent to follow Sheriff's cautious lead and to work with a lower, constant figure for the older trade of the Muslim world until someone can establish its dimensions and dynamics more securely.

The Expansion of the Slave Trade: African Responses

How did the people of East Central Africa respond to the growth of the European slave trade after 1785? Earlier in the eighteenth century, the increased demand for slaves along both the Kilwa and Mozambique coasts was supplied principally by Africans living near the coast. This same pattern of supply probably persisted at Kilwa over these years, where information is completely absent, but if comparisons with Mozambique are meaningful the impact of Kilwa's growing demand was also gradually extending deeper into the interior. At Mozambique, it will be recalled, Yao slaves were less favoured than the Makua because the combination of the long journey from the far interior and the different disease environment of the coast produced a high rate of mortality among them. Although evidence as to which Africans were supplying the slave trade is completely lacking for the decade of greatest French activity at Mozambique, there is no reason to believe that the brunt of the burden had been lifted from the Makua. An important point to be made here is that the beginning of this decade coincided with one of those rare periods of peace in Macuana, which remained undisturbed, except for desultory raids of no apparent consequence on Mossuril in the middle of 1789, for a full eleven years after the peace of 1784.[66] What is equally lacking is any record of how slaves were acquired in Macuana. Some may have been seized in Portuguese raiding, but in view of the repercussions which this sort of activity had caused in past years, it is most likely that the Portuguese were being supplied by the Makua chiefs of Uticulo, Cambira, and Matibane. And they, in turn, most likely were acquiring their captives by trading with or raiding Makua, and possibly Yao, who lived beyond the pale of Portuguese influence, for if they had been raiding each other it would have disrupted the peace on the mainland. In these circumstances, it seems not unreasonable to assume that a major factor in sustaining this calm was the prosperity which the slave trade brought to all who participated in its profits. Granted that this is a purely conjectural reconstruction of the relationship between trade and politics on the Mozambique mainland in the decade after 1784, it nevertheless has the merit of providing a framework for understanding the return to conflict in Macuana in 1795.

In the past, longer periods of peaceful relations between the Portuguese and their African neighbours had been characterized by the building up of petty grievances which eventually led to the recommencement of open hostilities by the latter. In any case, it should be remembered that conflict, not cooperation, was the normal state of affairs between Portuguese and Africans in Macuana. After 1787 this process of attrition was probably exacerbated by the decision in that year to permit the residents of Mozambique legally to trade firearms and gunpowder to the Makua, with whom a brisk trade was at once begun by leading Portuguese, whose agents negotiated these goods exclusively for slaves.[67] It is important to emphasize that the sanctioning of this trade came about only in the wake of the total commitment of the Portuguese at Mozambique to the slave trade. Arguments about the threat to the safety of the colonists no longer held much force when they were confronted with the huge profits that could be turned in the slave trade. Moreover, whereas formerly the weight of economic reasoning had been placed on the damage to the ivory trade which could be caused by hostile Africans armed with firearms, the same logic now argued that a high investment in firearms would bring about an even higher profit in slaves.

Peace was finally broken in 1795 by the eruption of fighting between the Sheikh of Quitangonha and the Portuguese. The specific reasons for this turn of events are not recorded, but as early as 1778 the Portuguese had encountered difficulties and threats of violence in their relations with this Swahili-Makua community which was traditionally a Portuguese ally.[68] Perhaps the sudden drop in the volume of the French slave trade after 1794 created a situation in which there was a greater supply of slaves on the mainland than the demand at Mozambique Island could handle. This sort of development would have increased competition among the Africans who were supplying slaves to the Portuguese. It would also have cut into the long-established contraband trade which the French had carried on to the north and south of the island-capital.

A declared state of war existed from 1795 to 1796, and, after an uneasy truce, from 1799 through 1801. The sheikh commanded an extensive following not only on the island of Quitangonha, but also on the mainland of Matibane. From the beginning of the conflict, the Portuguese sought to ally the important Makua chiefs of the coastal hinterland to their side. The Portuguese repulsed an attack on Mossuril in 1799 and by late August of that year had made preparations for a major expedition against

Quitangonha. Including the forces of their allies, this army is said to have numbered 14,000 men. For the occasion, both the Mwaviamuno and the Mauruça had agreed to join the Portuguese against the Sheikh of Quitangonha. In December, the Mauruça carried out a damaging raid into Matibane. But despite the grandiose plans of the Portuguese for large expeditions, most of the warring was carried out by individual Makua chiefs acting independently and for their own purposes.[69]

Several years later the roles were reversed, with the Portuguese lined up with the new Sheikh of Quitangonha, Zafir Salimo, who had come to power at the death of his recalcitrant predecessor in 1804, against the Murimuno, who had submitted to Portuguese rule in 1784.[70] Here the catalysts of the conflict were known to be the robbery of trade goods sent by the Portuguese into the interior and the harbouring of fugitive slaves. To make matters worse, the Murimuno was demanding a stiff ransom of 20 *cruzados* for each of these slaves. During 1807 the Portuguese carried out several strikes against his territory. While these were considered successful, only limited damage was inflicted on the Makua, who soon retaliated with a raid on Mossuril. It was the same sort of conflict which had prevailed throughout most of the eighteenth century between these two foes. If anything, however, the Portuguese were even less capable of imposing their own solution on affairs on the mainland than they had been in the past. A report by the Governor-General on the progress of the war reveals the extent to which the Portuguese were involved in the court intrigues of their Makua neighbours, a policy which was dictated by their military weakness on the mainland. At first, Amaral Cardoso was hopeful of appointing a disgruntled relative of the previous Murimuno as chief. When this candidate balked, the Portuguese sought to install a kinsman of the deceased Uticulo chief, Impahiamuno, as a more pliant Murimuno. At the writing of his report, the Governor-General was planning to convoke 'a public congress in conformity with African manners' for his nomination.[71]

While it is not known if a rival Murimuno was actually installed by the Portuguese, it is clear that the situation in Macuana remained very confused and potentially explosive. In 1808, the robberies committed by the Napitamuno, whose territory was located on the coast just north of Quitangonha, in Matibane, constituted a nuisance for the Portuguese, as did a variety of petty disorders around Mossuril, But the outbreak of serious fighting in Uticulo, early in the following year, posed a far more serious challenge.[72] As early as March 1809, civil strife had driven the reigning Impahiamuno to the Portuguese Crown Land which served as a buffer zone between the coastal settlements and the coastal hinterland. The Impahiamuno soon sought retaliation against his chief rival, the Mauruça, but by early May the Portuguese were actively seeking to maintain peace with this most powerful Makua ruler. There had recently been some skirmishes between the Mwaviamuno and the Mocaromuno, and the Portuguese feared that a confrontation with the Mauruça might lead to a more dangerous situation. For the Portuguese, António Alberto Macedo emphasized their desire for peace with the Mauruça, courting him with presents and assuring him that 'you can freely send your people to the coast to trade'. A week after writing to the Mauruça, however, Macedo reported that the Impahiamuno had turned up at his residence in the middle of the night, having again been driven from Uticulo.[73]

The outcome of that year's struggle is not known, but the events of 1810 indicate that there was no resolution of the differences between the various Makua chiefs on the mainland. As always, each pursued his own interests and alliances of convenience abounded. No single power on the mainland was able to enforce its will on the others, a situation which had prevailed since the decline of Maravi domination in the last decades of the seventeenth century, so that there was a constant jockeying for position which kept Macuana seething. In May, after first seeking Portuguese approval, the Sheikh of Quitangonha joined the Mauruça in a successful war against a certain Madulamuno, whose territory appears to have been located well to the north of Uticulo. Following some indeterminate warring among various Makua chiefs in the neighbourhood of Mossuril in June—skirmishes which the Portuguese discreetly observed without daring to intervene—the Sheikh of Quitangonha began in August an extensive campaign, at specific Portuguese request, against a number of Makua chiefs. In the following week he was instructed to pacify not only dissident chiefs near his own territory, such as the Cherepomuno (or Cherepwemuno), but also those to the south of Mozambique Island, like the Moveramuno and the Sheikh of Mogincual, which involved an amphibious attack. Yet in entrusting this extensive punitive expedition to the Sheikh of Quitangonha, the Portuguese harboured certain fears about the ultimate intentions of their sudden ally. That these proved to be unfounded for the moment does not alter the fact that in 1810 the Portuguese were perched atop a very precariously balanced system of shifting alliances close to Mozambique.[74]

On 16 November a combined force of some 1,300 men, armed with guns and under the orders of the Mwasemuno, the Cherepomuno, and the Moveramuno, attacked Sanculo and Lumbo on the coast. For once Portuguese retaliation on their withdrawal to the interior was unusually effective, and the ever active Sheikh Zafir followed up their sweep immediately with a raid involving more than 3,500 men. Scenting a victory, and badly needing relief from the ceaseless plague of skirmishes on the mainland, the Portuguese decided to mount a final, crushing expedition against these Makua chiefs. This brief campaign was notable chiefly for the fact that in it the Portuguese utilized field artillery for the first time against the Makua. Like previous definitive Portuguese expeditions against the Makua, this one was successful only up to a point. The general effect of these combined efforts was to restore a temporary semblance of Portuguese hegemony over parts of the immediate interior, but the whole of Macuana was in such a state of unrest that complete order remained unattainable.[75]

In the decade after 1784 the Portuguese had learned that they could make sure of a steady supply of slaves by providing their trading partners in Macuana with firearms. But the success of this system depended on a delicate balance of all the elements which were then at play in the slave trade at Mozambique. The decline in the French demand for slaves after 1794 seems to have upset this equilibrium, while the gradual growth of the Brazilian trade did not restore it, and the Portuguese were suddenly ensnared in a web of their own making. Arming the local Makua with firearms was no longer altogether beneficial to the trade of Mozambique. Instead, as it had been in the middle of the eighteenth century, when ivory was the staple trade of the island, possession of large numbers of firearms simply transformed the Makua into a more formidable enemy than sheer numbers and traditional weaponry had made them already. Portuguese weakness in these circumstances is emphasized by their willingness to let their African 'allies' on the mainland do virtually all of their fighting for them. Unlike 1784, in the first decade of the nineteenth century the Portuguese were once again unable to impose a solution of their own choice to the problems of Macuana.

One of the most interesting changes in the Mozambique slave trade during the first decade of the nineteenth century is the appearance of large numbers of Yao for sale. According to Colin, who spent the peak trading months of August and September 1804 on the island, 'The blacks whom the traders prefer to all the others are the Makua; they reach Mozambique in good health, having made a journey of only 30 leagues, and sometimes less. They withstand the rigours of the sea better . . . than the other blacks.' In the myth-making and stereotyping that Europeans engaged in when describing different groups of African slaves, the Makua were reputed to be gay and enterprising, but cruel. They were also said to be more prone to rebellion aboard ship than were other slaves, whom they were believed to scorn and with whom they refused to eat. But despite the continued preference for Makua slaves,

> The Yaos are the most common type of blacks at Mozambique. One recognizes them by the stars which they make on their bodies, as well as the two or three horizontal bars below their temples. Their humour is melancholic; they are much attached to their master, provided that they are not maltreated; they are better made, in general, than the Makua, but rather less robust. One must realize that when they reach Mozambique, they have made a journey of 250 leagues, and are prostrated with fatigue; this is undoubtedly the reason why so many of them die at sea.

Colin also identified Maravi slaves at the coast, and noted that the Makonde were reputed for their intelligence; slaves from Sofala and Inhambane were also observed.[76]

Another new important source of slaves at Mozambique was the Rivers of Sena. In 1806 a total of 1,484 slaves had been exported from Quelimane to Mozambique, while in the following year, when the total volume of the trade at Mozambique was about 5,000 individuals, 1,080 came from the Rivers. Only a little trade was carried on in Macuana by the *patamares* of Portuguese merchants.[77] This was probably the result of the disturbances there.

By this time, too, the impact of the slave trade had extended to the farthest marches of East Central Africa. At Kazembe's in 1799, Fr. Pinto observed:

The trade goods could be many: but presently two are known,

which are ivory and slaves. A tusk of ivory weighing one *arroba* to one and a half *arrobas*, is purchased for two, or three pieces of cloth, and some ten hides. A slave is evaluated at a bit of cloth which is two fathoms, or a fathom and a half in length. A tusk of two and a half to three *arrobas* costs five or six pieces with a little hide, or *velório*. Copper ingots also appear which are sold for four fathoms of cloth, or forty or fifty hides. The small ingots regularly cost a fathom of beads (*missanga*). The rough green stones [*malachite*] of different sizes are sold cheap; however these last two goods are foreign.[78]

A decade later, Baptista confirmed this impression of trading priorities at the Kazembe's:

> The trade of the Cazembe's country consists of ivory, slaves, green-stones, and copper bars, which they sell to the travellers from Tete and Senna, and to blacks of the Huiza [Bisa] nation, who are established on the road to Tete . . . Colonist travellers from Tete and Senna give for each slave they buy in Cazembe's land at the present time five Indian sheetings, and for ivory six or seven sheetings and other extra articles for every large tusk, as Cazambe's people understand that ivory is more valued in Tete than slaves.[79]

It is very likely that the price differential between ivory and slaves during this decade at the Kazembe's reflected the continued domination of the ivory trade over the interior of East Africa. At the same time, the careful distinction made between different items of trade and different categories within items again reveals the commercial acumen of the African traders of the interior.

Perhaps a few of the Kazembe slaves were already reaching Mozambique and Kilwa in Yao caravans. Undoubtedly, some of the Maravi were, as were many Yao slaves. The surprising predominance of Yao slaves at Mozambique in 1804 may, however, also indicate that the search for slaves for the Macuana trade now reached as far as Yaoland. Unfortunately, information on Yao trading to Mossuril in the two decades after 1784 is almost nonexistent, consisting entirely of inconsequential notes indicating no more than their continued involvement in this traffic.[80] One feature which seems to have distinguished their trade, and which may partially explain the large numbers of Yao slaves on the market at this time, was their willingness to do business at a regular fair at Mossuril.

The Yao Fair at Mossuril:
an Early Example of Unequal Exchange

The Portuguese administration was keen to have all trade on the mainland conducted at controlled fairs, as is shown by the remarks of Manuel Loureiro, who served as *Ouvidor* (Crown Judge) and Judge of the Customs-house at Mozambique from 1798 into 1802: 'It would be very convenient if the trade of the interior were conducted only at the National Settlements [e.g., Mossuril], where the free negroes come to offer us gold, ivory, and some foodstuffs, in exchange for the cloths which they value, as happens on the Mainland of the Capital with the Yao negroes'.[81] Here again, however, it is not the Portuguese who provide us with a description of Yao trade on the mainland, but the British ambassador plenipotentiary to Abyssinia, Henry Salt.

Salt was at Mozambique for just over three weeks in August–September 1809, but his natural curiosity and the lack of other diversions turned his attention to the Yao fair at Mossuril.

> In the afternoon [29 August] we walked to the house of one of the planters, about a mile distant, in the village of Mesuril, for the purpose of seeing some native traders from the interior, of a nation called Monjou [Yao], who had come down with a cafila of slaves, (chiefly female) together with gold and elephants' teeth for sale.[82]

On the next day, Salt returned 'to the house of the planter where the Monjou traders resided', where he bought a bow and some arrows from one of the Yao.

> In the cool of the evening, the planter took us to a kind of fair held in the neighbourhood for the purpose of bartering with the traders lately arrived. The articles displayed to tempt these simple savages were very trifling, such as salt, shells, beads, tobacco, coloured handkerchiefs and coarse cloths from Surat; a circumstance that proves how artfully the Portuguese have carried on this species of traffic, otherwise they could not have kept the natives in an ignorance thus suitable to their purposes. I was informed that in the interior, the traders are still able to purchase for about the value of two dollars, in the above articles, either a slave, or an elephant's tooth from sixty to eighty pounds weight. This fair was superintended by a guard of the Portuguese native troops. . . . [83.]

It would appear that the Yao whom Salt met were primarily slave traders. He also provides some insight into the way in which the Yao actually negotiated their business at Mossuril. Official evaluations notwithstanding, trade was still a matter of individual, undoubtedly slow, bargaining between buyer and seller. It would also seem that some sort of 'landlord and stranger' relationship existed between these Yao and the Portuguese planter who provided them with shelter during their stay at the coast. What the Portuguese 'landlord' received in return for his services to the Yao traders is not known, but if the West African example is valid here, he probably was compensated by either direct payment in the form of Yao merchandise or by some other mutually agreed upon arrangement.[84] Retrospectively, it also seems likely that the situation which Salt observed was well established at Mossuril and that it was analagous to the Banyan system of trade with the Yao which was discussed earlier. (See Chapter 5, pp. 145–6). As for his remarks on the cleverness of the Portuguese as traders, they reveal both his ignorance of the history of trade at Mozambique and his own contempt for the Yao as Africans, whom he belittled as ugly and child-like. Within the international trading system of East Central Africa, Yao traders were resourceful, intelligent, and selective. Certainly they were far more sophisticated in their ability to evaluate the factors at play within this closed system than were the Portuguese, whose myopic policies frequently brought trade to a standstill during the second half of the eighteenth century.

Yet Salt put his finger on something which the Yao and other Africans were unable to perceive at the beginning of the nineteenth century. Indeed, it is improbable that the local Portuguese were capable of recognizing this fundamental point, since they were always wholly absorbed in their immediate setting, where they knew themselves to be ineffective traders. What Salt correctly identified was the disparity in real value between the ivory, gold, and slaves which were traded by Africans to Europeans (and by extension Indians) for a variety of beads, trinkets, and cloths. In his eyes, Africans were being completely hoodwinked in this unequal trade. In the wider context of world economic history there can be little doubt that his analysis was just. But it is important here to strike a balance of perceptions, a balance which recognizes that from the point of view of people like the Yao they were receiving otherwise unobtainable goods of both great practical and prestige value in exchange for raw materials which were of little intrinsic value in their own societies. The fact that the slave trade was a trade in humans might seem to challenge this perception, but so long as slaves could be provided from the outcasts of society or from other societies, this dilemma could be avoided. It is wrong, then, to assume as some do that because of the economic exploitation of East Africa by European, Indian, and Arab traders, those Africans who traded with them were necessarily their dupes or lackeys. This would imply a high level of economic and political consciousness and shared economic perceptions, neither of which existed in East Africa at this time. Rather, the pre-colonial trade of East Africa was governed by the congruence of different economic systems with different sets of perceptions.

At the beginning of the nineteenth century, African economies like those of the Yao were confronted mainly by the developing industrial capitalism of the West, the mercantile capitalism of India, which backed most Arab trade in East Africa, and the re-invigorated mercantile capitalism of Masqat. But already, as in the profits which Indian merchants reaped from supplying Surat cloths for the European-dominated slave trade and in the in-creasing subordination of the ivory trade of Surat to that of Great Britain, the penetration of European capital was beginning to dominate the economic development of East Africa. And from this mercantile domination would grow Europe's imperial con-quest at the end of the century.

NOTES

1. A.H.U., Moç., Cx. 31, D. Diogo de Sousa to M. de Melo e Castro, Moç., 22 August 1795.
2. Varella, 'Descrição', in Carvalho Dias, 'Fontes', pp. 295–6, and in Andrade, *Relações*, pp. 388–9; A.H.U., Moç., 25, António José Teixeira Tigre to A. M. de Melo e Castro ,Ibo, 24 December 1788; A.H.U., Moç., Cx. 26, Manuel de Nasci-mento Nunes to Crown, Moç., 10 June 1790, paragraph 19; A.H.U., Moç., Cx. 54, Sheikh of Quitangonha, Zafir Salimo, *requerimento*, n.d., but definitely post-1804 and probably *c.* 1810; see also, Lobato, *Lourenço Marques*, II, pp. 298, 312, for further evidence of Melo e Castro's and Sousa's toleration of the Banyans.
3. M. G. J. Loureiro, *Memorias dos Estabellecimentos Portuguezes a l'Este do Cabo da Boa Esperança* . . . (Lisbon, 1835), p. 289; A.H.U., Moç., Cx. 41, petition of José Mariano Ribeiro, n.d., granted by Governor, Moç., 4 July 1803; A.H.U., Moç., Cx. 42, petition of Tanaclande Gopal, n.d., granted Moç., 20 August 1803; Epidariste Colin, 'Notice sur Mozambique', in Malte-Brun, *Annales des Voyages, de la Géographie et de l'histoire* (Paris, 1809), IX, p. 314.
4. A.H.U., Cod. 1374, fl. 31–62, 'Registo de Requerimento e mais Documentos de Lacamichande Matichande que deio a informar a este Governo', n.d., but last of

the appended documents is dated 29 November 1808; A.H.U., Moç., Cx. 46, 'Mappa das Embarcaçoens, que possuem os Banianes, e mais Gentios nesta Capital de Mossambique', Moç., 13 November 1805; A.H.U., Moç., Cx. 62, Sir Evan Nepean to José Francisco de Paula Cavalcanti de Albuquerque, Bombay, 11 November 1817, and enclosures; A.H.U., Cod. 1383, no. 1013, Crown to António de Melo Castro e Mendonça, Rio de Janeiro, 20 April 1810, enclosing same to *Senado da Câmara* of Mozambique, Rio de Janeiro, 19 April 1810; A.H.U., Cod. 1377, fl. 22, Francisco Carlos da Costa Lacé to Subachande Seuchande, Moç., 5 February 1810.

5. A.H.U., Moç., Cx. 32 and Cod. 1478, fl. 7–9, *alvará*, A.M. de Melo e Castro, Moç., 21 July 1787; A.H.U., Moç., Cx. 29, Sousa to M. de Melo e Castro, Moç., 28 July 1794. For voices raised against these measures, see A.H.U., Moç., Cx. 33, merchants of Mozambique to Sousa, Moç., 17 October 1796; ibid., decision taken by the Deputies of the *Junta da Fazenda Real*, Moç., 8 April 1797. The later adjustments can be followed in A.H.U., Cod. 1472, fl. 155–6, Crown to Francisco Guedes de Carvalho e Meneses da Costa, Queluz, 2 April 1799; *A.C.U.*, p.n.o., V (1864), pp. 65–6; and Lobato, *Lourenço Marques*, II, pp. 291–8, 308–13, 397–402. See also A.H.U., Moç., Cx. 33, João da Silva Guedes, 'Declaração expecificada do modo por que se cobravão os Direitos nesta Alf.ª por entrada e Sahida . . .', n.d., but perhaps *c.* 1797; A.H.U., Cod. 1472, fl. 176–83, D. Rodrigo de Sousa Coutinho to Isidro de Almeida de Sousa e Sá, Lisboa, 28 February 1801; A.H.U., Cod. 1500, fl. 59, Vicente da Silva Negrão, 'Pautta da Regulação dos Direitos da entrada, e Sahida da Alfandega de Moss.ᵉ', Moç., 10 August 1809.

6. A.H.U., Moç., Cx. 32, Silva Guedes, 'Relação exacta dos despachos do Marfim . . . que desta Capital se exportou em o anno de 1793', Moç., 18 July 1796; A.H.U., Moç., Cx. 38, Silva Guedes, 'Mapa do marfim . . . q̃. se despachar.ᵃᵒ p.ʳ sah.ª p.ª a India . . .', Moç., 3 September 1801, enclosed in Sousa e Sá to Sousa Coutinho, Moç., 5 November 1801; A.H.U., Cod. 1381, fl. 4, Silva Guedes, 'Mapa do Marfim . . . nesta Monção de Agosto de 1809'.

7. A.H.U., Moç., Cx. 39, Joaquim Giraldes Rosa, 'Mappa da Carga que tras a Goleta Maria do Porto de Inhambane para esta Capital dado pello Capitão . . .', [Moç.], 11 April 1802 (2070 tusks, weighing 64 *bares*, 11 *arrobas*); ibid., José Sebastião Jorge de Brito, 'Mapa do Estado atoal do Brique S.ᵗᵃ Ant.º Delingente', August 1802 (420 *arrobas*); A.H.U., Moç., Cx. 50, Prov. Govt. to Crown, Moç., 22 October 1807, reporting that in 1806 a total of 4375 tusks of ivory were sent from the Rivers of Sena to Mozambique; but see Isaacman, *Mozambique*, p. 86, Table 6 and source, where the figure given is 4375 *arrobas*. See also A.H.U., Moç., Cx. 43, anonymous, 'Mapa da Carga da Cruveta Felis Costa', n.d. (30 *bares*); ibid., António Norberto de Barbosa de Vilasboas Truão to Felix Lamberto da Silva Bandeira, Tete, 5 November 1804; Lobato, *Lourenço Marques*, II, pp. 414–15. By this time a *bar* was composed of 15 *arrobas* and therefore weighed the equivalent of 220·320 kg.

8. A.H.U., Cod. 1472, fl. 176–7, Sousa Coutinho to Sousa e Sá, Lisboa, 28 February 1801.

9. A.H.U., Moç., Cx. 53, Joaquim José de Melo e Costa, 'Acrescimo que houve da antiga Pauta da Alfandega formalizada no anno de 1787, para a que se formalizou no prezente de 1810', Moç., 12 December 1810; Salt, *Voyage to Abyssinia*, p. 82.

10. Sheriff, 'Rise of a Commerical Empire', pp. 99–100. The top price quoted by Salt for Mozambique in 1809 was equal to that paid at Zanzibar two decades later. See ibid., p. 469, Graph II.

11. Milburn, *Oriental Commerce* (London, 1813), I, p. 62.

12. C. S. Nicholls, *The Swahili Coast: Politics, Diplomacy and Trade on the East African Littoral, 1798–1856*, St. Antony's Publication No. 2 (London, 1971), pp. 81–2, 85, 99, 101, 373; Gray, *History of Zanzibar from the Middle Ages to 1856* (London, 1962), pp. 92–108, quoting the more important sources at length.

13. See Nicholls, *Swahili Coast*, p. 217, for the most recent variation of this theme; but cf. Sheriff, 'Rise of a Commercial Empire'.

14. Francisco José de Lacerda e Almeida, *Travessia da Africa* (Lisbon, 1936), p. 155; Isaacman, *Mozambique*, p. 80.

15. Lacerda e Almeida, *Travessia*, pp. 208, 233, 385–7.

16. Pedro João Baptista and José Amaro, 'Journey of the Pombeiros from Angola to the Rios de Senna', in Burton, *The Lands of Cazembe* (London, 1873), p. 228.

17. Lacerda e Almeida, *Travessia*, p. 387.

18. ibid., p. 388.

19. Jerónimo José Nogueira de Andrade, 'Descripção do Estado em que ficavão os Negocios da Capitania de Mossambique nos fins de Novembro de 1789 com algumas Observaçoens, e reflecçoens sobre a causa da decadencia do Commercio dos Estabellecimentos Portuguezes na Costa Oriental da Affrica', 1790, in *A.C.*, I (1917), p. 126; A.H.U., Moç., Cx. 36, Meneses da Costa to Sousa Coutinho, Moç., 29 July 1800; a copy of this letter is also in A.H.U., Cod. 1366, fl. 94, where it is misdated to 29 June 1800; excerpts from this copy are published in Lacerda e Almeida, *Travessia*, pp. 69–71.

20. ibid., pp. 208, 385–6.

21. Salt, *Voyage to Abyssinia*, pp. 32–3.

22. Baptista and Amaro, 'Journey of the Pombeiros', p. 188; Shorter, 'The Kimbu', in Roberts (ed.) *Tanzania before 1900* (Nairobi, 1968), p. 106. Salt seems to have known only of the principal Nyamwezi route to the Mrima coast. See B. M., Add. Ms. 19,419, fl. 14, where he notes that 'the Monjou—trade up as far as Quiloa—the Ambeze or Eveze higher up'.

23. See Chapter 5, p. 161

24. See Chapter 5, p. 159,

25. Lacerda e Almeida, *Travessia*, pp. 233, 71; A.H.U., Moç., Cx. 34, Meneses da Costa to Crown, Lisboa, 1 February 1804.

26. Truão, 'Extracto', p. 414; cf. Baptista and Amaro, 'Journey of the Pombeiros', pp. 168, 200, 226–7.

27. A.H.U., Moç., Cx. 29, Manuel António Correa to Sousa, Ibo, 10 June 1794, enclosed in Sousa to M. de Melo e Castro, Moç., 20 August 1794.

28. ibid., Correa to Sousa, Ibo, 27 January 1794; ibid., Sousa to Correa, Moç., 6 November 1794; A.H.U., Moç., Cx. 31, *bando*, Constantino António Álvares da Silva, Ibo, 27 August 1795; A.H.U., Moç., Cx. 30, same to Sousa, Ibo, 18 October 1795; A.H.U., Moç., Cx. 32, same to same, Ibo, 26 March 1796, and series of letters dated 10–12 October 1796; cf. Teixeira Botelho, *História*, I, pp. 551–3; Mabel V. Jackson, *European Powers in South-East Africa: A Study of Internal Relations on the South-East Coast of Africa, 1796–1856* (London, 1942), pp. 47–8.

29. A.H.U., Moç., Cx. 35 and Cod. 1472, fl. 149–50, royal *alvará*, Lisboa, 13 or 14 March 1798; A.H.U., Moç., Cx. 35, Álvares da Silva to Meneses da Costa, Ibo, 2 June 1798; ibid., twenty-four colonists to same, Querimba, 28 February 1799; ibid., António da Silva Pinto to same, Ibo, 21 November 1799; A.H.U., Moç., Cx. 36, Meneses da Costa to Silva Pinto, Moç., 19 June 1800; ibid., Álvares da Silva to Nicolau Luís da Graça, Ibo, 8 March 1799.

30. See Raymond K. Kent, *Early Kingdoms in Madagascar, 1500–1700* (New York, 1970), p. 203.

31. A.H.U., Moç., Cx. 38. Silva Pinto to Meneses da Costa, Ibo, 24 February 1801.

32. A.H.U., Moç., Cx. 48, Prov. Govt. to Pereira, Moç., 20 September 1808; ibid. and Cod. 1372, fl. 32–3, same to Visconde de Anadia, Moç., 10 November 1808; A.H.U., Moç Cx. 52, Pereira to Prov. Govt., Ibo, 1 April 1809; A.H.U., Moç., Cx. 54, Jerónimo Fernandes Viana to same, Ibo, 16 and 19 February 1810; Guillain, *Documents sur l'Histiore, la géographie et le commerce de la partie occidentale de Madagascar* (Paris, 1845), pp. 200–1.

33. *Dicionário Corográfico da Província de Moçambique* (Lisbon, 1919), I, pp. 96–7, 115, 165.

34. A.H.U., Moç., Cx. 38, Silva Pinto to Sousa e Sá, Ibo, 5 November 1801; A.H.U., Moç., Cx. 40, same to António Francisco Fernandes, Ibo, 24 March 1802; A.H.U., Moç., Cx. 46, Rodrigo Berri to Sousa e Sá, Ibo, 16 February 1805; ibid., *parecer*, *Senado da Câmara*, Ibo, 12 November 1805; A.H.U., Moç., Cx. 48, Pereira to Amaral Cardoso, Ibo, 26 February 1807.

35. ibid., Amaral Cardoso to Pereira, Moç., 23 March 1807.

36. ibid., João Gonzales Delgado to António da Costa Portugal, Mocimboa, 25 November 1806, ibid., Costa Portugal to Pereira, Muluri, 12 January 1807.

37. A.H.U., Moç., Cx. 38, Silva Pinto to Sousae Sá, Ibo, 25 February and 5 November 1801; A.H.U., Moç., Cx. 46, Berri to same, n.d., but probably 1805; ibid., same to same, Ibo, 17 January 1805; A.H.U., Moç., Cx. 50, Pereira to Amaral Cardoso, Ibo, 26 February 1807; A.H.U., Moç., Cx. 48, same to same, Ibo, 10 March 1807; A.H.U., Moç., Cx. 54, Francisco António de Sousa Cesar to Mendonça, Ibo, 28 December 1810, enclosing *requerimento* of the colonists of the Kerimba Islands, n.d., but post-July 1810.

38. A.H.U., Moç., Cx. 38, Silva Pinto, 'Descripção das Terras do Cabo Delgado pertencentes a Coroa', Ibo, 24 November 1801; for a verbatim citation of this report, see A.H.U., Moç., Cx. 50, Prov. Govt. to Crown, Moç., 22 October 1807.

39. Louis Dermigny, *Cargaisons Indiennes—Solier et Cie, 1781–1793* (Paris, 1959–60), I, p. 110, n. 23, 98. Although no comparative figures for slave mortality are known from French sources, one Portuguese document records that there was a 30 per cent death rate for slaves transported from Mozambique to Rio de Janeiro, as compared with a 20 per cent rate on the West Africa to Brazil passage: A.H.U., Moç., Cx. 13, anonymous, 'Os Francezes extraem . . .', n.d.; see also, Chapter 7, p. 211, and ibid., n. 13.

40. A.H.U., Moç., Cx. 26, A.M. de Melo e Castro to M. de Melo e Castro, Moç., 14 August 1789; A.H.U., Moç., Cx. 27, same to same, Moç., 24 August 1790 and 20 August 1791.

41. Nogueira de Andrade, 'Descripção', in *A.C..*, II (1918), pp. 32–6, estimated that the Mozambique coast provided some 4,000 to 5,000 or more, slaves each year.

42. Jackson, *European Powers*, p. 85, n. 2;

	1805	January–8 October 1806
Ivory to India	11:549$162	11:293$429
Gold in powder	2:261$280	:891$520
Slaves in national ships	7:416$000	16:211$700
Slaves in foreign ships	18:630$400	4:320$800

43. A.H.U., Cod. 1472, fl. 107–11, M. de Melo e Castro to Sousa, Queluz, 12 October 1792, paragraph 10; A.H.U., Moç., Cx. 32, Sousa to Luís Pinto de Sousa, Moç., 26 September 1796.

44. Santana, *Documentação*, I, pp. 83–4.

45. Isaacman, *Mozambique*, p. 86.

46. A.H.U., Cod. 1370, fl. 16, Sousa e Sá to Sousa Coutinho, Moç., 28 August 1802.

47. Salt, *Voyage to Abyssinia*, pp. 34–5, 80.

48. Earl of Caledon to Nicholas Vansittart, Cape of Good Hope, 27 June 1810, in Theal, *Records*, IX, p. 12.

49. A.H.U., Moç., Cx. 25, Correa to A. M. de Melo e Castro, Ibo, 4 March 1788.

50. A.H.U., Moç., Cx. 26, Tigre to same, Ibo, 2 April 1789, enclosing Tigre, 'Rellação das Embarcaçoens de Mouros da Costa q̃ tem a Porta do nesta Ilha de S. João do Ibo passagem p.^a a Capital de Moss.^e, outras, que ficarão p.^a algum Portos piquenos desta jurisdição . . .', Ibo, 2 April 1789. Of forty craft, seventeen were reportedly from Pate, bound for Mozambique; ten from around Pate, of which four were destined for Mozambique, while three were staying at Ibo, two at Arimba, and one at Querimba; five were from Zanzibar, bound for Mozambique; two were from Mombasa and one from Kilwa, with the same destination; an

additional five were from Anjouan Island, in the Comoros, and were at ports in the Kerimba Islands.

51. ibid., same to same, Ibo, 22 February 1789; pursuant correspondence ibid., and A.H.U., Cod. 1478, fl. 25-28, dated Moç., 3-6 April 1789; A.H.U., Moç., Cx. 26 and Cod. 1500, fl. 18, *bando*, Tigre, Ibo, 18 April 1789; A.H.U., Moç., Cx. 26, same to A. M. de Melo e Castro, Ibo, 16 July 1789.

52. A.H.U., Moç., Cx. 27, same to same, Ibo, 8 November 1790.

53. A.H.U., Moç., Cx. 25, same to same, Ibo, 24 December 1788; A.H.U., Moç., Cx. 26, A. M. de Melo e Castro to M. de Melo e Castro, Moç., 14 January 1789; Nogueria de Andrade, 'Descripção', in *A.C.*, I, p. 125.

54. See Alpers, 'French Slave Trade', pp. 118-19.

55. A.N.F., Colonies C⁴80, Saulnier de Mondevit, 'Memoire sur la Baye *de Lindy* et le Rivière *de Mongalo*, située à la côte orientale de l'Afrique', dated internally to 1786.

56. A.H.U., Moç., Cx. 48, António Alberto Pereira to Prov. Govt., Ibo. 16 August 1808.

57. A.N.F., Colonies C⁴80, Saulnier de Mondevit, 'Mémoire sur la nécessité'.

58. J. M. Gray, *History of Zanzibar*, pp. 92-108; Nicholls, *Swahili Coast*, p. 199; A.H.U., Moç., Cx. 44, Meneses da Costa to Crown, Lisboa, 6 January 1804.

59. Nicholls, *Swahili Coast*, p. 199.

60. See Alpers, *The East African Slave Trade*, Historical Association of Tanzania Paper No. 3 (Nairobi, 1967), pp. 1-2.

61. Nicholls, *Swahili Coast*, chapter 8. Cf. J. B. Kelley, *Britain and the Persian Gulf, 1795-1880* (Oxford, 1968), pp. 412-17.

62. Sheriff, 'Rise of a Commercial Empire', pp. 157-71.

63. Nicholls, *Swahili Coast*, p. 204.

64. ibid., pp. 96-9.

65. Cf. Alpers, *East African Slave Trade*, p. 11.

66. See A.H.U., Moç., Cx. 22, Manuel Galvão da Silva to Governor (?), Moç., n.d., but dated from other sources to August 1785; A.H.U., Moç., Cx. 26, A. M. de Melo e Castro, Moç., 14 January and 19 August 1789.

67. A.H.U., Moç., Cx. 23, same to same, Moç., 27 August 1787 (two letters bearing the same date); A.H.U., Moç., Cx. 26, same to same, Moç., 13 August 1789. For a reference to the forging of musket balls at this time by Makua smiths, see A.H.U., Moç., Cx. 22, Galvao da Silva, 'Noticia Sobre as duas Minas de ferro . . .', Moç., 21 August 1785.

68. A.H.U., Moç., Cx. 15, Pereira do Lago to Crown, Moç., 15 August 1778.

69. A.H.U., Moç., Cx. 31, Sousa to Manuel Pereira Baptista, Moç., 8 February 1795; A.H.U., Moç., Cx. 28, Álves da Silva to Sousa, Ibo, 9 October 1795; A.H.U., Moç., Cx. 35, Meneses da Costa to Sousa Coutinho, Moç., 25 August 1799; A.H.U., Moç., Cx. 36, Luís Correa Monteiro de Matos to Governor (?), Mossuril, 5 December 1799; ibid., same, or José António Caldas, to Governor (?), Mossuril, 1799 (fragment); A.H.U., Moç., Cx. 37, António Álvares de Macedo to Governor, Uticulo, 16 February 1801; A.H.U., Moç., Cx. 38, Meneses da Costa to Sousa Coutinho, Moç., 21 September 1801; ibid., Sousa e Sá to same, Moç., 23 September 1801; cf. Teixeira Botelho, *História*, I, pp. 501-3, 529-30.

70. A.H.U., Moç., Cx. 44, Sousa e Sá to Anadia, Moç., 28 October 1804.

71. A.H.U., Cod. 1372, fl. 26-8, [Amaral Cardoso] to same, Moç., 9 October 1807.

72. B.N.L., F.G., Cod. 8470, no. 4, Caldas to Prov. Govt., Moç., 5 November 1808; A.H.U., Moç., Cx. 50, same to same, Moç., 17 August 1808.

73. A.H.U., Moç., Cx. 52, Macedo to Prov. Govt., Moç., 10 April 1809; ibid., same to the Mauruça, Mossuril, 9 May 1809, enclosed in same to Prov. Govt., Mossuril, 10 May 1809; ibid., same to same, Mossuril, 16 and 17 May 1809.

74. A.H.U., Moç., Cx. 53, Macedo to Mendonça, Moç., 7 May 1810; A.H.U., Cod. 1380, fl. 35-6, Mendonça to Conde das Galveâs, Moç., 8 November 1810; A.H.U.,

Cod. 1377, fl. 38, 45–7, same to Sheikh of Quitangonha, Mossuril, 1 August, 29 September, and 7 October 1810; ibid., fl. 49, same to same, Moç., 3 November 1810 (two letters bearing same date); A.H.U., Moç., Cx. 53, Sheikh of Quitangonha Zafir Salimo, to Mendonça (?), Campo de Chagan, 6 October 1810. For the location of Moveira Muno's territory, see A.H.U., Moç., Cx. 56, *requiremento* of Cangi Petambor, n.d., but approved at Moç., 14 September 1812.

75. A.H.U., Moç., Cx. 54 and Cod. 1374, fl. 85–6, Cardenas e Mira, Campo de Impoença, 24 November 1810; A.H.U., Cod. 1380, fl. 46–8, Mendonça to Galveâs, Moç., 28 November 1810; A.H.U., Moç., Cx. 53, Cardenas e Mira to Mendonça, Mossuril, 12 December 1810.

76. Colin, 'Notice sur Mozambique', pp. 304, 312, 320–23. It is only fair to note that Colin's observation's on the volume of the trade in ivory and slaves at Mozambique are grossly inflated. But for his ability to recognize the provenance of slaves, see W. F. W. Owen, *Narrative of Voyages to explore the shores of Africa, Arabia, and Madagascar* (London, 1833), I, p. 295: 'The practice of tatooing is here universal, and, as each tribe has its distinguishing mark, a slave-dealer can at first sight tell to which particular one his victim belongs'.

77. Isaacman, *Mozambique*, p. 88, Table 6; A.H.U., Moç., Cx. 50, Prov. Govt. to Crown, Moç., 22 October 1807; see also, J. Tomkinson to Albermarle Bertie, Mozambique, 11 June 1809, in Theal, *Records*, IX, pp. 4–5.

78. Lacerda e Almeida, *Travessia*, pp. 297–8.

79. Baptista and Amaro, 'Journey of the Pombeiros', pp. 228–9.

80. Tigre to A. M. de Melo e Castro, Moç., 28 March 1790, in Caetano Montez, Inventário', *Moçambique*, 76 (1953), p.134, Document 69; B. N.L, F.G., Cod. 8105, anonymous, 'Moçambique', n.d., but post–1783; cf. Varella, 'Descrição', who merely echoes earlier descriptions of this trade.

81. Loureiro, *Memorias*, pp. 289–90. It is unclear why Loureiro fails to mention slaves in this passage.

82. Salt, *Voyage*, pp. 32–3.

83. ibid., pp. 35–6.

84. The 'landlord and stranger' concept has not previously been suggested in the context of pre-colonial trade in East Africa. In West Africa it has been explored most extensively by C. Fyfe and V. R. Dorjahn, 'Landlord and Stranger: Change in Tenancy Relations in Sierra Leone', *Jl. of African History*, III, 3 (1962), pp. 391–7; Polly Hill, 'Landlords and Brokers: A West African Trading System', *Cahiers d'Etudes Africaines*, VI (1966), pp. 351–66; and Abner Cohen, *Custom and Politics in Urban Africa: A Study of Hause Immigrants in Yoruba Towns* (London, 1969), especially chapters 1 and 3. It is also possible that African traders from the far interior returned each year to trade with the same merchant, be he Portuguese or Indian. This was certainly the case at Bagamoyo in the nineteenth century, as current research is demonstrating.

CHAPTER SEVEN

The Growth and Impact of the Slave Trade after 1810

❁❁❁❁❁❁❁❁❁❁❁❁❁❁❁❁❁❁❁❁❁❁❁❁❁❁❁❁❁❁

The Mozambique Coast

The first half of the nineteenth century in East Africa was marked by the continued rapid growth of the slave trade. All along the coast the demand for slaves steadily mounted, as Arabs, Brazilians, French, Spanish slavers from Cuba, and Americans discovered East Africa in the wake of the British anti-slave trade campaign in West Africa. East Africa was not completely ignored in the British campaign to abolish the slave trade, but it clearly was considered to be of secondary importance until the successful eradication of the West African traffic. Treaties were sought and sometimes secured with the Portuguese, the French, 'Uman, and the Hova rulers of Madagascar, but severe limitations on the rights of the British navy to seize and search suspected offending vessels, the inadequate size of the antislave trade patrol in the Indian Ocean, and the desire of virtually no body of traders in East Africa to abandon a most lucrative business rendered the campaign largely ineffective until the second half of the century.[1] Thus there were no serious obstacles to the unprecedented expansion of the exportation of slaves from East Africa for the half century after 1810.

At Mozambique Island slaves were already established as the most important item of commerce. In 1809 ivory exports had declined to about 7,300 *arrobas*; in 1817 they had sunk to less than 4,000 *arrobas*.[2] By the following year revenue collected on the exportation of slaves (52:815$600 *réis*) was more than five times that accruing from exportations of ivory and other goods (10:089$215 *réis*), alone accounting for 32·26 per cent of the total revenue of the customs-house (163:673$288 *réis*.[3] And in 1819 the Governor-General of Mozambique, João da Costa de Brito Sanches, observed that 'the present commerce of the Colony only consists of the principal article of slaves, and some ivory, which is exported to the North in two, or three vessels'.[4] A few years later, this impression was substantiated by the visiting Captain Owen, who observed that 'the commerce of Mozambique has much decreased, and at present it is little more than a mart for slaves, together with a small quantity of ivory, gold dust, and a few articles of minor value'.[5]

According to Governor-General Sebastião Xavier Botelho, whose memoirs on the colony are often fanciful and unreliable, there was a marked revival of the ivory trade of Macuana during his administration in the late 1820s. But Botelho's figures are undoubtedly inflated, and his description of this trade looks suspiciously derivative from several later eighteenth-century accounts of this trade during its heyday.[6] Perhaps there was a temporary increase in the ivory trade of Macuana in those years—it was never abandoned completely—but official customs-house figures for 1829 demonstrate convincingly the commanding position of the slave trade at Mozambique. Slaves (110:667$790 *réis*) produced some 55 per cent of the revenue received from total exports (201:909$792 *réis*) in that year, with coinage accounting for slightly less than 3 per cent and 'diverse goods', among which ivory must have been included, accounting for the remaining 42 per cent.[7] Since 1818 revenue from the slave trade had more than doubled, while that of the colony as a whole had increased by not quite 24 per cent. The export economy gradually ceased to be dominated by the slave trade in the 1850s, when the colonial encyclopaedist, Francisco Maria Bordalo, wrote of the customs-house at Mozambique: 'For a long time the duties from this customs-house were the principal revenue of the colony; almost exhausted by the extinction of the slave trade, a new expansion is today promised with the gradual development of legitimate commerce'.[8]

Most of the demand for slaves at Mozambique came from Brazil. Following Great Britain's abolition of the slave trade by British subjects in 1807, much pressure was brought to bear on the Portuguese Crown first to restrict and then to abolish the slave trade carried on by Portuguese subjects and in Portuguese territories. These measures did not achieve their purpose until the second half of the century, but by legally limiting, in 1815 and 1817, the Portuguese slave trade to Portuguese possessions in Africa lying south of the equator, they encouraged the diversion of much of the Brazilian traffic from West Africa to Portuguese East Africa. The achievement of Brazilian independence in 1822 further frustrated Britain's attempts to abolish the slave trade south of the equator.[9] Thus, although slaves from Mozambique were less in demand than those coming from the Congo region and Angola —in Maranhão they simply did not flourish—this trans-Atlantic trade was pursued vigorously.[10]

As usual, quantification of the slave trade is a risky undertaking, especially after 1830, when the trade at Brazil was declared illegal. Milburn's estimate that some 10,000 slaves annually were exported from Mozambique at the beginning of the second decade of the nineteenth century seems to be exaggerated; but by the end of that decade this was probably a minimal figure.[11] In 1818 export duties were collected on 8,164 slaves, but in order to appreciate the significance of that figure it is necessary to recognize that these were not the only slaves brought to the market at Mozambique.[12] Generally, some fifteen to eighteen Brazilian vessels arrived at Mozambique between July and October to trade for slaves in return for money. According to D. Fr. Bartolomeu dos Mártires, Prelate of Mozambique from 1819 to his death in 1828, in 1819 sixteen Brazilian ships embarked from that port with cargoes of slaves. Fr. Bartolomeu recorded that the Brazilians bought 9,242 slaves, 1,804 of whom died at Mozambique; and of the 7,920 who were embarked, 2,196 died on the voyage to Brazil, so that only 5,234 were landed there, at Rio de Janeiro, Bahia, and Pernambuco, a mortality rate of 27·7 per cent on the sea passage alone. Furthermore, some 1,200 slaves who were awaiting sale at Mozambique died before they could be purchased. In 1819, then, at least 10,442 slaves were known to have been carried to Mozambique for sale to Brazilian slavers alone. Of these, only half ever reached their intended destination.[13]

Figures compiled by British consulate officials in Brazil, in particular Rio de Janeiro, reflect the increasing volume of the Mozambique slave trade during the 1820s, but they are undoubtedly incomplete. Many slaves were disembarked in Brazil without paying duties at Rio de Janeiro, just as untold numbers were taken on illegally along the coast running north and south from Mozambique Island. In 1821, for example, the first year for which these detailed figures exist, only 2,941 slaves were reported by the British as having been embarked at Mozambique aboard Brazilian vessels. In the same year, dos Mártires, who was by then a member of the Revolutionary Provisional Government, reports that export duties were collected on 12,272 slaves at Mozambique.[14] However, even official figures from Mozambique tended to be conservative. In 1826, the Captain of a British cruiser anchored at Mozambique wrote:

> Between eight and ten thousand [slaves] are entered at the Custom house annually as being exported from the Port of Mozambique to the Brazils—however I consider that about $\frac{1}{4}$ or more may be added to that number as being shipped off to the Brazils in these vessels. This additional fourth is smuggled on board to cheat the Custom house.[15]

Portuguese objections to this contraband trade from Quitangonha to Brazilian vessels anchored in Mozambique harbour became particularly vocal in 1830.[16] Accordingly, although they are better than no index at all, the figures reproduced in Table 5 primarily from British consular dispatches in Brazil for the 1820s, the last decade of the legal slave trade in Brazil, must be recognized for what they are—seriously deficient, especially when the primary consideration is not how many slaves were landed in Brazil, but how many were brought to the Mozambique coast as a result of the increased demand for slaves to be exported. Nevertheless, they do indicate that at least more than 4,950 slaves each year were being shipped from Mozambique Island to Brazil.[17]

After 1830–1831, it is impossible to match even this level of quantification for the slave trade from Mozambique to Brazil. In the absence of official Brazilian records, British consuls were reduced to an exercise in intelligent guesswork. In most cases they greatly underestimated the volume of the illicit trade. Bethell's compilation of British Foreign Office statistics for the last two decades of the Brazilian slave trade indicate that at least 500,000 slaves were illegally imported into Brazil during this period.[18] How many of these came from Portuguese East Africa, let alone Mozambique Island, is impossible to establish. Nevertheless, it seems reasonable to assume that the proportion for Portuguese East Africa of nearly one quarter of all slaves imported at Rio de Janeiro in the flush years of 1828–1830 immediately preceding

TABLE 5

Slaves Exported from Mozambique, 1818–1830

Year	Number of slaves
1818	8,164[a]
1819	7,920[b]
1820	——
1821	12,272[a] (2,941[c])
1822	4,973[d]
1823	4,204[e]
1824	3,173[c]
1825	3,753[c]
1826	——
1827	2,810[c]
1828	6,655[c]
1829	7,789[f]
1830	6,350[c]
Total	68,063

Sources: A.C.L., Azul Ms. 648, no. 17; Mártires, 'Memoria,' fl. 35; P.R.O., F.O. 84/17, Hayne to Earl of Clanwilliam, Rio de Janeiro, 15 May 1822, enclosure, and 21 August 1822, enclosure; P.R.O., F.O. 84/24, H. Chamberlain to George Canning, Rio de Janeiro, 25 January 1823, enclosure, and 15 August 1823, enclosure; P.R.O., F.O. 84/31, same to same, Rio de Janeiro, 5 January 1824, enclosure, and 31 March 1824, enclosure; P.R.O., F.O. 84/42, same to same, Rio de Janeiro, 4 January 1825, enclosure; P.R.O., F.O. 84/55, same to same, Rio de Janeiro, 4 January 1826, enclosure; P.R.O., F.O. 84/71, A. McCarthy to John Bidwell, Rio de Janeiro, 10 November 1827, enclosure; P.R.O., F.O. 84/84, A. J. Heatherly to same, Rio de Janeiro 15 January 1828; ibid., McCarthy to same, Rio de Janeiro, 26 April 1828, enclosure, and 9 August 1828, enclosure; P.R.O., F.O. 84/95, same to same, Rio de Janeiro, 26 February 1829, enclosure, and 30 April 1829, enclosure; ibid., same to Earl of Aberdeen, Rio de Janeiro, 11 July 1829, enclosure; P.R.O., F.O. 84/112, William Pennell to same, Rio de Janeiro, 25 January 1830, enclosure, and 15 July 1830, enclosure; ibid., Charles G. Weiss to same, Bahia, 6 February 1830, enclosure; ibid., John Parkinson to same, Pernambuco, 13 February 1830, enclosure; P.R.O., F.O. 84/112, Pennell to same, Rio de Janeiro, 8 January 1831, enclosure; see also, P.R.O., F.O. 84/95, Arthur Aston to same, Rio de Janeiro, 30 September 1829, enclosure no. 3, 'List of National Vessels to which Passports have been granted for the Slave Trade to Moçambique', Secretary of State's Office, 15 September 1829.

[a]Based upon customs-house duties.
[b]Exports to Brazil only.
[c]Exports to Rio de Janeiro only.
[d]Exports to Rio and Maranhão.
[e]Exports to Rio and Bahia.
[f]Exports to Rio, Bahia, and Pernambuco.

the end of the legal traffic continued unabated in the 1830s and 1840s.[19]

Throughout this half century, however, Brazil was not the only source of demand for slaves at Mozambique. Though less important now, a considerable business in slaves continued to be carried on by the French at the island-capital. Operating from the Seychelles and Comoro Islands, ships from Bourbon and Mauritius boldly traded there despite British efforts to end this particularly localized trade and renewed Portuguese efforts to prohibit foreign trading in their East African empire. Mozambique slaves were also carried on Arab and Swahili vessels to the Comoros, where French traders purchased and then transported them to the Seychelles, before introducing them to the Mascarenes. The key to this system was the period of *francisation* which the slaves experienced at the Seychelles. After acquiring a smattering of French, they were imported to Bourbon and Mauritius under the pretext that they were already the slaves of French residents of the islands, not new slaves being brought in for sale there.[20] In 1826, Captain Acland remarked that 'I have been given to understand that 35 Cargoes of Slaves have been shipped off in French vessels within the last 2 years from the Portuguese settlements. These vessels are not large perhaps averaging about 200 Slaves each Cargo.'[21] Many of these vessels operated outside Mozambique— at Ibo, Quelimane, Inhambane, and Delagoa Bay—but there is no doubt that some of them did their business at the capital, where the District Judge observed in 1829 that the French were the most frequent foreign traders.[22] French traders continued to ply their trade there in the next two decades, but they appear to have shifted their attention away from Mozambique during these years. Not until the extension to Mozambique of the thinly disguised system of slave trading which was known as the 'free labour emigration scheme' in the early 1850s did the French traders again become a major factor in the slave trade of the island.

Even less is known about the slave trade to Cuba, but in 1819 four or five Spanish vessels from Havana entered Mozambique harbour, certainly to take on slaves, before continuing on to Zanzibar to complete their cargoes.[23] Cuban slavers, and even a few American slavers, continued to put in occasional appearances at Mozambique right through the 1840s. Mention should also be made of the Arab and Swahili slave trade to Madagascar, much of which was supplied from the coast adjacent to Mozambique. These slaves were transported to several ports on the north-west shore of Madagascar, the most important of which was Bombetoka. Most of these slaves, the majority of whom were Makua, were absorbed by the Sakalava, but as time wore on some of them were also traded by the Sakalava to the Hova in the interior of the island.[24] Wholly beyond the control of the Portuguese, this trade dragged on unabated into the last quarter of the nineteenth century (see below, p. 227 and n. 73).

Considering all this activity, then, the frequently expressed estimate that at least 15,000 slaves were exported each year from Mozambique Island during the 1820s and 1830s seems quite reasonable.[25] The abolition of slave trading in Portuguese territory in 1836 was fiercely resisted in Portuguese East Africa and was certainly unenforceable by the Governor-General, the Marquês de Aracaty. However, a British blockade of Mozambique harbour in 1840, which was a preamble to the Anglo-Portuguese Slave Trade Treaty of 1842, does appear to have brought about a temporary abatement in the level of slave trading at the capital.[26] But by mid-century the last fling of the Brazilian trade probably stimulated the renewed demand for slaves which produced a surplus of slaves being held for export at the coast in the early 1850s (see below, p. 225). Indeed, despite yearly fluctuations in the volume of the export trade from Mozambique, it seems unlikely that African slave traders were able to adjust their supplies on a seasonal basis, for fear of being caught empty-handed when the port was full of vessels ready to take on cargoes. Thus, there was probably less seasonal variation in the numbers of slaves carried to the coast than in the numbers actually purchased there for export. Furthermore, Bishop Mártires' evidence that large numbers of slaves brought to Mozambique for export died before being purchased suggests that perhaps nearly 20,000 slaves were gathered each year in the vicinity of Mozambique during this period. Clearly, the slave trade from Mozambique in the first half of the nineteenth century imposed an unprecedented demand on the peoples of the coastal hinterland and the farther interior.

Until the nineteenth century, no direct trade had been allowed between the subordinate ports of Portuguese East Africa and the metropole. But in a very few years after the transferral of the Royal Court to Rio de Janeiro in 1808, Brazilian slave traders were clamouring for permission to open up other East African ports besides Mozambique for direct commerce. As early as 1807, a Brazilian slaver had been granted permission by the Provisional Government to carry a cargo of slaves directly from Quelimane to Ile de France, but this was an unusual exception.[27] The Governors-General of Mozambique were violently opposed to this trade, some because it hurt Mozambique and the Crown's finances, others more probably because it affected their own pockets. Their pleas were not successful, however, and on 4 February 1811, a royal decree was promulgated which opened the subordinate ports of Portuguese East Africa to direct trading by Brazilian vessels, without requiring them to call at the capital.[28] In no time at all Quelimane became a thriving slave port. Official figures compiled at Quelimane in 1820 show that in the previous six years, 15,055 slaves were exported from that port to Rio de Janeiro, Bahia, and Pernambuco. A third of these were accounted for in 1819.[29] In 1823, Lieutenant Thomas Boteler estimated that the town yielded 10,000 slaves annually and considered it to be 'now the greatest mart for slaves on the east coast'. Three years later another British naval officer observed that many French slavers from Bourbon also traded there.[30] His impressions were verified in the next year by a notorious French slave trader named Charles Letord, better known as Dorval, who testified before the British Commission of Enquiry at Mauritius in exchange for personal amnesty. Dorval told the Commissioners that he thought that perhaps 12,000 to 15,000 slaves were taken away from Quelimane each year by 1827.[31] How many of these slaves were carried to Brazil and how many to the Mascarenes is difficult to ascertain. The statistics compiled by the British at Rio de Janeiro for slaves shipped from Quelimane for the period 1820–1832, plus the lone Portuguese set of statistics from 1821, total 45,205, an annual average of slightly more than 4,100 individuals during each of the eleven years for which statistics are available.[32] The incompleteness of these consular figures for the Mozambique trade has already been noted, but nevertheless they provide a useful base line for the Brazilian trade against which to weigh the estimates of British naval officials and men like Dorval. In fact, by this time the transformation of Quelimane and the Rivers of Sena to a slave trading economy was virtually complete, and even more stunning than that of Mozambique. In 1806 ivory and gold accounted for 57 per cent of the total value of exports from

Quelimane, with slaves taking only 17 per cent. In 1821 slaves yielded 85 per cent of export revenue, while ivory and gold brought in only 7 per cent.

After 1832, knowledge of the slave trade at Quelimane again depends entirely upon the observations of occasional visitors. In general, these random reports suggest the same level of trading which existed at Mozambique, a continued brisk trade in the 1830s and a slight decline during the 1840s. In 1838, Texugo condemned Quelimane as a place wholly committed to the slave trade and noted that 'during the whole year the harbour was never without some slavers'.[34] If Quelimane prospered somewhat less in the 1840s, like at Mozambique its slave trade was revitalized in the following decade by the French engagé system.

Ibo, too, enjoyed a marked revival as a result of the slave trade during the first half of the nineteenth century. Until 1820, the continual threat and realization of Sakalava raids, as well as attacks from the neighbouring Makua, completely paralysed the trade of the Kerimba Islands. The low point for the Portuguese was probably reached in 1811, when the Makua routed an expedition sent against them on the mainland and killed the Governor of the Kerimba Islands.[35] By the end of the decade, however, the Portuguese had finally reorganized themselves at Ibo, and the power of the Sakalava raiders was being broken at its root by the imperial expansion of the Hova. During these desperate years, only a few bold Swahili continued to ply their coastal trade. Soon after an end had been put to the Sakalava threat, French slave traders began to return to the islands, which had been one of their favourite haunts in the eighteenth century. In 1827, Dorval gave evidence that there were nearly always slaves ready for purchase there, a statement which conforms to the impression of the responses of African suppliers at Mozambique. According to Dorval, the export slave trade at Ibo was exclusively French, as Brazilian vessels never went there. A man named Fortuné Bataille (Batalha), who was a friend of the Governor of the Kerimba Islands, was the principal supplier to the French slavers at Ibo.[36] In 1829, Governor-General Botelho warned the new Governor of the islands against admitting any foreign vessels to trade there, indicating that the majority of the 'fantastic arrivals' were French ships from Bourbon. Botelho's admonishment had about as much effect as similar warnings had in the past, and this traffic continued to flourish. After 1830 Brazilian traders seem to have put in at Ibo occasionally and in the late 1850s Cuban slavers took on cargoes there.[37] In 1858, H. Lyons McLeod, the first British Consul at Mozambique, reported that Ibo had acquired a reputation as 'the great Warehouse for Slaves'.[38]

As Mozambique and Quelimane were the principal markets for the Brazilian slave traders, and Ibo served in a similar capacity for the French in Portuguese East Africa, the independent Sultanate of Angoche provided perhaps the most important outlet for the Swahili traders on the Mozambique coast. Angoche had been marking time since the first half of the sixteenth century, when it served as a major way-station for Swahili traders who were operating in Zambesia (see Chapter 2). Although it was theoretically subject to Portuguese rule, Angoche continued to survive under the leadership of its own Swahili dynasty, trading on a small scale with the hinterland of the northern lower Zambesi. The growing demand for slaves all along the coast of East Africa in the nineteenth century elevated Angoche to a position of renewed importance, however, as Arab and Swahili dhows took port there in search of slaves for the growing markets in Madagascar and the Comoro Islands. They very likely also transported some of their cargoes to the subordinate ports flanking Mozambique, like Sanculo and Quitangonha, so that some of the slaves taken on at Angoche probably found their way to Brazil eventually. In 1823, Captain Owen reported sighting 'a small schooner in the River Angozha, where much traffic is carried on by the Arabs, which the Portuguese term contraband, though the country is subject to independent Regulos [chiefs], and no Portuguese dare approach it'.[39] Fifteen years later, Texugo heard news at Mozambique of two French slavers at Angoche, where they could deal openly.[40]

In the 1840s Angoche increasingly became an embarrassment for the Portuguese, whom the British held responsible for the slave trade carried on there because of their empty claims to political authority over the town. In 1846, the intrusion of a British vessel at Angoche prompted the mounting of a joint Anglo-Portuguese expedition later in the year. Typically, the Portuguese regarded this assault as a success, but in spite of a second joint mission four years later, Angoche remained quite independent right through the next decade.[41] McLeod reckoned its population at about 1,000 inhabitants, and noted that it drove a thriving trade with the towns of the Swahili coast. The Sultan controlled ninety miles of the coast, from twenty miles north of Angoche to some seventy miles south. His political authority was reputed to be recognized by thirty to forty chiefs on the mainland.[42] McLeod also reported to the Cape Station that Angoche's prosperity arose from its recent abandonment of the slave trade, but when the Portuguese succeeded in forcing the submission of Angoche in 1861, the town was described as 'the focus of an immense contraband in cloths and in slaves'.[43]

The Makua of Macuana

The volume of the slave trade at Angoche and at Ibo was not guessed at even by contemporary observers, but taken together with the trade to Quelimane and Mozambique, there can be no doubt that an immense demand for slaves was imposed upon the peoples of what is now northern Mozambique during the first half of the nineteenth century. How was the impact of the slave trade felt by these people? By their proximity to the coast, the Makua continued to suffer most from the slave trade to the Mozambique coast. It is, of course, important to recognize that the rise of the slave trade and the eclipse of the ivory trade provided Makua chiefs near the coast with an unprecedented opportunity to build up their own power at the expense of their neighbours farther inland, both Makua and Yao. But the advantages of slaving for these chiefs operated only in the short run, and in any case did not alter the basic political configuration of Macuana. Such was the nature of the slave trade that in the long run it worked to weaken the economic, social, and political structure of the Makua who inhabited the coastal hinterland of Mozambique.

Following a Portuguese expedition against the Uticulo chiefs in 1811, there appears to have been nearly a full decade of peaceful relations between the Makua and the Portuguese of Mozambique.[44] During these years, there is no way of ascertaining the adjustments which were being made by the Makua in response to the rapidly growing demand for slaves at the coast. By 1819, however, rivalry over control of the slave trade had clearly become the main bone of contention among the major powers in Macuana. The chief contestants against the Portuguese were the Mauruça, chief of Uticulo, and the Impahiamuno, chief of Mutipa. A decade earlier, the Impahiamuno had been closely allied with the

Portuguese against the Mauruça. Now the Makua chiefs were allies. The cause of the strife in Macuana were the robberies to which coastal traders had been subjected in the hinterland.[45] According to Mártires, most of the slaves who were sent to Brazil came from this part of Macuana, a fact which surely accounts for the willingness of the Portuguese to forget the long history of surprise attacks and humiliating defeats which they had suffered at the hands of the Makua of Uticulo, so that the Bishop could write of their present '*boa-inteligencia*'—'amiable understanding' or 'harmony of interests'—with the State.[46] But the Portuguese were not content to depend on this arrangement, so that one of the features of the heyday of the slave trade in Portuguese East Africa was the more active participation of the local Portuguese (and to a lesser extent, Indian) traders in actually procuring slaves for themselves in the interior.

During the eighteenth century, when ivory had dominated the trade of the colony, the carrying trade was exclusively in the hands of the Africans, especially those of the Yao. Banyan merchants used to send out *patamares* to negotiate with the Yao caravan leaders on their march to the coast, but the Banyans did not themselves organize trading or hunting expeditions on their own account. Nor did the Portuguese, who used *patamares* only on a limited scale in connection with the petty trade of the immediate hinterland. But so great was the demand for slaves along the coast after 1810, and so rapidly were the leading Portuguese traders able to amass their fortunes and to command large retinues of personal slaves, that they soon began to send their own parties into the interior in search of slaves at the source. This development posed a serious challenge to the control which the African traders of the interior, in this case those of Matibane and Uticulo, exercised over the carrying trade in slaves. The '*boa inteligencia*' of which Fr. Bartolomeu spoke could not long survive such a threat. Similarly, it must have been clear to the Portuguese that this conflict involved a fundamental problem in the economics of the slave trade, particularly since Matibane and the Impahiamuno were supposed to be subject to the authority of the Crown.[47] Despite the urging of the Crown to seek a peaceful conciliation with the Impahiamuno and the Mauruça, then, the local interests at stake were too great to let their robberies pass without censure. Prudence and political reality argued against an attack on the Mauruça, but towards the end of 1820 the Portuguese waged a campaign against the Impahiamuno in Mutipa. Notwithstanding the usual glowing reports of a crushing defeat of the rebel, the problem persisted for at least the next few years.[48]

By 1830, relations with the Makua of Mutipa and Uticulo were good,[49] but now a new conflict erupted in Matibane with the ambitious Sheikh of Quitangonha, Selimane bin Agy. It, too, was rooted deep in the struggle for control of the slave trade in the vicinity of Mozambique Island. In this case, the problem focused on the contraband export trade in slaves from Quitangonha itself and from Fernão Veloso Bay, at the north end of Matibane. Quitangonha had for years carried on a desultory contraband trade with the Swahili, although its sheikhs were nominally subordinate to the Portuguese Government at Mozambique, but in 1829 both French and Portuguese vessels put in there to make up cargoes of slaves.[50] This the Portuguese could not tolerate. When they started to investigate the matter more carefully, however, they discovered that Sheikh Selimane was already in the process of developing a lucrative slave trade at Fernão Veloso Bay with the Swahili and the French.[51] Repeated warnings to the Sheikh, who guilelessly claimed no responsibility for affairs over which he had no control and proclaimed his continued loyalty to the Portuguese Crown, were to no avail. As the Sheikh wrote to Governor-General Paulo José Miguel de Brito at the end of 1830, the slave trade was 'a tree with sweet fruit which all wish to eat'[52]. No less the Portuguese. Already in May of that year they had begun to attack the trade at Fernão Veloso at its source by establishing an outpost there.

The *Estabelecimento de El-Rei o Senhor D. Miguel Primeiro* was the first serious attempt by the Portuguese to bridge the gap between their outlying coastal colonies since these were first conquered in the sixteenth century.[53] Then the logic underlying the establishment of bases in the Kerimba Islands and at Quelimane was to protect against what the Portuguese considered to be the contraband trade in gold from Zambesia. Now the same mercantilist logic of imperial expansion prevailed, only the colony at Fernão Veloso was designed to protect Portuguese control of the slave trade. Almost at once it came under attack from the Sheikh of Quitangonha and his Makua allies and subordinates in Matibane.

For the next three years the Portuguese attempted to eradicate the thorn in their side which was Sheikh Selimane of Quitangonha. Elaborate overtures were made to the chiefs of Uticulo. At the end of October 1830, the Governor-General wrote to pledge his friendship to the Mauruça, and assured him that he could send his people freely to the mainland of Mozambique.[54] By the last week of November, negotiations were being conducted between the Portuguese, represented by the Captain-Major of the Mainland, Gabriel José de Sousa Ferreira, and the Makua of Uticulo, represented by Mwaviamuno Napu.[55] On 25 November 1830, Sousa Ferreira and the Mwaviamuno negotiated a five-point treaty which began by asserting that 'an inalterable peace and all the relations of friendship' would obtain between the Portuguese and Uticulo. Points two to four specified that the Mwaviamuno would immediately sever all communication with Matibane, that his forces would be at the ready to attack Matibane and that the Portuguese would supply him with gunpowder and shot to that end, and that the Portuguese would provide him with an appropriate gift in trade goods upon the fulfillment of his part of the bargain. Finally, the treaty called upon Mwaviamuno Napu to secure the assent of his 'uncles'—the other chiefs of Uticulo—to these terms. The Mwaviamuno was especially implored to gain the unfailing support of the Mauruça, who had considered his earlier agreement with a past Captain-Major of the Mainland to be a personal treaty of friendship, rather than a contract between his nation and that of the Portuguese.[56] To this end the Governor-General promised the Mauruça a special present of 'bone encrusted with gold filigree, and a pair of good pistols', as well as the items usually given in exchange for a tusk of ivory which the Makua paramount had sent to him.[57]

At the beginning of 1831, Brito was still attempting to line up African allies against the Sheikh of Quitangonha, using his understanding with the chiefs of Uticulo to dragoon those of Marezane and Simuco, immediately to the north of Fernão Veloso Bay, into the Portuguese camp.[58] Typically, alliances were tenuous, and the Portuguese never succeeded in mounting an outright assault against Quitangonha. By 1833 rumours were circulating on the mainland of an impending invasion by the Makua of Uticulo. Embassies were sent to Mozambique Island by the Mauruça and the Mwaviamuno to complain about the insufficient gift which the Mauruça had received from the now deceased Brito in exchange for the tusk of ivory which the Makua chief had sent to the former Governor-General.[59] By the end of that year, the alignments of 1830 were almost completely reversed, with the contrite, but still independent Sheikh Selimane first offering to 'clear the road to Macuana' and then launching an attack on the Makua around Fernão Veloso on his own initiative.[60] And less than two months later, the Mwaviamuno himself appeared in the Crown Lands lying between Uticulo and the coastal settlements to claim the return of two slaves belonging to him.[61]

The efforts made by the Provisional Government to treat the Makua chiefs of Uticulo with all due respect, and their inability to curb the rambunctious Sheikh of Quitangonha, reveal once again how little control the Portuguese were able to exercise over affairs on the mainland. The feeble establishment at Fernão Veloso was abandoned in April 1834.[62] When he visited Mozambique a decade earlier, Captain Owen had commented on this situation:

> Even at Mozambique the Portuguese jurisdiction and settlements do not extend ten miles in any direction, and to the southward not at all. The natives, who are termed Makwomas [Makua] and Majowjes [Yao], form an insurmountable barrier; they will trade with them, but have a great objection to their entering the country, which often leads to wars, that only in the end impress more strongly on the minds of the Portuguese the determination of their neighbours to support themselves in their native territorial possessions.[63]

Three decades later, Bordalo tersely reiterated Owen's dismal account of the extent of Portuguese authority on the mainland at Mozambique after three and a half centuries of imperial presence in East Africa: 'Our effective dominion on this side does not extend to more than three leagues inland.'[64] To be sure, in the mid-1850s a column sent to restore order in Matibane was routed and the mainland settlements at Ampoense and Nandoa razed in retaliation, while as late as 1864 the Mauruça and the Impahiamuno were still being described as 'brigands' as a consequence of their intermittent raiding on the mainland.[65]

Yet if the Portuguese were no more able to impose order on the mainland in the middle of the nineteenth century than they had been in the previous centuries, their involvement in the slave trade had turned them into more effective agents for disruption than ever before. I have already mentioned the increased use of *patamares* and of organized slave trading expeditions mounted by coastal traders in the 1820s, as well as the resistance which these evoked from the Makua. By the 1850s these agents seem to have been used much more extensively in the hinterland, and among the Makua may well have seized the initiative in their trade with the coast. According to Jeronimo Romero, writing about the operations of these traders inland from the Cape Delgado coast, the *patamares*—some of whom may themselves have been independent small traders—were generally from the coast and they spoke Makua and other languages of the interior well. They travelled in company with anywhere from five to fifteen skilled slaves (*ladinos*), each of whom was armed with a rifle and supplied with a load of trade goods which was designed for easy travelling. They also carried beads with them for purchasing food in the hinterland. These caravans could take anywhere from two to six months going and coming, depending on how far inland they travelled. Most trips varied between thirty and ninety leagues (perhaps 170 to 450 kilometres). With their trade goods these *patamares* purchased ivory, rhinocerous horn, slaves, and malachite, as well as other products of lesser importance. Travel was not without risk, but so long as they avoided trouble and kept to themselves, they appear to have been relatively free to pursue their business. Romero also writes that these small caravans set out from the coast in every month of the year.[66] This change in the pattern of trade in the Mozambique hinterland was not by itself disruptive, of course, although it does indicate that the initiative in the trade of the interior was passing from the Makua to the people on the coast. But without this initial shift in the trade of the continent, it would not have been possible for the Portuguese to employ these coastal traders as *agents provocateurs* when the demand for slaves at the coast to supply the French 'free labour emigration scheme' met with no response from the chiefs of Macuana in the 1850s.

The source for our knowledge of this new stage in the direct intervention by the Portuguese in the affairs of the people of Macuana is the headstrong British consul at Mozambique, Lyons McLeod. McLeod never attempted to understand the Portuguese and finally came to despise them.[67] Nevertheless, and allowing for the verbal barbs which he aimed at Governor-General Vasco Guedes de Carvalho e Meneses, who seems to have been neither better nor worse than most of his predecessors, McLeod's description of this change bears careful consideration.

In the early 1850s, the slave trade at Mozambique was moribund. The sudden end of the Brazilian trade in 1851—the result of stringent measures taken by the Brazilian Government— made it realistic for the Portuguese administration to enforce the 1836 abolition of the slave trade for the first time since it had been ordered from Lisbon. Thus, when the French free labour scheme was inaugurated in 1854,

> there was a surplus of slaves in all the Portuguese settlements on the east coast of Africa; and the Governor-General of Mozambique, and his subordinates, found no difficulty in supplying the demand for the first twelve months, that is to say, from 1854 to 1855; for the Portuguese residents were only too glad to sell to the Portuguese officials those slaves whom the orders of the government of Portugal had prevented being supplied to the regular slave ships from Cuba, and the southern parts of the United States; and the effect of this trade was to rid Mozambique of a great portion of its slave population, with which it was over-burdened. After the first twelve months of the traffic, the price rose, the demand still increased, but the French slave-dealers were unwilling to give the prices now demanded by the residents in Mozambique. To supply the demand, keep prices low, and secure the enormous profits which the Governor-General of Mozambique, and his partners in this nefarious traffic, were enjoying, it became necessary to send into the interior for slaves.[68]

McLeod does not mention it, but the fact that an epidemic of smallpox took the lives of more than 5,000 slaves in Mozambique was a factor at play in this situation.[69]

In a wonderfully ironic turnabout, the Swahili agents of the Portuguese were refused by the chiefs whom they approached, who said that the slave trade was against the wishes of the Portuguese government. This episode provides a vivid index of how thoroughly colonized in outlook the chiefs of Macuana had become by the 1850s, even though they were still politically independent of the Portuguese. Their attitude, if McLeod is correct, was the historical outcome of the prolonged contact of Macuana with European mercantile capitalism.

> To prove to the chiefs in the interior that the Moors went with the consent of the Portuguese authorities in search of slaves for the French Free Labour Emigration, some of the Portuguese soldiers, who had been living with the women of the country, and had acquired the Makua language, were despatched with

the Moors into the interior, and the uniforms of the soldiers of the King of Portugal were found a sufficient guarantee to the chiefs of the interior that the slave trade was authorized by the Portuguese government, and immediately they set to work to supply the traffic in earnest; by these means the prices of slaves were kept low at Mozambique, the Portuguese officials made enormous gains, and the French Free Labour Emigration flourished.

At first, McLeod tells us that these slaves were produced from those at hand in the interior, but in a very little time the renewed demand for slaves led to extensive slave raiding among the Makua of Macuana.

At last a reaction took place: the natives found that they were destroying each other to obtain a few prisoners for the supply of the slave-trade which the Portuguese were carrying on; and, for a time, they ceased from warfare, and again there was a scarcity in the slave market at Mozambique.

When the Portuguese attempted to send troops into Macuana for slaves in 1857, the Makua beat them off and threatened to attack the mainland. Only the Governor-General's expedient promise not to seek slaves from their country prevented war.[70]

Knowing very little about the way in which slaves were procured before the middle of the nineteenth century, when British abolitionists first began to examine the interior trade closely, it is difficult to determine how much of a departure the system described by McLeod represents. Although he nowhere identifies the Makua to whom the Portuguese sent their agents, the principal focus of their activity must have been Uticulo, which continued to be 'the nearest slave preserve to Mozambique' right into the 1870s.[71] The chiefs of Uticulo had almost certainly been raiding their neighbours to capture slaves for the Mozambique trade for many decades by mid-century. From the 1850s, however, it would appear that a half century of intensive slaving had driven many of these victimized societies away from the immediate reach of raids launched from Uticulo and the other regions of the immediate coastal hinterland, so that the chiefs of Macuana had now to turn to raiding each other's people in order to satisfy the demand for slaves at the coast. Inexorably fettered to the international slave trading economy, they were unable to do otherwise, since their mid-century strength had been built upon the profits of the slave trade. Accordingly, the Makua reaction of the mid-1850s was only a temporary assertion of African over Western economic values. Now most of the Makua chiefs were to pay dearly.

Two decades after McLeod observed the first signs of this process, Frederic Elton, the second British consul at Mozambique and a remarkable perceptive traveller, commented upon its effects.

> In the hill and forest districts of Okuso, Maridi, and Nangiri, through which I travelled [north] from Tugulu [Uticulo] to reach the neutral ground of Namoti upon the Nkomburi [Mocubúri] river, flowing into Mwendazi [Memba] Bay, narrow, tortuous ways, and thorny paths choked up with brambles and undergrowth, lead one to the villages and water, the broader paths almost invariably terminating in a *cul-de-sac*. The fear of slave-dealers' raids—their tracks are marked by many a burned and desolated settlement—has engendered a suspicious uneasiness among the villagers for so many years, that is has now become an innate feature of the Makua character, is marked upon their faces, and colours every action of their lives at the present day. No communication with a stranger or with an adjoining tribe is allowed without express permission from a 'baraza' of chiefs. The Lomwé country, lying between Makuani and the Lake Nyassa, Mosembé, and Mwendazi, may not be visited under pain of capital punishment, without the headman of the subdivision of the tribe to which the intending traveller belongs referring for leave to higher authority. Tracks of land are purposely laid waste and desolated upon the frontiers, where armed scouts, generally old elephant hunters, continually wander, their duty being to report at the earliest moment any approach of strangers, who are invariably treated as enemies.[72]

Matters were scarcely any better on the eastern marches of Uticulo.

> For years past Makuani has furnished the main supply of slaves and 'libres engagés' for the Portuguese, French, and Madagascar markets. Fighting is constantly going on, dissensions being actively promoted by the unscrupulous dwellers on the coast, anxious to purchase the prisoners taken by the successful side, and utterly careless as to who is the winner. So long as the Makua held together they were formidable enemies to the Portuguese; but the breaking-up of the tribe into fragments, and faction-fighting among the chiefs for the supreme power,

eventually placed them at the mercy of any Arab intriguer who chose to instigate hostilities in order to secure a slave cargo.[73]

In truth, the Makua had never been united politically, but they had almost always 'held together' in the face of Portuguese attempts to undermine their strength and to subordinate them to Portuguese rule. It was their ability to submerge petty rivalries which had served them so well since the eighteenth century in their relations with the Portuguese. That lost, the very resiliency of coastal Makua society soon succumbed to the increasing pressures emanating from the coast. When Elton met in 1876 the reigning Mauruça, who was still the most important chief in Uticulo, the consul found him unable to influence affairs beyond Uticulo, where a triple alliance with his brother and another related chief rendered him strong. Caravans travelling the short distance from Uticulo to the coast to trade provisions were always subject to raids and had to 'take the precaution of throwing out scouts and establishing nightly patrols round their bivouacs'. The country between Uticulo and the coast was thoroughly depopulated, except for a few isolated pockets, and although the Mauruça had recently concluded a peace treaty with the authorities at Mosembe, on the mainland opposite Quitangonha Island, 'putting an end to the kidnapping of the inhabitants of the flats as slaves by either side, and arranging a division of the land; yet it is still with fear and trembling that the Makuas venture down to till the soil'.[74]

If, then, the Makua of Uticulo seemed to be as formidable an obstacle to the Portuguese in the 1850s as they had been for nearly three centuries of intimate commercial contact, they were much weakened within two decades as a result of changes in the pattern of the slave trade at Mozambique, which had its roots in the middle years of the century. On the threshold of the modern colonial era their reduction was complete. When Mousinho de Albuquerque opened his disputed and inconclusive operations on the mainland against the *namarrais* in 1896, Uticulo and the reigning Mauruça cooperated with the Portuguese against this upstart aggressive Makua confederacy whose chiefs were too deeply wedded to the slave trading system to abandon it without a prolonged struggle.[75] But although the Mauruça and the *namarrais* were on opposite sides in the wars of colonial conquest, which stretched into the twentieth century, both were the products of their historical relationship with international trade. Indeed, from the African perspective, the nature of these wars must have seemed no different from the constant struggles which had characterized the political economy of Macuana since the beginning of the slave trade in the eighteenth century.

The Yao Trade to Mossuril

While there is no doubt at all that most of the slaves exported from Mozambique during the nineteenth century were Makua, it is equally clear that the Yao were the second greatest suppliers of the Mozambique slave market until about mid-century.[76] In 1819, Governor-General Brito Sanches wrote that the reason Brazilian ships were leaving Mozambique laden with slaves

> is due to the abundance which some types of cafilas called Yao, who come from the interior near Tete, the farthest of the Rivers of Sena, bring to the Mainland of Mossuril, so that this year they brought more than 3,500 slaves, and not due to those which come from the environs of this City . . .[77]

1819 was, in fact, a bad year for Luso-Makua relations, but as more than 10,000 slaves were brought to the coast for export in that year, Brito Sanches' comments probably reflect a decline in the supply of slaves from Mutipa and Uticulo, rather than from Macuana as a whole. As for his remarks on the Yao, these are vividly borne out by the detailed observations of Bishop Mártires. The Yao, he said, were 'a great, and numerous Nation . . . , who have always maintained a trade with the Portuguese which has been very profitable to the Colony'. Each year the Yao came to Mossuril bringing 2,000 to 3,000 slaves, together with only 'some ivory, and a small quantity of provisions', as well as tobacco and iron wares. Their slaves were bought at a low price, for although they were thought to be superior in many respects, many of them perished or were seriously debilitated before making the adjustment to the disease environment—what Mártires calls 'climate'—of the coast, a factor which had been mentioned by earlier sources on the Yao. Fr. Bartolomeu also provides a lengthy and fascinating description of the organization of Yao slave caravans, which in turn helps us to understand the nature of Yao slave trading in about 1820.

According to what he could learn, all the slaves were Yao. In passing through the hostile territory of the Makua, the caravan was defended by 'a few Kaffirs, their compatriots'. Mártires believed that the slaves did not know that they were to be sold at the coast, 'because the secret of their business is only confided to a few: out of 3,000, fewer than 30 return to their lands'. That they did not forcibly seize their freedom he attributed to the fact that they were outcasts in their own country and that they would surely be killed or enslaved in foreign lands. In effect, they had no alternative but to submit.

> Now these Yao are certainly not prisoners of war, because they are of the same nation as their sellers: but all are victims of some crime, either real, or supposed; and among them there are some crimes which, though committed by only one individual, the onus falls upon his entire family, and most remote relatives; thus it is not rare to see the father, mother, sons, daughters, nephews, etc., being sold in the same fair.[78]

Mártires was surely mistaken in his belief that there was no internecine warfare among the Yao at this time; in any case, the Yao have never been a nation in any political sense. But he is probably correct in his analysis that the increased demand for slaves may have caused criminal liability to be more widely and arbitrarily applied in Yao law than ever before.

On a less grand scale, Bishop Mártires' account of the organization of Yao caravans was echoed a quarter-century later by Froberville. Writing about the slave trade in general, he observed that 'The caravans are usually composed of twenty or thirty persons, without counting the captives who are often as numerous as their masters, but who rarely seek to regain their liberty by force'. Kidnapping was common practice on the march to the coast, and it was this problem which forced most traders to band together in large caravans, a practice which also served to reinforce the authority of the big trading chiefs, who could employ large numbers of armed guards. However, most slaves were prisoners of war, 'because domestic slavery is absolutely unknown in East Africa'.[79]

After Mártires, there is little substantive evidence on the trade of the Yao to Mozambique.[80] According to Vasconcelos e Cirne, who was Governor at Quelimane and then in the Rivers of Sena from 1829 until his death at Tete in 1832, the Yao continued to bring 'a great number of slaves, and some ivory' to Mossuril during this period, although 'they have given up coming in the past few years owing to the robberies and wars which they have suffered at the hands of the chiefs near Mozambique'.[81] Warfare in Macuana, then, appears to have continued to obstruct Yao trade to Mozambique well into the nineteenth century. Yao slaves continued to be sold at Mozambique in the 1830s, and Yao caravans seem to have come there as well, but information for these years is very scarce.[82] Accordingly, it is impossible even to speculate about the changes which might have been taking place in the trade of the Yao to Mozambique in the years following Fr. Bartolomeu's detailed observations in 1822.

Before long, however, the rise of Ibo and Quelimane as major trading towns in their own right provided the Yao and other traders from the far interior with alternate coastal outlets to Mozambique Island along that stretch of the East African coast. According to a memoir written by the Marquis of Bemposta Subserra in December 1853, but quite possibly referring more generally to the second quarter of the nineteenth century,

> each year, 'great *mangas* [caravans] of Negroes, some Bisa, who come from the lands of the Kazembe, others Yao, and of different tribes or nations, all of them traders, show up on that peninsula [Cabaceira], in order to trade their merchandise for others which they need; a makeshift fair is set up for this purpose, in which everyone cheats with the greatest expertise and perspicacity. These Negroes do not enter our territory without permission, nor do they usually commit any acts of violence there; when, however, they are unable to overcome the difficulties which they encounter in the interior on the part of other nations, they go to Quelimane or Ibo.'[83]

Whatever the exact provenance of his information, his remarks throw a valuable light on the way in which the growth of the slave trade in East Central Africa during the first half of the nineteenth century fostered the development of two major overland routes to the coast.

During the eighteenth century, when the trade in ivory dominated the foreign trade of East Central Africa, neither Ibo nor Quelimane was capable of emerging as a major outlet for this trade. Quelimane suffered from the same onerous tax structure as the rest of the Rivers of Sena, while Ibo lacked a body of merchants who could finance the credit base of the ivory trade, concentrating instead on the more localized trade in cowrie shells and slaves. The opening of the subordinate ports to direct trade from Brazil at the beginning of the second decade of the nineteenth century, the revival of the French slave trade, and the fact that the slave trade was primarily in European hands and did not depend on Indian capitalization, combined to raise both Ibo and Quelimane to the status of major trading ports. Together with Kilwa and the other towns along that coast, they further undermined the once dominant position of Mozambique Island as a principal entrepôt for the trade of the far interior.

As early as about 1830, the Yao were trading slaves directly to Ibo, while by about 1844 the route linking the Lake Nyasa region to Ibo was already being plied by Swahili slave trading caravans, as John Rebman learned at Mombasa from the freed slave who served as his informant in compiling his *Kiniassa Dictionary*. This man

> was an Mniassa, who in consequence of international expeditions for slave-catching was seized by a tribe called Wapogera, who sold him to the Wamaravi, and these to the Swahili slave merchants who had come from Uibu (a small island belonging to Moçambique and on the map called Ibo). At Uibu which was reached after two months' travelling at a very slow rate (in effective march only half the time is wanted), he was at last bought by slave-merchants from Mombas.[84]

Similarly, by 1859, after the beginning of the great Yao migration into the Shire valley, Yao traders were well known at Quelimane, where they traded slaves, ivory, and Maravi iron hoes.[85] During the second half of the nineteenth century, both Ibo and Quelimane, as well as Angoche, were to remain important termini of long-distance trade routes in East Central Africa. The trade of Mozambique, on the other hand, was progressively limited to its own immediate hinterland as a result of the changes in the pattern of the slave trade which were described earlier in this chapter. The increasing incidence of violence in the hinterland of Mozambique and of man-stealing at the coast probably combined with the greater accessibility of markets such as Ibo, Angoche, Quelimane, and those of the southern Swahili coast, to make the journey to the fair at Mossuril an unnecessarily risky venture. Indeed, the changes in the operation of the slave trade at the coast itself made even that once protected fair a convenient arena for man-stealing. As McLeod observed, 'In 1856 many of these Natives who came down to trade, were seized by the

Portuguese to supply the so-called French Free Labour Emigration, since which occurrence they have not made their appearance at Messuril'.[86] Already by 1854, when the *pombeiros* of the important Angolan trader, António Francisco Ferreira da Silva Porto, crossed the continent to the coast of East Africa, they followed the increasingly popular route which crossed the Shire, held to the east of the Lujenda River, and debouched at the coast between Ibo and Kilwa.[87] After nearly three centuries of serving as one of the most important coastal entrepôts for the overland trade of the interior of the continent, by about 1860 Mozambique Island was reduced in all but administrative terms to a minor position in the export trade of East Central Africa.[88]

The Indians of Mozambique

The changing context of trade at Mozambique during the first half of the nineteenth century had as profound an effect on the Indian community of the island as it did on the Africans of the continent. Not only was the demand for slaves beyond the control of the Indians, but they also found their control over the importation of African trade cloths was being challenged by British and American cotton sheeting. British cottons first entered the Mozambique trade as a consequence of the Anglo-Portuguese Treaty of Commerce and Navigation, which was concluded at Rio de Janeiro on 19 February 1810. According to at least one overly pessimistic Portuguese trader, they had struck a death blow to the trade in Indian textiles by the early 1820s.[89] That this was not the case is demonstrated by the detailed accounting of a standard bale of trade cloths current in the Rivers of Sena in 1832 which A. C. P. Gamitto appended to his remarkable narrative of the Portuguese expedition to the Mwata Kazembe in 1831–1832. Each bale contained ninety-eight pieces of cloth, of seven different varieties, all of Indian manufacture. But Gamitto notes that 'Since the author left Mozambique, this kind of trade has altered considerably, and today (1853) good cotton cloths of English and American manufacture are preferred to the Indian weaves'.[90] At Tete, three years later, Livingstone also observed that 'English or American unbleached calico is the only currency used'.[91] Indeed, so important had American cottons become to the trade of Mozambique by this time that the Portuguese Minister of the Navy and Overseas Provinces was moved to comment upon the impact which the American Civil War had upon their availability in his annual report to the Chamber of Deputies at Lisbon in January 1864.[92] Indian traders still remained an important factor in the trade of the colony as a whole, but their influence was now exerted more in the trade with the subordinate ports than in that of the mainland opposite the island-capital. Finally, trade from East Africa to Portuguese India was depressed throughout this period. Encouraged during the second and harried during the fourth decade of the nineteenth century—though always defended by the Crown—the varying fortunes of the Indian traders at Mozambique seem to have had little decisive effect on African trade during this era.[93] Only with the slow development of 'legitimate' trade, that harbinger of impending colonial conquest, for the securing of cheap raw materials from Africa, did Indian traders come forward again to dominate the trade of Mozambique.[94]

Zanzibar and the Kilwa Coast

By contrast, to the north of Portuguese jurisdiction Indian traders and Indian merchant capital were two of the most important factors in the phenomenal rise of Zanzibar in the economy of the Indian Ocean under the energetic 'Umani ruler, Seyyid Sa'id ibn Sultan al-Bu Sa'idi (1804–1856). The growth and impact of Zanzibar on the trade of East Africa is a well-known story. Here it is important to stress not only the more spectacular rise in the slave trade—which was brought about by the creation of a colonial plantation economy on the islands of Zanzibar and Pemba—but also the concommitant growth of the ivory trade at Zanzibar, where American traders, in particular, augmented the long-standing demand of the Indian market.[95] The wealth produced by the industrial revolution in America and western Europe brought with it the fashion for a number of amusements and trinkets—billiards, pianos, and carved curios and jewellery—which gave rise to this new trade in ivory. In 1856, according to the French consul at Zanzibar, Western exports of ivory totalled some 242,975 pounds, with American merchants carrying more than three-quarters of the trade.[96] Three years later, his British counterpart gave the total export of ivory from Zanzibar as 488,600 pounds, with some 243,600 pounds going to Western countries and the remainder clearly destined for the Indian market.[97] And although it is impossible to break down the volume of the ivory trade to Zanzibar from the various ports on the mainland, there is no doubt that Kilwa continued to maintain a thriving ivory trade alongside its booming export trade in slaves right through the period of this study. The continued importance of ivory there was probably one of the main reasons why most Yao continued to prefer carrying their merchandise to Kilwa, instead of to Mozambique, during the first half of the nineteenth century.

But it is for the slave trade that Kilwa gained its greatest notoriety in the history of East Africa during the nineteenth century. In 1811, Captain Smee commented that the various tribes which supplied the Zanzibar slave market were 'too numerous to describe', but that the chief one was the Nyamwezi. Among the other peoples whom he identified were the Makua, the Yao, and the Ngindo.[98] A year later, when H.M.S. *Nisus* visited Kilwa, a temporary decline in the slave trade seems to have set in there as a result of the recent British seizure of the Mascarene Islands, and James Prior, the ship's surgeon, took particular note of the ivory trade. Prior also made a passing reference to the slave and ivory trade carried on at Lindi and Mongalo.[99] In both 1816 and 1817, Kilwa and the Mafia Islands were attacked by large Sakalava fleets. After suffering considerable losses during the first raid, a combined expedition of local Swahili and 'Umani forces from Zanzibar inflicted a crushing defeat on the Sakalava at Msimbati Bay, just north of the mouth of the Ruvuma River.[100] Thus, for much of the second decade of the nineteenth century conditions in the Western Indian Ocean may have been less than ideal for the successful prosecution of the slave trade from Kilwa.

Not long after the defeat of the Sakalava, the Sultan of Kilwa, Yusuf bin Hasan, died. In 1819, when the gifted French linguist and Orientalist, Fortuné Albrand, visited Kilwa, a successor to the deceased Sultan had not yet been chosen. By now, however, real political and commercial power were firmly in the hands of the 'Umani. Alluding to its medieval splendour, Albrand remarked that it was 'now only a miserable village to which the slave trade alone gives any importance'. He was nevertheless sceptical of the assurance he received at Zanzibar that 13,000 slaves were imported there from Kilwa each year. Albrand also noted that 'in addition to the traffic in blacks, Zanzibar also does as extensive a trade in ivory', although he does not specifically comment on the ivory trade at Kilwa.[101] During the next decade the Arab slave trade at Kilwa was supplemented by a renewed spurt of activity by French slavers at the several ports dotting the coast below it, where 'Umani hegemony was less than effective. Of these, Mongalo seems to have been more important than either Lindi or Mikindani, for in 1826 the 'Umani governor of Zanzibar told Captain Acland that 'Mongalo was the principal depot for the French'.[102] Indeed, article 10 of the interim agreement concluded between the ambassador of Seyyid Sa'id and Governor-General Botelho at Mozambique on 28 March 1828 recognized that the coast between Mongalo and Tungui, which lay immediately to the south of Cape Delgado, was not subject to the jurisdiction of either 'Uman or Portugal.[103]

In the 1830s, Kilwa Kisiwani finally succumbed to a combination of continuing political dissension within the Swahili community and an increasingly violent environment.[104] By the end of the decade the once insignificant mainland village of Kivinje, which was situated some twenty-seven kilometres to the north of Kilwa Kisiwani, fell heir to the mantle of the once great island-state, assuming the popular name of Kilwa Kivinje and emerging as the principal collection point for slaves on the coast of East Africa. Already the 'Umani had put a governor there by 1819.[105] But the rise of Kilwa Kivinje represents something more than the simple re-location of a townsite. As G. S. P. Freeman-Grenville pointed out a decade ago, it also stands as a symbol of the changed orientation of trade at Kilwa from the pre-Portuguese to the early modern period of East African history, the one being dominated entirely by the Indian Ocean and the sea lanes north to Western Asia and south to Sofala, the other drawing its strength as much from the overland trade of East Central Africa as from the seaborne trade of Zanzibar and the north.[106] Moreover, there can be little doubt that one of the most important factors in the rise of Kilwa Kivinje to prominence in the trade of East Africa was the contribution made by individuals from the far interior like the Masaninga Yao adventurer, Mwinyi Mkwinda, who settled at Kivinje during the late eighteenth century.[107]

By the 1840s Kilwa Kivinje had become a thriving market town. Although its fame was justifiably built on the slave trade, its export trade was not so thoroughly dependent upon slaves as was that of Mozambique Island. Even Atkins Hamerton, who served as British Consul at Zanzibar from May 1841 to his death in July 1857, and was the source of many irresoluble estimates of the slave trade, was able to comment in 1842 that Kilwa Kivinje was 'the port to which the ivory, gum copal, &c., are brought from the interior and chiefly sent to Zanzibar for sale'. His remark that the rebellious 'Umani Governor of Kilwa Kivinje had levied a special tax on ivory exported to Zanzibar also suggests that this trade may well have been at least as important as the slave trade in the early 1840s.[108] The slave trade expanded even further in the following years, largely in response to the increasing need for hands to work the mature clove and coconut palm plantations on Zanzibar and Pemba. During these years perhaps an average of 13,000 to 15,000 slaves entered Zanzibar each year from the mainland, and most of these came from Kilwa.[109] In 1850, J. L. Krapf described Kilwa Kivinje as 'the most important town on the coast between Mozambique and Zanzibar', and a great trading centre. Its population he estimated to be between 12,000 and 15,000 inhabitants. He reckoned slaves to be the principal item of trade there and he was told that some 10,000 to 12,000 slaves, both from central Tanzania and from the vicinity of Lake Nyasa, passed through Kilwa Kivinje each year. At the same time, however, Krapf also observed that the town 'drives a very considerable trade in ivory, rice, copal, tobacco . . . '.[110] If slaves were the mainstay of Kilwa Kivinje's trade, this was not so to the exclusion of all other products.

Yearly fluctuations in the volume of the slave trade could be considerable. Hamerton informed Richard Burton that the average annual importation into Zanzibar was 14,000, but that the extremes varied from 9,000 to 20,000.[111] In 1851 the American Consul at Zanzibar, Charles Ward, judged the annual rate of importation to be between 8,000 and 10,000, 'and they mostly from Kilwa'.[112] Not all slaves exported north from Kilwa went to Zanzibar, however, as Krapf learned during his brief visit to the mainland port at mid-century.

> Although the Sultan of Zanzibar has prohibited the slave-trade with Arabia, yet many slave-ships proceed there annually, starting from Kiloa and sailing round Zanzibar on the eastern side of the island, so as to evade the sultan's police; and slaves are often smuggled to Arabia by the aid of a declaration of the captain that they are sailors.[113]

Similarly, slaves from Kilwa had been exported to the south for

TABLE 6

Slaves Exported from Kilwa Kivinje, 1862–1869

Year	Number of slaves
1862–1863	18,500[a]
1863–1864	17,500[a]
1864–1865	16,821[a]
1865–1866	22,344[a]
1866–1867	22,038[a]
1867–1868	————
1868–1869	14,944[b]
Total	112,147

Source: Burton, *Zanzibar*, II, p. 347.

[a]Exports through customs to Zanzibar and elsewhere.
[b]Exports for year ending 23 August 1869.

many years in small numbers in order to supply the Brazilian trade at Mozambique.[114] During the late 1850s French slavers also were active in direct trading at Kilwa.[115] In fact, by the 1860s, returns from the customs-house at Kilwa Kivinje show that nearly one-fifth of all slaves exported were destined for markets other than Zanzibar.[116] This decade in all likelihood marked the apogee of the export trade from Kilwa Kivinje. The export trade from the mainland was officially abolished during the 1870s, but slaves continued to be driven to Kilwa from the interior of East Africa, and from Kilwa north to the towns of the Mrima coast, whence they could be smuggled more easily to Zanzibar, as Elton discovered during his march behind the Swahili coast in 1873, when he was Vice-Consul at Zanzibar.[117] Thereafter, although the export trade continued from the many smaller ports along the Kilwa coast, the slave trade in East Africa was largely internalized, and slaves brought down to the coast from the interior frequently ended up working on Arab or Indian plantations on the coast itself. This aspect of the slave trade does not concern us here. The question remaining is to determine the impact of a half-century of intensive slave trading to Kilwa on the peoples of the southern interior of East Africa.

The Peoples of the Lake Nyasa Region

Perhaps the most reliable information on this problem was compiled by Consul Rigby. In his extensive 'Report on the Zanzibar Dominions', completed on 1 July 1860, Rigby observed:

> During the past year, 19,000 slaves were brought to Zanzibar from the coast of Africa. Of these, four thousand were from the 'Marima', or coast opposite to Zanzibar, and fifteen thousand were from the neighbourhood of the great lake of Nyassa, situated about forty days' journey south-west of Keelwa. The tribes which formerly furnished most of the slaves are now nearly exhausted, and this miserable traffic is being carried further into the interior every year, and is depopulating vast tracts of fertile country. . . . The majority of the slaves belong to the great tribes of M'Nyassa, Miyan, and Magindo.

Later on in his report, Rigby adds that 'many of the Manganga are now amongst the slaves brought to Zanzibar from Keelwa'.[118] Concerning the depopulation of the coastal hinterland,

> Natives of India who have resided many years at Kilwa . . . state that districts near Kilwa, extending to ten or twelve days' journey, which a few years ago were thickly populated, are now entirely uninhabited; and an Arab who has lately returned from Lake Nyasa informed me that he travelled for seventeen days through a country covered with ruined towns and villages which a few years ago were inhabited by the Mijana and Mijan [Yao] tribes and where no living soul is to be seen.[119]

Rigby was not alone in his impression of the depopulation of large tracts of territory along the march to Lake Nyasa, as a reading of von der Decken and Livingstone reveals.[120] It is important, however, not to give too much weight to these accounts, as they can lead to completely erroneous statements like Burton's assumption that 'the Wahiáo tribe has been so favoured in the slave-market that it is now nearly extinct' and 'nearly annihilated by the slave-trade'.[121] Clearly this was not so. Yet it is true that by the middle of the nineteenth century, most of the slaves coming to Kilwa were from the region around the lake, rather than from the immediate hinterland. In an earlier note on the slave trade at Kilwa, when he was not defending his interpretations of East African geography against his critics, as he was in the notes to Lacerda's travels, Burton singled out the Yao and Ngindo among the various peoples exported as slaves from Kilwa to Zanzibar. A decade later he included a variety of other peoples from both far and near in a list of the ethnic derivation of the slave population of Kilwa Kivinje, but also noted that in the export market it was the Yao who were 'preferred to all others'.[122] Similarly, von der Decken learned during his exploration in the Kilwa hinterland in December 1860 that most of the slaves exported from Kilwa were Bisa and Yao.[123]

But it is not necessary to rely exclusively on European accounts of the sources and operation of the slave trade in East Central Africa. For the later nineteenth century there are a number of published freed-slave accounts which, although they must often be set in the context of their mission origin or in that of their British interrogators, nevertheless do represent a genuine African voice. The individuals from whom these personal accounts come include several Yao, Nyasa, Makua, two Bisa, one Ngindo, and one Bemba. Some of their stories are long, others include but a few brief details. Most of these people were enslaved when children as a result of warfare. The captors of Petro Kilekwa, a Bisa, are described as Maviti, which in the late nineteenth century was more often a euphemism for any brigand rather than an Ngoni party. In the case of another Bisa and one Nyasa child, the war was carried to their homes by Mpezeni's Ngoni, while the Bemba child was seized in a Gwangwara raid.[124] The Ngindo woman was captured in a war with the Yao, as was another Nyasa boy, while one Yao was enslaved by Ngindo. Many of the Yao slaves interviewed by Speke in 1860 stated that they had been 'captured during wars in their own country'.[125] James Mbotela's father, a Yao, was captured in a raid on his country by a party of Arabs led by Makua from Mozambique, and one of the Makua children was seized in a raid by the Lomwe.[126] Kidnapping was another widely practised form of acquiring a slave for sale, and this was the fate of several of the Kiungani children. It was also common practice among the Chewa.[127] The Chewa also acquired slaves for their own use and for sale as a result of internal warfare, while the Nsenga traded large numbers of slaves to them for foodstuffs during periods of famine. Certain crimes, especially murder, also required payment in slaves among the Chewa, and some of these slaves found their way into the hands of Yao slave traders. One of the Makua children lost his freedom by first being pawned in this fashion in payment for his elder brother's adulterous behaviour, after which he was sold and re-sold to an Arab.[128] Finally, at least one Yao was apparently sold by his father (or more probably his uncle) for what was very likely the simple acquisition of trading goods.[129]

The main slave traders who emerge from these accounts are the Yao, Makua, and Arabs. Abdallah confirms and extends the sources of slaves for the Yao trade by listing Nyasa, Bisa, Senga (possibly Nsenga?), and Chikunda.[130] All of Isaacman's Chewa informants stress the importance of Yao as slave traders, whom they preferred to the Portuguese or their agents because they gave the Chewa a better price for both their slaves and their ivory. The Yao travelled among the Chewa of Makanga in small groups of from three to six men. When they reached a village they were greeted warmly by the headman, who gave them a place to sleep and food to eat. The next day they would begin to do business with their host, trading cloth and, less commonly, guns for slaves. Among the Bisa, according to Rashid bin Hasani, it was also the chief who reaped by far the largest profit from the slave trade with the Yao. This same pattern was repeated by coast traders who came to trade at Yao villages.[131] All of those captives coming from the area west of Lake Nyasa passed through a number of hands, several changing owners three or four times before reaching the coast at or near Kilwa. In several instances freed slaves reported that they lived with their masters for a period of one or two years before finally being sold to the coast.[132] The same was true for those whose homes were at any distance from the coast, so that the normal pattern of the trade was clearly the passage of individual slaves, or small groups of them, from their point of origin until they reached either the coast or a major caravan town in the interior—such as those of the Yao chiefs Mponda, Makanjila, and Mataka—from whence they were assembled in large numbers and driven to the coast. By the last decades of the century this part of the trade was largely in Arab hands, although it was not so in previous years.

The obvious point about the profits to be made from the sale of slaves is that prices were lowest in the interior and highest at the point of final destination. That is not surprising. The nature of the business and the evidence makes it almost impossible to calculate the percentage of profit involved, and European observers tended to exaggerate, but it is clear that a handsome profit could be made by all parties concerned. In particular, it was the more prosperous Indian merchants at Zanzibar who profited

most from the trade, by virtue of their capitalization of its operation in East Africa.[133] In the interior there is no doubt that the
main item involved in trading for slaves was cloth. Isaacman's
Chewa informants all mention cloth, in general, and one gives the
price of a slave as three *peças* or pieces of cloth. According to
another Chewa elder, an important distinction was made between male and female slaves, the latter being valued more
highly because of their reproductive capacity. Indeed, he also
gives higher prices of one gun and five *peças* for a male, and two
guns and ten *peças* for a female slave.[134] Abdallah, on the other
hand, mentions a price of 'a wide piece of calico about four
yards long for one slave, double that for others'. But he also
mentions that coast people normally paid 'two lengths and eight
yards of fringed cloth' for a slave, which at least gives a rough
notion of the middleman's profits which were turned in the
interior. Again, after his capture and sale to slave dealers from the
coast, Petro Kilekwa was taken back to his village where his
mother offered to buy him back for three yards of cloth. She was
refused, the price being eight yards, and he was carried away.
Similarly, when the father of one of the Makua captives attempted
to ransom him for a new gun, four hoes, some beads, and some
iron, he was refused because only cloth was wanted.[135] In all of
these cases the only sale in the interior which did not involve
cloth was that of the young Bemba, who was sold by his Gwangwara captors for seven hoes.[136]

It is apparent that most contemporary observers attributed the
prominence of slaves from the lake region at Kilwa to the fact
that the country lying immediately behind Kilwa had been so
thoroughly depopulated by the ravages of the slave trade in
previous decades that it could no longer meet the insatiable
demands of the Kilwa market. How accurate an interpretation
is this? In certain respects it is very likely correct. At first, most
slaves were taken from the peoples living nearest to the coast, as
happened at Mozambique. There, however, the coastal hinterland
remained the primary region from which slaves were taken for
exportation right through the nineteenth century. Perhaps one
reason for the different distribution of slave supplies to Kilwa is
that the Kilwa hinterland was never as thickly populated as that
of Mozambique. Turning to the historical sources, in 1616 Gaspar
Bocarro found almost the entire line of march from the Ruvuma
River to Kilwa to be uninhabited, while the late eighteenth-

century French commentators like Crassons and Saulnier de Mondevit suggest that it was only in the more fertile river valleys of the hinterland that a significant population existed.[137] Further support for this interpretation may be found in Froberville's notes on the Ngindo, which state plainly that their settlement pattern was one of small, isolated family homesteads.[138] Finally, the large Makua population of the Kilwa hinterland seems not to have begun to enter this region from across the Ruvuma River until after the middle of the nineteenth century.[139] At Mozambique, on the other hand, the general impression which emerges from the Portuguese documentation is that the hinterland was more thickly populated. Perhaps, then, the Kilwa hinterland was exhausted as a major source of slaves for export by the middle of the nineteenth century because it began with a smaller and less dense population than that of Macuana, which remained at the centre of the Mozambique trade. Similarly, it was no accident that the Lake Nyasa region became the chief supply area for the slave trade from the middle decades of the century. The country surrounding the lake is one of the richest, most densely settled areas in all Africa, and was ideally suited to the slave trade for the simple reason that it sustained an unusually high population.[140]

Bisa—Yao Competition for Control of the Ivory Trade

Equally interesting changes were taking place in the ivory trade to Kilwa and in the interior during this period, changes which may have influenced the concentration of the Yao on slaves by the middle decades of the nineteenth century. The arrival of the two Angolan *pombeiros* at Tete in February 1811 re-animated Portuguese hopes for developing a prosperous trade with the Mwata Kazembe.[141] As late as 1814 there is evidence of trade in ivory between individual colonists at Tete and the Bisa, who dominated the carrying trade from the eastern Lunda state.[142] But by 1820, private trading by Portuguese colonists was restricted by the Governors of the Rivers of Sena in view of the hostilities which beset relations with Africans both north and south of the Zambesi. At the same time, Governor Barbosa was determined to revive the trade of the Rivers, particularly 'the trade with the hinterlands of the Bisa'. An official trading expedition composed of six local traders and a detachment of troops was outfitted at Tete under his direction for that specific purpose.[143] The arrival of envoys from the Mwata Kazembe in about 1822 suggests that his policy was beginning to take effect.[144]

Barbosa believed that it was not sufficient to operate exclusively from the Zambesi, however, and recommended that Portugal establish an official trading fair on the banks of the Luangwa River, the boundary between Bisa and Chewa territory. In this he was almost certainly influenced by the advice of the *prazeros* of northern Zambesia, in particular by that of the Caetano Pereiras of Makanga.[145] Official support from the Governor-General was first given to his plan at the end of 1822, although in 1825 the Crown recommended that it be suspended in favour of a concerted effort to resuscitate the Portuguese fair at Zumbo.[146] Nevertheless, two years later land was acquired by the Portuguese from the important Chewa chief Mwase for the establishment of what was to be called the *Nova Feira de Aruangua do Norte*. By November 1827 the expedition sent out from the Rivers had reached the Luangwa.[147] The potential importance of the new outpost for the Portuguese was of major proportions. As in previous years, their main purpose was to recapture the trade of the interior from the Kilwa market. The earliest notice of this problem during this period dates to 1820, when Governor-General Brito Sanches remarked that both the Yao and the Bisa were carrying their slaves and ivory to Zanzibar, that is, Kilwa, where the Arabs bought both items at a high price. By April 1827, just as the plans for the Luangwa fair were coming to fruition, a report on Barbosa's achievements as Governor of the Rivers vividly reveals the extent of Portuguese hopes for the revival of trade in northern Zambesia and emphasizes the principal role of the Bisa in that trade. Barbosa's acquisition of the Luangwa outpost, it was asserted,

> facilitates, consolidates and augments the trade of the Rivers with the Bisa Nation, who are great traders and who are in touch with the hinterlands which look to Benguela, and whose chief has already sent ambassadors on several occasions to Tete for the purpose of establishing commercial relations. As a result of this acquisition the extraction of ivory will be greatly increased, because various tribes which live thereabouts go annually to carry ivory to Zanzibar, owing to the injustice and mistreatment which they received at Mozambique during the administration of Francisco de Paula Albuquerque.[148]

It was not long before the Portuguese were disillusioned about their new station in the interior. Trade was limited to a small amount of ivory and slaves, principally the latter. The land which they had been granted by Mwase, they soon discovered, was virtually a no-man's land as a result of repeated assaults by the important Bisa chief Kazembe, whose country bordered the fair on the other bank of the Luangwa River.[149] According to the first commander of the fair, those Bisa who were seriously involved in the ivory trade simply did not come to the fair, travelling instead

> to the site of the Nyanja [Shire] river, in the hinterlands of the Zimba, or Nguru, with whom they exchange ivory for the superior and inferior goods of Zanzibar and Madagascar, which they call *fazendas dos Mujojos*, good pieces of red cloth, various glass beads of all colours, and fine coloured stones; in which trade they make great profits; since the manner in which they sell ivory is by placing the tusk on the ground with the hump lying up, and the buyer will go on placing boxes of beads and pieces of cloth on either side of the tusk until it covers it completely; accordingly, if the tusk is large they receive a roll of cloth and beads, besides more stones, etc., etc.; and they prefer those cloths and effects to ours, and they carry them throughout all this interior.[150]

Nevertheless, the Portuguese continued their campaign to attract the trade of the Bisa and the Mwata Kazembe to the Rivers of Sena and away from the enticements of the Zanzibar market.[151] The culmination of these efforts was a second major expedition to the court of the Mwata Kazembe in 1831–1832.

In his invaluable account of that futile expedition, Gamitto reinforces the impression that the Bisa had firmly asserted their control of the traffic between the Shire and the Luapula Rivers, largely at the expense of the Yao, judging by the situation in the later eighteenth century. According to Gamitto, the Bisa traded ivory and slaves from the Mwata Kazembe's and their own country to the Nguru, who subsequently carried them to the Kilwa coast. Much of this trade was done directly between the Bisa and the Nguru along the banks of the upper Shire. There was also a considerable boat traffic across Lake Nyasa from the south to perhaps as far north as Tumbukaland.[152] It is not entirely clear who these Nguru were. As used by people living to the west of Lake Nyasa, the word simply meant 'easterners', and Gamitto uses it in connection with both Maravi and Yao.[153] With respect to the boat traffic on the lake at this time, in 1850 Krapf learned from a Kilwa-born Mwera who had travelled in a caravan to Yaoland 'many years ago' that 'the caravan procured slaves and ivory, the latter being brought by the Waniassa from the western side of the lake. The Waniassa construct light but water-tight boats of the bark of trees, in which they cross the lake to buy ivory from the Mawisa-tribes.'[154] By the fourth decade of the nineteenth century, then, it would seem that the Yao had lost much of the ivory trade to the west of the lake and the Shire River, a development which probably dates to the last decade of the eighteenth century.

By the 1850s, the Bisa were also posing a challenge to the carrying trade of the Yao to Kilwa. At the beginning of 1849, the American Consul at Zanzibar wrote to one of the leading ivory merchants in Salem, Massachusetts, the centre of American commercial involvement with East Africa, that 'There are reports of the Beshu tribe near Kilwa with 3,000 frs [upwards of 100,000 pounds] ivory. The Banians have dispatched upwards of $100,000 worth of goods & 10,000$ in specie. . . .' A few days later he wrote to confirm these reports and mentioned that 'Other tribes are reported to be near.'[155] By the late 1850s, Burton's description of the ivory trade at Kilwa leaves little doubt as to why the Bisa were able to wrest much of this trade from the Yao. 'The "Bisha ivory" formerly found its way to Mozambique, but the barbarians have now learned to prefer Zanzibar; and the citizens welcome them, as they sell their stores more cheaply than the Wahiao, who have become adept in coast arts.'[156] What Burton is saying here needs little explication. Through their long contact with the coast, the Yao had become very much aware of the value of their ivory at the coast. Indeed, despite their concentration on the slave trade during the middle of the nineteenth century, ivory continued to be valued more highly by the Yao in the interior, being worth more than a female slave among the Chewa. Abdallah gives the price of a large tusk as thirty to sixty yards (one or two *taka*) of cloth, or one hundred *matemanya* beads (small, white, elongated—i.e., *velório*), which was equal to the price of between seven and fifteen slaves.[157] Had the Yao been able to maintain their monopoly over the carrying trade to Kilwa, they would likely have been able to demand and receive a higher price for their stock in trade than they had been receiving in the past. But the presence of another, equally vigorous African trading people who were attempting to break their control of that trade by undercutting their prices put them in a position of asking for more goods in exchange for their ivory than the merchants of Kilwa were now prepared to pay.

From the perspective of the Indian traders of the coast, the problem presented itself differently. According to an American trader at Zanzibar in 1844, the Indians—most of whom were Banyans—'trade with the natives who are very ignorant and know not the value of these articles. The Banyans obtain the ivory of these people for almost nothing, giving a string of beads or a small coil of brass wire for a tooth weighing 140 pounds or even more. But the natives within a few years have found out something the value of this article and charge a much higher price for it.'[158] No wonder the appearance of the Bisa at Kilwa was so well received at the coast, where their competition with the Yao enabled the Banyans to continue to extract the greatest margin of profit from the trade of East Africa. In the widest context, then, African competition for the international trade of East Africa can be seen to have played right into the hands of foreign traders by allowing them to pay artificially deflated prices for raw materials which were of increasing value on the world market.[159]

Finally, in coming to grips with the way in which African traders were viewed in this sytem of international trade, it is important to remember that throughout the nineteenth century there was the most intense competition for control of the carrying trade between up-country African traders and coastal traders, be they Arab or Swahili. The well-known cases of the Nyamewzi, Kimbu, and Kamba admirably demonstrate this point.[160] At the same time, a less well-known distinction in the ivory trade was also made at the coast which worked to the disadvantage of African traders and was intended to restrict as much as possible their participation in even the carrying trade. According to a report on the state of commerce at Zanzibar in 1865 submitted by Edward D. Ropes, American Consul to the Sultanate, 'A distinction is made in favor of Ivory expeditions which are fitted out from Zanz., they paying five dollars the frassil less duty than the Natives from the interior who bring their own Ivory to the coast for sale'.[161] For all their pains and acquired skills, then, African traders were as much captives of the system of international trading in East Africa at Kilwa and Zanzibar as they were at Mozambique.

So by about 1860, it is arguable that the Yao were in the process of losing their long-established control of the ivory trade of East Central Africa to the Bisa. The Kilwa market was the main focus of their competition, but in view of our knowledge of what was happening there, it seems possible that a similar situation was developing at Mozambique. It is noteworthy, for instance, that the Marquis of Bemposta Subserra places the Bisa first, before the Yao, in his description of the caravan trade from the interior to Mozambique. Similarly, whereas in the middle of the eighteenth century it was the Yao who were blamed for introducing goods from Mozambique into the hinterland of Zumbo, in 1856 Livingstone observed that English cottons carried by the Bisa from Mozambique were finding their way into the country beyond the Kafue Gorge.[162] Perhaps it is the growth of Bisa control of the ivory trade, as much as the growth of the demand for slaves at the coast, which turned the Yao increasingly to the slave trade during the first half of the nineteenth century. At about this time, however, this trend was violently disrupted by a combination of forces which had been slowly gathering strength in the years preceding the 1860s. Some of these were the result of processes which we have been examining in this chapter, others represented entirely new developments in the history of this part of Africa. The result of their conjoining was that in the space of a very few years the Bisa trading network was completely dismantled, and both the economic and political strength of the Yao considerably enhanced.

As early as the late 1820s, the Bisa were beginning to be pressured again by the expansion of the Bemba state in northeastern Zambia. At about the same time they began to encounter serious competition for control of the ivory trade of the Mwata Kazembe from Swahili and Arab traders who were developing the trade route leading north through the corridor between Lakes Tanganyika and Nyasa on the way to the coast.[163] In response to these challenges, the Bisa seem to have cultivated the ivory trade beyond the Kafue Gorge, while maintaining control of that lying to the west of Lake Nyasa. The final blow to Bisa trade was delivered not by other traders in the interior, however, but by the devastating raid of Mpezeni's Ngoni in the 1860s to the west of the Luangwa River after his people had settled into the country immediately to the east of the river.[164]

The general outline of the impact of the Ngoni migration on

the peoples of East Africa after their crossing of the Zambesi River from southern Africa in 1835 is well known.[165] The main body of the Ngoni was led by Zwangendaba. After a sojourn of a few years in Nsenga country, just east of the Luangwa, the Ngoni pushed on north until they settled near the Fipa plateau, to the south-east of Lake Tanganyika, in about 1840. By this date their numbers were swollen by the incorporation of many peoples through whose country they had marched to the west of Lake Nyasa. Not long after Zwangendaba's Ngoni crossed the Zambesi, a smaller Ngoni group led by Mputa Maseko also crossed the river, settling for a while among the Chewa. In about 1846 the Maseko Ngoni travelled north-east across the Shire at Mpingangila, near Fort Johnston, where the Shire leaves the southern end of Lake Nyasa, continued north along the hills lying to the east of the lake, and finally settled in the country around what is now Songea in southern Tanzania. Abdallah is silent on the question of what impact the migration of the Maseko Ngoni had on the Yao at this time, but Ngoni traditions specifically mention fighting the Yao, who fled to the hills above the lakeside. Equally, the incorporation of what appear to have been large numbers of Yao by the Maseko Ngoni, and Ebner's claim that the name 'Mputa' was derived from the Yao verb 'to beat', suggest that either Abdallah or his informants may have been suppressing information on this important point.[166]

In about 1848, or possibly a few years earlier, Zwangendaba died and there was a major dispersal of the main body of the Ngoni from the Fipa area. One of the Ngoni sections, led by Zulu-Gama and Mbonani, moved east across the mountains at the north end of Lake Nyasa until they reached the country around the headwaters of the Ruvuma River where the Maseko Ngoni were already settled. After a period of uneasy co-existence, rivalries between the two groups came to a head and an open struggle took place between them. Mputa Maseko was killed and his successor, Chikuse, led a retreat of his Ngoni back along the route which they had originally followed north to the east of Lake Nyasa. Eventually they settled to the south-west of the lake in the hills of what is modern Dedza District in Malawi. The date of the Ngoni retreat through western Yaoland is not known with any certainty, but it probably took place sometime late in the 1850s. Its immediate impact on the Yao is difficult to assess, but once the issue of supremacy among the Ngoni around Songea was settled in favour of the successors of Zulu-Gama and Mbonani, there is no question that these Ngoni, who became widely known by their Yao nickname of Gwangwara, were a major threat to the Yao. In about 1866, for example, they raided extensively to the east of Songea and perhaps across the Ruvuma into north-western Yaoland.[167] When Livingstone travelled from the Kilwa coast into Yaoland in the middle of that year, he found vast stretches of unpopulated country which were probably much more immediately the product of these Ngoni raids than of the slave trade.[168] The instability created among the peoples surrounding Lake Nyasa who were not directly incorporated into one of the several Ngoni kingdoms established after the death of Zwangendaba did, however, contribute to the availability of slaves for those who would prey upon refugees from the Ngoni (see above, p. 240).

Foremost among these refugees were the Yao, who were themselves involved in a massive migration south into the Shire highlands in 1859–1861. The causes and development of this migration are difficult to isolate.[169] Most sources point to raids on the Yao from the east by both the Makua and the Lomwe, although Livingstone understood that internal raiding among the Yao to supply the slave trade was the root cause. Others mention raids by the Ngoni, one of them specifically naming the Gwangwara.[170] Yet another includes the Bisa among those who attacked the Yao at this time.[171] A decade earlier, Krapf was told at Mombasa 'that in the year 1847 about 7000 Wahiau were captured and sold to Kiloa, or destroyed by the Mabiti or Mawizi, a tribe residing on the South-Western bank of the lake'.[172] This is an almost hopelessly vague reference, as it could be interpreted to mean either an Ngoni group, or the Bisa, or both. In any case, it is indicative of the complexity of the pressures which were coming to bear upon the Yao in the middle of the nineteenth century, while the intensely localized nature of the variant accounts of the causes of the Yao migration render a satisfactory synthesis from the available sources impossible.

Of particular interest in the context of this study are the reasons for the attacks by the Makua on the Yao. Most sources point to the central importance of the Meto Makua in causing the dispersal of the Yao, although there is little agreement as to what forces drove the Makua to fall upon the Yao. Abdallah attributes their outburst to famine and resultant clashes among the Makua in their own country, although he specifically mentions the outstanding leadership of a Makua named Namauwa from Meto district.[173] An old Makua living among the Yao near Lake Nyasa told W. P. Johnson 'that we came across fighting and killing because our chief wanted more elbow room'.[174] But there is at least one version of the involvement of the Meto Makua in attacking the Yao which directly raises the question of the impact of the slave trade. According to a Yao story entitled 'On Our Home' which was collected by Duff Macdonald sometime between 1878 and 1881,

> The Walolo lived on the other side of the (river) Lujenda, on the road to Chisanga [Kisanga]. The Walolo were capturing the Machinga to carry them to Chisanga and exchange them for cloth. The Walolo were brave, and had many guns. The Machinga dwelt at Mandimbi, and the Walolo made them flee.[175]

On the other hand, traditions gathered by British colonial officers in southern Tanzania in about 1930 suggest that there were a variety of internal causes of dissension among a large number of Makua groups in and around the Meto area.[176] Faced with such a bewildering range of sources and possible interpretations, it would be imprudent to attempt to argue too strenuously for the primacy of the impact of the slave trade on developments among the Meto Makua leading up to their raids against the Yao. But in view of our knowledge about the growing dimensions of the slave trade to Mozambique and to Ibo, it is an important possibility to bear in mind when it becomes possible to explore some of these fundamental questions in the field.

By about 1860, then, the historical environment of East Central Africa was much altered from what it had been for many years. The arrival of the Ngoni effectively laid to rest what appears to have been the successful challenge of the Bisa to the entrenched supremacy of the Yao in the carrying trade of the region. At the same time the presence of the Ngoni contributed significantly to the general disruption of life around Lake Nyasa. The Yao, on the other hand, were able at once to convert their situation from one in which they were victims of attacks from their neighbours to another in which they were marauding invaders who rapidly established their hegemony over the Maravi-speaking peoples of the upper Shire valley.[177] Those

Yao who remained in the heart of Yaoland seem to have responded with equal vigour to the challenges of the period, producing a series of remarkable innovative leaders who developed trading states of unprecedented vitality among the Yao from about this period.[178] Control of the upper Shire valley immediately put the Yao in touch with Portuguese slavers from Tete, who were only too willing to supply the Yao with firearms in exchange for slaves, while Yao control of the route to Quelimane probably dates only from this period.[179] By 1863, African trading agents of a Portuguese colonist from Tete reported encountering Englishmen from Natal, Portuguese from Benguela, 'as well as many Yao and Moors from Zanzibar' trading for ivory and some copper at the court of Sekeletu, Litunga of Barotseland, on the upper reaches of the Zambesi River.[180] From what may have been the beginning of a major decline in their importance in the trade of East Central Africa, the Yao moved rapidly and confidently from strength to strength, from the time of their invasion of what is today southern Malawi until their subjugation to colonial rule by the British in Malawi, the Germans in Tanzania, and, finally in 1912, the Portuguese in Mozambique.[181]

For all that, however, the fact remains that the Yao were not better served in their international trading relations at the end of the nineteenth century than they had been at the beginning. In particular, the linking of ivory sales at the coast to the cash economy of Mozambique provided yet another mechanism for robbing Africans of a fair exchange value for their goods. According to one of the new Portuguese colonial administrators, in the early 1890s Yao caravans of one thousand or more individuals arrived annually at Ingode, near Quelimane, bearing ivory in exchange for cotton, silks, guns, and powder. Smaller numbers even traded directly at Quelimane.

> The trade carried on with them by the Indian dealers frequently follows a curious process; these dealers almost always prefer to buy ivory from them in exchange for money, employing the greatest diligency in order to convince the Yao to accept it; consequently the black goes out by one door and enters the next, to leave all his money in exchange for spirits or other goods which are then sold to him for an exorbitant price.
>
> The black is a born trader, and is such more through natural tendency than through his own interest. Thus it is curious to see how, always trading, many times intelligent blacks allow them-

selves to be fooled by this process, and not being content with five pieces of cotton in exchange for a tusk of ivory, go to sell it there for a quantity of money which scarcely allows them to buy two pieces afterwards.[182]

Once again, control over the system of international trade in East Central Africa can be seen to have remained in the hands of foreign merchants, who used every new opportunity to increase their own profits at the expense of their African trading 'partners'.

NOTES

1. For a full treatment of the British anti-slave trade campaign in the Western Indian Ocean, see G. S. Graham, *Great Britain in the Indian Ocean, 1810–1850* (Oxford, 1967), especially chapters 2, 3, and 5.

2. A.H.U., Moç., Cx. 62, Silva Guedes, 'Relação do Marfim e mais generos q̃ se despacharão nesta Alf.ª p.r Sahida p.ª os Portos da Azia no mes de Agosto de prezente ano de 1817'. The exact figure is 3,959 *arrobas* and 10¾ *arráteis*. Of this, 70·4 per cent went to Daman, 17·3 per cent to Diu, and 12·3 per cent to Bengal.

3. A.C.L., Azul Ms. 648, no. 17. It is worth noting, too, that the duty paid on ivory in 1818 was now raised to 6 per cent *ad valorem*.

4. A.H.U., Cod. 1394, fl. 15–17, Brito Sanches to Conde dos Arcos, Moç., 10 October 1819.

5. Owen, *Narrative*, I, p. 191.

6. S. X. Botelho, *Memoria Estatistica sobre os Dominios Portuguezes na Africa Oriental* (Lisbon, 1835), pp. 371–3.

7. Santana, *Documentação*, II, p. 835. Moreover, the price of Mozambique ivory remained well above that paid at Zanzibar during these years. In 1832 it was 28 to 33 dollars per *arroba* of large ivory, equivalent to 30·6 to 36·1 dollars per *frasila* (*faraçola*) of the same, which was higher even than the price current at Bombay. See Gamitto, *King Kazembe*, II, p. 84, and Sheriff, 'Rise of a Commercial Empire', p. 469, Graph II.

8. Bordalo, *Ensaio*, p. 167.

9. For a detailed description of British attempts to restrict the Brazilian and Portuguese slave trade at this time, see Leslie Bethell, *The Abolition of the Brazilian Slave Trade: Britain, Brazil, and the Slave Trade Question, 1807–1869* (Cambridge, 1970), chapters 1–2.

10. See Caledon to Vansittart, Cape of Good Hope, 27 June 1810, in Theal, *Records*, IX, p. 12; P.R.O., F.O. 84/122, Robert Hesketh to Lord Palmerston, London, 3 August 1831, enclosure no. 2, 'State of the Slave Trade on the Northern Coast of Brazil'.

11. Milburn, *Oriental Commerce*, I, p. 59.

12. A.C.L., Azul Ms. 648, no. 17. See also A.H.U., Moç., Cx. 61 and Cx. 62, Silva Guedes, *despachos* issued for twelve Brazilian merchant vessels, Moç., 9 February 1817 to 26 March 1818.

13. Arquivo da Casa da Cadaval, Cod. 826 (M VI 32), D. Fr. Bartolomeu dos Mártires, 'Memoria Chorographica da Provincia e a Capitania de Moçambique na Costa d'Africa Oriental Conforme o estado em que se achava no anno de 1822', fl. 29–30. I am most grateful to the Marqueza de Cadaval for allowing me to see this important manuscript and to Fr. Francisco Leite de Faria, Keeper of the

Arquivo, who enabled me to use it in Lisbon. Lengthy extracts have been published with an introduction by Virgínia Rau, 'Aspectos étnico-culturais da ilha de Moçambique em 1822', *Studia*, 11 (1963), pp. 123–62, especially 148–51. Cf. A.H.U., Moç., Cx. 64, Pedro Simião, 'Mappa das Embarcaçoens, que entrarão e Sahirão do Porto de Mossambique no ano de 1819', Moç., 31 December 1819.

14. P.R.O., F.O. 84/17, Henry Hayne to Marquis of Londonderry, Rio de Janeiro, 16 January 1822, enclosing, 'Slaves imported at Rio de Janeiro during the year 1821'; Mártires, 'Memoria', fl. 35.

15. P.R.O., C.O. 415/7, A. No. 172, pp. 12–13, Captain Acland's Journal No. 2, Moç., 9 October 1826; see also ibid., p. 34, Captain Polkinhome's Journal, post-12 December 1826.

16. A.H.U., Cod. 1425, fl. 3–5, Paulo José Miguel de Brito to Sheikh of Quitangonha, Moç., 9 and 17 March 1830.

17. Mártires' 1819 figures yield a higher mortality rate (27·7 per cent) than the 23·3 per cent which Herbert Klein has obtained from Brazilian notarial records for all slaves shipped (4,665) and imported (3,577) from Portuguese East Africa during the transitional period of 1795–1811, but the British consular figures for Mozambique and Quelimane importations in the 1820s (which together totalled 74,173 embarked and 64,688 landed, with 9,485 deaths at sea), yield a much lower mortality rate of 12·8 per cent. If these figures are at all reliable, they suggest that from about 1820 the Atlantic slave trade from East Africa became a much less hazardous business than in previous years. See Klein, 'The Trade in African Slaves to Rio de Janeiro, 1795–1811: Estimates of Mortality and Patterns of Voyages', *Jl. of African History*, X, 4 (1968), p. 540; Table 5 and sources.

18. Bethell, *Abolition*, Appendix.

19. I have calculated the percentage of slaves imported from Portuguese East Africa during 1828–1830 by dividing the total figures supplied by Bethell by the Foreign Office statistics cited in Table 5 for those years for both Mozambique and Quelimane. See ibid., p. 71. For references to the slave trade from Mozambique to Brazil in the 1830s, see ibid., pp. 79, 85, 127, 150, 168.

20. H. Lynne to Stopford, H. M. Sloop *Eclipse*, 21 May 1812, and C. R. Moorsom to Christian, H.M.S. *Andromache*, Simon's Bay, 24 May 1825, both in Theal, *Records*, IX, pp. 16, 51; A.H.U., Moç., Cx. 57, *autos da visita* issued to eleven vessels with British passports, from Mauritius and the Seychelles; A.H.U., Cod. 1386, no. 1167, António de Araujo de Azevedo to Marco Caetano de Abreu e Meneses, Rio de Janeiro, 18 June 1814; ibid., no. 1213, Marquês de Aguiar to same, Rio de Janeiro, 31 July 1815; A.H.U., Cod. 1380, fl. 240–3, Brito Sanches to Conde dos Arcos, Moç., 27 September 1819; A.H.U., Cod. 1391, no. 1414, Arcos to Brito Sanches, Rio de Janeiro, 11 February 1820; A.H.U., Cod. 1394, fl. 69, Brito Sanches to Arcos, Moç., 15 July 1820.

21. P.R.O., C.O. 415/7, A. No. 172, pp. 14–15.

22. A.C.L., Azul Ms 847, 'Estado das Relações Commerciaes da Capitania de Mossambique ate o dia 21 de Agosto de 1829 dado pelo Juiz de Fora de Mossambique Dionisio Ignacio de Lemos Pinto em sua informação de 2 de Novembro de 1829 dirigido ao Gov.ᵒʳ e Cap.ᵃᵐ General da d.ᵃ Capitania Paulo Jose Miguel de Brito', fl. 13.

23. A.H.U., Moç., Cx. 64, Simião, 'Mappa', Moç., 31 December 1819.

24. See A.H.U., Cod. 1379, fl. 43, 46, 50, 90–1, being licences granted to eight Swahili and Arab traders to embark slaves at Mozambique, the average request being for fifty slaves, 14 March–12 April 1810, 1 February and 16 March 1812; ibid., fl. 66, licence granted for buying forty slaves to 'Massane Bunu Portador da Rainha Vaine de Bom-Bottoque', 8 January 1811; A.H.U., Moç., Cx. 60, *requerimento*. Said bin Saif, from Zanzibar, to go to Madagascar, granted, Moç., 2 April 1817; ibid., *requerimento*, Sidi Hasan, returning from Madagascar, to go to Zanzibar, granted, Moç., 25 September 1817; P.R.O., Admiralty 1/69, no. 63, Joseph

Nourse to John Wilson Croker, H.M.S. *Andromache*, at Sea, in the Mozambique Channel, 15 December 1823; Mártires, 'Memoria', fl. 31–2, also in Rau, 'Aspectos', pp. 152–3; P.R.O., C.O. 415/4, no. 61, 'Interrogatories addressed to Mr. Copall and Mr. Copall's Answers relative to the State of Madagascar', nos. 200 and 202, Port Louis, 8 October 1827.

25. Owen to Croker, H.M.S. *Leven*, Mozambique, 9 October 1823, in Theal, *Records*, IX, pp. 32–3; cf. ibid., pp. 18, 50; F. T. Texugo, *A Letter on the Slave Trade still carried on along the Eastern Coast of Africa* . . . (London, 1839), p. 34; Eduardo Correia Lopes, *A escravatura (subsidios para a sua história)* (Lisbon, 1944), p. 169. In assessing Texugo's evidence it is worth knowing that he was a political exile from Portugal: see A.H.U., Cod. 1444, no. 198, [Crown to Governor of Mozambique], 27 June 1839.

26. See Jackson, *European Powers*, pp. 195–6, 198–201, 222; Marquês da Bemposta Subserra, *et al*, Untitled memorandum on Portuguese East Africa directed to the the Crown, Lisboa, 28 April 1856, pp. 19–20; Lyons McLeod, *Travels in Eastern Africa; with the Narrative of a Residence in Mozambique* (London, 1860), I, pp. 304–311, 313, 316–21, 325; James Duffy, *A Question of Slavery* (Oxford, 1967), p. 41.

27. A.H.U., Moç., Cx. 49, petition of Joaquim da Rosário Monteiro, granted, [Moç.], 28 April 1807; A.H.U., Moç., Cx. 50, Prov. Govt. to Crown, Moç., 22 October 1807.

28. A.C.L., Azul Ms. 847, fl. 11, 16; A.H.U., Moç., Cx. 59 and Cod. 1380, fl. 152–3, Abreu e Meneses to Azevedo, Moç., 1 October 1815; ibid., fl. 189, José Francisco de Paula Cavalcanti de Albuquerque to Conde da Barca, Moç., 23 September 1817.

29. Jackson, *European Powers*, p. 189.

30. Owen to Croker, H.M.S. *Leven*, Mozambique, 9 October 1823, in Theal, *Records*, IX, p. 33; Thomas Boteler, *Narrative of a Voyage of Discovery to Africa and Arabia, performed in His Majesty's Ships Leven and Barracouta, from 1821 to 1826* (London, 1835), I, pp. 248–9; Owen, *Narrative*, I, 292–3; P.R.O. C.O. 415/7, A. No. 172, pp. 34–5, Polkinhome's Journal.

31. P.R.O., C.O. 415/9, A. No. 238, 'Correspondence and Documents furnished to Captains *Polkinhome* and Acland . . . 29 Sept.ʳ 1827 relative to the Slave Trade on the Coast of Africa', Document No. 1, article no. 4; see also A.H.U., Cod. 1414, no. 1837, José António de Oliveira Leite de Barros to Botelho, Ajuda, 19 April 1828.

32. See sources for Table 5; for the annual figures, see Isaacman, *Mozambique*, p. 92, Table 8.

33. ibid., pp. 88, Table 6, 93.

34. Texugo, *Letter*, p. 34; for references from the 1840s, see Coupland, *East Africa and Its Invaders*, pp. 496–8.

35. For the Makua conflicts, see A.H.U., Cod. 1478, fl. 233, Caetano José Resende to Mendonça, Ibo, 1 September 1811; A.H.U., Moç., Cx. 55, Mendonça to Resende, Moç., 1 October 1811; A.H.U., Cod. 1380, fl. 79, same to Galveâs, Moç., 11 December 1811; A.H.U., Cod. 1385, no. 1116, Aguiar to Mendonça, Rio de Janeiro, 20 May 1812; A.H.U., Moç., Cx. 57, Manuel Onofre Pantoja to Abreu e Meneses, Ibo, 23 February 1813; ibid., Costa Portugal to same, Ibo, 23 February 1813; A.H.U., Cod. 1377, fl. 154, Abreu e Meneses to Pantoja, Moç., 12 August 1814. There is a rich body of documentation on the Sakalava raids against the coast of East Central Africa during this decade: see A.H.U., Moç., Cx. 54, 55, 56, 58, 59, 60, 64, 66, and Cod. 1380, 1394, 1478; B.N.L., F.G., Cod. 8470; Mártires, 'Memoria', fl. 39–42.

36. P.R.O., C.O. 415/9, A. No. 238, Document No. 1, article no. 6; A.H.U., Cod. 1402, fl. 105, Prov. Govt. to Caldas, Moç., 14 February 1824; Boteler, *Narrative*, II, pp. 55, 64; Owen, *Narrative*, II, pp. 9–10, 14; P.R.O., C.O. 415/7, A. No. 172, pp. 3–4, Acland's Journal No. 1, Ibo, 24 June 1826; Santana, *Documentação*, I, pp. 119, 457.

37. A.H.U., Cod. 1413, fl. 110, Botelho to José Amanti da Lima, Moç., 2 June 1829; A.H.U., Cod. 1427, fl. 8, Brito to Bernardes, Moç., 5 October 1830; A.H.U., Cod. 1207, fl. 91–2, *portaria*, Joaquim Pereira, Moç., 29 August 1840; P.R.O., F.O. 84/1050, F.O. to McLeod—Slave Trade Draft No. 2, 5 January 1858.

38. P.R.O., F.O. 63/836, McLeod to Malmesbury, Hyde Park, 30 November 1858.

39. Owen, *Narrative*, I, p. 199.

40. Texugo, *Letter*, p. 34.

41. Teixeira Botelho, *História*, II, pp. 164–5; C. G. L. Sullivan, *Dhow Chasing in Zanzibar Waters and On the Eastern Coast of Africa. Narrative of Five Years' Experience in the Suppression of the Slave Trade* (London, 1873), pp. 21–4; P.R.O., Admiralty 1/5596, T. V. Anson to B. Reynolds, H.M.S. *Eurydice*, Simon's Bay, 3 March 1849.

42. Jackson, *European Powers*, p. 222; McLeod, *Travels*, I, pp. 247–9; see also, Bordalo, *Ensaio*, p. 49.

43. P.R.O., F.O. 63/836, McLeod to Sir J. Grey, Mozambique, 2 March 1858; *A.C.U.*, p.n.o., III (1862), p. 95. See Newitt, 'Angoche, the slave trade and the Portuguese, *c.* 1844–1910', *Jl. of African History*, XIII, 4 (1972), pp. 659–72.

44. A.H.U., Cod. 1385, no. 1074, Galveâs to Mendonça, Rio de Janeiro, 4 June 1811; A.H.U., Moç., Cx. 55, same to same, Rio de Janeiro, 5 June 1811; A.H.U., Moç., Cx. 54, Mendonça to Galveâs, Moç., 31 October 1811; A.H.U., Cod., 1380, fl. 110, Abreu e Meneses to same, Moç., 5 February 1813.

45. A.H.U., Cod. 1394, fl. 31–2, Brito Sanches to Arcos, Moç., 11 November 1819.

46. Mártires, 'Memoria', fl. 17–18.

47. ibid.

48. A.H.U., Cod. 1391, no. 1437, and Moç., Cx. 67, Arcos to Brito Sanches, Rio de Janeiro, 2 August 1820; ibid., Brito Sanches to Arcos, Moc., 10 November 1820; A.H.U., Cod. 1394, fl. 78 and Moç., Cx. 67, same to same, Moç., 7 December 1820; ibid., same to same, Moç., 8 and 9 December 1820; Mártires, 'Memoria', fl. 27, also in Rau, 'Aspectos', pp. 142–3. In January 1823, a British naval officer reported that 'The Merchants who had recently gone into the interior to purchase slaves, I was informed, had been murdered, and their goods seized'. Joseph Nourse to Croker, H.M.S. *Andromache*, At Sea, 5 January 1823, in Theal, *Records*, IX, p. 18.

49. See Santana, *Documentação*, I, p. 169; A.H.U., Moç., maço 11, Brito to Conde de Basto, Moç., 8 August 1830; A.H.U., Cod. 1432, fl. 19–20, same to same (?), Moç., 27 October 1830.

50. Santana, *Documentação*, II, p. 381.

51. ibid., II, pp. 625, 756.

52. ibid., II, p. 381.

53. There is a mass of documentation on this subject, much of it presented, in detail in ibid., II; for specific references, see Santana's index.

54. A.H.U., Cod. 1425, fl. 11, Brito to the Mauruça, Moç., 30 October 1830.

55. A.H.U., Moç., maço 11, Sousa Ferreira to Brito, Mossuril, 22 and 24 November 1830.

56. ibid., same to same, Mossuril, 25 November 1830.

57. A.H.U., Cod. 1425, fl. 12, Brito to the Mauruça, Moç., 14 December 1830.

58. A.H.U., Cod. 1432, fl. 23–4, Brito to Manuel da Silva Gonçalves, Moç., 8 January 1831. The chief of Simuco, or Samuco, was called Nampustamuno, a Makua name, but correspondence to him was translated into Swahili. A.H.U., Cod. 1425, fl. 26–7, Brito to Chief of Samuco, Moç., 10 August 1831, and fl. 41, Prov. Govt. to same, Moç., 21 August 1832.

59. A.H.U., Cod. 1440, and unfoliated, Silva Gonçalves to José António Pereira, Moç., 13 and 19 March 1833; ibid., *portaria*, Prov. Govt., Moç., 23 April 1833; ibid., Prov. Govt. to Dez.ᵒʳ Ouv.ᵒʳ Geral, Moç., 23 April 1833; ibid., Silva Gonçalves to Interim Commander of the Mainland, Moç., 3 May 1833.

60. B.N.L., Cod. 8470, fl. 61, Selimane bin Agy to Prov. Govt., Quitangonha, 1

December 1833; A.H.U., Cod. 1440, Silva Gonçalves to António de Vasconcelos e Carvalho, Moç., 3 December 1833.
61. ibid., Silva Gonçalves to Pereira, Moç., 25 January 1834.
62. Bordalo, *Ensaio*, p. 37.
63. Owen, *Narrative*, I, p. 192.
64. Bordalo, *Ensaio*, p. 50.
65. Maria José Galvão Mousinho de Albuquerque, *Moçambique, 1896–1898* (Lisbon, 1934; 1st ed., 1899), p. 61, no. 1, where he gives the date of the Matibane campaign as 1857; cf. Ministério dos Negocios da Marinha e Ultramar, *A Campanha contra os Namarraes. Relatorios enviados ao Ministerio e Secretario d'Estado dos Negocios da Marinha e Ultramar pelo Commissario Regio da Provincia de Moçambique* (Lisbon, 1897), p. 5, where Mousinho dates it to 1854, while noting that 'there are no written documents to this point'; *A.C.U.*, p.n.o., VII (1866), pp. 28–9.
66. Jeronymo Romero, *Supplemento á Memoria Descriptiva e Estatistica do Districto de Cabo Delgado com uma Noticia Ácerca do Estabelecimento da Colonia de Pemba* (Lisbon, 1860), pp. 117–19.
67. For a capsule account of McLeod's activities at Mozambique, see Duffy, *A Question of Slavery*, pp. 51–3.
68. McLeod, *Travels*, I, pp. 316–17.
69. Bordalo, *Ensaio*, p. 133.
70. McLeod, *Travels*, I, pp. 317–21; see Duffy, *A Question of Slavery*, pp. 53–4.
71. Elton, *Travels*, p. 195.
72. ibid., pp. 199–200.
73. ibid., p. 195. Very little is known about the slave trade to Madagascar at this time. The Anglo-Malagasy Treaty of 1817 specifically prohibited it, but the Malagasy took this to mean only the export of slaves from the island. Treaties aside, in the 1860s perhaps 3,000 to 4,000 slaves were exported annually to Mauritius, the United States of America, and the West Indies. There was a flourishing system of slavery in Madagascar, the economy of which Mutibwa has described as 'dependent largely on the use of slave labour'. Thus there was a vigorous slave trade until the final imposition of French colonial rule over Madagascar at the end of the nineteenth century. It is important to note, however, that slave labour on Madagascar did not serve only the domestic economy of the island. The Hova hierarchy was deeply involved in commercial agriculture for export, especially in the rice trade to Mauritius, and the entire economy was oriented outward after the early 1860s. Like the slave trade to Zanzibar, then, that to Madagascar cannot be dismissed simply as the product of an anomalous Arab or Malagasy slave economy, but must also be seen in the context of Madagascar's becoming an economic satellite of the West. See Phares M. Mutibwa, 'Patterns of Trade and Economic Development in Nineteenth Century Madagascar', *Transafrican Jl. of History*, II, 1 (1972), pp. 37–40, 51, 59, n. 12. For another source on the volume of this slave trade, see Colomb, *Slave-Catching*, pp. 308–12. According to Colomb, the general term for African slaves at Madagascar was 'Mozambiques'. ibid., p. 309. More specifically, Elton writes:

> That there are thousands of Makua slaves on the west coast of Madagascar, and that they are sold and bartered to the Hovas for service is a matter of notoriety to everybody who knows Mozambique and anything about the Sakalava, whose principal trade consists in the purchasing of the slaves from the dhows and re-selling them to their neighbours.

Elton, *Travels*, p. 162; see also, Hubert Descamps, *Histoire de Madagascar*, 2e ed. (Paris, 1961), pp. 87, 295, map 12.
74. Elton, *Travels*, pp. 145, 196–9, also 215; cf. Daniel J. Rankin, *Arab Tales translated from the Swahili language into the Túgulu Dialect of the Mákua Language, as spoken in the Immediate Vicinity of Mozambique. Together with comparative vocabularies of five*

dialects of the Makua language (London, n.d.), p. xii; O'Neill, 'Journey from Mozambique, pp. 643, 735.

75. The name *namarral* (pl. *namarrais*), the etymology of which I have been unable to ascertain, was given to the Makua confederacy headed by chief Mucutomuno, whose aggressive behaviour first made an impression at Mozambique in about 1875 or 1876. Mello Machado identifies the *namarrais* as Central Makua and gives their localities as Monapo, Quixaxe, and Mossuril. During the later eighteenth century, the stronghold of Mucutomuno was Cambira, in the same general country to the west of Mossuril and northwest of Mutomunho as Monapo. So although all sources agree that they were recent arrivals in the immediate coastal strip opposite Mozambique Island, they may only have shifted their centre of activities coastward in the last quarter of the nineteenth century, rather than having come from the far interior. See O'Neill, 'Journey from Mozambique', pp. 632–3; Mello Machado, *Entre os Macuas*, p. 111, maps facing pp. 16 & 61, & Table 1, facing p. 112; see above, Ch. 5, p. 153; Camizão, *Indicações*, p. 16; cf. Nancy Jane Hafkin, 'Trade, Society, and Politics in Northern Mozambique, *c.* 1753–1913', unpublished Ph.D. thesis, Boston University, 1973, pp. 365–9. For a full account of local resistance to the imposition of Portuguese colonial rule, see ibid., Ch. 11.

76. A.C.L., Azul Ms. 847, fl. 10.

77. A.H.U., Cod. 1394, fl. 16, Brito Sanches to Arcos, Moç., 10 October 1819; for passing references to the Yao, see A.H.U., Moç., Cx. 59, *requerimento*, Muhamad Hasan, n.d., with enclosure, Moç., 12 August 1815; A.H.U., Cod. 1380, fl. 235–6, Prov. Govt. to Arcos, Moç., 19 February 1819.

78. Mártires, 'Memoria', fl. 27, 63, also in Rau, 'Aspectos', pp. 143–4, 158–9.

79. Froberville, 'Notes sur les . . . amakoua', pp. 323–4, and n. 1. For kidnapping and caravan protection, see J. Lewis Krapf, *Travels, Researches, and Missionary Labours, during an Eighteen Years' Residence in Eastern Africa* (London, 1860), pp. 423–5.

80. See Santana, *Documentação*, I, pp. 163, 300–1.

81. Manuel Joaquim Mendes de Vasconcelos e Cirne, *Memoria sobre a Provincia de Moçambique*, Ministério dos Negócios da Marinha e Ultramar, Documentos para a História das Colónias Portuguezes (Lisbon, 1890), p. 6.

82. Botelho, *Memoria*, p. 311, but see also p. 389; cf. anonymous arhill, 'Botelho *on the Portuguese Colonies*', *The Edinburgh Review, or Critical Journal*, LXIV (1837), p. 421. For Botelho's retort, see his *Segunda Parte da Memoria Estatistica sobre os Dominios Portuguezes na Africa Oriental* (Lisbon, 1837), p. 59. See also, Texugo, *Letter*, pp. 34–5.

83. Bemposta Subserra, 'Resumo sôbre a Província de Moçambique', *Boletim da Sociedade de Geografia de Lisboa*, LV, 7–8 (1937), p. 303.

84. Vasconcelos e Cirne, *Memoria*, p. 41; Rebman, *Kiniassa Dictionary*, pp. iv–v; for the Wapogera, see Young, *Notes*, pp. 25–6.

85. Livingstone, *Narrative*, pp. 125–6, 363, 496–7; Peirone, *O Tribo Ajaua*, p. 25; *A.C.U.*, p.n.o., III (1862), p. 87.

86. P.R.O., F.O. 63/836, McLeod to Malmesbury, Hyde Park, 30 November 1858.

87. Sousa Dias, *Silva Porto*, pp. 148–66 and map at end.

88. In the early 1860s the ivory exported through the customs-house at Mozambique rose dramatically from less than half that handled at Zanzibar in 1859 to almost three times that total (see Chapter 7, p. 234). This rise seems to have been stimulated as part of a concerted official effort to replace the slave trade with 'legitimate' commerce, and was marked by gradually rising prices that were at this time below those obtaining at Zanzibar. These favourable prices may have attracted Indian and European ivory merchants back to Mozambique. From the available statistics, however it is quite clear that most of this ivory was coming from Quelimane, Inhambane, and Lourenço Marques. In particular, the enormous rise in exports in 1863 was attributed to the opening up of 'the vast hinterland between Inhambane and Lourenço Marques'. Only at Quelimane was there a direct

impact on the trade of East Central Africa, and by 1890 the Yao were major traders there (see below, Chapter 7, p. 252). For the 1861–1863 ivory figures and prices, see *A.C.U.*, p.n.o., III (1862), pp. 85–8; ibid., IV (1863), pp. 66, 74, 85; ibid., V (1864), pp. 15, 66; ibid., VI (1865), p. 36; ibid., VII (1866), p. 57. For prices at Zanzibar, again see Sheriff, 'Rise of a Commercial Empire', p. 469, Graph II.

89. A.N.T.T., Junta do Comércio, maço 62, n.º d'ordem 122, report on the trade of Mozambique by António José Baptista de Sala, Lisboa, 24 May 1824.

90. Gamitto, *King Kazembe*, II, p. 197.

91. Livingstone, *Missionary Travels*, p. 680.

92. *A.C.U.*, p.n.o., V (1864), p. 14.

93. See, e.g., A.H.U., Moç., Cx. 60, Aguiar to Conde de Sarzedas, Rio de Janeiro, 25 January 1816; A.H.U., Moç., Cx. 66, *requerimento* of twelve Banyan traders, [Moç.], n.d., but *c.* 1817; A.H.U., Moç., Cx. 63, Arcos to Cavalcanti de Albuquerque, Rio de Janeiro, 4 July 1818; A.H.U., Moç., Cx. 64, Cardenas to Governor, Moç., 27 September 1819; A.H.U., Cod. 1402, fl. 41, Prov. Govt. to Simião and António José Segundo, Moç., 6 November 1821; A.H.U., Cod. 1413, fl. 8, João Faustino da Costa to José António Marcelino Pereira, Moç., 26 July 1827; ibid., fl. 105, Botelho to Silva, Moç., 6 May 1829; A.H.U., Moç., maço 11, petition of Lauchande Cancadas, granted, Moç., 18 October 1830; A.H.U., Cod. 1445, no. 2117 (or 2108), António Abrucísio Jarvis de Atongonia to Governor of Mozambique, Paço do Ramalhão, 12 September 1835; Botelho, *Resumo*, pp. 11–14, and *Memoria*, p. 376; Texugo, *Letter*, pp. 38–9, 41; Santana, *Documentação*, II, p. 482.

94. See O'Neill, 'On the Coast Lands', p. 602, for reference to the growth of coastal trade in oilseeds, rubber, ivory, copra, and wax 'in the hands of these subjects of British and Portuguese India, and the complete web which has been woven upon it by them'.

95. See Gray, *History of Zanzibar*, pp. 194–6; Sheriff, 'Rise of a Commercial Empire', especially chapter 4; Nicholls, *Swahili Coast*, chapter 12; and see above, Chapter 3, p. 87.

96. A.N.F., Affaires Étrangères B^III 438, Ladislas Cochet, 'Importations et Exportations de principales merchandises en 1856', Zanzibar, 2 January 1857; cf. Nicholls, *Swahili Coast*, p. 371. See also, Norman R. Bennett and George E. Brooks, Jr. (eds.), *New England Merchants in Africa, A History through Documents, 1802 to 1865* (Boston, 1965), pp. 246, n. 83, 385.

97. Nicholls, *Swahili Coast*, pp. 370–71. The most authoritative analysis of the ivory trade at Zanzibar is Sheriff, 'Rise of a Commercial Empire'.

98. In Burton, *Zanzibar*, II, pp. 510–11.

99. James Prior, *Voyage along the Eastern Coast of Africa, to Mosambique, Johanna, and Quiloa; . . . in the Nisus Frigate* (London, 1819), pp. 80, 64; cf. W. H. Smyth, *The Life and Service of Captain Philip Beaver, late of Her Majesty's Ship Nisus* (London, 1829), p. 279.

100. See A.H.U., Cod. 1374, fl. 96–7, Caldas to Abreu e Meneses, Ibo, 3 December 1816; A.H.U., Cod. 1377, fl. 210, Cavalcanti de Albuquerque to Sultan of Kilwa, Moç., 29 March 1817; A.H.U., Moç., Cx. 60, Sultan of Tungui to Caldas, Tungui, 24 May 1817; ibid., Caldas to Cavalcanti de Albuquerque, Ibo, 13 November 1817; B.N.L., F.G., Cod. 8470, fl. 71, Salimo Bono Sahi Bono Saude Usaiude Seleman to Governor of Mozambique, Zanzibar (?), n.d., but *c.* 1817–1818; Freeman-Grenville, *Select Documents*, pp. 224, 198–9; T.N.A., Mafia District Book; Fortuné Albrand, 'Extrait d'un Memoire sur Zanzibar et sur Quiloa', *Bulletin de la Société de Géographie*, 2e Serie, X (1838), p. 82; Nicholls, *Swahili Coast*, pp. 130–1; Kent, *Madagascar*, p. 297.

101. Albrand, 'Extrait', pp. 81, 75; also Nicholls, *Swahili Coast*, p. 213.

102. See B.M., Add. Ms. 41,265, Volume V, fl. 3–6, R. T. Farquhar to Imam of Muscat

(*sic*), Port Louis, 10 May 1821; ibid., fl. 7–8, same to Marquis of Hastings, Port Louis, 11 May 1821; ibid., fl. 67–70, 'Memorandum connected with the final Suppression of the Slave Trade on the *East* Coast of Africa', *c.* December 1821; P.R.O., C.O. 415/7, A. No. 171, pp. 1–5, 16–19, 'Observations by Captain Owen on the Slave Trade in Aug.ᵗ 1824 . . . with Dorval's remarks thereon, 30 May 1827', articles 1–6; ibid., A. No. 172, pp. 5–8, 17–20, 25–29.

103. Santana, *Documentação*, II, p. 784.
104. Freeman-Grenville, *Select Documents*, pp. 224–5; Boteler, *Narrative*, II, p. 47.
105. Nicholls, *Swahili Coast*, p. 86.
106. Freeman-Grenville, 'The Coast', p. 131.
107. See Chapter 5, p. 164.
108. Hamerton's letter is quoted in J. M. Gray, 'A History of Kilwa: Part II', p. 35.
109. See Nicholls, *Swahili Coast*, p. 215; Sheriff, 'Rise of a Commercial Empire', p. 171.
110. Krapf, *Travels*, p. 423.
111. Burton, *The Lake Regions of Central Africa* (New York, 1861), II, p. 377.
112. Bennett and Brooks, *New England Merchants*, p. 479.
113. Krapf, *Travels*, p. 424.
114. See, e.g., Santana, *Documentação*, II, pp. 835, 881.
115. Bennett and Brooks, *New England Merchants*, p. 502.
116. Burton, *Zanzibar*, II, p. 347.
117. Elton, *Travels*, chapter 2. For still another major work on the suppression of the East African slave trade from this time, see François Renault, *Lavigerie, l'Esclavage africain et l'Europe, 1868–1892* (Paris, 1971).
118. C. E. B. Russell (ed.), *General Rigby, Zanzibar and the Slave Trade* (London, 1935), pp. 333, 352.
119. Quoted in Coupland, *The Exploitation of East Africa, 1856–1890* (London, 1939), p. 140, from the Report of the Select Committee of 1871.
120. Carl Claus von der Decken, *Reisen in Ost-Afrika in der Jahren 1859 bis 1865*, ed. O. Kersten (Leipzig and Heidelberg, 1869), I, Book 2; Livingstone, *Last Journals*, I, pp. 70, 79.
121. Burton, *The Lands of Cazembe*, pp. 37, 39, footnotes only.
122. Burton, *Lake Regions*, II, p. 376, and *Zanzibar*, II, pp. 346–7.
123. Decken, *Reisen*, I, p. 185.
124. Petro Kilekwa, *Slave Boy to Priest: The Autobiography of Padre Petro Kilekwa*, trans. from Cinyanja by K. H. Nixon Smith (London, 1937), p. 9; A. C. Madan, *Kiungani* (Zanzibar, 1886), pp. 14–23, 33–4; Rashid bin Hassani, 'The Story of Rashid bin Hassani of the Bisa Tribe, Northern Rhodesia', recorded by W. F. Baldock, in Margery Perham (ed.), *Ten Africans*, (London, 1936), pp. 92–5.
125. Colomb, *Slave-Catching*, pp. 28–30; Speke, *Journal*, p. 7.
126. James Mbotela, *Uhuru wa Watumwa* (Nairobi, 1967; 1st ed., London, 1934), p. 10. There is an English translation available as *The Freeing of the Slaves in East Africa*, but I was unable to obtain it when writing this section. Madan, *Kiungani*, p. 46.
127. Colomb, *Slave-Catching*, p. 29; Madan, *Kiungani*, pp. 30, 51, 56; African Studies Association Oral Data Archives, Archive of Traditional Music, Indiana University, Bloomington: Allen F. Isaacman Collection, interviews with Capachika Chúau, 10 October 1968 (Translated Tape No. 14, side no. 2; Edited Tape No. 11, side no. 1), and Chiponda Cavumbula, 16 October 1968 (T.T. No. 15 (2); E.T. No. 11 (2)), both conducted in the region of Makanga.
128. Isaacman Collection, joint interview with Chetambara Chenungo and Wilson John, 15 October 1968 (T.T. No. 15 (2); E.T. No. 11 (2)), and interview with Chiponda Cavumbula: Madan, *Kiungani*, p. 39.
129. Colomb, *Slave-Catching*, p. 28.
130. Abdallah, *The Yaos*, p. 31.
131. Isaacman Collection, interviews with Simon Biwi, 10 October 1968, region of

Makanga (T.T. No. 14 (2); E.T. No. 11 (1)), Capachika Chúau, and Chiponda Cavumbula; joint interviews with Calavina Couche and Zabuca Ngombe, 14 October 1968, region of Makanga (T.T. No. 15 (1); E.T. No. 11 (2)), and Chetambara Chinungo and Wilson John; Rashid bin Hassani, 'Story', p. 91; Abdallah, *The Yaos*, p. 32.

132. Madan, *Kiungani*, pp. 24, 34, 36; Kilekwa, *Slave Boy*, p. 13; Rashid bin Hassani, 'Story', p. 98.

133. For slave prices, see, e.g., Steere, *The Universities' Mission to Central Africa. A Speech delivered at Oxford* (London, 1875), pp. 8–9; and cf. Colomb, *Slave-Catching*, pp. 55–9. For prices at the coast, see Nicholls, *Swahili Coast*, pp. 201–2, 209–11, 216–17. For an example of an Arab who was trading for slaves on credit, and the way in which this affected a young Makua when agents of the money-lender came to collect on the Arab's debt, see Madan, *Kiungani*, p. 40.

134. Isaacman Collection, interviews with Capachika Chúau and Chiponda Cavumbula. It is not at all clear what is meant by a *peça* here. According to Burton, *Zanzibar*, II, p. 419, 'The Takah or piece varies greatly. That of "Merikani", American domestics, is generally of 30 yards.' He also notes that the *taka* ranges down to twenty yards of cloth. This would indicate an unusually high price for slaves among the Chewa of Makanga. If, however, a *peça* is taken to indicate a *doti* of either two yards of wide cloth or four yards of narrow, then the price of a slave in Makanga, while still high, is within the range of prices cited by Abdallah and others.

135. Abdallah, *The Yaos*, pp. 31–2; Kilekwa, *Slave Boy*, p. 10; Madan, *Kiungani*, p. 46.

136. ibid., p. 34.

137. See Chapter 1, pp. 5–6; Chapter 2, p. 60; Chapter 5, p. 160.

138. Froberville, 'Notes sur les Va-Ngindo', *Bulletin de la Société de Géographie*, 4ᵉ Série, III (1852), pp. 426–7.

139. See T.N.A., Masasi District Book, 'The Ekoni Clan (Makua Tribe) of Masasi-District', trans. of an article in Swahili by Marko Gwaja in *Mambo Leo* (June 1936); T.N.A., Secretariat 42186, 'Preliminary Report', p. 9.

140. See also Isaacman, *Mozambique*, pp. 89–90.

141. Baptista and Amaro, 'Journey of the Pombeiros', p. 233; A.H.U., Moç., Cx. 56, Aguiar to Mendonça, Rio de Janeiro, 20 May 1812; ibid., Abreu e Meneses to Galveâs, Moç., 19 September 1812; ibid., same to Constantino Pereira de Azevedo, Moç., 24 November 1812.

142. A.H.U., Moç., Cx. 58, *requerimento* of Pascoal José Fernando de Rosário, n.d., but prior to 7 November 1814, when judgment was passed on his petition; Felipe Gastão de Almeida de Eça, *História das Guerras no Zambeze*, I (Lisbon, 1953), p. 159.

143. A.H.U., Moç., Cx. 66, decree of José Francisco Alves Barbosa, Tete, 10 June 1820; A.H.U., Moç., Cx. 65, Barbosa to Brito Sanches, [Tete], 14 June 1820.

144. A.H.U., Cod. 1402, fl. 75, Sinfónio Maria Pereira Sodré to Barbosa, Moç. 8 October 1822.

145. For a detailed history of the Caetano Pereira family, see Isaacman, *Mozambique*, pp. 124–34, 219–21, n. 2.

146. A.H.U., Cod. 1402, fl. 80, Sodré to Barbosa, Moç., 19 December 1822; A.H.U., Cod. 1413, fl. 62, Botelho to Francisco Henriques Ferrão, Moç., 16 June 1823; A.H.U., Cod. 1409, no. 1666, Joaquim José Monteiro Tôrres to Botelho, Mafra, 28 March 1825.

147. Santana, *Documentação*, I, pp. 312, 315–16, 439, 440.

148. A.H.U., Cod. 1394, fl. 46, Brito Sanches to Arcos, Moç., 12 January 1820; Santana, *Documentação*, I, p. 140. Governor-General Cavalcanti de Albuquerque took office at Mozambique on 2 February 1817 and died on 12 November 1818: Bordalo, *Ensaio*, p. 126.

149. A.H.U., Moç., maço 3, José Manuel Correia Monteiro to Ferrão, Aruangua do

Norte, 15 June 1828, partially summarized in Santana, *Documentação*, I. pp. 463–5.

150. *A.C.U.*, p.n.o., II (1861), p. 207.
151. Santana, *Documentação*, II, pp. 330, 946.
152. Gamitto, *King Kazembe*, I, p. 144, and II, pp. 87, 169–71.
153. Rebman, *Kiniassa Dictionary*, p. 120; Gamitto, *King Kazembe*, I, p. 65, and II, p. 169.
154. Krapf, *Travels*, p. 419. See also, Abdallah, *The Yaos*, pp. 30–31, for Maravi control of the lake traffic; cf. Stannus, 'Notes', pp. 331–2.
155. Bennett and Brooks, *New England Merchants*, pp. 437–8.
156. Burton, *Lake Regions*, II, p. 412.
157. Isaacman Collection, interviews with Simon Biwi and Chiponda Cavumbula; Abdallah, *The Yaos*, pp. 31, 33.
158. Bennett and Brooks, *New England Merchants*, pp. 262–3.
159. For rising prices of ivory in East Africa during the nineteenth century, see Sheriff, 'Rise of a Commercial Empire', p. 469, Graph II; also Nicholls, *Swahili Coast*, p. 355.
160. For the Nyamwezi and Kamba, see Roberts and Lamphear in Gray and Birmingham, *Pre-Colonial African Trade*; for the Kimbu, see Shorter, 'The Kimbu'.
161. Bennett and Brooks, *New England Merchants*, p. 540; also pp. 531–2.
162. See above, p. 122, and Chapter 5; Livingstone, *Missionary Travels*, p. 567.
163. Gamitto, *King Kazembe*, II. pp. 119–20, 161.
164. For a brief description of the collapse of Bisa trade, see Roberts, 'Pre-Colonial Trade in Zambia', p. 730; for the rise of the Bemba, see Roberts (Madison, 1974 *A History of the Bemba: political growth and change in north-eastern Zambia before 1900*.
165. See J. D. Omer-Cooper, *The Zulu Aftermath: A Nineteenth-Century Revolution in Bantu Africa* (London, 1966), Chapter 5; for a somewhat different overview, see Alpers, 'The Nineteenth Century: Prelude to Colonialism', in Ogot and Kieran, *Zamani*, pp. 240–44.
166. See Y. M. Chibambo, *My Ngoni of Nyasaland* (London, 1942), p. 31; Elzear Ebner, *History of the Wangoni*, mimeographed (Peramiho, 1959), pp. 58, 61; Ian Linden, 'Some Oral Traditions from the Maseko Ngoni', *The Society of Malawi Jl.*, XXIV, 2 (1971), pp. 64–5, 71.
167. Charles Stewart Smith, 'Explorations in Zanzibar Domains', Royal Geographical Society, *Supplementary Papers*, II, 1 (London, 1887), pp. 103–4. Smith travelled in the Kilwa hinterland in the middle of 1884 and learned at the coast that the Gwangwara raid occurred 'about eighteen years ago'.
168. Livingstone, *Last Journals*, I, p. 70.
169. For the Yao migration into southern Malawi, see Alpers, 'The Yao in Malawi: the importance of local research', in Pachai, *Early History*, pp. 168–73.
170. Livingstone, *Narrative*, p. 497; Stannus, 'The Wayao', p. 231.
171. Rowley, *Story*, p. 185.
172. Krapf, *Vocabulary of Six East-African Languages.* (*Kisuáheli, Kinika, Kikámba, Kipokómo, Kihiáu, Kigálla*) (Tübingen, 1850), p. viii.
173. Abdallah, *The Yaos*, pp. 35–6; see also, Assabel Jonassane Mazula, 'História dos Nianjas', *Portugal em África*, XIX (1962), p. 242.
174. Johnson, *Nyasa*, p. 100.
175. Macdonald, *Africana*, II, p. 334. For a vivid account of a Makua-led slave raid on a Yao village and the journey to the coast, see Mbotela, *Uhuru wa Watumwa*, pp. 9–31; see also, Sousa Dias, *Silva Porto*, p. 150.
176. T.N.A., Masasi District Book, 'Tribal History and Legend', p. 1; Lindi District Book, 'Tribal History and Legend', p. 6; Mikindani District Book, 'Tribal History and Legend', pp. 4–6.
177. Vivid documentation of the Yao invasion of southern Malawi is to be found in the journals of the members of Livingstone's Zambesi expedition and in the

papers of the members of the U.M.C.A. who were attempting to establish themselves in the Shire highlands with the aid of Livingstone's party at this time. Some of these are quoted in Alpers, 'The Yao in Malawi', pp. 170–3.

178. See Alpers, 'Trade, State, and Society'.

179. The traditions collected by Klass include several references to the Ciwambo coast, which was just south of Quelimane, where the Zambesi enters the sea. The principal trade at the end of the century was ivory for guns and gunpowder. See Klass, 'The Amachinga Yao', interviews with N. A. Mwikuna, 17 July 1970, Malundani Ct., Kasupe District; Masten, 20 May 1970, Ndumundu Ct., Fort Johnston District; and Abu Mkumba, 24 May 1970, Pasekele Village, Kasupe District. See also A. J. Hanna, *The Beginnings of Nyasaland and North-Eastern Rhodesia, 1859–1895* (Oxford, 1956).

180. *A.C.U.*, p.n.o., V (1864), pp. 15–16. For the wider context of Lozi trade, see Roberts, 'Pre-Colonial Trade in Zambia', pp. 730–34.

181. See Alpers, 'Trade, State, and Society'.

182. João Coutinho, *Do Nyassa a Pemba—Os Territorios da Companhia do Nyassa* (Lisbon, 1893), p. 47.

CHAPTER EIGHT

International Trade in the History of East Central Africa: Some Conclusions

꩜꩜꩜꩜꩜꩜꩜꩜꩜꩜꩜꩜꩜꩜꩜꩜꩜꩜꩜꩜꩜꩜꩜꩜꩜꩜꩜

This study has attempted to describe and analyse the long history of international trade in ivory and slaves in East Central Africa before the imposition of European colonial rule upon its peoples. Until recently, European colonialism in Africa was regarded as a radical break with the past, but of late many scholars have come to argue that it was, instead, a brief interlude in the history of the African peoples, whose civilizations continue to draw primarily upon their own cultural traditions. From the perspective of cultural history, the revisionist position is surely correct, but from that of economic history it is only partly applicable. With respect to the technology of agricultural production, for example, a strong case can be made for this point of view, but for an understanding of the present underdevelopment of the economies of Africa we must seek different causes. Here, too, however, it is a mistake to regard the period of direct European colonial rule, even where it still persists, as the original cause of underdevelopment in Africa. Rather, as I hope this book has demonstrated for East Central Africa, the roots of underdevelopment lie in the entanglement of African societies in the mercantile capitalist systems of the world through the nexus of international trade.

At both Mozambique and Zanzibar it is clear that several different sets of actors played a critical role in underwriting the mercantile empires that were constructed in the eighteenth and nineteenth centuries by the Portuguese and the 'Umani Arabs. Indian and French merchant capital sustained the trading economy of Mozambique in the eighteenth century, while Brazilian capital assumed the major role in the first half of the nineteenth century. Similarly, Indian and British-supported Arab capital enabled the rulers of 'Uman to establish a commercial empire in East Africa, while American capital, in particular, helped to entrench it there until later in the nineteenth century. And if it is true that Indian merchant capitalism declined in importance at Mozambique during the nineteenth century, and was increasingly tied to British capitalism in India from the middle of the eighteenth century, the fact remains that the exploitation of East Central Africa before the early nineteenth century was to a very large extent dependent upon non-Western capital. Nor were African economies served any better by linking their external trade to Indian merchant capitalism rather than to developing Western capitalism. In each situation there emerged a definite structural subordination of African economies to a capitalist economy, with the main powers of decision-making resting outside Africa. In the long run, of course, the main architect of Africa's underdevelopment was, and remains, Western capitalism. But the dangers of attempting to achieve economic development, as opposed to mere economic growth, by linking a significant sector of one's economy to capitalist economies, and of surrendering basic decision-making power over the developmental path to be followed by one's society exist whatever the nationality of the dominating capitalist power, or the multinational combinations in which capitalism frequently appears nowadays. That this is not a new problem facing African societies is demonstrated by the role played by international merchant capitalism in the economic exploitation of East Central Africa in the eighteenth and nineteenth centuries.

In assessing the impact of these centuries of international trade on the African societies of this region it would be a great advantage to have more information from within each society. Yet this handicap should not obscure those conclusions which do emerge from the evidence now available. First, it is clear that the international trading economies of the Maravi, Makua, and Yao (to take only the peoples whose histories have dominated this book), were excessively dependent upon the foreign markets that brought them into being. For while it is true that the Yao and others showed themselves to be resourceful and adaptable traders within the system of international trade in East Central Africa, still they were in no ways masters of that system. Indeed, such adaptations as were made in response to the international market were virtually all connected with the exploitation of either the human or natural resources of the country for export. If Africans wished to continue to receive goods from abroad, they necessarily had to provide those goods that were required.

Second, it is important to reiterate that what Africans received in exchange for ivory, even though it had little intrinsic economic value in their own societies, were goods that in no way equalled the value placed on ivory by the merchant capitalists of India, Europe, and America. And, even more emphatically, it is evident that what they received in exchange for slaves in no way equalled the labour power lost to each society. Here there was no mutually advantageous exchange of manufactured products; here there was no compensatory exchange of technology for the debilitating depletion of the African working force; here there was no possible way of rectifying the cruel distortions which the slave trade induced in the fabric of African societies. All that Africans received in exchange for ivory and slaves and the other raw materials of the continent were luxury items, inexpensive consumable goods, and Western means of destruction which were always inferior to those which Europeans maintained for their own use.

Third, and finally, it is essential to emphasize that the multiplier effects of this trade did nothing to promote either economic development or social equality in African societies. If the foreign trade goods which were acquired in exchange for ivory and slaves were widely distributed among the peoples of East Central Africa, the main effect of this trade was to put more wealth in the hands of fewer people, who then used the profits of the trade to build up their own personal or dynastic power. This process is best known among the Yao in the later nineteenth century, but it is also strongly suggested for the great Maravi paramount chiefs of an earlier period and for the Makua chiefs of Macuana. Certainly, the political economies of the major Yao and Makua chiefdoms of East Central Africa, intimately linked as they were to a suddenly obsolete system of mercantile capitalism based upon international trade between politically independent societies, made their resistance to the imposition of direct colonial rule inevitable. For these chiefdoms colonialism meant the abrupt end to one line of historical development and the beginning of a quite different one in which chiefs generally became government functionaries, and economic exploitation took the principal forms of enforced labour migration or enforced production of cash crops which were bought at artificially depressed prices for the benefit of the metropolitan economies. Nevertheless, what took place during colonialism was only a change in the form of the economic exploitation which marked Europe's historic relationship with East Central Africa.

That all of these conclusions reflect a disproportionate attention to external determinants of African history is no mistake. This is not to deny the importance of the internal dynamics of African history, such as the impact of the Ngoni invasions of the nineteenth century. Nor does it imply a disregard of determining factors within African societies, such as the structural weaknesses of Maravi political organization and the socio-economic organization of the Makua, Yao, and Mang'anja. What these conclusions do represent is an attempt to isolate the main elements in the historical process of underdevelopment in East Central Africa. Interpretations which look to the structure of African societies for the roots of underdevelopment err in confusing a lack of economic development for the dynamic of underdevelopment. Those which seek these roots in colonialism err in assuming that trade between Europe and Africa, not to mention that between India and Africa, was equally beneficial to all parties. The evidence presented here suggests, quite to the contrary, that the historical roots of underdevelopment in East Central Africa must be sought in the system of international trade which was established by Arabs by the thirteenth century, seized and extended by the Portuguese in the sixteenth and seventeenth centuries, dominated by Indians in the eighteenth century, and finally commanded by a complex admixture of Indian, Arab, and Western capitalisms in the nineteenth century.

Sources

MANUSCRIPTS IN ARCHIVES

England
British Museum, London:
Additional Mss. 19,419; 20,890; 20,906; 28,163; 41,265, Volume
V Sloane Ms. 197.
London Missionary Society:
Journal of Alexander Carson
Public Record Office, London:
Admiralty 1/69, 1/5596
Colonial Office 415/4, 415/7, 415/9
Foreign Office 63/836
Foreign Office 84/17, 84/24, 84/31, 84/42, 84/55, 84/71, 84/84,
84/95, 84/112, 84/122, 84/1050
United Society for the Propagation of the Gospel, London:
Universities' Mission to Central Africa A/I/iii/2, A/I/iv

France
Archives Nationales, Paris:
Affaires Étrangères B^{III} 438
Colonies série C^4 (Ile de France) 7, 80

India
National Archives of India, Panaji, Goa:
Livros das Monções 2–B, 3–A, 9, 12, 17, 18, 21–A, 21–B, 22–B, 69,
70, 71, 73, 74–A, 75, 77, 78, 80, 81, 83, 92, 93-A, 94–A, 95–B, 97–B,
103–A, 105, 111–A, 125–B
Códices 832, 2323

Italy
Archivum Romanum Societatis Jesu', Rome:
Goa, 33 II

Portugal
Academia das Ciências de Lisboa:
Azul Mss 648, 847
Vermelho Ms 273
Arquivo da Casa da Cadaval:
Códice 826 (M VI 32)

Arquivo Histórico Ultramarino, Lisboa:
  India, Maços 18, 19, 23, 29, 37
  Moçambique, Caixas 1–44, 46, 48–50, 52–67
  Moçambique, Maços 3, 11
  Códices 211, 1207, 1307, 1310, 1313, 1317, 1320, 1321, 1322, 1323,
    1324, 1325, 1327, 1328, 1329, 1331, 1332, 1333, 1340, 1344, 1345,
    1355, 1357, 1366, 1370, 1372, 1374, 1377, 1379, 1380, 1381, 1383,
    1385, 1386, 1391, 1394, 1402, 1409, 1413, 1414, 1425, 1427, 1432,
    1440, 1444, 1445, 1471, 1472, 1478, 1500
Arquivo Nacional da Tôrre do Tombo, Lisboa:
  Junta do Comércio, Maço 62
  Ministério do Reino, Maços 602, 603, 604
Biblioteca Nacional de Lisboa:
  Colleção Pombalina 742
  Fundo Geral, Caixa 12
  Fundo Geral, Códices 1603, 2320, 4406, 4408, 8105, 8470

Spain
Biblioteca Nacional de Madrid:
  Codice 2362

Tanzania
National Archives, Dar es Salaam:
  District Books: Kilosa, Lindi, Mafia, Masasi, Mikindani, Newala
  Secretariat, Local Government 42186

United States of America
Indiana University, Bloomington, Indiana, Huntington Library:
  C. R. Boxer Collection, Castello-Novo Codex

UNPUBLISHED MANUSCRIPTS

Franz, Mary Louise. 'The Masking Complex of the Makonde-Speaking People of East Central Africa'. M.A. thesis, University of California, Los Angeles, 1970.

Hafkin, Nancy Jane. 'Trade, Society, and Politics in Northern Mozambique, *c.* 1753–1913'. Ph.D. thesis, Boston University, 1973.

Noël, Karl. 'L'Esclavage à l'Ile de France pendant l'Occupation française (1715–1810)'. Ph.D. thesis, University of Paris, 1953.

Sheriff, Abdul Mohamed Hussein. 'The Development of Underdevelopment: The role of internal trade in the economic history of the East African coast before the sixteenth century'. Seminar paper, University of Dar es Salaam, 1972.

——. 'The Rise of a Commercial Empire: An Aspect of the Economic History of Zanzibar, 1770–1873'. Ph.D. thesis, School of Oriental and African Studies, University of London, 1971.

Shorter, Aylward. 'Ukimbu and the Kimbu Chiefdoms of Southern Unyamwezi'. D. Phil. thesis, University of Oxford, 1968.
Smith, Alan K. 'The Struggle for Control of Southern Mozambique, 1720–1835'. Ph.D. thesis, University of California, Los Angeles, 1970.

ORAL DATA

Alpers, Edward A. Interviews with Mzee Mbrisho Kipindula, Wami Station, Miono Division, Bagamoyo Area, Coast Region, Tanzania, 14 November 1972, and Mzee Ali Rusewa Pangapanga, Mziha, Turiani Division, Morogoro Area, Morogoro Region, Tanzania, 14 February 1973. Copies of these tapes and edited transcripts in Swahili and English will be deposited in the Swahili Collection of the library of the University of Dar es Salaam.
Gregson, Ronald E. Interview with G. Tadeyu Harawa, Mhuju, Malawi, 1968. A copy of the relevant section is in the author's possession.
Isaacman, Allen F. Isaacman Collection, African Studies Association Oral Data Archives, Archive of Traditional Music, Indiana University, Bloomington.

Region of Makanga
Simon Biwi, interview, 10 October 1968. Translated Tape No. 14, side 2; Edited Tape No. 10, side no. 1.
Capachika Chúau, interview, 10 October 1968.
T.T. No. 14 (2); E.T. No. 10 (2).
Calavina Couche and Zabuca Ngombe, joint interview, 14 October 1968. T.T. No. 15 (1); E.T. No. 11 (2).
Chetambara Chenungo and Wilson John, joint interview, 15 October 1968. T.T. No. 15 (2); E.T. No. 11 (2).
Chiponda Cavumbula, interview, 16 October 1968. T.T. No. 15 (2); E.T. No. 11 (2).

Klass, Lance J. 'The Amachinga Yao of Malawi: Field Research Papers'. Chancellor College Library, University of Malawi, Zomba.

Fort Johnston District
Masten, interview, Ndumundu Ct., 20 May 1970.

Kasupe District
Chikwisimbi, interview, Kalambo Village, 2 May 1970.
Abu Mkumba, interview, Pasekele Village, 24 May 1970.
N. A. Mwikuna, interview, Malundani Ct., 17 July 1970.
Edwin Nyambi, interview, Nyambi Village, 20 July 1969.

PUBLISHED SOURCES

Abdallah, Yohannah B. *The Yaos*. Arranged, edited, and translated by M. Sanderson. Zomba, 1919.

Abraham, Donald P. 'Tasks in the Field of Early History'. In *Conference of the History of the Central African Peoples*, pp. 1–6. Lusaka, 1963.

Agnew, Swanzie. 'Environment and History: the Malawian setting'. In B. Pachai (ed.), *The Early History of Malawi*, pp. 28–48. London, 1972.

'l Ajjemy, Abdallah bin Hemedi. *The Kilindi*. Translated and edited by J. W. T. Allen and William Kimweri. Nairobi, 1963.

Albrand, Fortuné. 'Extrait d'un Memoire sur Zanzibar et sur Quiloa', *Bulletin de la Société de Géographie*, 2ᵉ Série, X (1838), pp. 65–84.

Alcântara Guerreiro, Jerónimo de. 'Episódios inéditos das lutas contra os macuas no reinado de D. Maria I, segundo o Códice CXVI, fls. 179 a 184 da Biblioteca Pública de Évora', *Boletim da Sociedade de Estudos da Colónia de Moçambique*, XV, 52 (1947), pp. 79–109.

——. *Quadros da História de Moçambique*. 2 vols. Lourenço Marques, 1954.

Almeida de Eça, Felipe Gastão de. *Historia das Guerras no Zambeze*. 2 vols. Lisbon, 1953–1954.

Alpers, Edward A. 'The Coast and the Development of Caravan Trade'. In I. N. Kimambo and A. J. Temu (eds.), *A History of Tanzania*, pp. 35–56. Nairobi, 1969.

——. *The East African Slave Trade*. Historical Association of Tanzania Paper No. 3. Nairobi, 1967.

——. 'The French Slave Trade in East Africa (1721–1810)', *Cahiers d'Études Africaines*, X, 37 (1970), pp. 80–124.

——. 'Introduction'. In Y. B. Abdallah, *The Yaos*. 2nd edition. London, 1973.

——. 'The Mutapa and Malawi Political Systems to the time of the Ngoni Invasions'. In T. O. Ranger (ed.), *Aspects of Central African History*, pp. 1–28. London, 1968.

——. 'The Nineteenth Century: Prelude to Colonialism'. In B. A. Ogot and J. A. Kieran (eds.), *Zamani*, pp. 238–54. Nairobi, 1968.

——. 'Re-thinking African Economic History: a contribution to the discussion of the roots of underdevelopment'. *Ufahamu*, III, 3 (1973). pp. 97–129.

——. 'Towards a History of Expansion of Islam in East Africa: The Matrilineal Peoples of the Southern Interior'. In T. O. Ranger and I. N. Kimambo (eds.), *The Historical Study of African Religions*, pp. 172–201. London, 1972.

——. 'Trade, State, and Society among the Yao in the Nineteenth Century', *Journal of African History*, X, 3 (1969), pp. 405–20.

——. 'The Yao in Malawi: the importance of local research'. In B. Pachai (ed.), *The Early History of Malawi*, pp. 168–78. London, 1972.

Alpers, Edward A. and Ehret, Christopher. 'Eastern Africa, 1600–1790'. Forthcoming in Richard Gray (ed.), *The Cambridge History of Africa*, IV.

Anrade, António Alberto de. 'Fundação do Hospital Militar de S. João de Deus, em Moçambique', *Stvdia*, 1 (1958), pp. 77–89.

——. *Relações de Moçambique Setecentista.* Lisbon, 1955.

Annaes do Conselho Ultramarino, parte não official. 7 vols. Lisbon, 1857–1895.

Anonymous. 'Botelho on the Portuguese Colonies', *The Edinburgh Review, or Critical Journal*, LXIV (1837), pp. 411–28.

——. 'Memorias da Costa d'Africa Oriental e algumas reflexões uteis para estabelecer melhor e fazer mais florente o seu commercio', Sena, 21 March 1762. In A. A. de Andrade, *Relações de Moçambique Setecentista*, pp. 189–224. Lisbon, 1955.

Arquivo das Colónias. Publicação oficial e mensal, Ministério das Colónias. 5 vols. Lisbon, 1917–1933.

Atlas de Moçambique. Lourenço Marques, 1962.

Axelson, Eric. *Portuguese in South-East Africa, 1600–1700.* Johannesburg, 1960.

——. 'Portuguese settlement in the interior of south-east Africa in the seventeenth century'. In Congresso Internacional de História dos Descobrimentos, *Actas*, V, 2, pp. 1–17. Lisbon, 1961.

——. *South-East Africa, 1488–1530.* London, 1940.

Baker, S. J. K. 'The East African Environment'. In R. A. Oliver and G. Mathew (eds.), *History of East Africa*, I, pp. 1–22. Oxford, 1963.

Baptista, Pedro João and Amaro, José. 'Journey of the Pombeiros from Angola to the Rios de Senna'. In R. F. Burton (ed.), *The Lands of Cazembe*, pp. 165–244. London, 1873.

Barreto, Manuel. 'Informação do Estado e Conquista dos Rios de Cuama', Goa, 11 December 1667. In G. M. Theal (ed.), *Records of South-East Africa*, III, pp. 436–95. London, 1899.

——. 'Supplimento da Informação do Estado e Conquista dos Rios de Cuama'. In G. M. Theal (ed.), *Records of South-East Africa*, III, pp. 498–506. London, 1899.

Barth, Heinrich. 'Routes from Kano to Nyffe, and from Mozambique to Lake Nyassi. Extracted from Letters from Dr. Barth to Dr. Beke, dated Kano, March 4th, and Kuka, July 25th, 1851', *The Journal of the Royal Geographical Society*, XXIV (1854), pp. 285–8.

Baumann, H. and Westermann, D. *Les Peuples et les civilisations de l'Afrique.* Translated by L. Homburger. Paris, 1948.

Bemposta Subserra, Marquês da (Théodore Estavam de la Rue de Saint Leger). 'Resumo sobre a Província de Moçambique', Lisboa, 11 December 1853, introduction by João Farmhouse, *Boletim da Sociedade de Geografia de Lisboa*, LV (1937), pp. 269–318.

Bemposta Subserra, Marquês da, *et al.* Untitled memorandum of Portuguese East Africa addressed to the Crown, Lisboa, 28 April 1856.

Bennett, Norman R. and Brooks, George E., Jr. *New England Merchants in Africa, A History through Documents, 1802 to 1865.* Boston, 1965.

Berg, F. J. 'The Coast from the Portuguese Invasion to the Rise of the

Zanzibar Sultanate'. In B. A. Ogot and J. A. Kieran (eds.), *Zamani*, pp. 119–41. Nairobi, 1968.

Berg, F. J. 'The Swahili Community of Mombasa, 1500–1900', *Journal of African History*, IX, 1 (1968), pp. 35–56.

Bethell, Leslie. *The Abolition of the Brazilian Slave Trade: Britain, Brazil, and the Slave Trade Question, 1807–1869*. Cambridge, 1970.

Biker, Júlio Firmino Judice. *Collecção de Tratados e concertos de pazes que o Estado de Índia Portuguesa com os Reis e Senhores com quem teve relações nas partes da Asia e Africa Oriental desde o principio da conquista até ao fim de seculo XVIII*. 14 vols. Lisbon, 1881–1887.

Boletim de Filmoteca Ultramarina Portuguesa. No. 14. Lisbon, 1960.

Bordalo, Francisco Maria and Lopes de Lima, José Joaquim. *Ensaios sobre a Estatistica das Possessões Portuguezas no Ultramar*. II Serie, Livro, IV, 'Ensaio sobre a Estatistica de Moçambique', Lisbon, 1859.

Boteler, Thomas. *Narrative of a Voyage of Discovery to Africa and Arabia, performed in His Majesty's Ships Leven and Barracouta, from 1821 to 1826*. 2 vols. London, 1835.

Botelho, Sebastião Xavier. *Memoria Estatistica sobre os Dominios Portuguezes na Africa Oriental*. Lisbon, 1835.

——. *Resumo para servir de introducção a Memoria Estatistica sobre os dominios portuguezes na Africa Oriental*. Lisbon, 1834.

——. *Segunda Parte da Memoria Estatistica sobre os Dominios Portuguezes na Africa Oriental*. Lisbon, 1837.

Boxer, Charles Ralph. 'Moçambique island and the "carreira da Índia" '. *Stvdia*, 8 (1961), pp. 95–132.

——. 'The Portuguese in the East, 1500–1800'. In H. V. Livermore (ed.), *Portugal and Brazil*, pp. 185–247. Oxford, 1953.

——. 'The Portuguese on the Swahili Coast, 1593–1729'. In C. R. Boxer and Carlos de Azevedo, *Fort Jesus and the Portuguese in Mombasa, 1593–1729*, pp. 11–86. London, 1960.

——. *The Portuguese Seaborne Empire: 1415–1825*. New York, 1969.

——. *Race Relations in the Portuguese Colonial Empire, 1415–1825*. Oxford, 1963.

Bragança Pereira, A. B. de. *Arquivo Português Oriental*. Nova edição. 11 vols. Bastorá, 1936–1940.

Bruwer, J. P. 'The composition of a Cewa village (mudzi)', *African Studies*, VIII, 4 (1949), pp. 191–7.

Bryan, M. A. *The Bantu Languages of Africa*. London, 1959.

Burton, Richard Francis. *The Lake Regions of Central Africa*. 2 vols. New York, 1861.

——. *The Lands of Cazembe: Lacerda's Journey to Cazembe in 1798*. London. 1873.

——. *Zanzibar; City, Island and Coast*. 2 vols. London, 1872.

Câmara Reis, Diogo da. 'Os Macuas de Mogovolas', *Boletim da Sociedade de Estudos de Moçambique*, 131 (1962), pp. 9–37.

Cambier, Ernest, 'Rapport de l'excursion sur la route de Mpwapwa addressé à l'Association Internationale Africaine', *Bulletin de la Société Belgé de Géographie*, II (1878), pp. 193–210.

Camizão, Antonio. *Indicações Geraes sobre a Capitania-Mór de Mossuril— Governo de Moçambique: Appendice ao Relatorio de l de Janeiro de 1901*. Mozambique, 1901.

Carvalho, Mário de. *A Agricultura Tradicional de Moçambique*. Lourenço Marques, 1970.

Carvalho Dias, Luís Fernando de. 'Fontes para a História, Geografia e Comércio de Moçambique (Sec. XVIII)'. Junta de Investigações Coloniais, Estudos de História da Geografia da Expansão Portuguesa, *Anais*, IX, Tomo I. Lisbon, 1954.

Castro, Soares de. *Os Achirimas (Ensaio Etnográfico)*. Lourenço Marques, 1941.

——. 'Os Lómuès no Larde', *Boletim Geral das Colónias*, 304 (1950), pp. 21–66.

Chafulumira, E. W. *Mbiri ya Amang'anja*. Zomba, 1948.

Chibambo, Yesaya M. *My Ngoni of Nyasaland*. London, 1942.

Chittick, H. Neville. 'The "Shirazi" Colonization of East Africa', *Journal of African History*, VI, 3 (1965), pp. 275–94.

Codrington, Robert. 'The Central Angoniland District of the British Central Africa Protectorate', *The Geographical Journal*, XI (1898), pp. 509–22.

Cohen, Abner. *Custom and Politics in Urban Africa: A Study of Hausa Immigrants in Yoruba Towns*. London, 1969.

Colin, Épidariste. 'Notice sur Mozambique'. In Malte-Brun, *Annales des Voyages, de la Géographie et de l'histoire*, IX, pp. 304–28. Paris, 1809.

Colomb, Captain. *Slave-Catching in the Indian Ocean. A Record of Naval Experiences*. London, 1873.

Commisão de Cartografia. *Carta de Moçambique 1889*.

Conceição, Frei António. 'Tratados dos Rios de Cuama', Sena, 20 June 1696, and Goa, 15 December 1696. In J. H. da Cunha Rivara (ed.), *O Chronista de Tissuary*, II, pp. 39–45, 63–9, 84–92, 105–11. Nova Goa, 1867.

Costa Mendes, Francisco da. *Catalogo Chronologico e Historico dos Capitães Generaes e Governadores da Provincia de Moçambique desde 1752, epoca da sua separação do Governo de Goa, ate 1849*. Mozambique, 1892.

Coupland, Reginald. *East Africa and Its Invaders from the earliest times to the death of Seyyid Said in 1856*. Oxford, 1938.

——. *The Exploitation of East Africa, 1856–1890*. London, 1939.

Coutinho, João. *Do Nyassa a Pemba—Os Territorios da Companhia do Nyassa*. London. 1893.

Couto, Diogo do. *Da Asia . . . dos feitos, que os Portuguezes fizeram na Conquista, e descubrimento das terras, e mares do Oriente*. Década Décima. Lisbon, 1788.

Cunha Rivara, Joaquim Heliodoro da (ed.), *Archivo Portuguez-Oriental.* 8 vols. Nova Goa, 1857–1876.

——. (ed.), *O Chronista de Tissuary.* 4 vols. Nova Goa, 1866–1869.

Cunnison, Ian. 'Kazembe and the Portuguese, 1798–1832', *Journal of African History*, II, 1 (1961), pp. 61–76.

——. *The Luapula Peoples of Northern Rhodesia.* Manchester, 1959.

Dalrymple, Alexander. *Plan of Querimboo and the Adjacent Islands, From a Portuguese MS. supposed by Capt.ⁿ Bento de Almedoe.* 1 November 1779.

——. *Plan of Quiloa and Its Environs on the East Coast of Africa from the Observations of Sieur Morice.* 9 May 1784.

Das Gupta, Ashin. 'Trade and Politics in 18th Century India'. In D. S. Richards (ed.), *Islam and the Trade of Asia*, pp. 181–214. Oxford, 1970.

Decken, Carl Claus von der. *Reisen in Ost-Afrika in den Jahren 1859 bis 1861.* Edited by Otto Kersten. 4 vols. Leipzig and Heidelberg, 1869.

Dermigny, Louis. *Cargaisons Indiennes—Solier et Cᵢᵉ, 1781–1793.* 2 vols. Paris, 1959–1960.

Deschamps, Hubert. *Histoire de Madagascar.* 2ᵉ édition. Paris, 1961.

Dias, Jorge, *et al. Os Maconders de Moçambique.* 5 vols. Lisbon, 1964–1970.

Dicionário Corográfico da Provincia de Moçambique. 3 vols. Lisbon and Coimbra, 1919–1923.

Documentos sobre os Portugueses em Moçambique e na África Central, 1497–1840. Documents on the Portuguese in Mozambique and Central Africa, 1497–1840. National Archives of Rhodesia and Centro de Estudos Históricos Ultramarinos. 7 vols. to date. Lisbon, 1962–1970.

Doke, C. M. and Cole, D. T. *Contributions to the History of Bantu Linguistics.* Johannesburg, 1961.

Douglas, Mary Tew. 'Matriliny and Pawnship in Central Africa', *Africa*, XXXIV, 4 (1964), pp. 301–13.

Duffy, James. *Portuguese Africa.* Cambridge, Mass., 1959.

——. *A Question of Slavery.* Oxford, 1967.

Duly, A. W. R. 'The Lower Shire District, Notes on Land Tenure and Individual Rights', *Nyasaland Journal*, I, 2 (1948), pp. 11–44.

Ebner, Elzear. *History of the Wangoni.* Peramiho, 1959.

Elton, J. Frederic. *Travels and Researches among the Lakes and Mountains of Eastern & Central Africa.* Ed. H. B. Cotterill. London, 1879.

Fagan, Brian M. 'Excavations at Ingombe Ilede, 1960–1962'. In B. M. Fagan, D. W. Phillipson, and S. G. H. Daniels, *Iron Age Cultures in Zambia, II: Dambwa, Ingombe Ilede and the Tonga*, pp. 57–184. London, 1969.

Figueiredo, Luís António de. 'Noticia de Continente de Mossambique, e abreviada Relação do seo Comercio', Lisboa, 1 December 1773. In L. F. de Carvalho Dias, 'Fontes para a História, Geografia e Comércio de Moçambique', pp. 251–67. Lisbon, 1954.

Filliot, J. M. *La traite des esclaves vers les Mascareignes au XVIIIᵉ siècle.* ORSTOM, Section Historique. Tananarive, 1970.

Foskett, Reginald. (ed.), *The Zambesi Journal and Letters of Dr. John Kirk, 1858–1863*. 2 vols. Edinburgh, 1965.

Freeman-Grenville, G.S.P. 'The Coast, 1498–1840'. In R. Oliver and G. Mathew (eds.), *History of East Africa*, I, pp. 129–68. Oxford, 1963.

——. *The East African Coast—Select Documents from the first to the earlier nineteenth century*. Oxford, 1962.

——. *The French at Kilwa Island—An Episode in Eighteenth-Century East African History*. Oxford, 1965.

——. *The Medieval History of the Coast of Tanganyika*. Berlin, 1962.

Froberville, Eugène de. 'Notes sur les moeurs, coutumes et traditions des amakoua, sur le commerce et la traite des esclaves dans l'Afrique Orientale', *Bulletin de la Société de Géographie*, 3ᵉ Série, VIII (1847), pp. 311–29.

——. 'Notes sur les Va-Ngindo', *Bulletin de la Société de Géographie*, 4ᵉ Série, III (1852), pp. 423–41.

Furber, Holden. *Bombay Presidency in the Mid-Eighteenth Century*. London, 1965.

Fyfe, Christopher and Dorjahn, V. R. 'Landlord and Stranger: Change in Tenancy Relations in Sierra Leone', *Journal of African History*, III, 3 (1962), pp. 391–7.

Galvão da Silva, Manuel. 'Diario das Viagens feitas pellas terras de Manica', 14 November 1788. In *Annaes do Conselho Ultramarino*, parte não official, I (1857)–II (1861), and J. F. de Carvalho Dias, 'Fontes para a História, Geografia e Comércio de Moçambique', Lisbon, 1954. pp. 323–32.

Gamitto, Antonio Candido Pedroso. *King Kazembe and the Marave, Cheva, Bisa, Bemba, Lunda, and other peoples of Southern Africa being the Diary of the Portuguese Expedition to that Potentate in the Years 1831 and 1832*. Translated by I. Cunnison. 2 vols. Lisbon, 1960.

Gerard, P.ᵉ 'Costumes dos Macua do Mêdo, região de Namuno, circunscrição de Montepuez', *Moçambique*, 28 (1941), pp. 5–22.

——. ' "Mahimo" Macuas', *Moçambique*, 26 (1941), pp. 5–22.

Gibb, H. A. R. (trans. and ed.) *The Travels of Ibn Battuta in Asia and Africa*. 3 vols. Cambridge, 1962.

Gomes, António. 'Viagem que fez o Padre Ant.º Gomes, da Comp.ª de Jesus, ao Imperio de de (sic) Manomotapa; e a assistencia que fez nas ditas terras d.ᵉ Alg'us annos'. Notes by E. Axelson. *Stvdia*, 3 (1959), pp. 155–242.

Gomes de Brito, Bernardo. *Historia Tragico-Maritima*. 12 vols. Lisbon, 1904–1909.

Graham, G. S. *Great Britain in the Indian Ocean, 1810–1850*. Oxford, 1967.

Grande Dicionário da Língua Portuguesa. 10th edition. Lisbon, n.d.

Grande Enciclopédia Portuguesa e Brasileira. 40 vols. Lisbon and Rio de Janeiro, n.d.

Grant, Charles. *The History of Mauritius or the Isle of France and the Neighbouring Islands;* . . . London, 1801.

Gray, Ernest, 'Notes on the Salt-Making Industry of the Nyanja Peoples near Lake Shirwa', *South African Journal of Science*, XLI (1945), pp. 465–75.

Gray, John Milner, 'A French Account of Kilwa at the end of the Eighteenth Century', *Tanganyika Notes and Records*, 63 (1964), pp. 224–26.

——. 'A History of Kilwa: Part II', *Tanganyika Notes and Records*, 32 (1952), pp. 11–37.

——. *History of Zanzibar from the Middle Ages to 1856*. London, 1962.

——. 'A Journey by Land from Tete to Kilwa in 1616', *Tanganyika Notes and Records*, 25 (1948), pp. 37–47.

——. 'The Recovery of Kilwa by the Arabs in 1785', *Tanganyika Notes and Records*, 62 (1964), pp. 20–6.

——. 'Zanzibar and the Coastal Belt, 1840–1884.' In R. Oliver and G. Mathew (eds.), *History of East Africa*, I, pp. 212–51. Oxford, 1963.

Gray, John Richard and Birmingham, David. (eds.), *Pre-Colonial African Trade: Essays on Trade in Central and Eastern Africa before 1900.* London, 1970.

Guillain, Charles. *Documents sur l'histoire, la géographie, et le commerce de l'Afrique Orientale.* 3 vols. Paris, 1856.

——. *Documents sur l'histoire, la géographie et le commerce de la partie occidentale de Madagascar.* Paris, 1845.

Guthrie, Malcolm. *The Classification of the Bantu Languages.* London, 1948.

Habib, Irfan, *Agrarian Systems of Mughal India.* Bombay, 1963.

——. 'Potentialities of Capitalistic Development in the Economy of Mughal India', *Journal of Economic History*, XXIX, 1 (1969), pp. 32–78.

——. 'Usury in Medieval India', *Comparative Studies in Society and History*, VI, 4 (1963–1964), pp. 393–423.

Hamilton, R. A. 'The Route of Gaspar Bocarro from Tete to Kilwa in 1616', *The Nyasaland Journal*, VII, 2 (1954), pp. 7–14.

Hanna, A. J. *The Beginnings of Nyasaland and North-Eastern Rhodesia, 1859–1895.* Oxford, 1956.

Hassani, Rashid bin. 'The Story of Rashid Bin Hassani of the Bisa Tribe, Northern Rhodesia'. Recorded by W. F. Baldock in Margery Perham (ed.), *Ten Africans*, pp. 81–119. London, 1936.

Hetherwick, Alexander. 'Some Animistic Beliefs among the Yao of British Central Africa', *The Journal of the Anthropological Institute of Great Britain and Ireland*, XXXII (1902), pp. 89–95.

Hill, Polly. 'Landlord and Broker: A West African Trading System', *Cahiers d'Études Africaines*, VI (1966), pp. 351–66.

Hommy, O. L. Report of the voyage of the *De Brack*, 9 November 1741.

In Alfred Grandidier *et al.* (eds.), *Collection des Ouvrages anciens concernant Madagascar*, VI. Paris, 1913.

Hoppe, Fritz, *A África Oriental Portuguesa no tempo do Marquês de Pombal (1750–1777)*. Lisbon, 1970.

Ingrams, W. H. *Zanzibar: Its History and its People*. London, 1930.

Isaacman, Allen F. *Mozambique—The Africanization of a European Institution: The Zambezi Prazos, 1750–1902*. Madison, 1972.

Jackson, Mabel V. *European Powers and South-East Africa: A Study of International Relations on the South-East Coast of Africa, 1796–1856*. London, 1942.

Johnson, William Percival. *Nyasa the Great Water*. London, 1922.

Kapferer, Bruce. *Co-operation, Leadership and Village Structure: a preliminary economic and political study of ten Bisa villages in the Northern Province of Zambia*. Zambia Paper No. 1. Manchester, 1967.

Kelly, J. B. *Britain and the Persian Gulf, 1795–1880*. Oxford, 1968.

Kent, Raymond K. *Early Kingdoms in Madagascar, 1500–1700*. New York, 1970.

Kilekwa, Petro. *Slave Boy to Priest: The Autobiography of Padre Petro Kilekwa*. Translated from Cinyanja by K. H. Nixon Smith. London, 1937.

Klein, Herbert S. 'The Trade in African Slaves to Rio de Janeiro, 1795–1811: Estimates of Mortality and Patterns of Voyages, *Journal of African History*, X, 4 (1969), pp. 533–49.

Krapf, J. Lewis. *Travels, Researches, and Missionary Labours, during an Eighteen Years' Residence in Eastern Africa*. London, 1860.

——. *Vocabulary of Six East-African Languages*. (*Kisuahéli, Kinika, Kikámba, Kipokómo, Kihiáu, Kigálla*). Tübingen, 1850.

Lacerda e Almeida, Francisco José de. *Travessia de África*. Lisbon, 1936.

Lamphear, John. 'The Kamba and the Northern Mrima Coast'. In R. Gray and D. Birmingham (eds.), *Pre-Colonial African Trade*, pp. 75–101. London, 1970.

Langworthy, Harry. 'Chewa or Malawi Political Organization in the Precolonial Era'. In B. Pachai (ed.), *The Early History of Malawi*, pp. 104–22. London, 1972.

——. 'Conflict among rulers in the history of Undi's Chewa kingdom', *Transafrican Journal of History*, I, 1 (1971), pp. 1–23.

Linden, Ian. 'Some Oral Traditions from the Maseko Ngoni', *The Society of Malawi Journal*, XXIV, 2 (1971), pp. 61–73.

Lislet Geoffrey, J. B. *Memoir and Notice Explanatory of a Chart of Madagascar and the North-Eastern Archipelago of Mauritius . . . together with some observations on the coast of Africa*. London, 1819.

Livingstone, David. *Last Journals*. Edited by Horace Waller. 2 vols. London, 1874.

——. *Missionary Travels and Researches in South Africa*. New York, 1858.

——, and Livingstone, Charles. *Narrative of an Expedition to the Zambesi and its Tributaries; and of the Discovery of the Lakes Shirwa and Nyassa, 1858–1864.* New York, 1866.

Lobato, Alexandre. *Colonização Senhorial da Zambézia e outros estudos.* Lisbon. 1962.

——. *Evolução Administrativa e Económica de Moçambique, 1752–1763.* 1.ª Parte—'Fundamentos da Criação do Governo-Geral em 1752'. Lisbon, 1957.

——. *A Expansão Portuguesa em Moçambique de 1498 a 1530.* 3 vols. Lisbon, 1954–1960.

——. *História do Presídio de Lourenço Marques.* 2 vols. Lisbon, 1949–1960.

Lopes, Eduardo Correia. *A escravatura (subsídios para a sua história).* Lisbon, 1944.

Lougnon, Albert. *Recueil Trimestriel de Documents et Travaux inédits pour servir à l'histoire des Mascareignes françaises.* 8 vols. Tananarive and Saint-Denis, 1932–1949.

Loureiro, Manuel José Gomes. *Memorias dos Estabelecimentos Portuguezes a l'Este do Cabo da Boa Esperança . . .* Lisbon, 1835.

Lupi, Eduardo do Couto. *Angoche—Breve memoria sobre uma das capitanais-mores do Districto de Moçambique.* Lisbon, 1907.

Macdonald, Duff. *Africana, or the Heart of Heathen Africa.* 2 vols. London, 1882.

Madan, A. C. *Kiungani.* Zanzibar, 1886.

Martin, Bradford G. 'Notes on Some Members of the Learned Classes of Zanzibar and East Africa in the Nineteenth Century', *African Historical Studies,* IV, 3 (1971), pp. 525–45.

Marwick, M. G. 'The kinship basis of Cewa social structure', *South African Journal of Science,* 48 (1952), pp. 258–62.

Mathew, Gervase. 'The East African Coast until the Coming of the Portuguese'. In R. Oliver and G. Mathew (eds.), *History of East Africa,* I, pp. 94–127. Oxford, 1963.

Mazula, Assabel, Jonassane. 'História dos Nianjas', *Portugal em África,* XIX (1962), pp. 155–66, 235–47.

Mbotela, James. *Uhuru wa Watumwa.* Nairobi, 1967.

Meillassoux, Claude. *Anthropologie Économique des Gouro de Côte d'Ivoire—De l'économie de subsistence à l'agriculture commerciale.* Paris and The Hague, 1970.

Mello Machado, A. J. de. *Entre os Macuas de Angoche—Historiando Moçambique.* Lisbon, 1970.

Milburn, William. *Oriental Commerce.* 2 vols. London, 1813.

——, and Thornton, Thomas. *Oriental Commerce.* London, 1825.

Miles, S. B. *The Countries and Tribes of the Persian Gulf.* 2 vols. London, 1919.

Miller, Joseph C. 'Cokwe Trade and Conquest in the Nineteenth Century'. In R. Gray and D. Birmingham (eds.), *Pre-Colonial African Trade,* pp. 175–201. London, 1970

Miller, Joseph C. 'Requiem for the "Jaga"'. *Cahiers d'Études Africaines*, XIII, 49 (1973), pp. 121–49.

Ministério dos Negócios de Marinha e Ultramar. *A Campanha contra os Namarraes. Relatorios enviados ao Ministerio e Secretario d'Estado dos Negocios da Marinha e Ultramar pelo Commissario Regio da Provincia de Moçambique*. Lisbon, 1897.

Miracle, Marvin. *Maize in Tropical Africa*. Madison, 1966.

Miranda, António Pinto de. 'Memoria sobre a costa de Africa', c. 1766. In A. A. de Andrade, *Relações de Moçambique Setecentista*, pp. 217–51. Lisbon. 1955.

Mitchell, J. Clyde. 'Marriage, Matriliny and Social Structure among the Yao of Southern Nyasaland', *International Journal of Comparative Sociology*, III, 1 (1962), pp. 29–42.

——. *The Yao Village—A Study in the Social Structure of a Nyasaland Tribe*. Manchester, 1956.

Monclaro, Padre. 'Relação da Viagem que fizeram os Padres da Companhia de Jesus com Francisco Barreto na conquista de Monomotapa no anno de 1569'. In G. M. Theal (ed.), *Records of South-East Africa*, III, pp. 157–253. London, 1899.

Montaury, João Baptista de. 'Moçambique, Ilhas Querimbas, Rios de Sena, Villa de Tete, Villa de Zumbo, Manica, Villa de Luabo, Inhambane', c. 1778. In A. A. de Andrade, *Relações de Moçambique Setecentista*, pp. 339–73. Lisbon. 1955.

Montez, Caetano. 'Inventário do Fundo do Século XVIII', *Moçambique*, 72–92 (1952–1957).

Moreland, W. H. *India at the Death of Akbar—An Economic Study*. London, 1920.

Morgan, W. B. 'The Lower Shire Valley of Nyasaland: A Changing System of African Agriculture', *The Geographical Journal*, CXIX (1953), pp. 459–69.

Mousinho de Albuquerque, Maria José Galvão. *Moçambique, 1896–1898*. Lisbon, 1934.

Murdock, G. P. *Africa—Its Peoples and their Culture History*. New York, 1959.

Murray, S. S. *A Handbook of Nyasaland*. London, 1932.

Mutibwa, Phares M. 'Trade and economic development in nineteenth century Madagascar', *Transafrican Journal of History*, II, 1 (1972), pp. 33–63.

McLeod, Lyons. *Travels in Eastern Africa: with the Narrative of a Residence in Mozambique*. 2 vols. London, 1860.

Newitt, M. D. D. 'Angoche, the slave trade and the Portuguese, c. 1844–1910', *Journal of African History*, XIII, 4 (1972), pp. 659–672.

——. 'The Early History of the Sultanate of Angoche', *Journal of African History*, XIII, 3 (1972), pp. 397–406.

Nicholls, C. S. *The Swahili Coast—Politics, Diplomacy and Trade on the East African Littoral, 1798–1856*. St. Antony's Publications No. 2. London, 1971.

Nogueira de Andrade, Jeronimo José. 'Descripção do Estado em que ficavão os Negocios da Capitania de Mossambique nos fins de Novembro de 1789 com algumas Observaçoens, e reflecçoens sobre a causa da decadencia do Commercio dos Estabelecimentos Portugueses na Costa Oriental da Affrica', 1790, *Arquivo das Colónias*, I (1917), pp. 75–96, 115–34, 166–84, 213–35, 275–88, and II (1918), pp. 32–49.

Ogot, B. A. and Kieran, J. A. (eds.) *Zamani—A Survey of East African History*. Nairobi, 1968.

Ojany, Francis F. 'The Geography of East Africa'. In B. A. Ogot and J. A. Kieran (eds.), *Zamani*, pp. 22–48. Nairobi, 1968.

Oliver, Roland. 'Discernible Developments in the Interior, *c.* 1500–1840'. In R. Oliver and G. Mathew (eds.), *History of East Africa*, I, pp. 169–211. Oxford, 1963.

——, and Mathew, Gervase. (eds.), *History of East Africa*, I. Oxford, 1963.

Omer-Cooper, John D. *The Zulu Aftermath: A Nineteenth-Century Revolution in Bantu Africa*. London, 1966.

O'Neill, Henry E. 'On the Coast Lands and some Rivers and Ports of Mozambique', *Proceedings of the Royal Geographical Society*, IV (1882), pp. 595–605.

——. 'Journey from Mozambique to Lakes Shirwa and Amaramba', *Proceedings of the Royal Geographical Society*, VI (1884), pp. 632–55, 713–41.

Owen, W. F. W. *Narrative of Voyages to explore the shores of Africa, Arabia, and Madagascar; performed in H. M. Ships Leven and Barracouta*. 2 vols. London, 1833.

Pachai, Bridglal (ed.) *The Early History of Malawi*. London, 1972.

Peirone, J. F. *A Tribo Ajaua do Alto Niassa (Moçambique) e Alguns Aspectos da sua Problemática Neo-Islâmica*. Lisbon, 1967.

Phillipson, D. W. and Fagan, B. 'The date of the Ingombe Ilede Burials', *Journal of African History*, X, 2 (1969), pp. 199–204.

Pissurlencar, Panduronga S. S. *Assentos do Conselho do Estado [da Índia]*. 5 vols. Bastorá-Goa, 1953–1957.

Portugal Durão, Albano Aujustida. 'Reconhecimento e Occupação dos Territorios entre o Messangire e os Picos Namuli', *Boletim da Sociedade de Geografia de Lisboa*, XX, 7 (1902), pp. 5–17.

Prakash, Ishwar, 'Organization of Industrial Production in Urban Centres in India during the 17th Century with special reference to textiles'. In B. N. Ganguli (ed.), *Readings in Indian Economic History*, pp. 44–52. London, 1964.

Prata, António Pires. 'Os Macuas Tem Outros Nomes', *O Missionário Católico*, XXIII, 200 (1946), p. 47.

Price, Thomas. 'Malawi Rain-cults'. In *Religion in Africa*, pp. 114–24. Edinburgh, 1964.

——. 'More about the Maravi', *African Studies*, XI (1952), pp. 75–9.

——. 'The Name "Anguru"', *The Nyasaland Journal*, V, 1 (1952), pp. 23–5.

——. 'Yao Origins', *The Nyasaland Journal*, XVII, 2 (1964), pp. 11–16.

Prior, James. *Voyage along the Eastern Coast of Africa, to Mozambique, Johanna, and Quiloa . . . in the Nisus Frigate.* London, 1819.

Qaisar, A. Jan. 'Shipbuilding in the Mughal Empire during the Seventeenth Century', *The Indian Economic and Social History Review*, V, 2 (1968), pp. 149–70.

Randles, W. G. L. 'South East Africa and the Empire of Monomotapa as shown on selected printed maps of the 16th century', *Stvdia*, 2 (1958), pp. 103–63.

Rangeley, W. H. J. 'The Arabs', *The Nyasaland Journal*, XVI, 2 (1963), pp. 11–25.

——. 'The Ayao', *The Nyasaland Journal*, XVI, 1 (1963), pp. 7–27.

——. 'Bocarro's Journey', *The Nyasaland Journal*, VII, 2 (1954), pp. 15–23.

——. 'Mbona—the Rain Maker', *The Nyasaland Journal*, VI, 1 (1953), pp. 8–27.

——. 'Two Nysaland Rain Shrines: Makewana—the Mother of all People', *The Nyasaland Journal*, V 2 (1952) pp. 31–50.

——. 'The Portuguese', *The Nysaland Journal*, XXII, 1 (1964), pp. 42–71.

Rankin, Daniel J. *Arab Tales translated from the Swahili language into the Tugulu Dialect of the Makua Language, as spoken in the Immediate Vicinity of Mozambique. Together with comparative vocabularies of five dialects of the Makua language.* London, c. 1886.

Rau, Virgínia. 'Aspectos étnico-culturais da ilha de Moçambique em 1822', *Stvdia*, 11 (1963), pp. 123–62.

Raychaudhuri, Tapan. 'European Commercial Activity and the Organization of India's Commerce and Industrial Production, 1500–1750'. In B. N. Ganguli (ed.), *Readings in Indian Economic History*, pp. 64–77. London, 1964.

Rebman, John. *Dictionary of the Kiniassa Language.* Ed. L. Krapf. St. Chrischona, 1877.

Renault, François. *Lavigerie, l'Esclavage africain et l'Europe, 1868–1892.* 2 vols. Paris, 1971.

Richards, A. I. 'Some Types of Family Structure amongst the Central Bantu'. In A. R. Radcliffe-Brown and D. Forde (eds.), *African Systems of Kinship and Marriage*, pp. 207–251. London, 1950.

Rita-Ferreira, António. *Agrupamento e Caracterização Étnica dos Indígenas de Moçambique.* Lisbon, 1958.

——. 'Os "Azimba" (Monografia Etnográfica)', *Boletim da Sociedade de Estudos de Moçambique*, XXIV, 84–5 (1954), pp. 47–140, 5–116.

Rita-Ferreira, António. *Os Cheuas da Macanga.* Lourenço Marques, 1966.

Roberts, Andrew D. 'Nyamwezi Trade'. In R. Gray and D. Birmingham (eds.), *Pre-Colonial African Trade*, pp. 39–74. London, 1970.

——. 'Pre-Colonial Trade in Zambia', *African Social Research*, 10 (1970), pp. 715–46.

Rodney, Walter. *How Europe Underdeveloped Africa.* London and Dar es Salaam, 1972.

Romero, Jeronymo. *Supplemento á Memoria Descriptiva e Estatistica de Districto de Cabo Delgado com uma Noticia Acerca do Establelecimento da Colonia de Pemba.* Lisbon, 1860.

Rowley, Henry. *The Story of the Universities' Mission to Central Africa.* London, 1866.

Russell, C. E. B. *General Rigby, Zanzibar and the Slave Trade.* London, 1935.

Salt, Henry. *A Voyage to Abyssinia . . . in the Years 1809 and 1810; in which are included, An Account of the Portuguese Settlements on the East Coast of Africa, visited in the Course of the Voyage. . . .* London, 1814.

Sanderson, G. Meredith. *A Dictionary of the Yao Language.* Zomba, 1954.

——. 'Inyago—The Picture-Models of the Yao Initiation Ceremonies', *The Nyasaland Journal*, VIII, 2 (1955), pp. 36–57.

Santana, Francisco (ed.), *Documentação Avulsa Moçambicana do Arquivo Histórico Ultramarino.* 2 vols. Lisbon, 1964–1967.

Santos, João dos. 'Ethiopia Oriental', 1609. In G. M. Theal (ed.), *Records of South-East Africa.* VII, pp. 1–370. London, 1901.

Santos Baptista, Abel dos. *Monografia Etnográfica sobre os Macuas.* Lisbon, 1951.

Sarmento, Z. 'Um santareno no Oriente: Nuno Velho Pereira—Notas biográficas'. In Congresso Internacional de História dos Descobrimentos, *Actas*, V, 1, pp. 263–75. Lisbon, 1961.

Saul, John S. and Woods, Roger. 'African Peasantries'. In Teodor Shanin (ed.), *Peasants and Peasant Societies*, pp. 103–14. Harmondsworth, 1971.

Schoffeleers, Matthew. 'The History and Political Role of the M'Bona Cult among the Mang'anja'. In T. O. Ranger and I. N. Kimambo (eds.), *The Historical Study of African Religion*, pp. 73–94. London, 1972.

Schurhammer, Georg. 'Die Entdeckung des Nyassa-Sees', *Stimmen der Zeit*, 99 (1920), pp. 349–56.

Scott, D. C. and Hetherwick, A. *Dictionary of the Nyasa Language.* London, 1929.

Scrivenor, T. V. 'Some Notes on *Utani*, or the Vituperative Alliances existing between the Clans in the Masasi District', *Tanganyika Notes and Records*, 4 (1937), pp. 72–4.

Shepperson, George (ed.). *David Livingstone and the Rovuma: A Notebook.* Edinburgh, 1965.

Shorter, Aylward. 'The Kimbu'. In A. D. Roberts (ed.), *Tanzania before 1900*, pp. 96–116. Nairobi, 1968.

Smith, Charles Stewart. 'Explorations in Zanzibar Domains'. Royal Geographical Society, *Supplementary Papers*, II, 1, pp. 99–125. London, 1887.

Smithies, Charles Alan. *A Journey to Lake Nyassa, and Visit to the Magwanwara and the Source of the Rovuma, in the Year 1886* . . . Kiungani, Zanzibar, n.d.

Smyth, W. H. *The Life and Service of Captain Philip Beaver, late of Her Majesty's Ship Nisus*. London, 1829.

Sousa Dias, Gastão de (ed.), *Silva Porto e a Travessia do Continente Africano*. Lisbon, 1938.

Sousa Lobato, A. 'Monografia Etnográfica Original sobre o Povo Ajaua', *Boletim da Sociedade de Estudos da Colónia de Moçambique*, XIX, 63 (1949), pp. 7–17.

Speke, John Hanning. *Journal of Discovery of the Source of the Nile*. London. 1863.

A Standard Swahili–English Dictionary. Oxford, 1939.

Stannus, Hugh. 'Some Notes on the Tribes of British Central Africa', *Man*, XL (1910), pp. 285–335.

——. 'The Wayao of Nyasaland'. Harvard African Studies, *Varia Africana III*, pp. 229–372. Cambridge, Mass., 1922.

Steere, Edward. *The Free Village in Yao Land*. Zanzibar, *c.* 1876.

——. *The Universities' Mission to Central Africa. A Speech delivered at Oxford*. London, 1875.

Stevenson-Hamilton, James. 'Notes on a Journey through Portuguese East Africa, from Ibo to Lake Nyasa', *The Geographical Journal*, XXXIV (1909), pp. 514–29.

Strandes, Justus. *The Portuguese Period in East Africa*. Translated by J. F. Wallwork; edited by J. S. Kirkman. Kenya Historical Society Publication No. 2. Nairobi, 1961.

Sullivan, C. G. L. *Dhow Chasing in Zanzibar Waters ond On the Eastern Coast of Africa. Narrative of Five Years' Experience in the Suppression of the Slave Trade*. London, 1873.

Summers, Roger. *Inyanga—Prehistoric Settlements in Southern Rhodesia*. Cambridge, 1958.

Sutherland-Harris, Nicola. 'Zambian Trade with Zumbo in the Eighteenth Century'. In R. Gray and D. Birmingham (eds.), *Pre-Colonial African Trade*, pp. 231–42. London, 1970.

Teixeira Botelho, José Justino. *História Militar e Política dos Portugueses em Moçambique*. 2 vols. Lisbon, 1934–1936.

Teixeira da Mota, A. *A Cartografia Antiga da África Central e a Travessia entre Angola e Moçambique, 1500–1860*. Lourenço Marques, 1964.

Texugo, F. Torres. *A Letter on the Slave Trade still carried on along the*

Eastern Coast of Africa, called the Province of Mosambique . . . London, 1839.

Theal, George McCall (ed.), *Records of South-East Africa*. 9 vols. London, 1898–1903.

Truão, António Norberto das Vilasboas. 'Extracto do Plano para um Regimento ou Nova Constituição Economica e Politica da Capitania de Rios de Senna', Tete, 20 May 1806. In *Annaes do Conselho Ultramarino*, parte não official, I (1857), pp. 407–17.

Vail, Leroy. 'Suggestions towards a reinterpreted Tumbuka history'. In B. Pachai (ed.), *The Early History of Malawi*, pp. 148–67. London, 1972.

Valdez Thomas dos Santos, Nuno Beja. *O Desconhecido Niassa*. Lisbon, 1964.

Varella, Joaquim José. 'Descrição da Capitania de Moçambique e suas povoações e produções, pertencentes a Coroa de Portugal,' 1788. In A. A. de Andrade, *Relações de Moçambique Setecentista*, pp. 375–405. Lisbon, 1955.

Vasconcelos e Cirne, Manuel Joaquim Mendes de. *Memoria sobre a Provincia de Mocambique*. Ministério dos Negócios da Marinha e Ultramar, Documentos para a História das Colónias Portuguezes. Lisbon, 1890.

Velten, Carl. *Prosa und Poesie der Suaheli*. Berlin, 1907.

Vilhena, Ernesto Jardim de. 'De Tete a Quiloa', *Revista Portugueza Colonial e Maritima*, V, 2 (1901), pp. 1–14, 49–59, 97–107.

Vincent, J. 'The Namuli Mountains, Portuguese East Africa', *The Geographical Journal*, LXXXI, 4 (1933), pp. 314–27.

Vito, João. 'Noticias que da João Vitto das Ilhas de Cabo Delgado'. In J. F. de Carvalho Dias (ed.), 'Fontes para a História, Geografia e Comércio de Moçambique,' pp. 268–80. Lisbon, 1954.

Watt, George. *A Dictionary of the Economic Products of India*. 6 Vols. London and Calcutta, 1890.

Wilson, Godfrey. *The Constitution of Ngonde*. Rhodes-Livingstone Papers No. 3. Livingstone, 1939.

Wilson, Monica. 'Reflections on the Early History of North Malawi'. In B. Pachai (ed.), *The Early History of Malawi*, pp. 136–47. London, 1972.

Xavier, Inácio Caetano. 'Noticias dos Dominios Portugueses na Costa de Africa Oriental', 26 December 1758. In A. A. de Andrade, *Relações de Moçambique Setecentista*, pp. 139–88. Lisbon, 1955.

Young, T. Cullen. *Notes on the History of the Tumbuka-Kamanga Peoples of the Northern Province of Nyasaland*. London, 1932.

Index

Abdallah, Y. B., 15, 16, 21, 22, 26, 58-9, 60, 63-4, 81, 242, 246, 249, 250

Abu'l-Mawahib dynasty, 40

Africa, East Central, xv-xvi; environment, 2, 4-5; demography, 6, and slave trade, 242-3; staple crops, 6; cultures, 6-8; resources and trade patterns, 29, 38n; historical environment, changed, 251

Africa, Portuguese East, commercial organization, 104-6, 121-2, 173-174, 179; subordinate to Goa, 105; slave trade, 186, 188, 210-11; and Brazil, 188-9, 254n; ivory trade, 258n; see also ivory trade, *Junta do Comércio*, Mozambique Island, slave trade

Alaum, Sharif, 61

Alley, William, at Mombasa, 62

Almeida, Nicolau Tolentino de, obstructs trade with Yao, 75-7

Amaral Cardoso, Francisco de Paula e Albuquerque, 196; obstructs trade, 173

American, War for Independence, 185; slave trade, 209; cloths, 233-4, 248; trade with Zanzibar, 246, 266

Ampoense, 233

Angoche, 4, 12, 42, 43; -Zambesi trade route, 44, 47; Zimba at, 52; slave trade, 218-19

Arabs, 24; at Kilwa, 71-6, 160; at Mongalo, 133; at Zanzibar, 159, 177; at Angoche, 218; as slavers, 209, 218-19, 240-1, 261n

Ataide, Nuno da Cunha de, 53

Axelson, Eric, xv; on gold trade, 47

Bahia, 127, 211

Balowoka, 161-4; trade route, 162

Bangweulu, Lake, 15

Banyans, 85-8, 89, 90-1, 92, 117, 220; from Diu, 92; harassed, 93-4, 114, 116; at Mozambique, 114-15, 143-9, 172-3; in Rivers of Sena, 122; at Kilwa, 246; profits, 247; see also Indian traders

Baptista, João, 129

Barbosa, José Francisco Alves, 243-4

Barotseland, Yao in, 252

Bataille, Fortuné, 217

Barreto, Manuel de, on ivory trade, 56; on Maravi empire, 57; on Portuguese, 112-13

Barros, João de, 41

Barth, Heinrich, 125

beads, *missanga*, 200; see also *velório*

Bemba, as slaves, 240, 242; and Bisa, 248

Bemposta Subserra, Marquis of, 248; on slave trade, 231

Bisa, and salt, 26; and Yao, 122, 125, 178-9, 245-8, 250, 251; and Kazembe, 124, 178-9, 200; at Quelimane, 179; and Portuguese, 178, 243-4; and slave trade, 240, 241; dominate trade, 244-6; and Nyasa, 246; at Kilwa, 246; decline, 248

Biwi (Bive), 121, 124

Bocarro, António, 54

Bocarro, Gaspar, 21; Tete to Kilwa, 59-61, 165, 242

Bombay, British at, 127

Bororo, 53, 54, 57

Boteler, Thomas, at Quelimane, 216

287